THE BETRAYAL
kNoWS MY NAME

8

Hotaru Odagiri

8
Contents

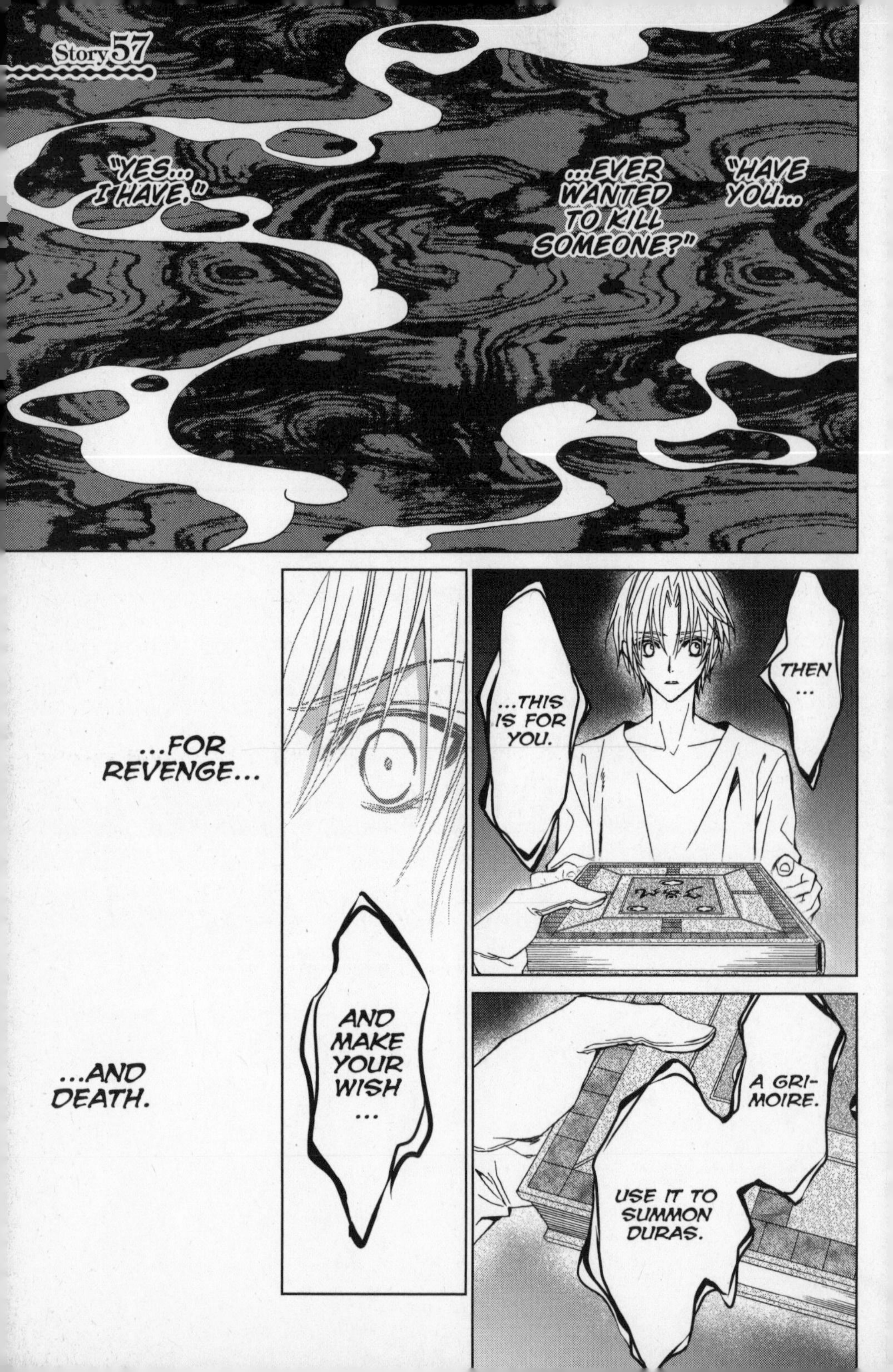
Story 57
"HAVE YOU...
...EVER WANTED TO KILL SOMEONE?"
"YES... I HAVE."
THEN...
...THIS IS FOR YOU.
A GRI-MOIRE.
USE IT TO SUMMON DURAS.
AND MAKE YOUR WISH...
...FOR REVENGE...
...AND DEATH.

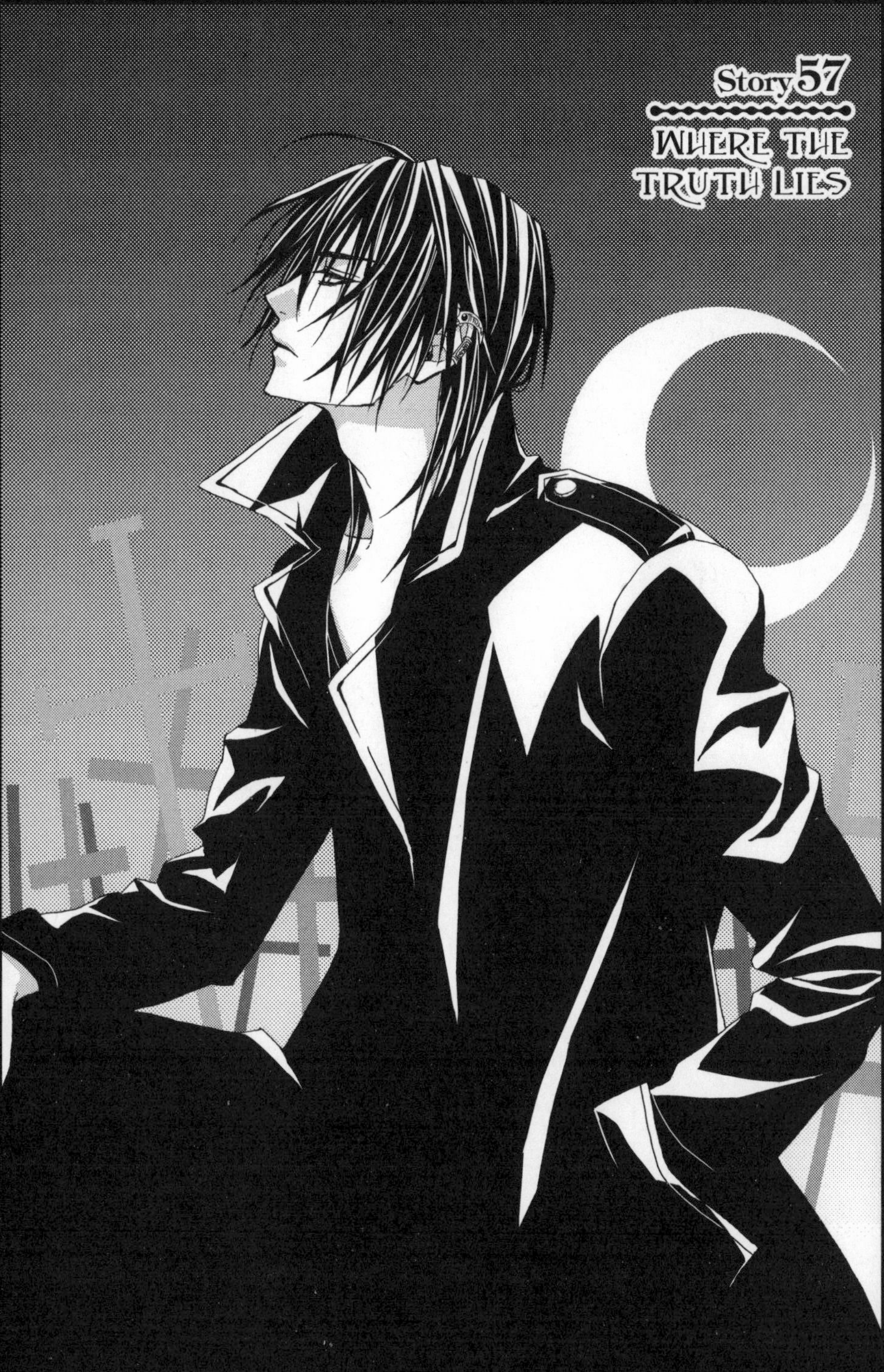
Story 57
WHERE THE TRUTH LIES

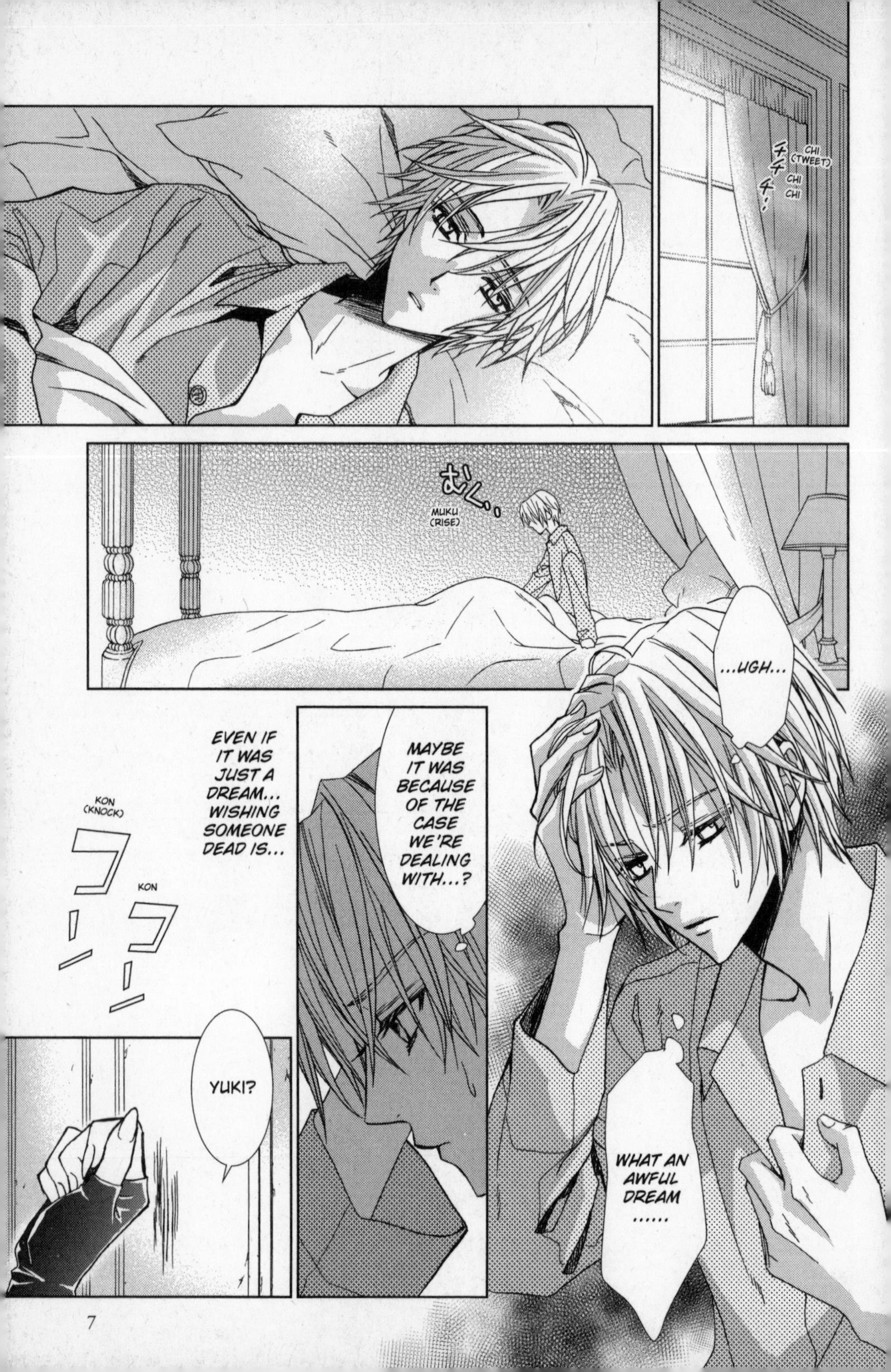

チチチ
CHI (TWEET) CHI CHI
むくっ
MUKU (RISE)
...UGH...
WHAT AN AWFUL DREAM ......
MAYBE IT WAS BECAUSE OF THE CASE WE'RE DEALING WITH...?
EVEN IF IT WAS JUST A DREAM... WISHING SOMEONE DEAD IS...
コン
KON (KNOCK)
コン
KON
YUKI?

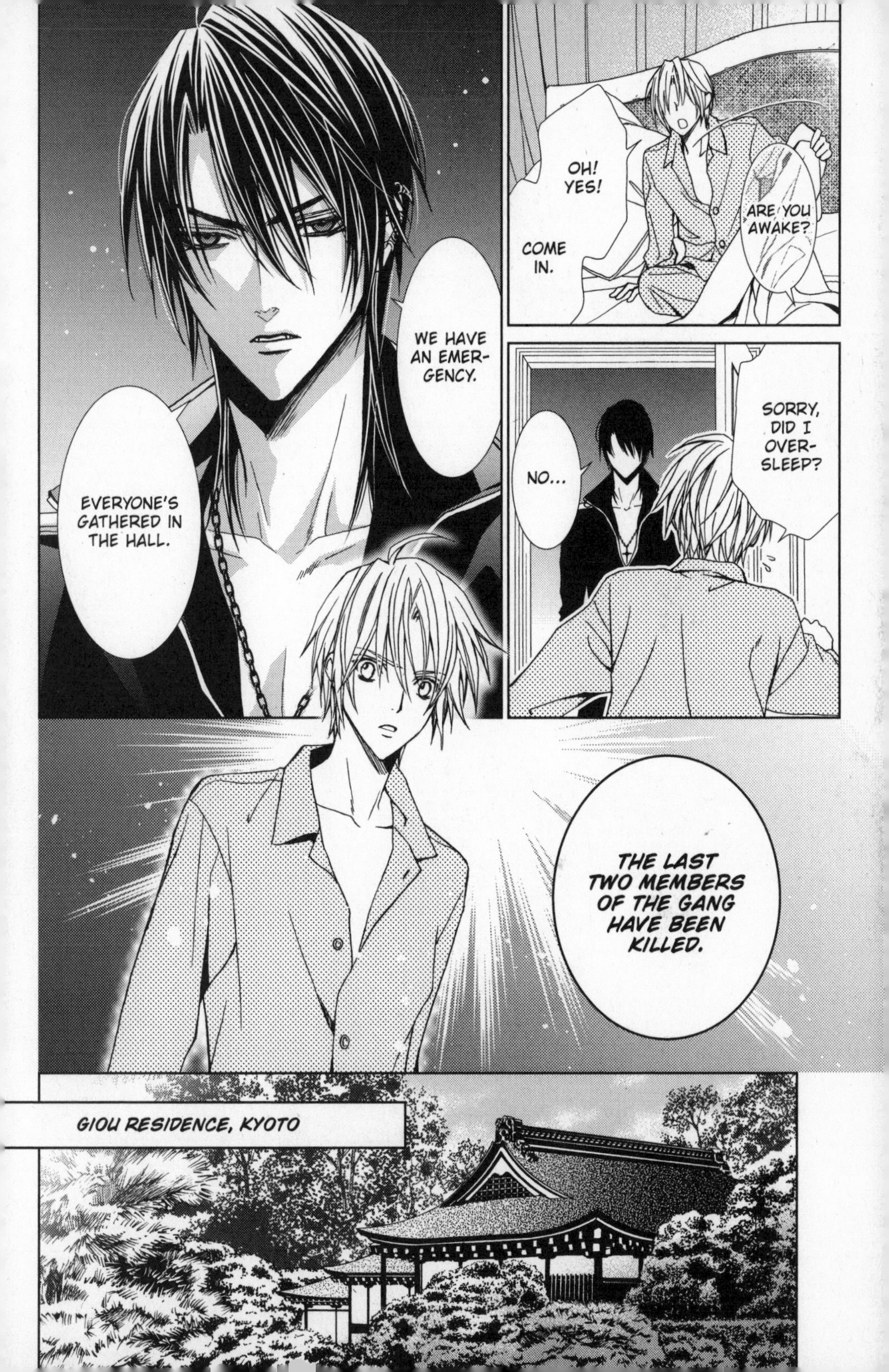
ARE YOU AWAKE?
OH! YES!
COME IN.
SORRY, DID I OVER-SLEEP?
NO...
WE HAVE AN EMERG-ENCY.
EVERYONE'S GATHERED IN THE HALL.
THE LAST TWO MEMBERS OF THE GANG HAVE BEEN KILLED.
GIOU RESIDENCE, KYOTO

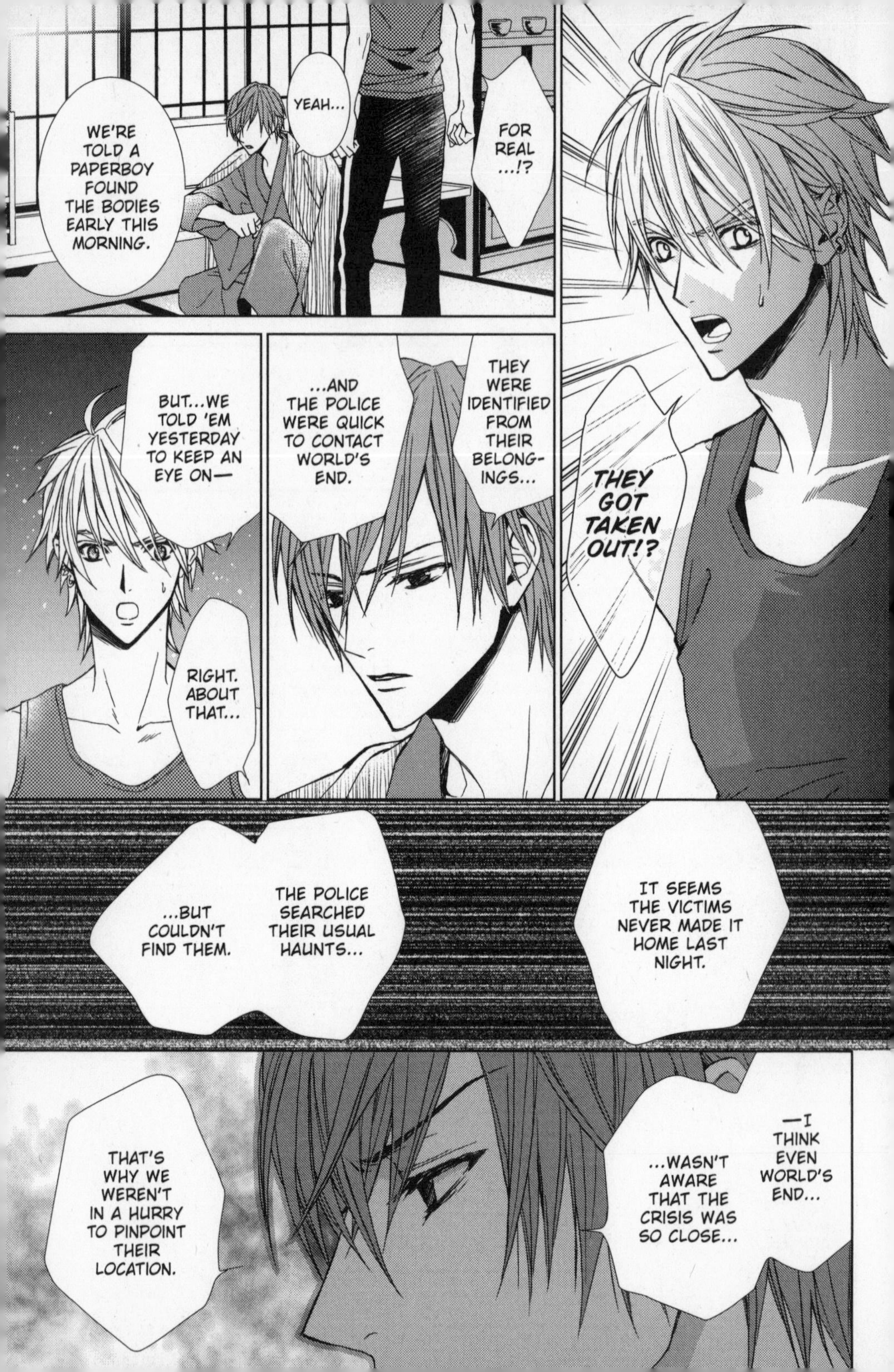
THEY GOT TAKEN OUT!?
FOR REAL ...!?
YEAH...
WE'RE TOLD A PAPERBOY FOUND THE BODIES EARLY THIS MORNING.
THEY WERE IDENTIFIED FROM THEIR BELONG-INGS...
...AND THE POLICE WERE QUICK TO CONTACT WORLD'S END.
BUT...WE TOLD 'EM YESTERDAY TO KEEP AN EYE ON—
RIGHT. ABOUT THAT...
IT SEEMS THE VICTIMS NEVER MADE IT HOME LAST NIGHT.
THE POLICE SEARCHED THEIR USUAL HAUNTS...
...BUT COULDN'T FIND THEM.
—I THINK EVEN WORLD'S END...
...WASN'T AWARE THAT THE CRISIS WAS SO CLOSE...
THAT'S WHY WE WEREN'T IN A HURRY TO PINPOINT THEIR LOCATION.

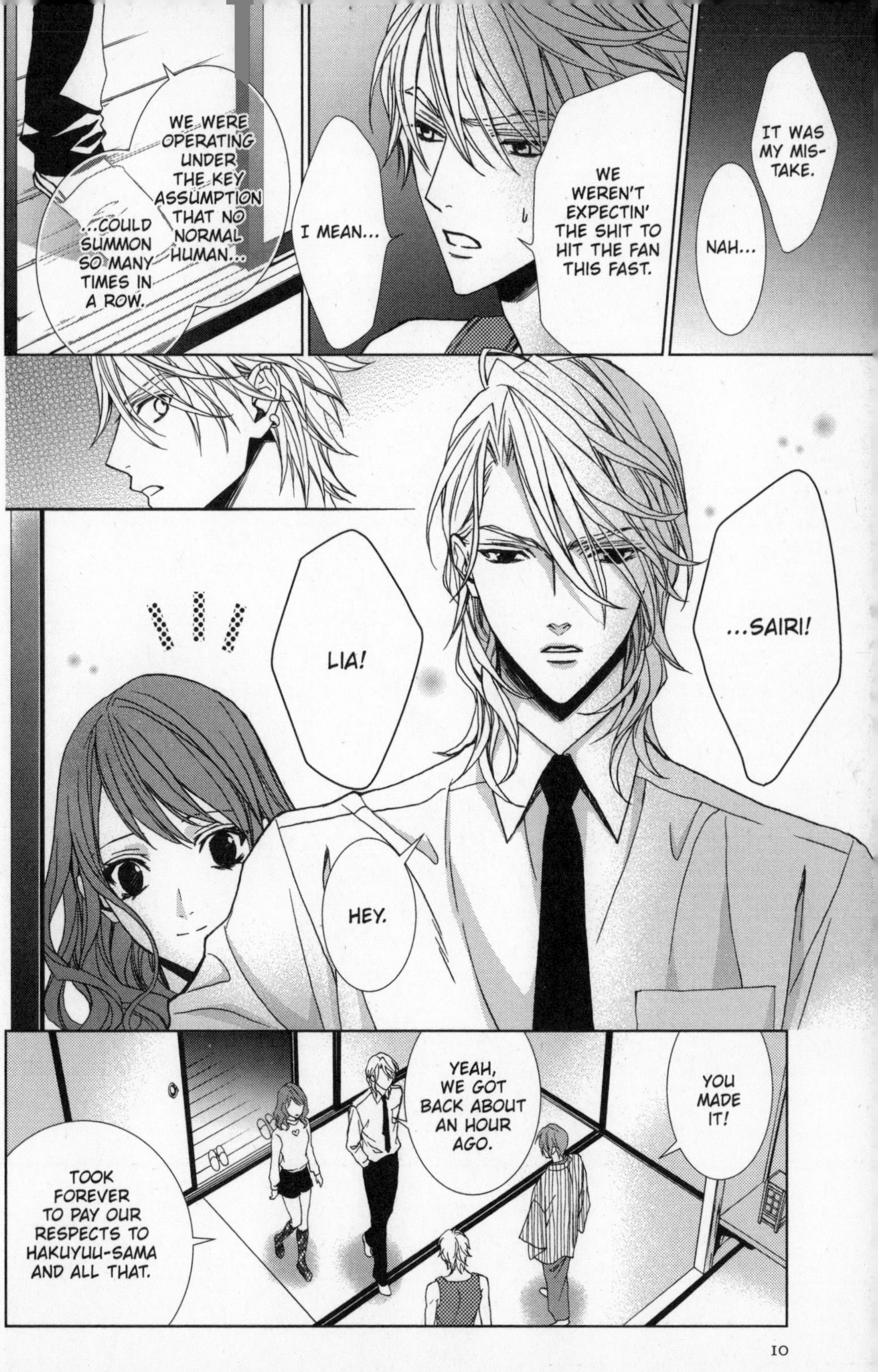
IT WAS MY MIS-TAKE.
NAH...
WE WEREN'T EXPECTIN' THE SHIT TO HIT THE FAN THIS FAST.
I MEAN...
WE WERE OPERATING UNDER THE KEY ASSUMPTION THAT NO NORMAL HUMAN...
...COULD SUMMON SO MANY TIMES IN A ROW.
...SAIRI!
LIA!
HEY.
YOU MADE IT!
YEAH, WE GOT BACK ABOUT AN HOUR AGO.
TOOK FOREVER TO PAY OUR RESPECTS TO HAKUYUU-SAMA AND ALL THAT.

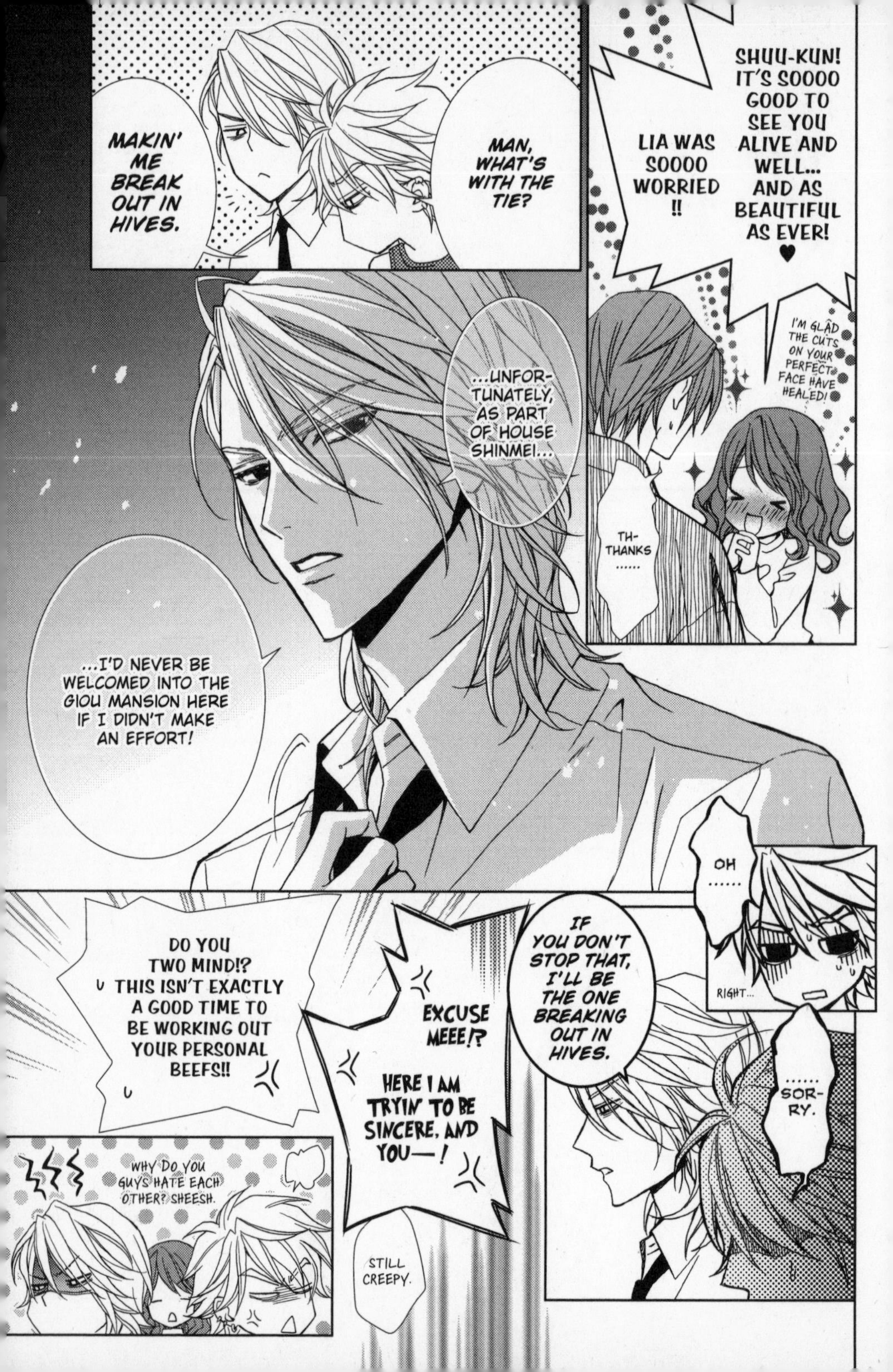
SHUU-KUN! IT'S SOOOO GOOD TO SEE YOU ALIVE AND WELL... AND AS BEAUTIFUL AS EVER! ♥
LIA WAS SOOOO WORRIED!!
I'M GLAD THE CUTS ON YOUR PERFECT FACE HAVE HEALED!
TH-THANKS......
MAN, WHAT'S WITH THE TIE?
MAKIN' ME BREAK OUT IN HIVES.
...UNFORTUNATELY, AS PART OF HOUSE SHINMEI...
...I'D NEVER BE WELCOMED INTO THE GIOU MANSION HERE IF I DIDN'T MAKE AN EFFORT!
IF YOU DON'T STOP THAT, I'LL BE THE ONE BREAKING OUT IN HIVES.
OH......
RIGHT...
......SORRY.
EXCUSE MEEE!?
HERE I AM TRYIN' TO BE SINCERE, AND YOU—!
DO YOU TWO MIND!? THIS ISN'T EXACTLY A GOOD TIME TO BE WORKING OUT YOUR PERSONAL BEEFS!!
STILL CREEPY.
WHY DO YOU GUYS HATE EACH OTHER? SHEESH.

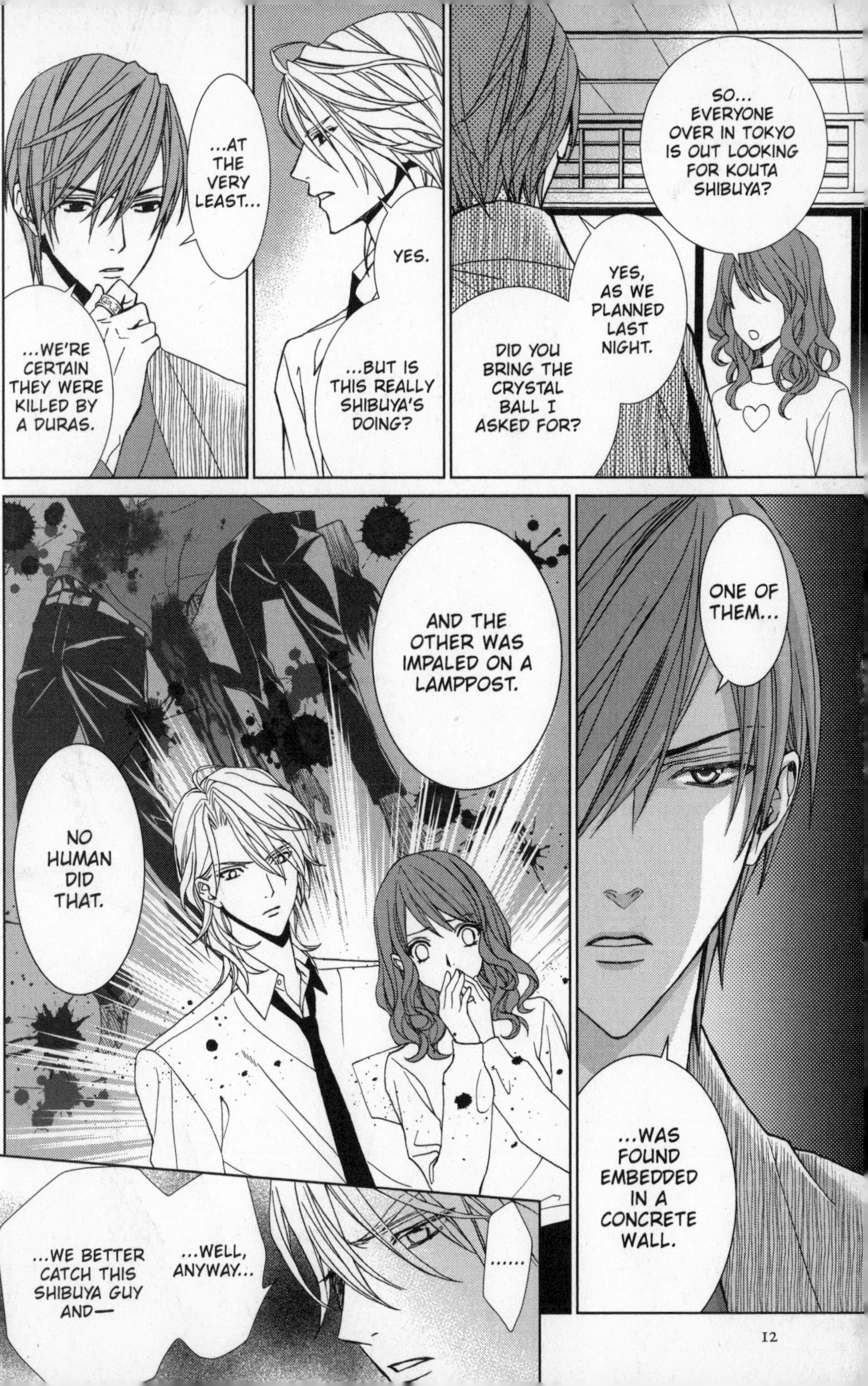
SO... EVERYONE OVER IN TOKYO IS OUT LOOKING FOR KOUTA SHIBUYA?
YES, AS WE PLANNED LAST NIGHT.
DID YOU BRING THE CRYSTAL BALL I ASKED FOR?
YES.
...BUT IS THIS REALLY SHIBUYA'S DOING?
...AT THE VERY LEAST...
...WE'RE CERTAIN THEY WERE KILLED BY A DURAS.
ONE OF THEM...
...WAS FOUND EMBEDDED IN A CONCRETE WALL.
AND THE OTHER WAS IMPALED ON A LAMPPOST.
NO HUMAN DID THAT.
......
...WELL, ANYWAY...
...WE BETTER CATCH THIS SHIBUYA GUY AND—

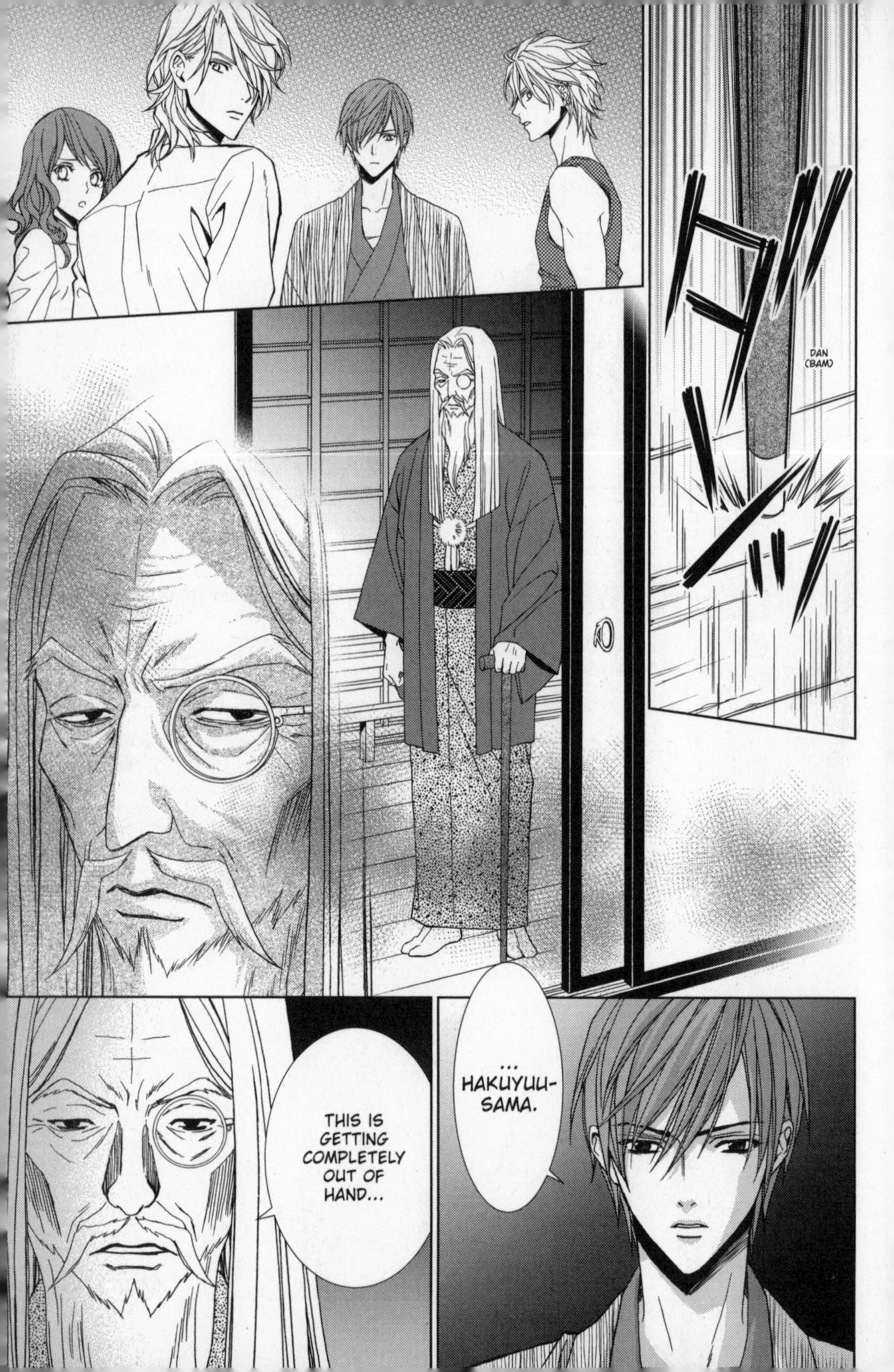
DAN (BAM)
... HAKUYUU-SAMA.
THIS IS GETTING COMPLETELY OUT OF HAND...

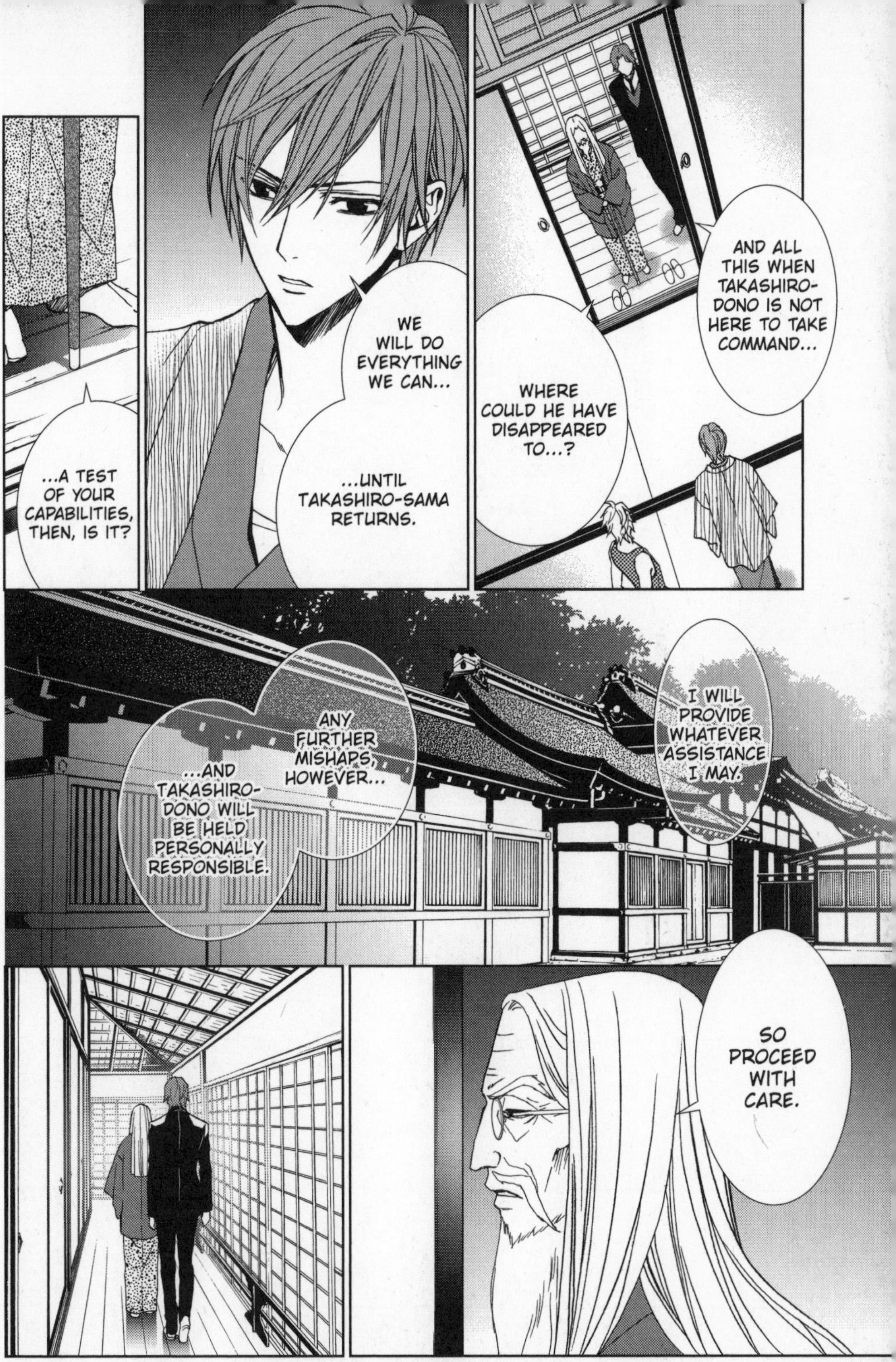
AND ALL THIS WHEN TAKASHIRO-DONO IS NOT HERE TO TAKE COMMAND...
WHERE COULD HE HAVE DISAPPEARED TO...?
WE WILL DO EVERYTHING WE CAN...
...UNTIL TAKASHIRO-SAMA RETURNS.
...A TEST OF YOUR CAPABILITIES, THEN, IS IT?
I WILL PROVIDE WHATEVER ASSISTANCE I MAY.
ANY FURTHER MISHAPS, HOWEVER...
...AND TAKASHIRO-DONO WILL BE HELD PERSONALLY RESPONSIBLE.
SO PROCEED WITH CARE.

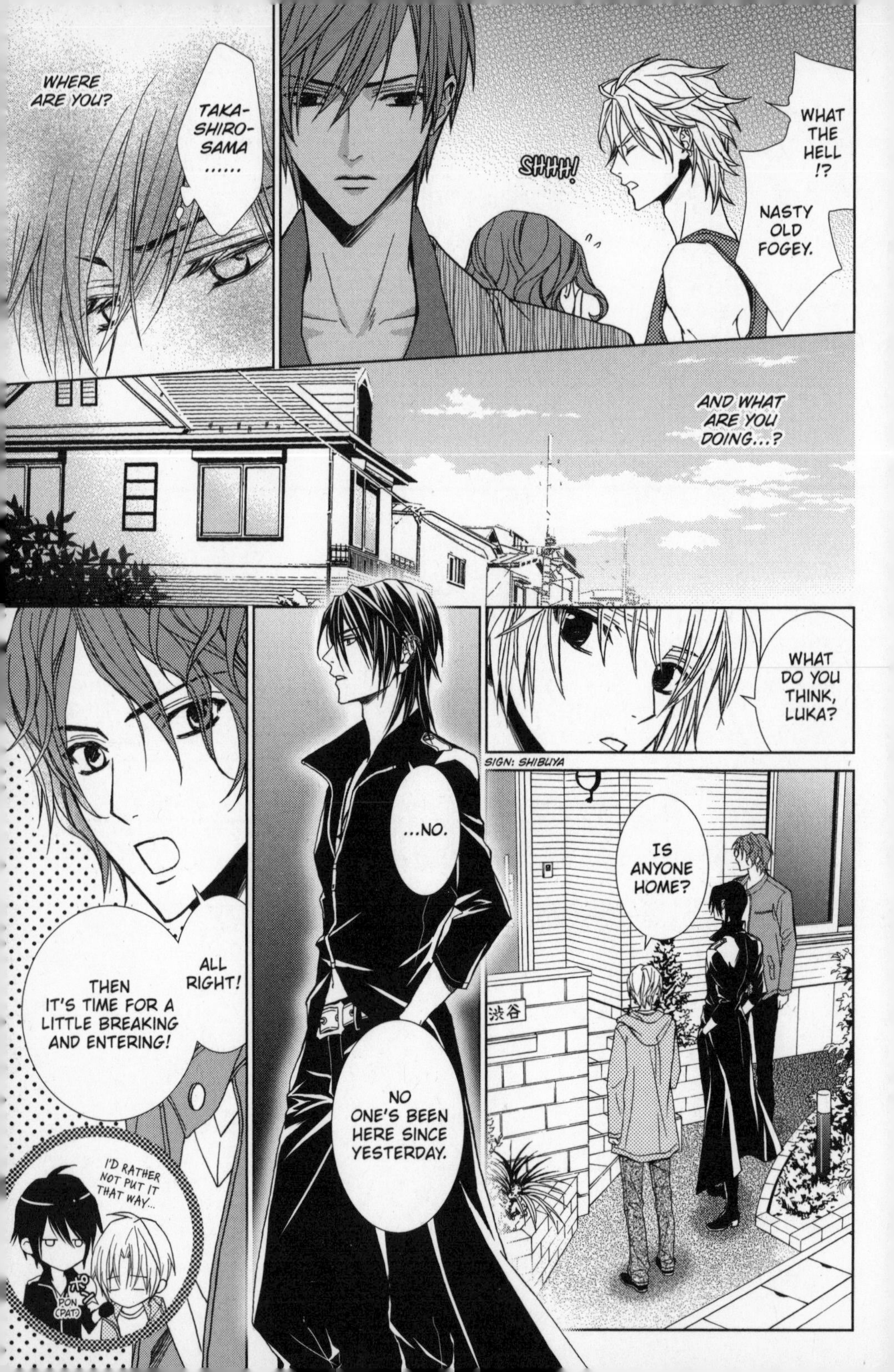
WHAT THE HELL !?
NASTY OLD FOGEY.
SHHH!
TAKA-SHIRO-SAMA ......
WHERE ARE YOU?
AND WHAT ARE YOU DOING...?
WHAT DO YOU THINK, LUKA?
SIGN: SHIBUYA
IS ANYONE HOME?
渋谷
...NO.
NO ONE'S BEEN HERE SINCE YESTERDAY.
ALL RIGHT!
THEN IT'S TIME FOR A LITTLE BREAKING AND ENTERING!
I'D RATHER NOT PUT IT THAT WAY...
PON (PAT)

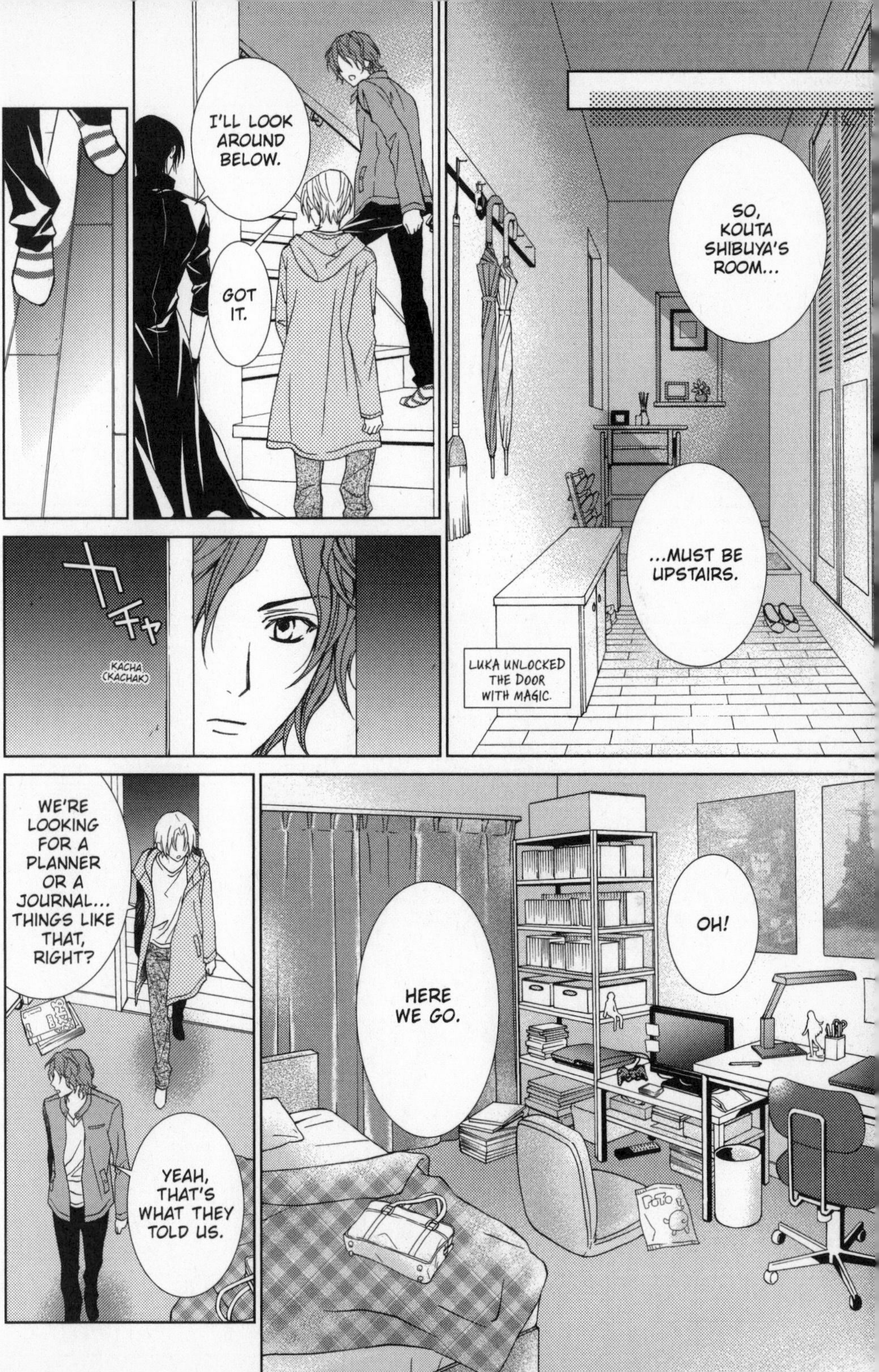
SO, KOUTA SHIBUYA'S ROOM...
...MUST BE UPSTAIRS.
LUKA UNLOCKED THE DOOR WITH MAGIC.
I'LL LOOK AROUND BELOW.
GOT IT.
カチャ
KACHA (KACHAK)
OH!
HERE WE GO.
WE'RE LOOKING FOR A PLANNER OR A JOURNAL... THINGS LIKE THAT, RIGHT?
YEAH, THAT'S WHAT THEY TOLD US.

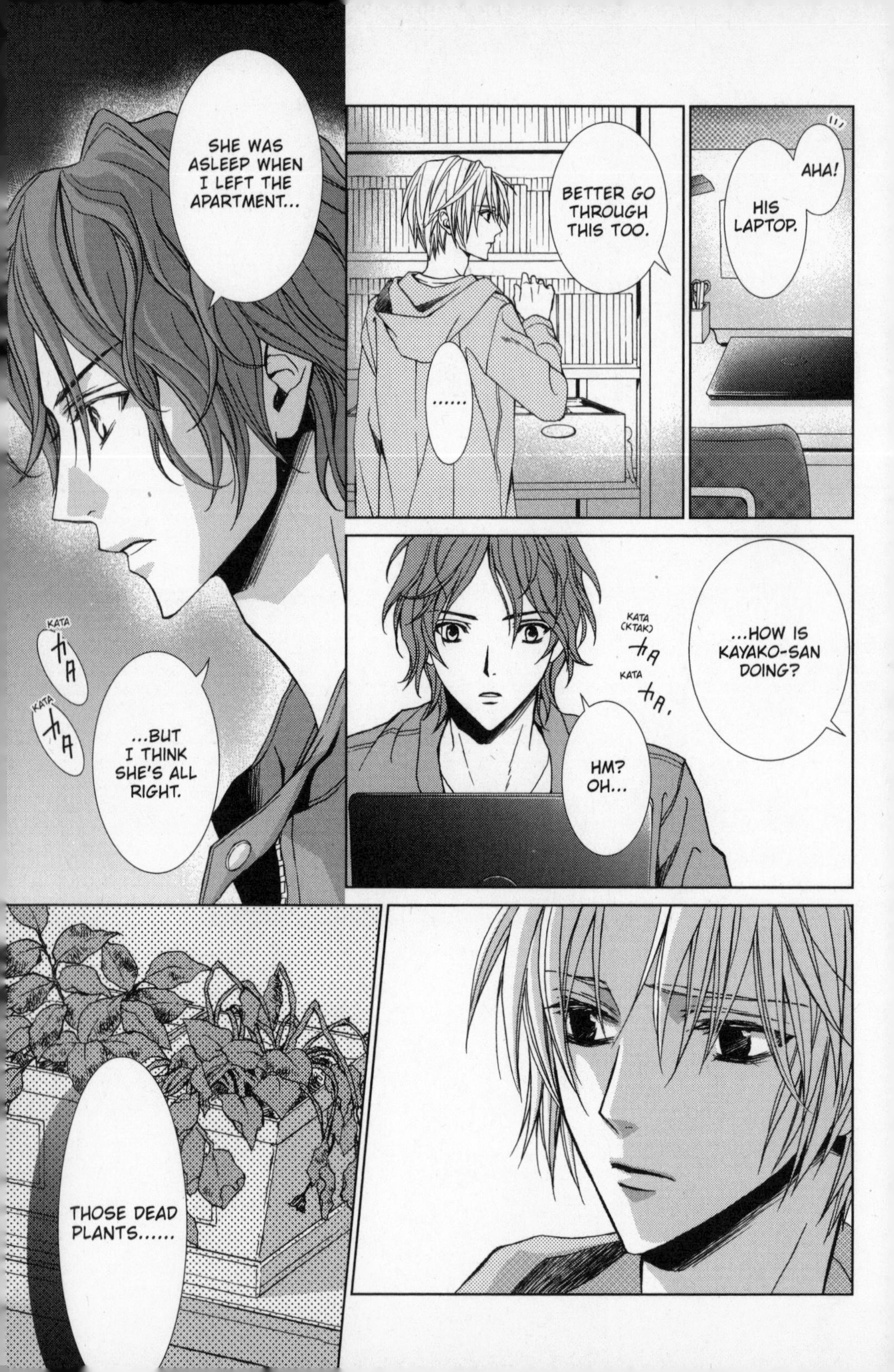
AHA!
HIS LAPTOP.
BETTER GO THROUGH THIS TOO.
......
...HOW IS KAYAKO-SAN DOING?
KATA (KTAK)
KATA
HM? OH...
SHE WAS ASLEEP WHEN I LEFT THE APARTMENT...
KATA
KATA
...BUT I THINK SHE'S ALL RIGHT.
THOSE DEAD PLANTS......

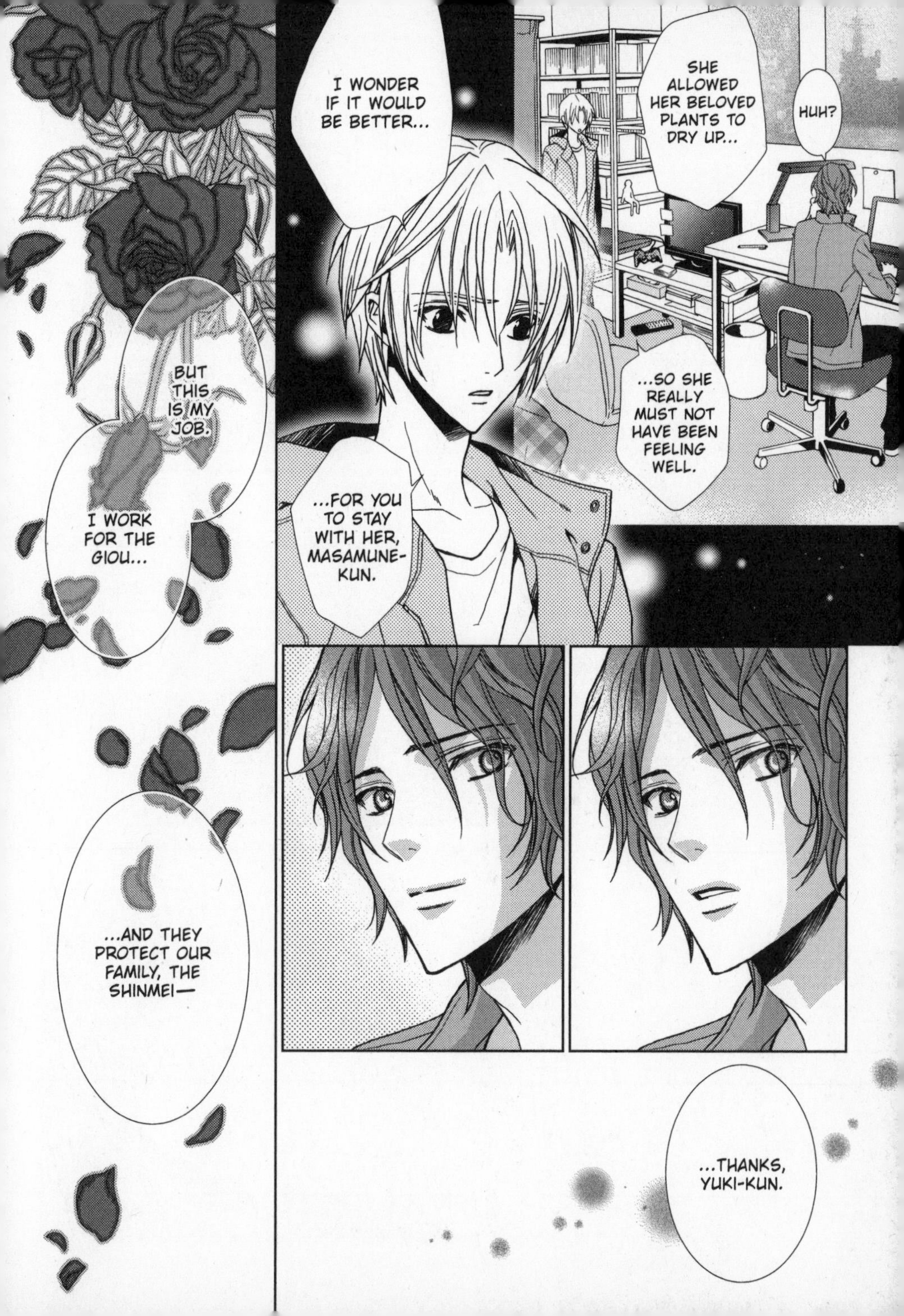
HUH?
SHE ALLOWED HER BELOVED PLANTS TO DRY UP...
...SO SHE REALLY MUST NOT HAVE BEEN FEELING WELL.
I WONDER IF IT WOULD BE BETTER...
...FOR YOU TO STAY WITH HER, MASAMUNE-KUN.
...THANKS, YUKI-KUN.
BUT THIS IS MY JOB.
I WORK FOR THE GIOU...
...AND THEY PROTECT OUR FAMILY, THE SHINMEI—

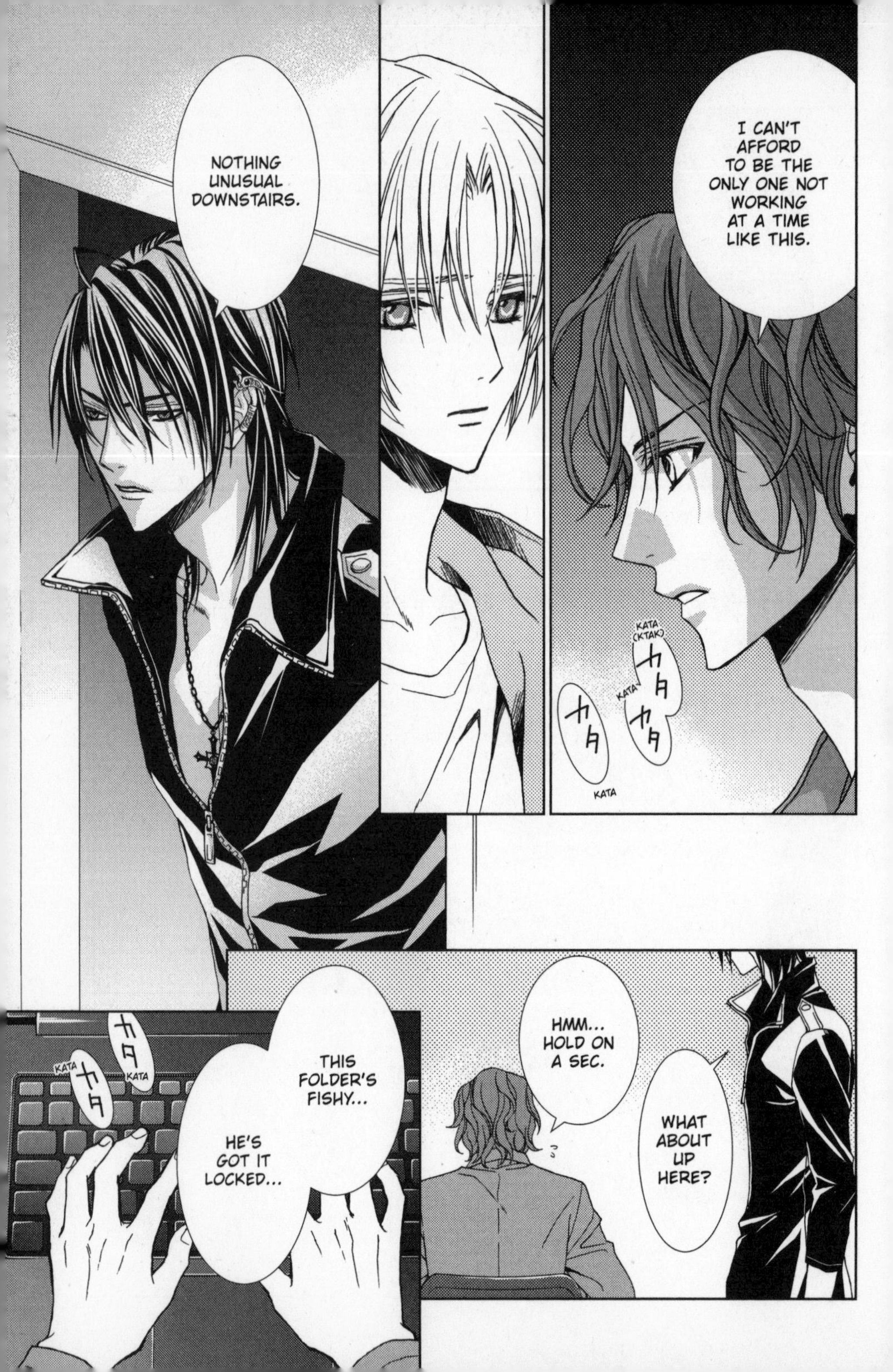
I CAN'T AFFORD TO BE THE ONLY ONE NOT WORKING AT A TIME LIKE THIS.
KATA (KTAK)
カタ
KATA
カタ
カタ
KATA
NOTHING UNUSUAL DOWNSTAIRS.
WHAT ABOUT UP HERE?
HMM... HOLD ON A SEC.
THIS FOLDER'S FISHY...
HE'S GOT IT LOCKED...
カタ
KATA
カタ
KATA

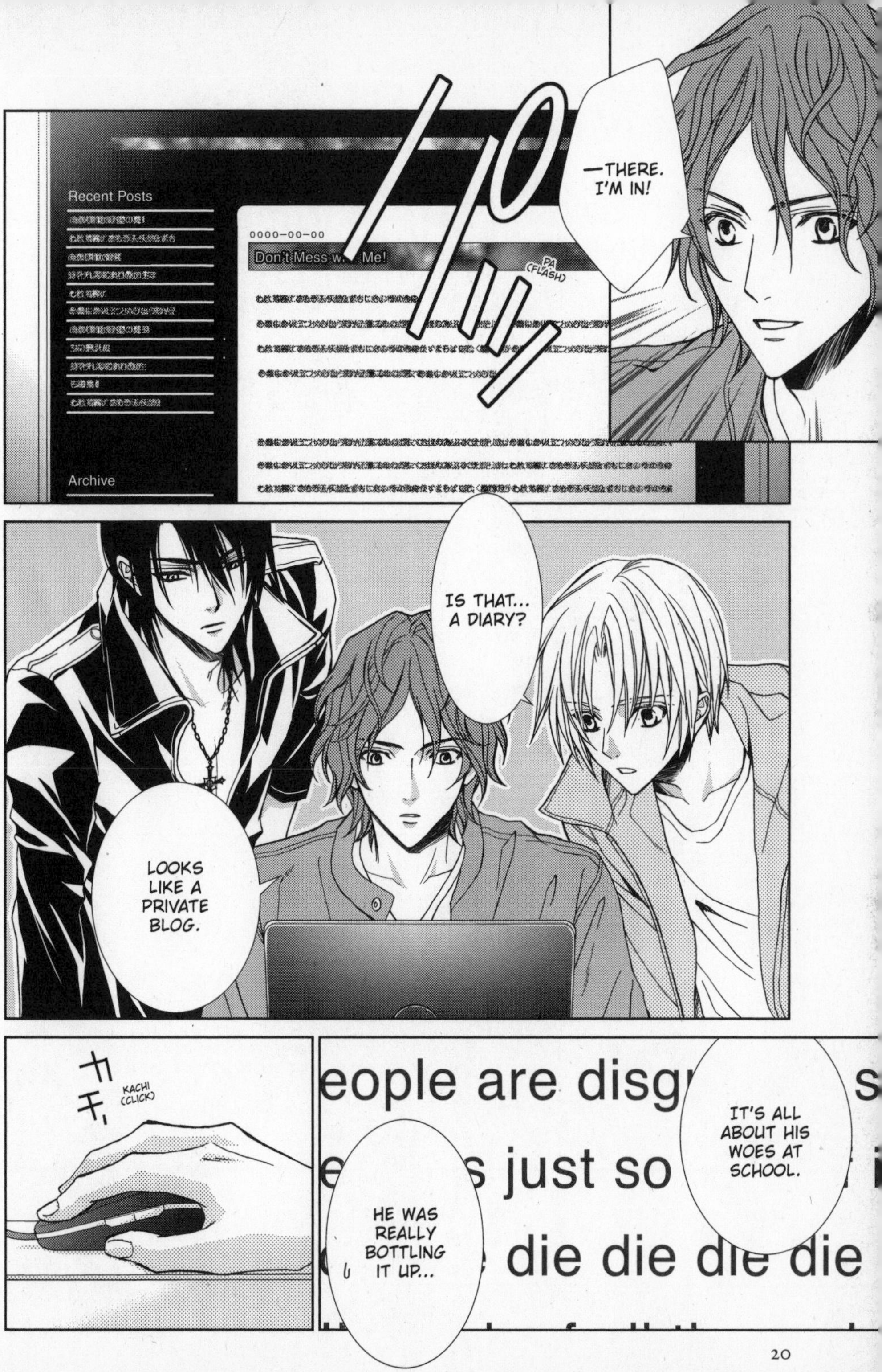
—THERE. I'M IN!
PA (FLASH)
Recent Posts
0000-00-00
Archive
IS THAT... A DIARY?
LOOKS LIKE A PRIVATE BLOG.
eople are disgr
s just so
die die die die
IT'S ALL ABOUT HIS WOES AT SCHOOL.
HE WAS REALLY BOTTLING IT UP...
KACHI (CLICK)

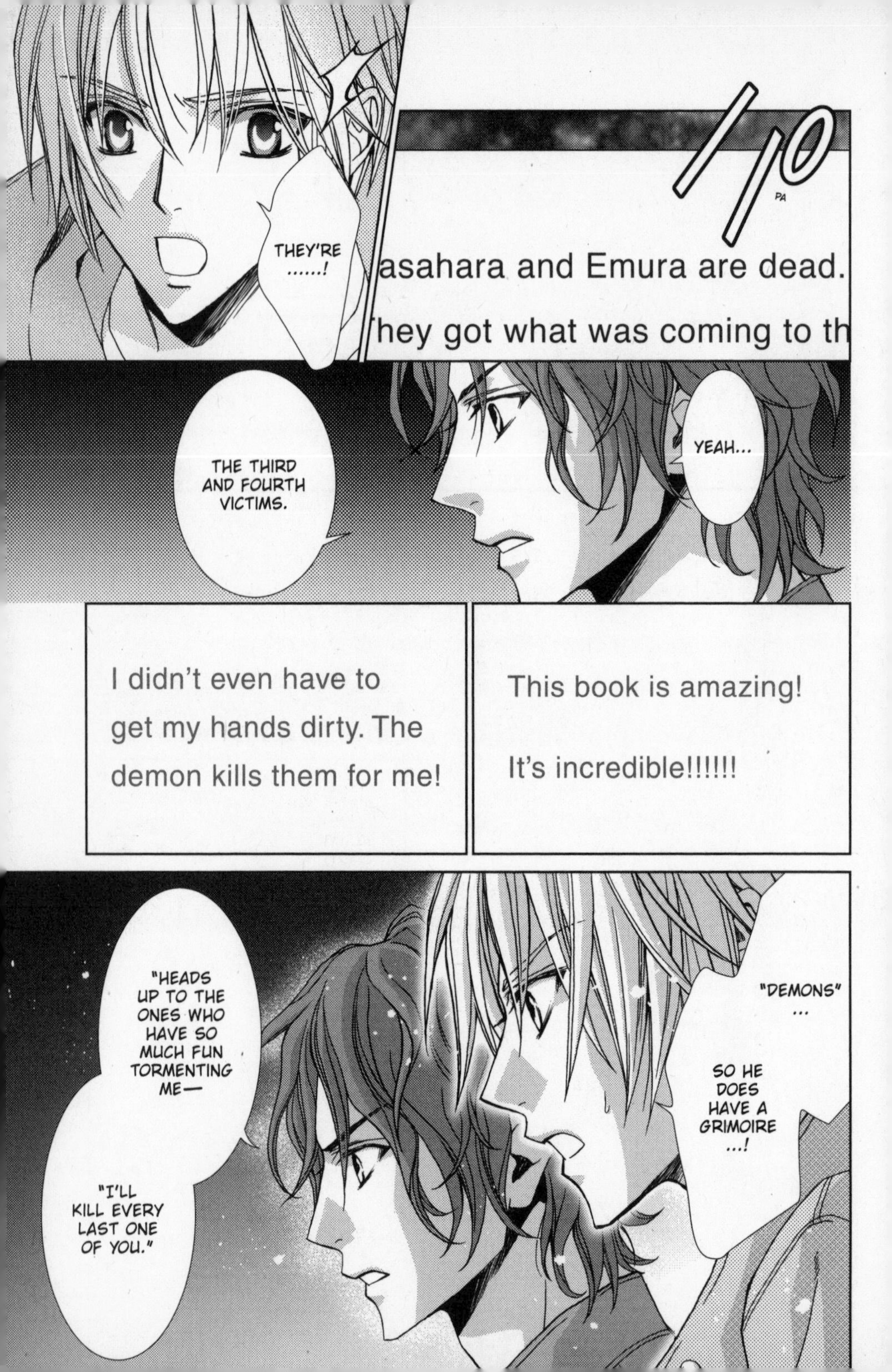
PA
asahara and Emura are dead.
They got what was coming to th
THEY'RE ......!
YEAH...
THE THIRD AND FOURTH VICTIMS.
This book is amazing! It's incredible!!!!!!
I didn't even have to get my hands dirty. The demon kills them for me!
"DEMONS" ...
SO HE DOES HAVE A GRIMOIRE ...!
"HEADS UP TO THE ONES WHO HAVE SO MUCH FUN TORMENTING ME—
"I'LL KILL EVERY LAST ONE OF YOU."

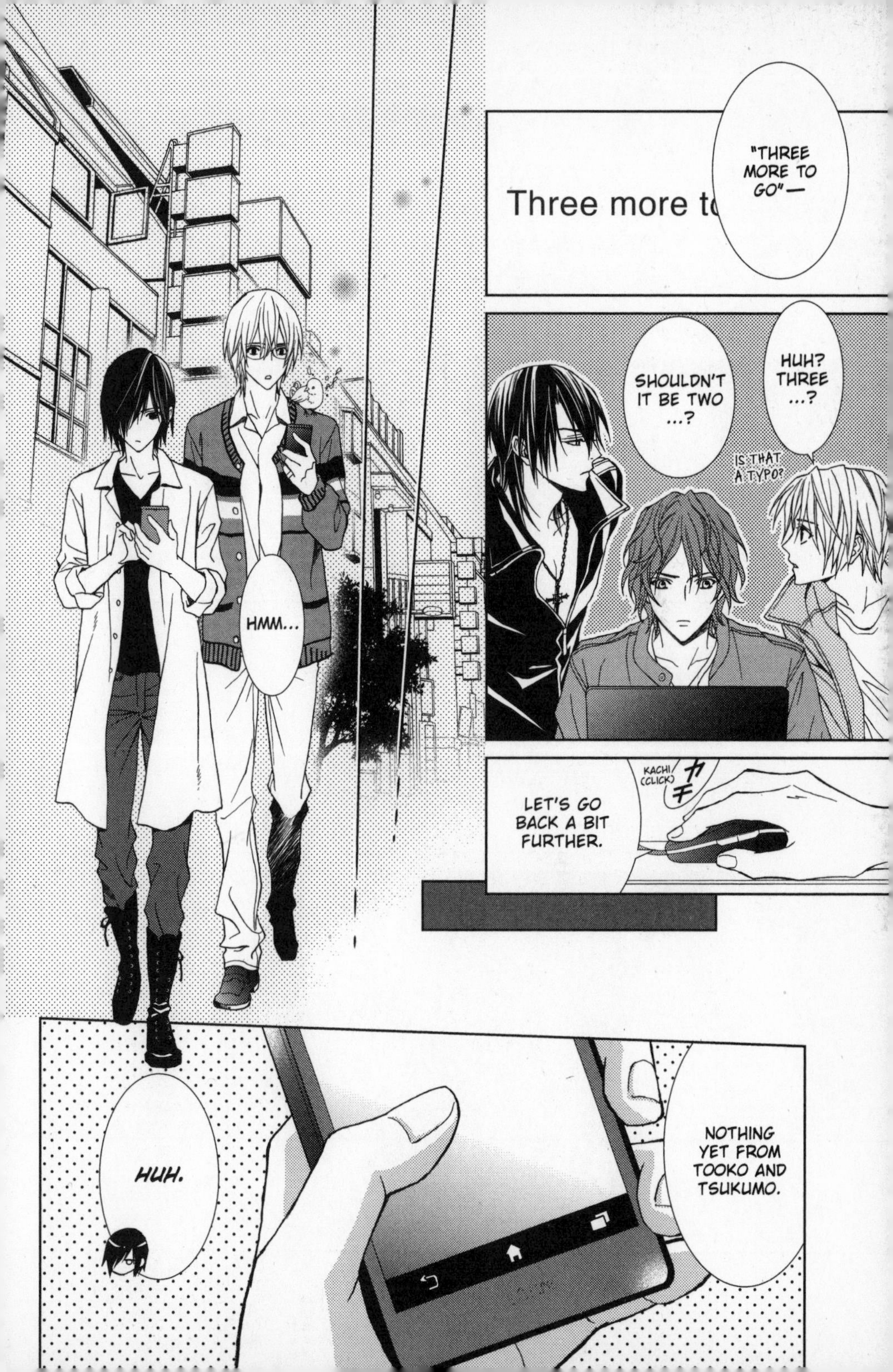
Three more to
"THREE MORE TO GO"—
HUH? THREE ...?
IS THAT A TYPO?
SHOULDN'T IT BE TWO ...?
KACHI (CLICK)
LET'S GO BACK A BIT FURTHER.
HMM...
NOTHING YET FROM TOOKO AND TSUKUMO.
HUH.

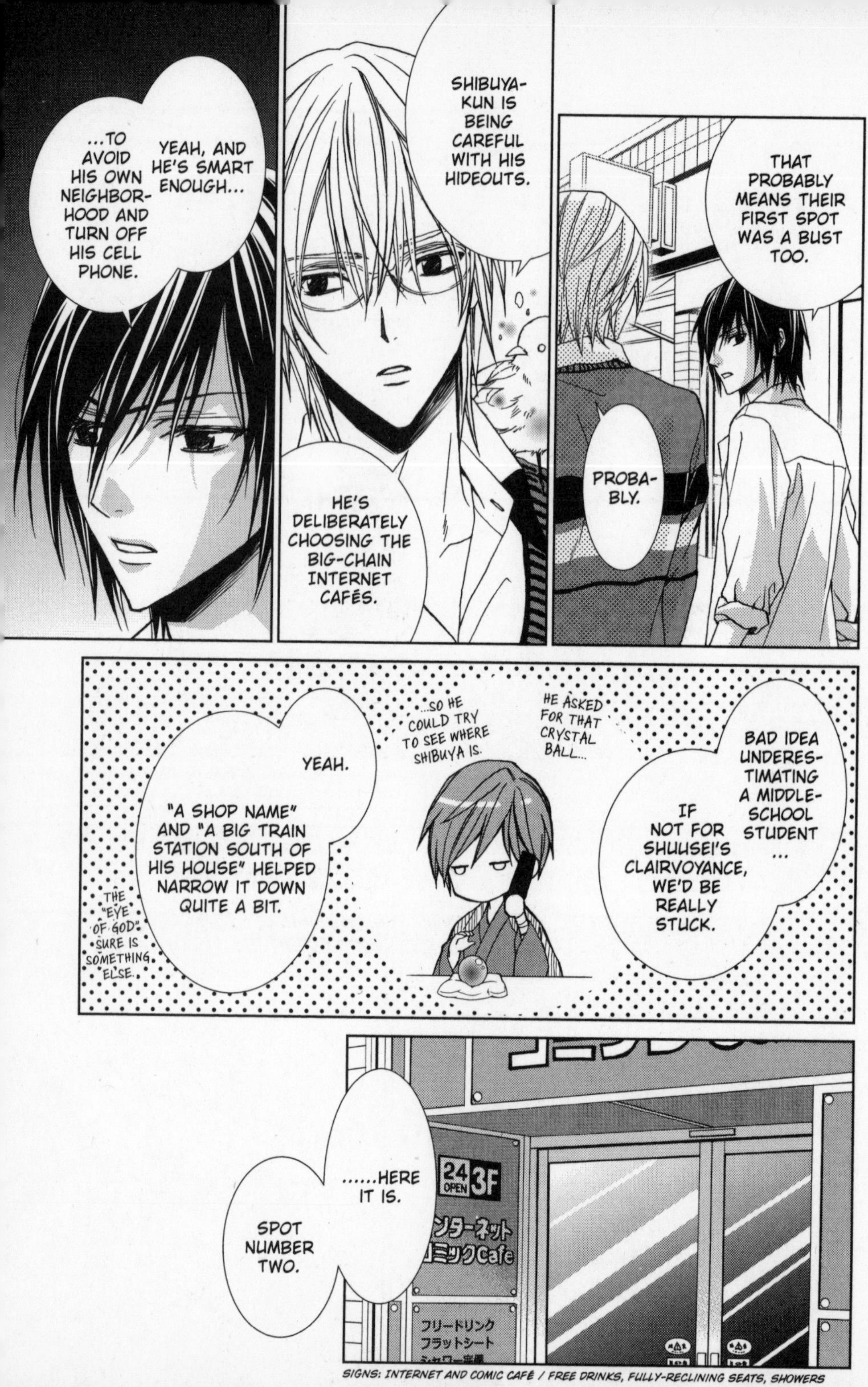
THAT PROBABLY MEANS THEIR FIRST SPOT WAS A BUST TOO.
PROBA-BLY.
SHIBUYA-KUN IS BEING CAREFUL WITH HIS HIDEOUTS.
HE'S DELIBERATELY CHOOSING THE BIG-CHAIN INTERNET CAFÉS.
YEAH, AND HE'S SMART ENOUGH...
...TO AVOID HIS OWN NEIGHBOR-HOOD AND TURN OFF HIS CELL PHONE.
BAD IDEA UNDERES-TIMATING A MIDDLE-SCHOOL STUDENT ...
IF NOT FOR SHUUSEI'S CLAIRVOYANCE, WE'D BE REALLY STUCK.
HE ASKED FOR THAT CRYSTAL BALL...
...SO HE COULD TRY TO SEE WHERE SHIBUYA IS.
YEAH.
"A SHOP NAME" AND "A BIG TRAIN STATION SOUTH OF HIS HOUSE" HELPED NARROW IT DOWN QUITE A BIT.
THE "EYE OF GOD" SURE IS SOMETHING ELSE.
......HERE IT IS.
SPOT NUMBER TWO.
24 OPEN 3F
フリードリンク
フラットシート

SIGNS: INTERNET AND COMIC CAFÉ / FREE DRINKS, FULLY-RECLINING SEATS, SHOWERS

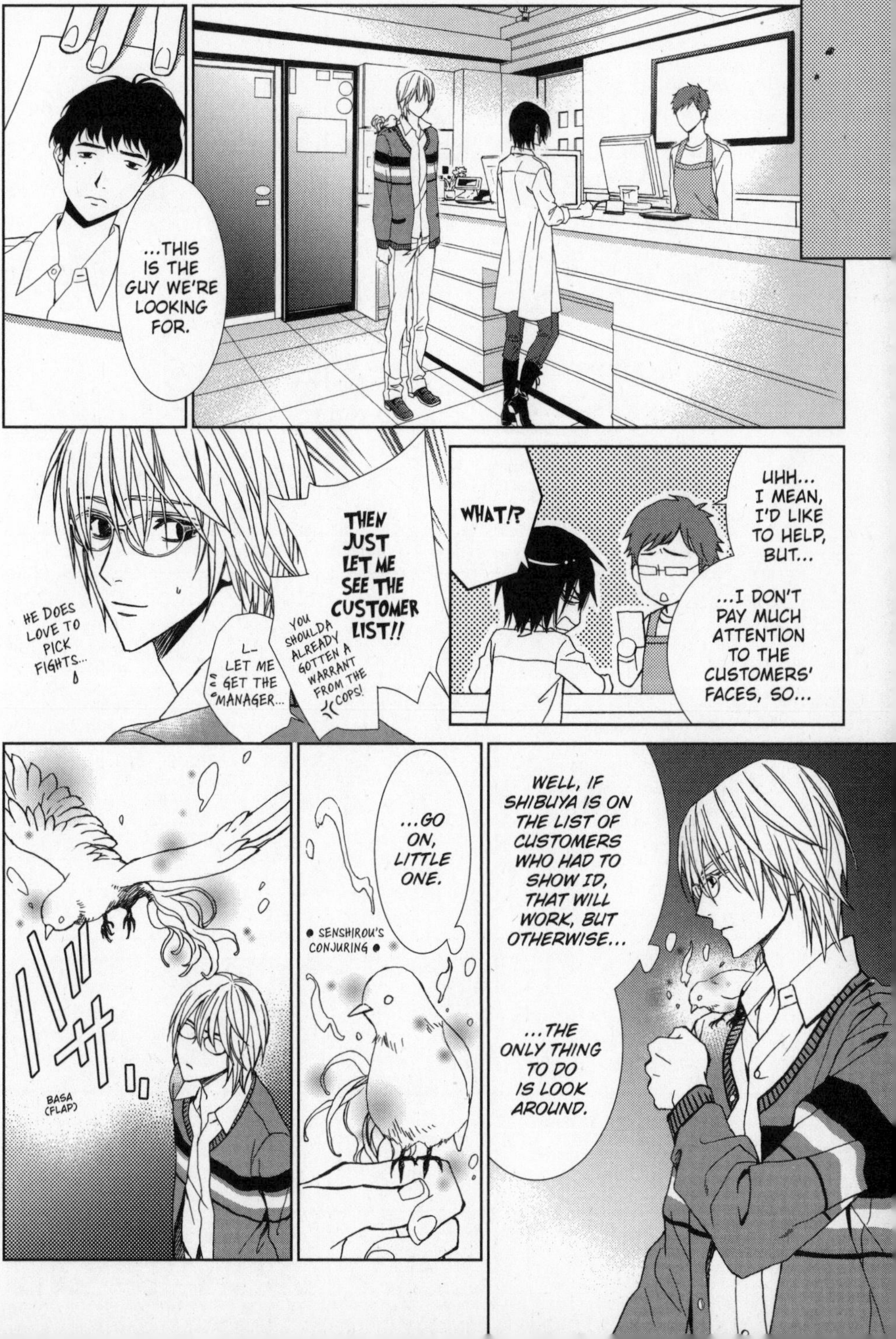
...THIS IS THE GUY WE'RE LOOKING FOR.
UHH... I MEAN, I'D LIKE TO HELP, BUT...
WHAT!?
...I DON'T PAY MUCH ATTENTION TO THE CUSTOMERS' FACES, SO...
THEN JUST LET ME SEE THE CUSTOMER LIST!!
YOU SHOULDA ALREADY GOTTEN A WARRANT FROM THE COPS!
L- LET ME GET THE MANAGER...
HE DOES LOVE TO PICK FIGHTS...
WELL, IF SHIBUYA IS ON THE LIST OF CUSTOMERS WHO HAD TO SHOW ID, THAT WILL WORK, BUT OTHERWISE...
...THE ONLY THING TO DO IS LOOK AROUND.
...GO ON, LITTLE ONE.
● SENSHIROU'S CONJURING ●
BASA (FLAP)

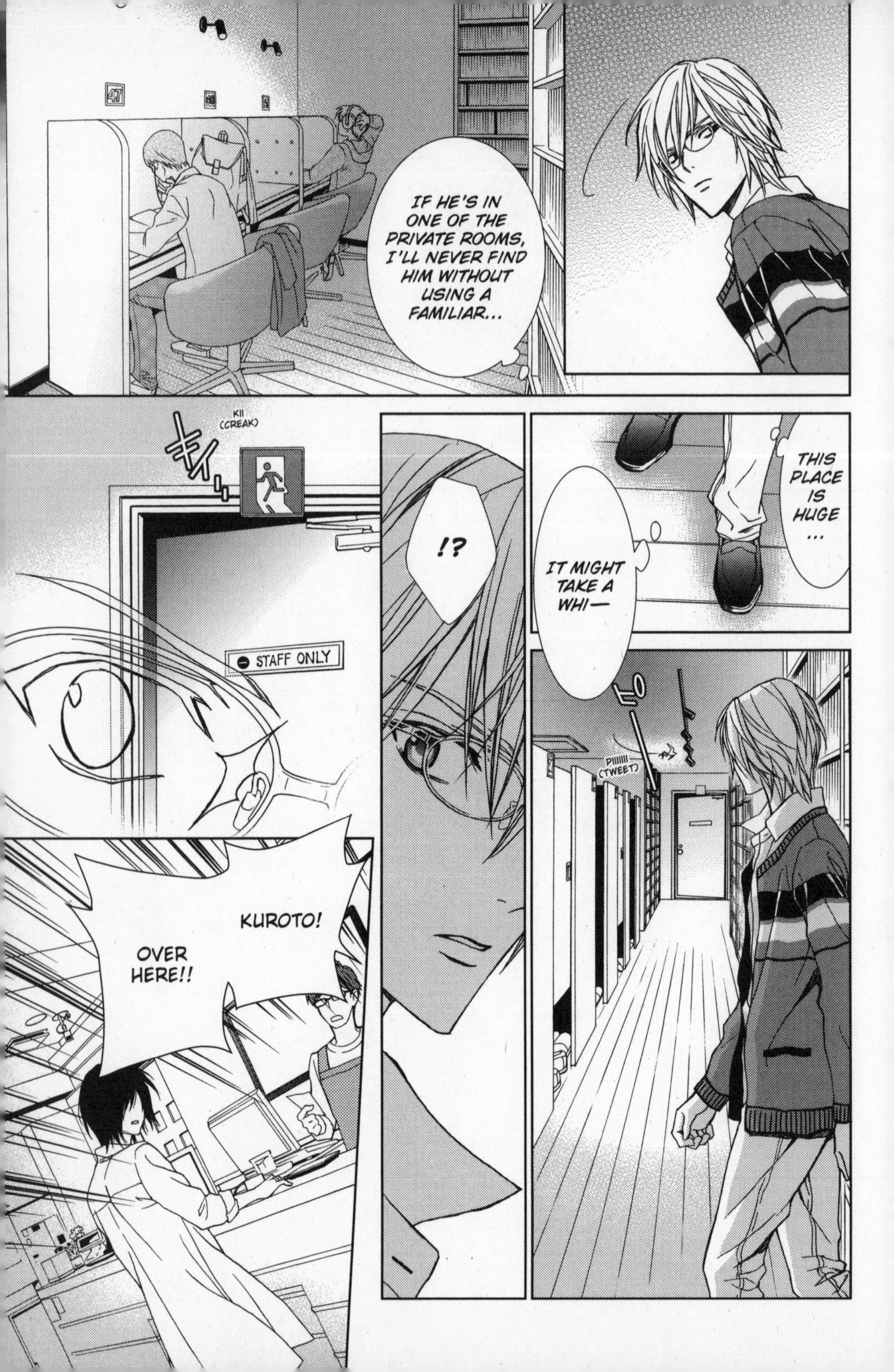
IF HE'S IN ONE OF THE PRIVATE ROOMS, I'LL NEVER FIND HIM WITHOUT USING A FAMILIAR...
THIS PLACE IS HUGE...
IT MIGHT TAKE A WHI—
PIIIIII (TWEET)
!?
KII (CREAK)
STAFF ONLY
KUROTO!
OVER HERE!!

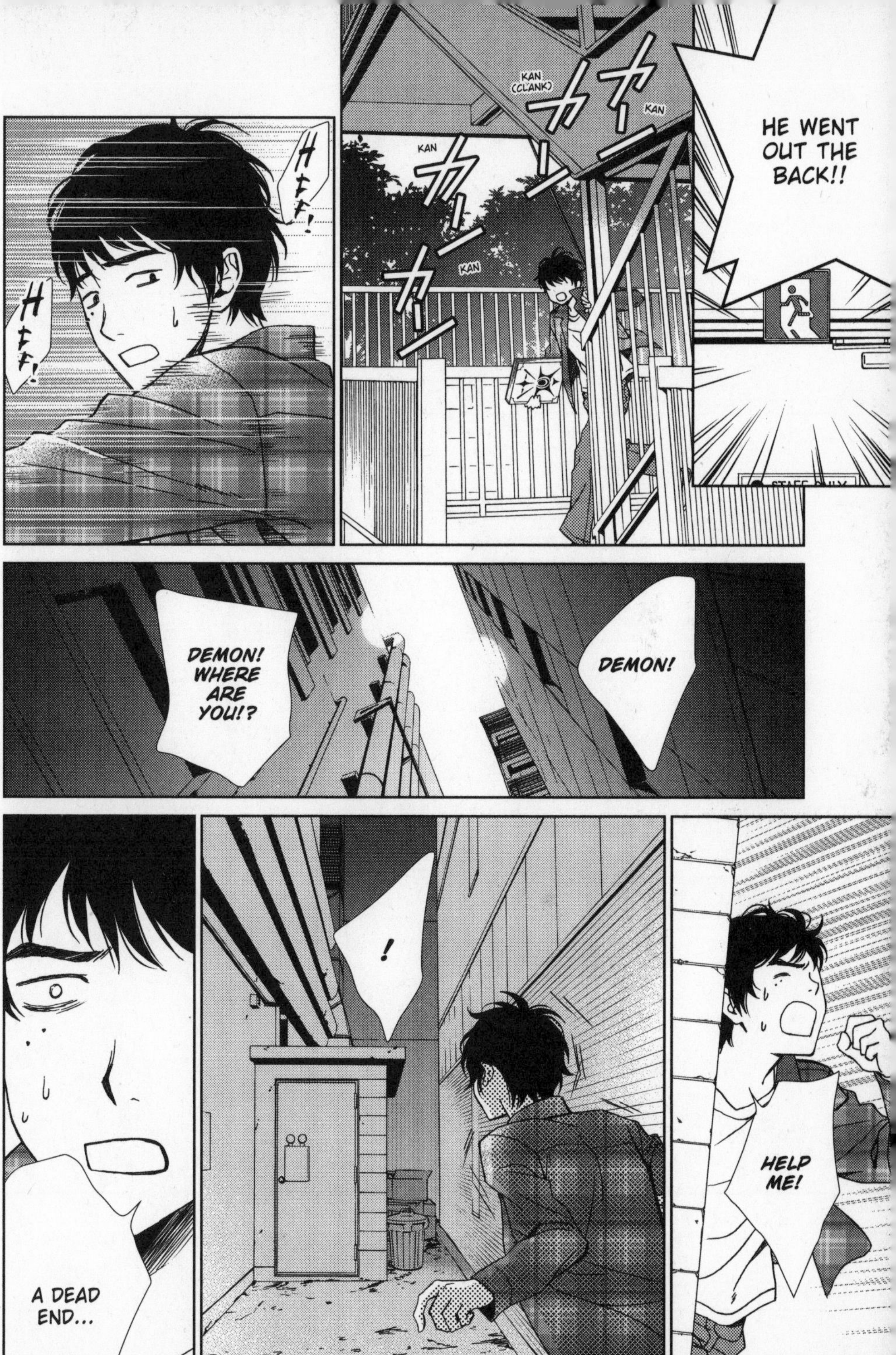
HE WENT OUT THE BACK!!
KAN (CLANK)
KAN
KAN
KAN
HFF!
HFF!
DEMON!
DEMON! WHERE ARE YOU!?
HELP ME!
!
A DEAD END...

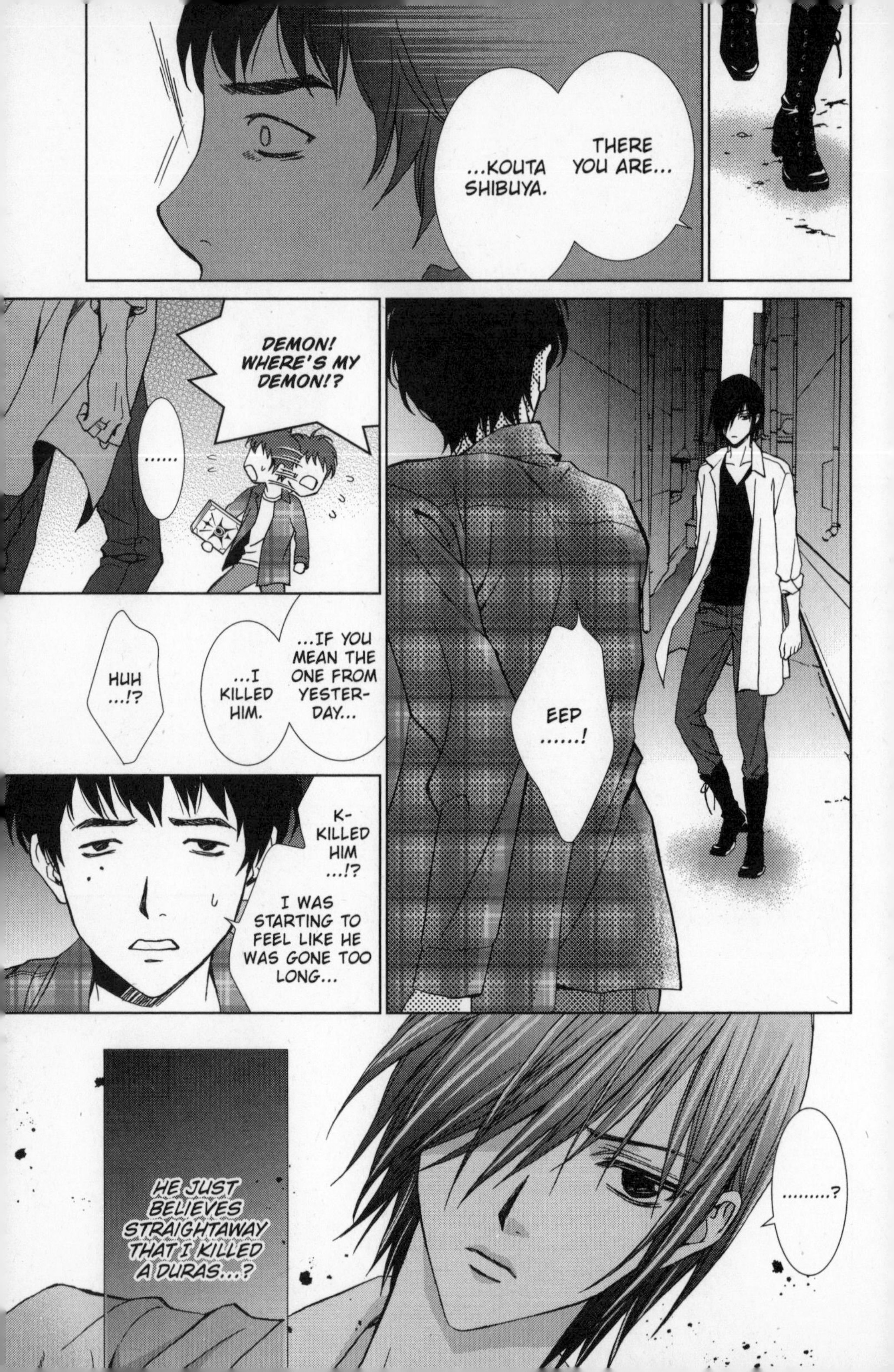
THERE YOU ARE...
...KOUTA SHIBUYA.
EEP ......!
DEMON! WHERE'S MY DEMON!?
......
...IF YOU MEAN THE ONE FROM YESTERDAY...
...I KILLED HIM.
HUH ...!?
K-KILLED HIM ...!?
I WAS STARTING TO FEEL LIKE HE WAS GONE TOO LONG...
.........?
HE JUST BELIEVES STRAIGHTAWAY THAT I KILLED A DURAS...?

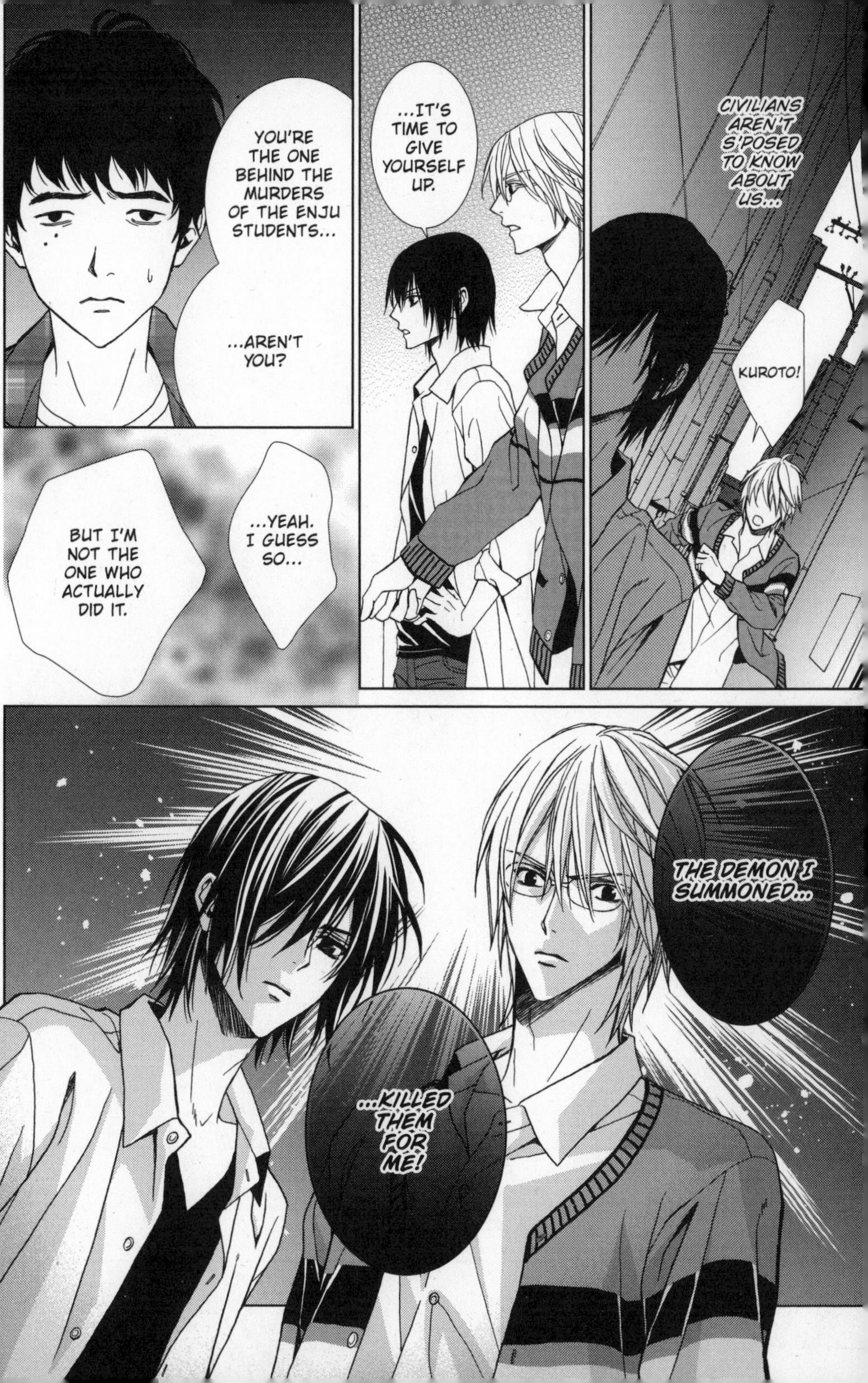
CIVILIANS AREN'T S'POSED TO KNOW ABOUT US...
KUROTO!
...IT'S TIME TO GIVE YOURSELF UP.
YOU'RE THE ONE BEHIND THE MURDERS OF THE ENJU STUDENTS...
...AREN'T YOU?
...YEAH. I GUESS SO...
BUT I'M NOT THE ONE WHO ACTUALLY DID IT.
THE DEMON I SUMMONED...
...KILLED THEM FOR ME!

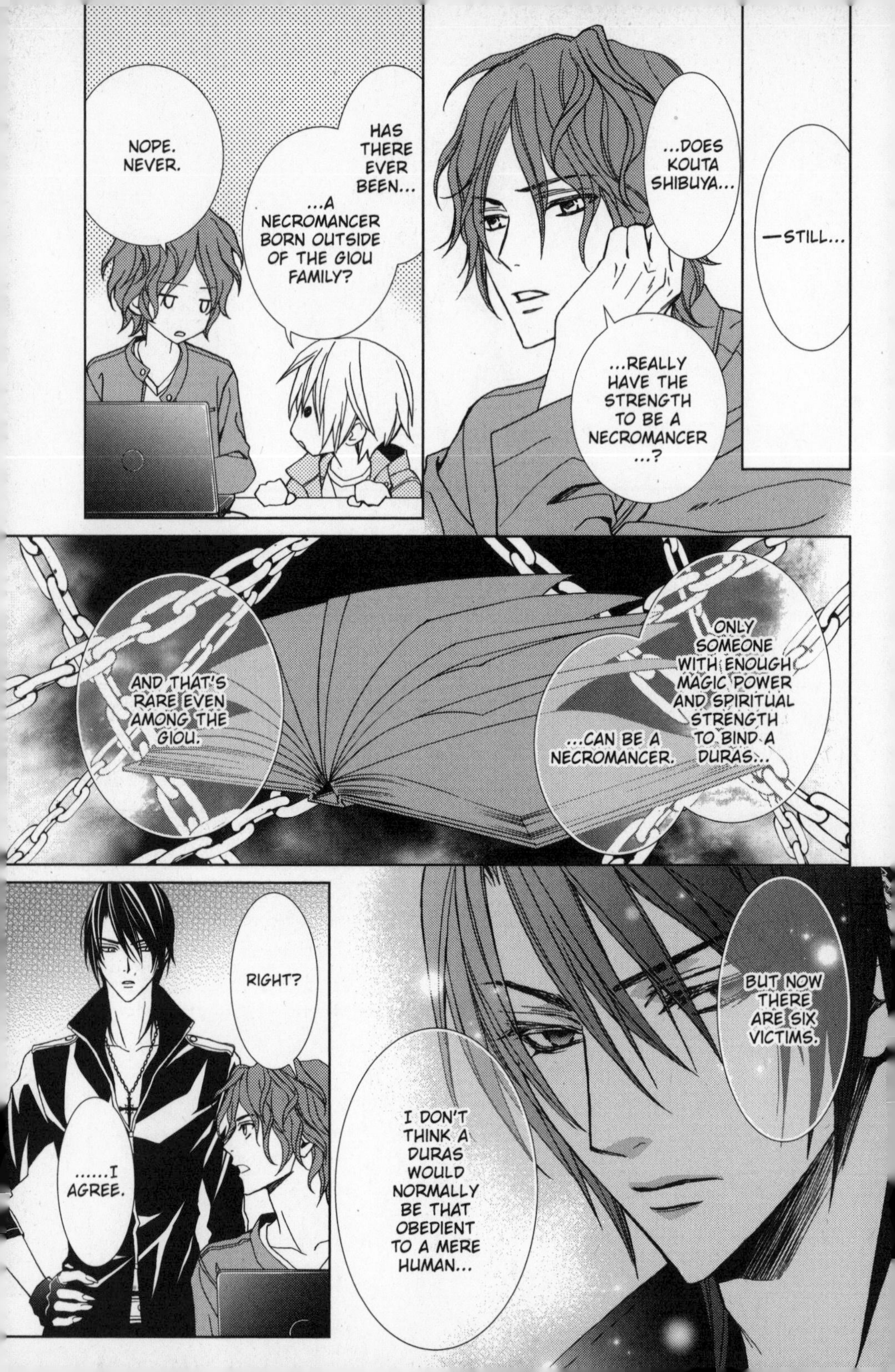
—STILL...
...DOES KOUTA SHIBUYA...
...REALLY HAVE THE STRENGTH TO BE A NECROMANCER ...?
HAS THERE EVER BEEN...
...A NECROMANCER BORN OUTSIDE OF THE GIOU FAMILY?
NOPE. NEVER.
ONLY SOMEONE WITH ENOUGH MAGIC POWER AND SPIRITUAL STRENGTH TO BIND A DURAS...
...CAN BE A NECROMANCER.
AND THAT'S RARE EVEN AMONG THE GIOU.
BUT NOW THERE ARE SIX VICTIMS.
I DON'T THINK A DURAS WOULD NORMALLY BE THAT OBEDIENT TO A MERE HUMAN...
RIGHT?
......I AGREE.

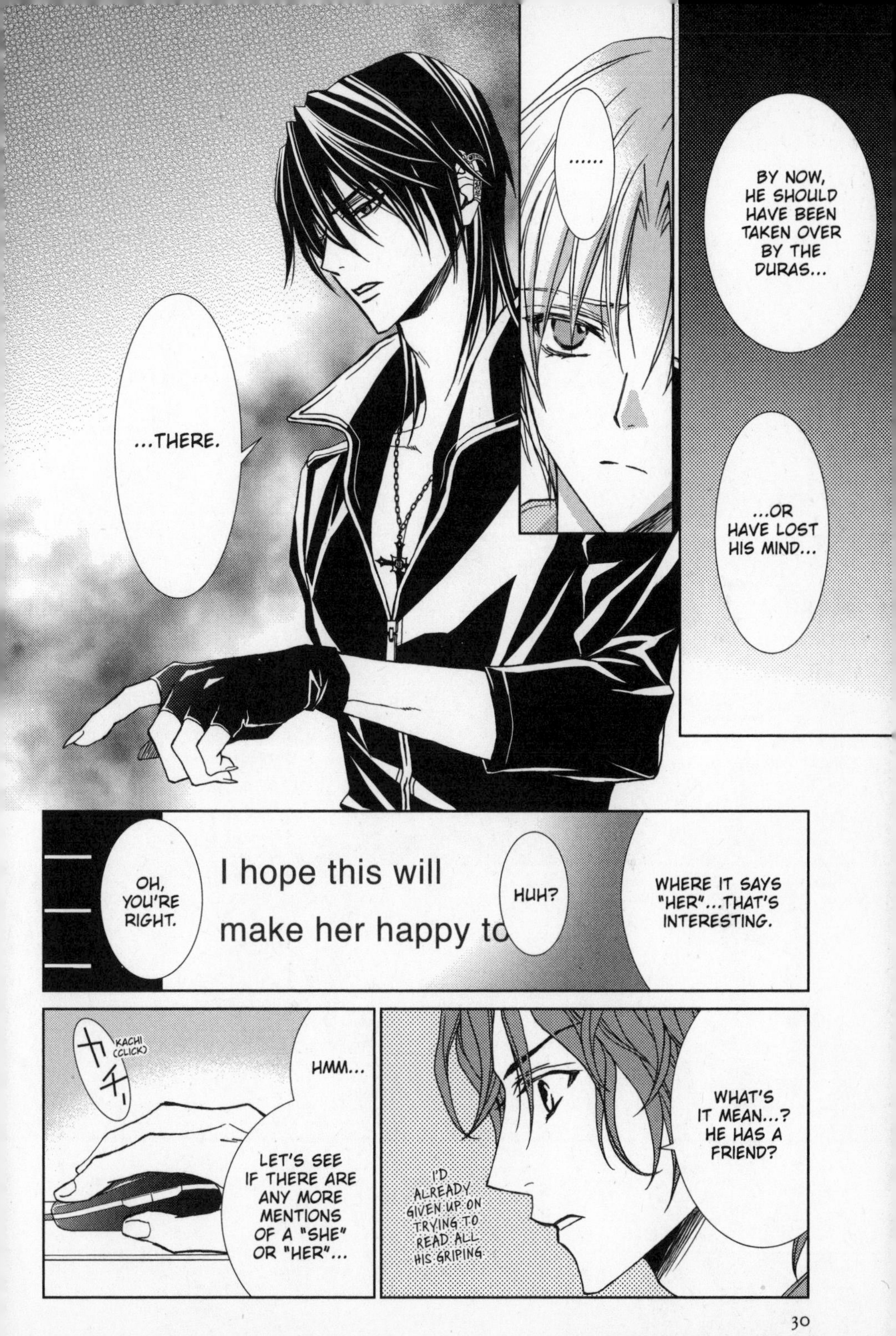
BY NOW, HE SHOULD HAVE BEEN TAKEN OVER BY THE DURAS...
...OR HAVE LOST HIS MIND...
......
...THERE.
WHERE IT SAYS "HER"...THAT'S INTERESTING.
HUH?
I hope this will make her happy to
OH, YOU'RE RIGHT.
WHAT'S IT MEAN...? HE HAS A FRIEND?
I'D ALREADY GIVEN UP ON TRYING TO READ ALL HIS GRIPING
HMM...
LET'S SEE IF THERE ARE ANY MORE MENTIONS OF A "SHE" OR "HER"...
カチー
KACHI (CLICK)

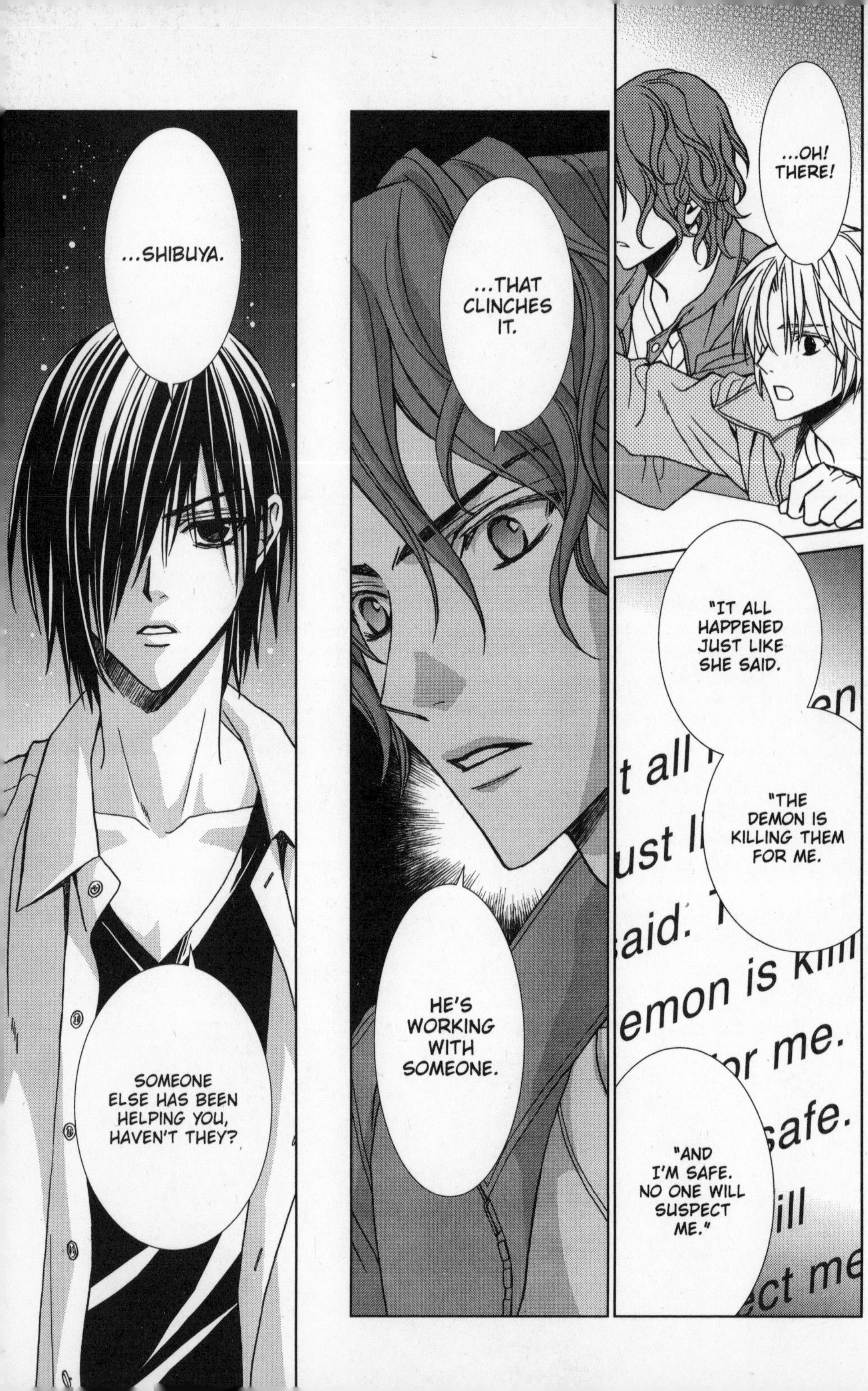
...OH! THERE!
"IT ALL HAPPENED JUST LIKE SHE SAID.
"THE DEMON IS KILLING THEM FOR ME.
"AND I'M SAFE. NO ONE WILL SUSPECT ME."
...THAT CLINCHES IT.
HE'S WORKING WITH SOMEONE.
...SHIBUYA.
SOMEONE ELSE HAS BEEN HELPING YOU, HAVEN'T THEY?

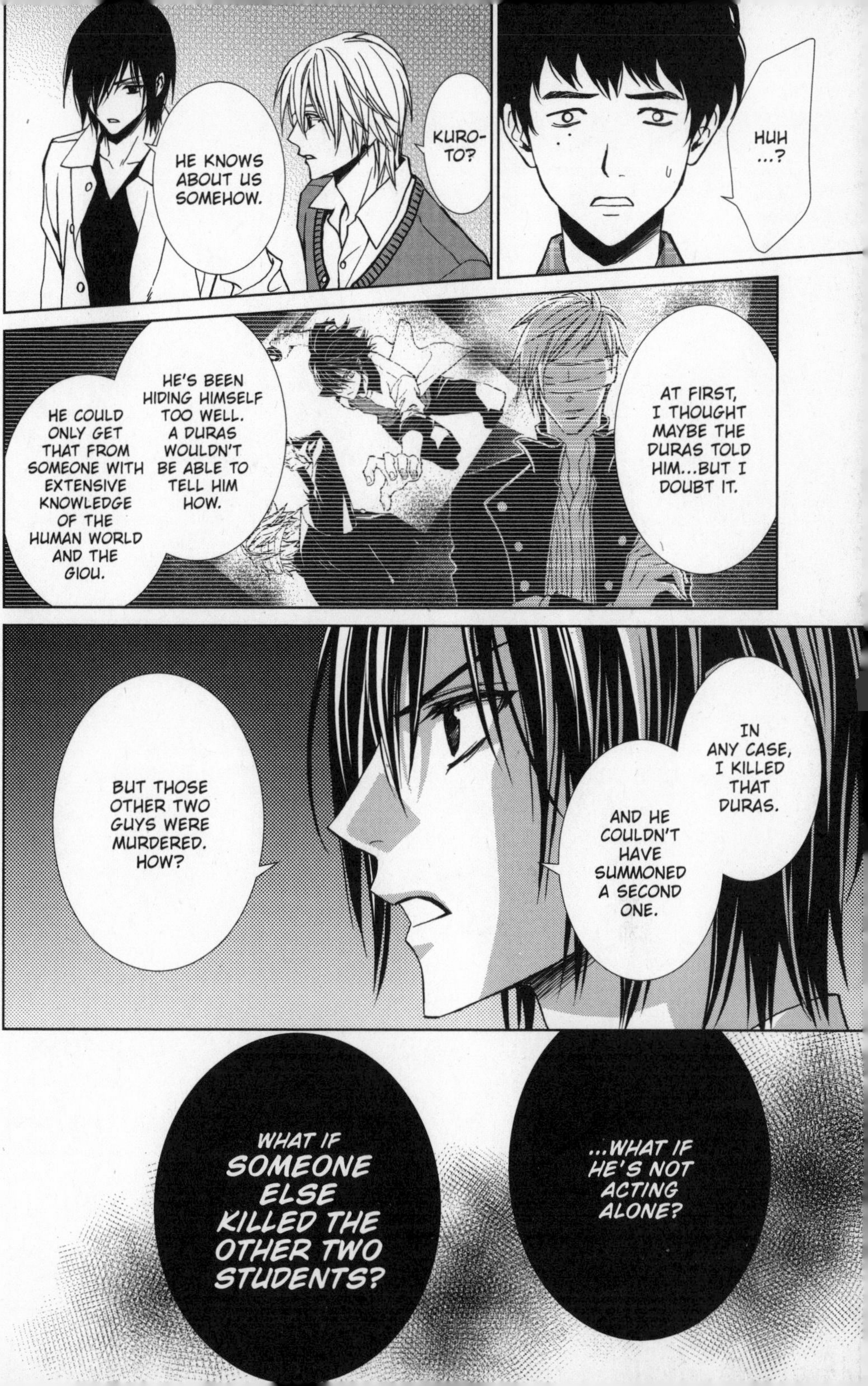
HUH ...?
KURO-TO?
HE KNOWS ABOUT US SOMEHOW.
AT FIRST, I THOUGHT MAYBE THE DURAS TOLD HIM...BUT I DOUBT IT.
HE'S BEEN HIDING HIMSELF TOO WELL. A DURAS WOULDN'T BE ABLE TO TELL HIM HOW.
HE COULD ONLY GET THAT FROM SOMEONE WITH EXTENSIVE KNOWLEDGE OF THE HUMAN WORLD AND THE GIOU.
IN ANY CASE, I KILLED THAT DURAS.
AND HE COULDN'T HAVE SUMMONED A SECOND ONE.
BUT THOSE OTHER TWO GUYS WERE MURDERED. HOW?
...WHAT IF HE'S NOT ACTING ALONE?
WHAT IF SOMEONE ELSE KILLED THE OTHER TWO STUDENTS?

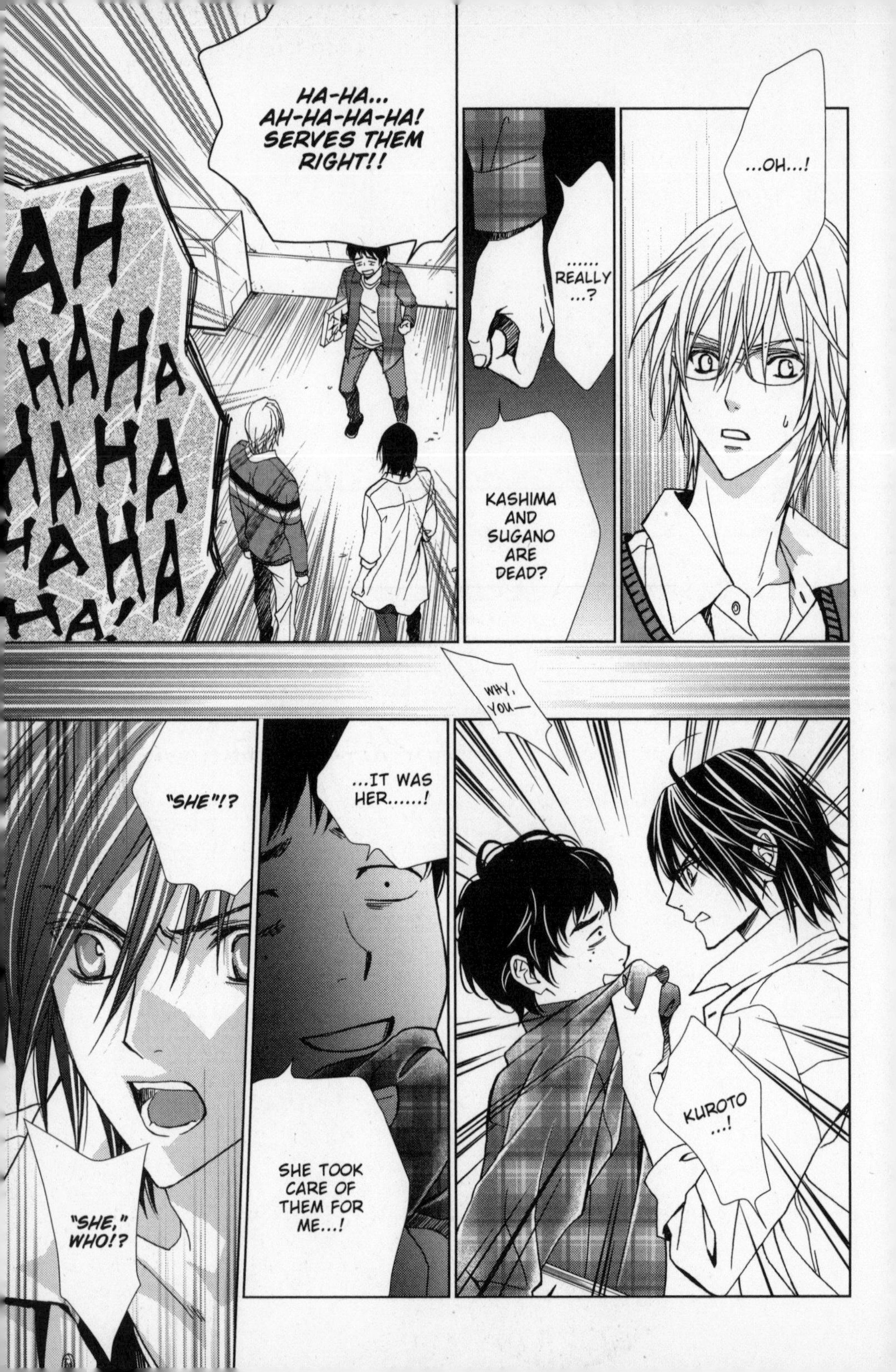
...OH...!
......REALLY...?
KASHIMA AND SUGANO ARE DEAD?
HA-HA... AH-HA-HA-HA! SERVES THEM RIGHT!!
AH HAHA HAHA HAHA HAHA HA!
WHY, YOU—
KUROTO...!
...IT WAS HER......!
SHE TOOK CARE OF THEM FOR ME...!
"SHE"!?
"SHE," WHO!?

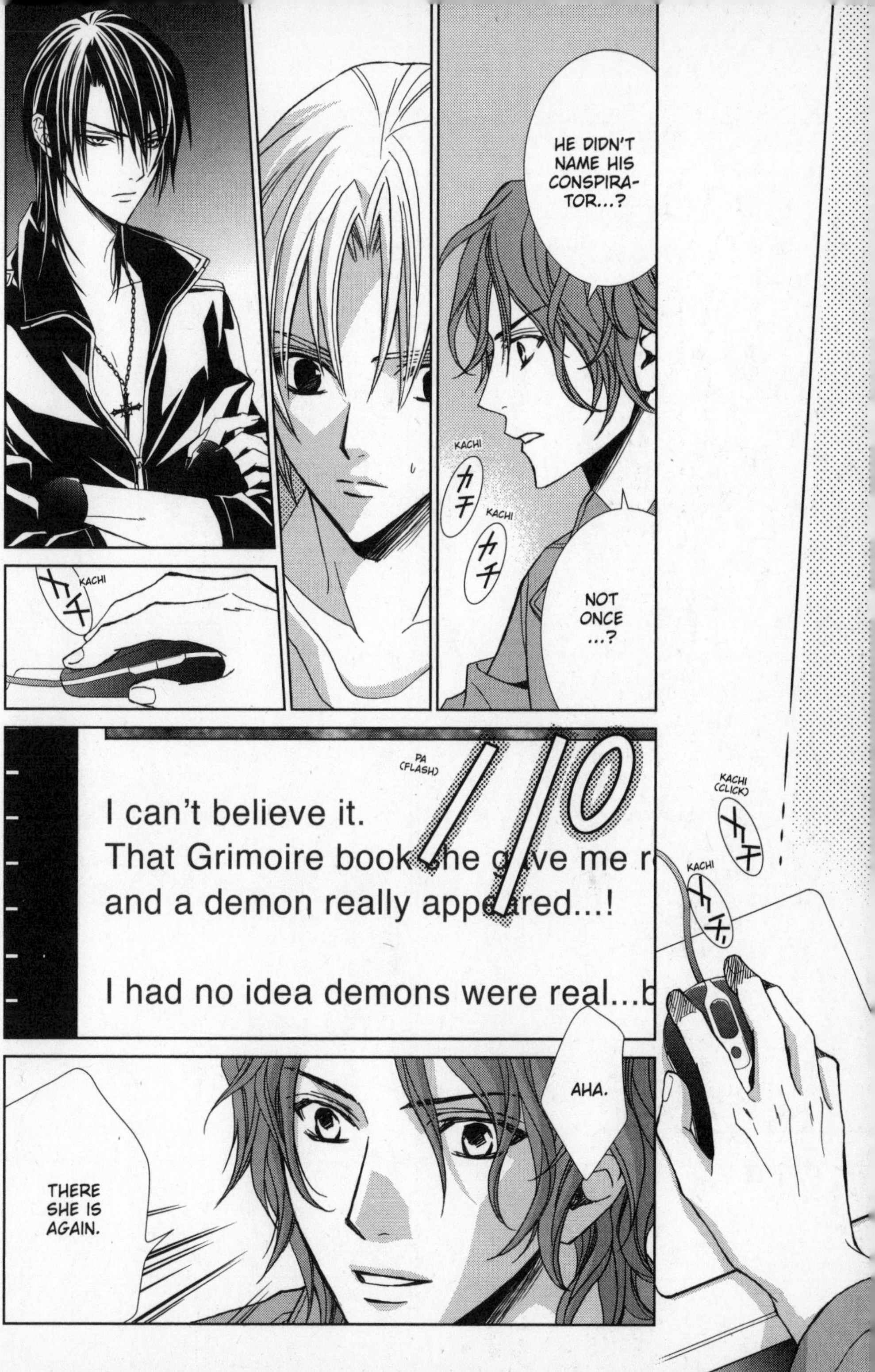
HE DIDN'T NAME HIS CONSPIRATOR...?
KACHI
KACHI
NOT ONCE ...?
KACHI
PA (FLASH)
KACHI (CLICK)
KACHI
I can't believe it.
That Grimoire book she gave me
and a demon really appeared...!
I had no idea demons were real...
AHA.
THERE SHE IS AGAIN.

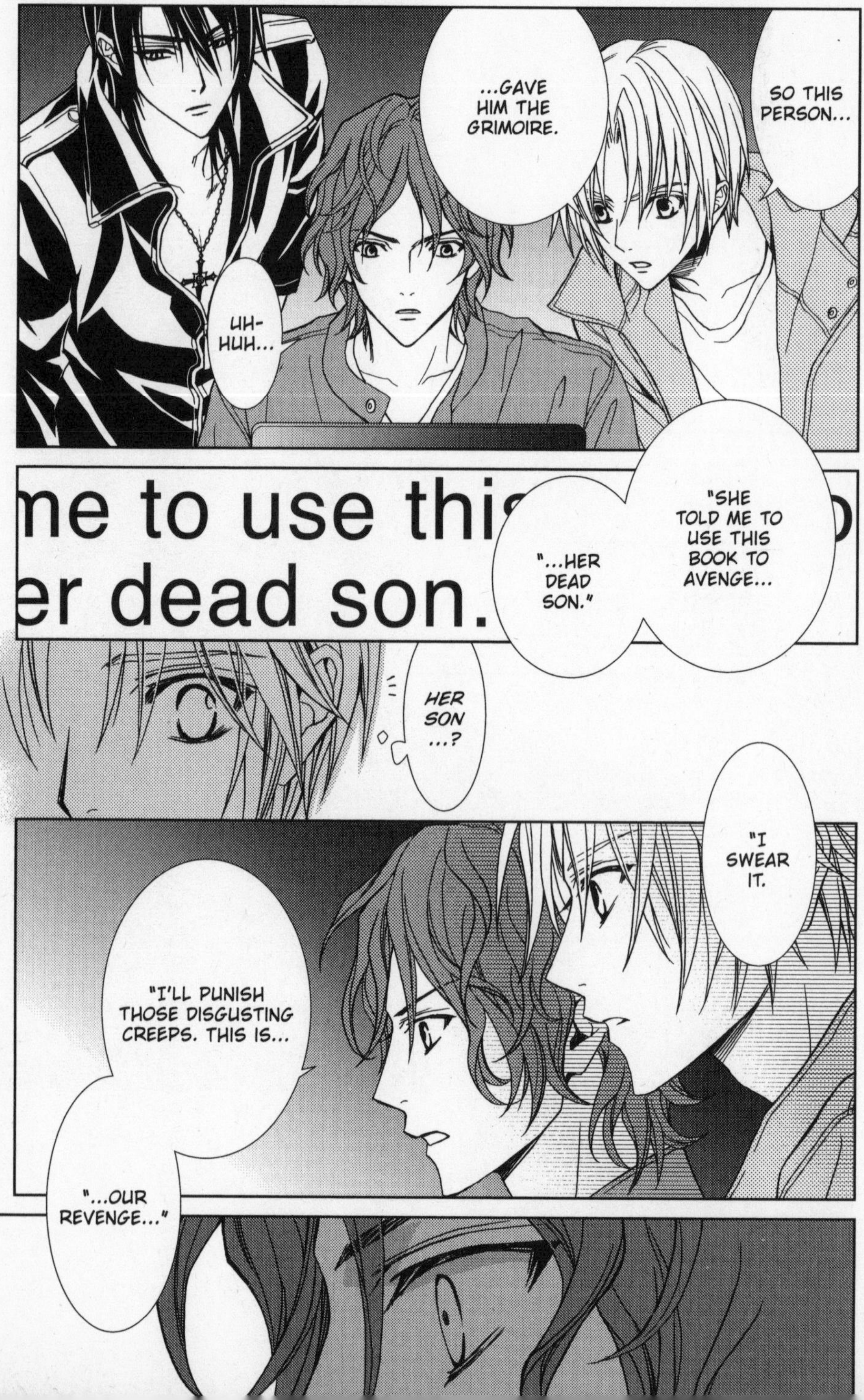
SO THIS PERSON...
...GAVE HIM THE GRIMOIRE.
UH-HUH...
me to use thi
er dead son.
"SHE TOLD ME TO USE THIS BOOK TO AVENGE...
"...HER DEAD SON."
HER SON ...?
"I SWEAR IT.
"I'LL PUNISH THOSE DISGUSTING CREEPS. THIS IS...
"...OUR REVENGE..."

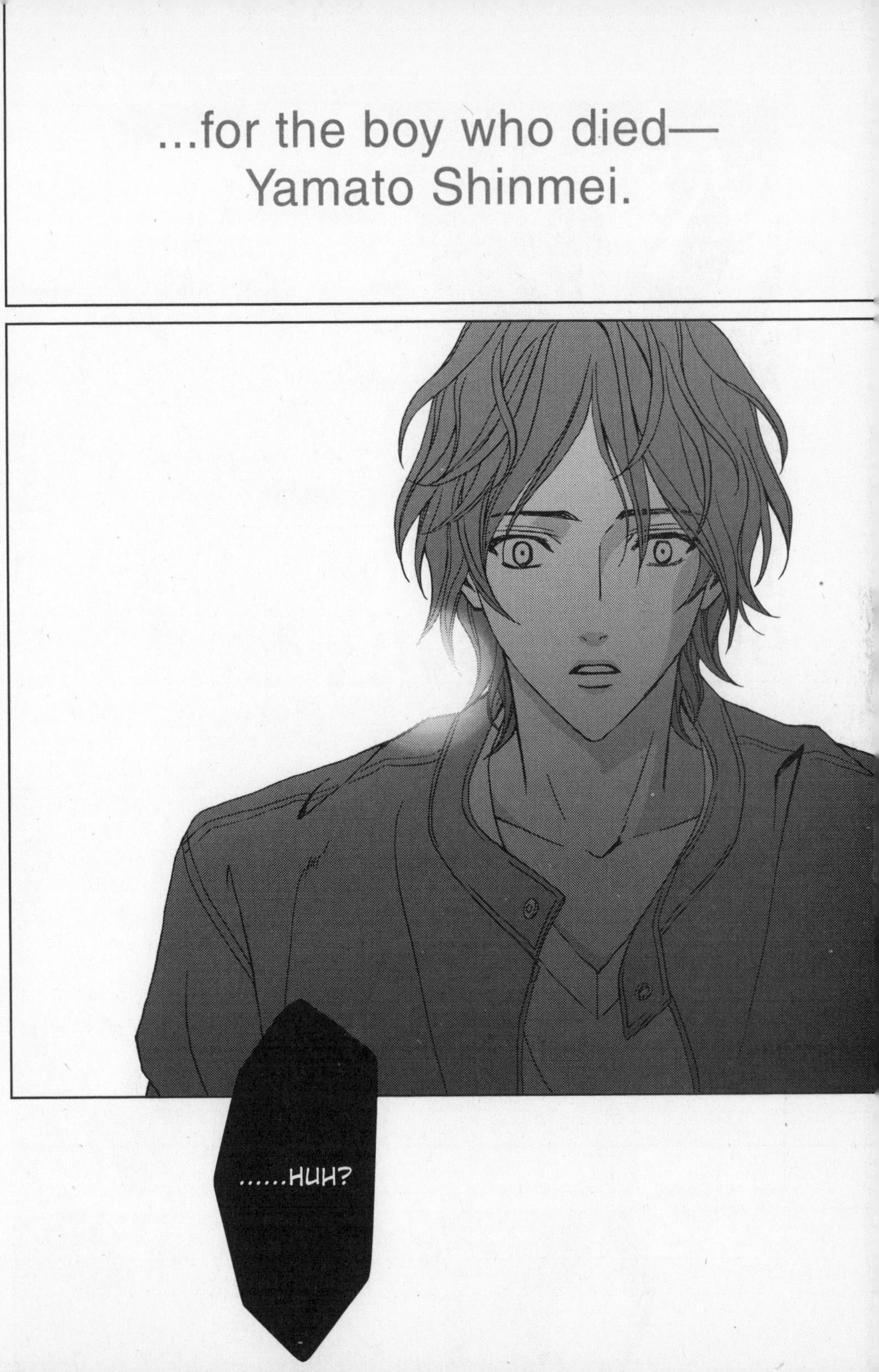
...for the boy who died—
Yamato Shinmei.
......HUH?

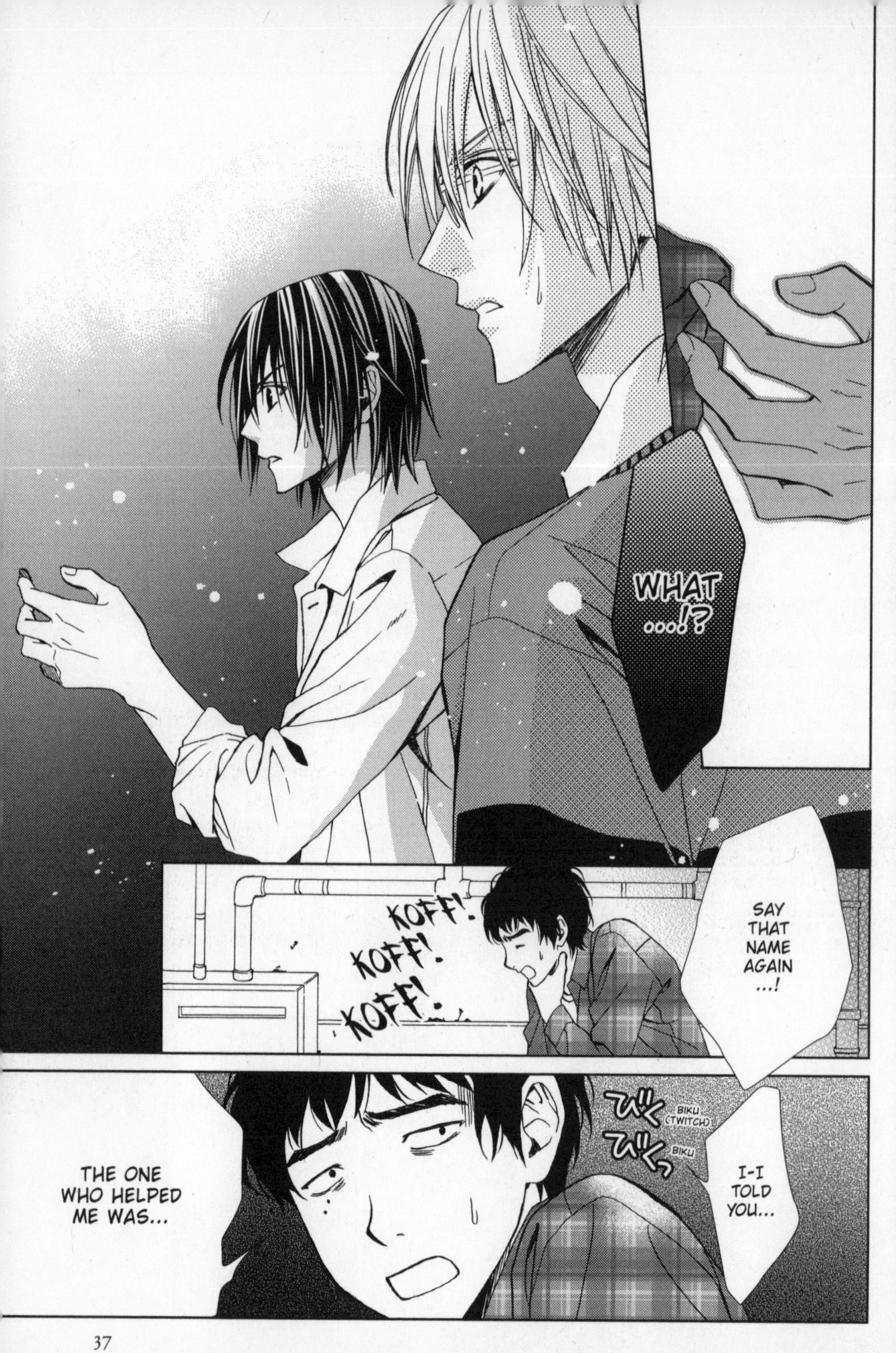
WHAT...!?
SAY THAT NAME AGAIN...!
KOFF! KOFF! KOFF!
びく
BIKU (TWITCH)
びくっ
BIKU
I-I TOLD YOU...
THE ONE WHO HELPED ME WAS...

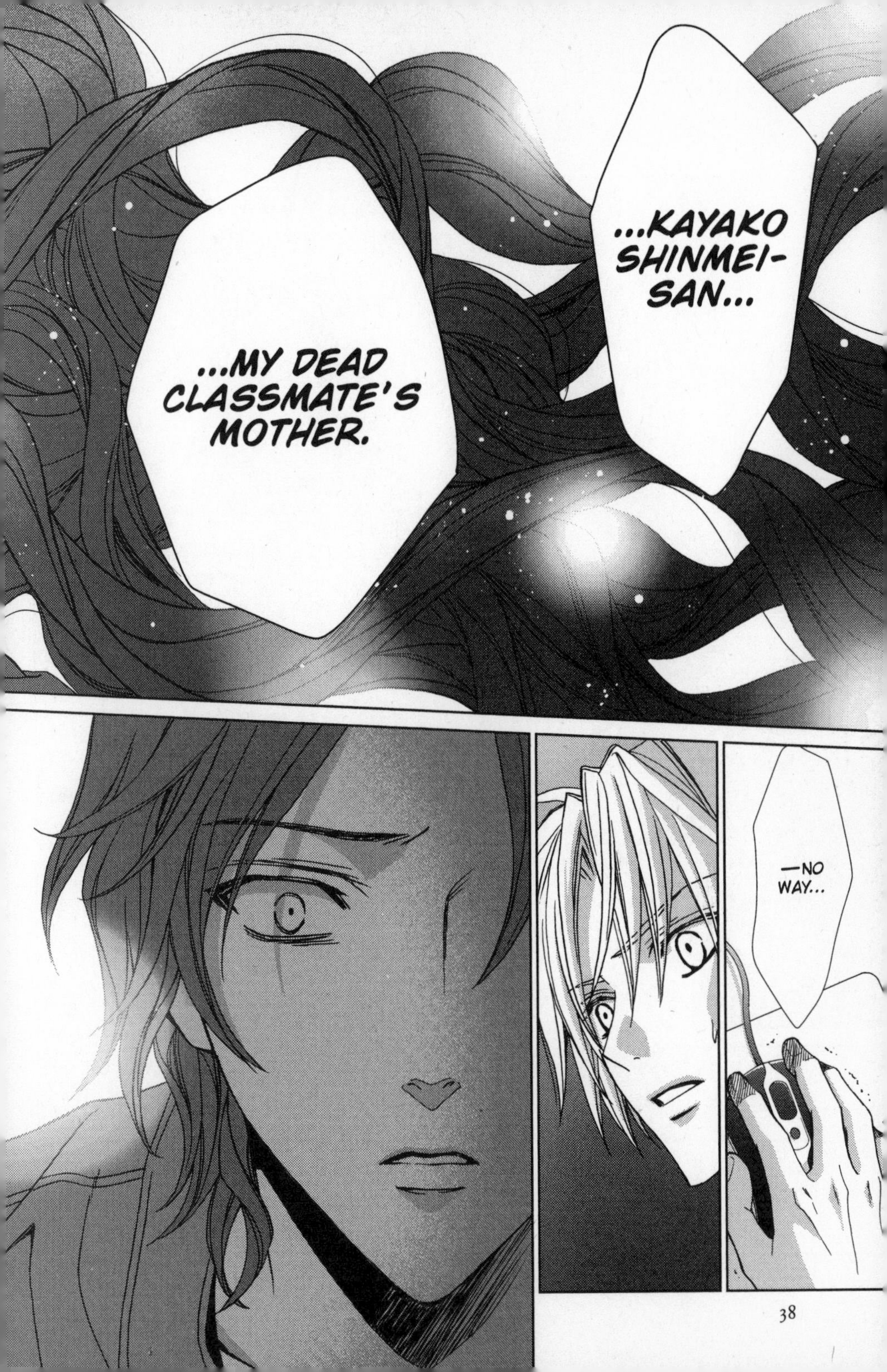
...KAYAKO SHINMEI-SAN...
...MY DEAD CLASSMATE'S MOTHER.
—NO WAY...

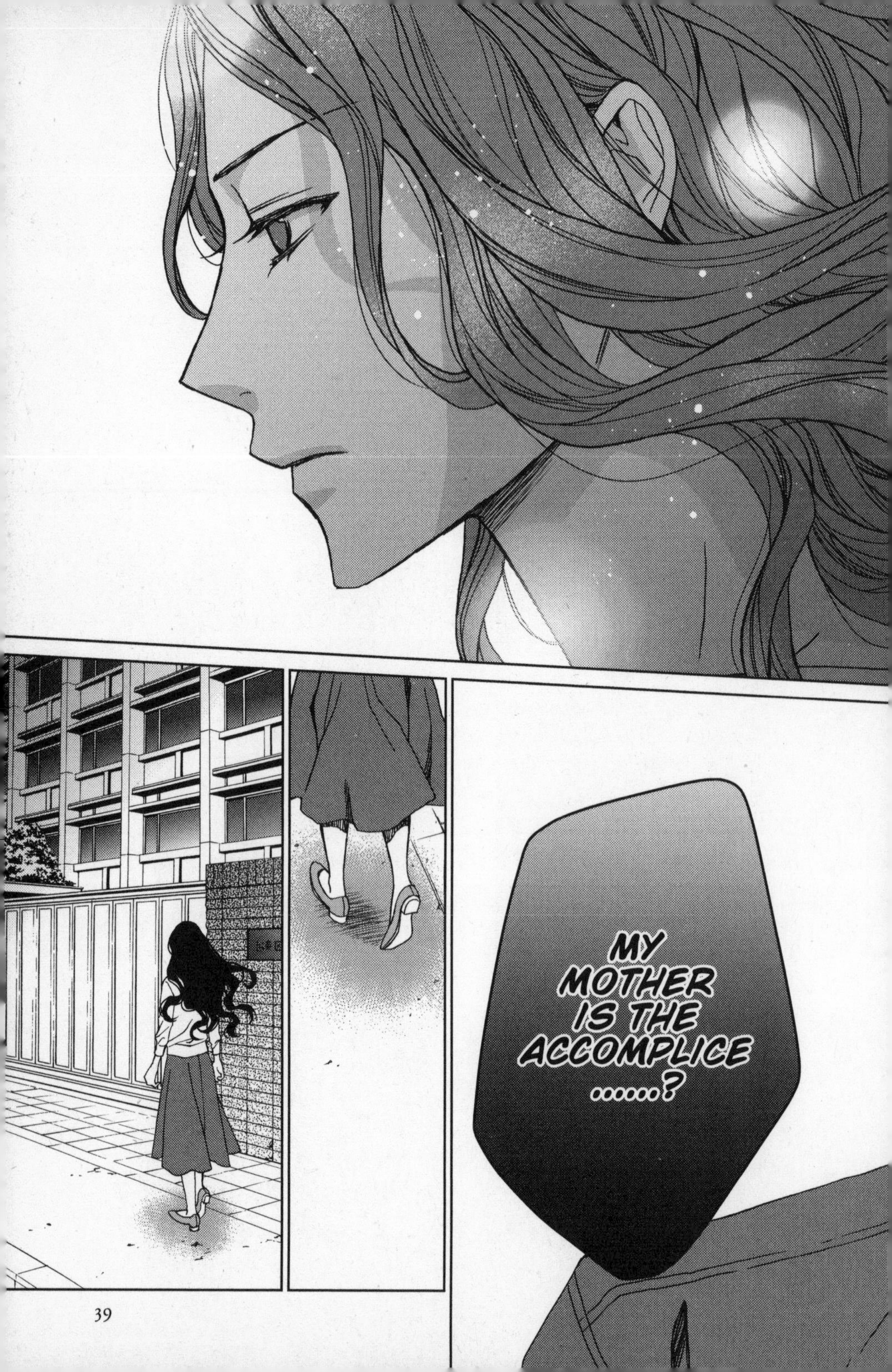
MY MOTHER IS THE ACCOMPLICE ......?

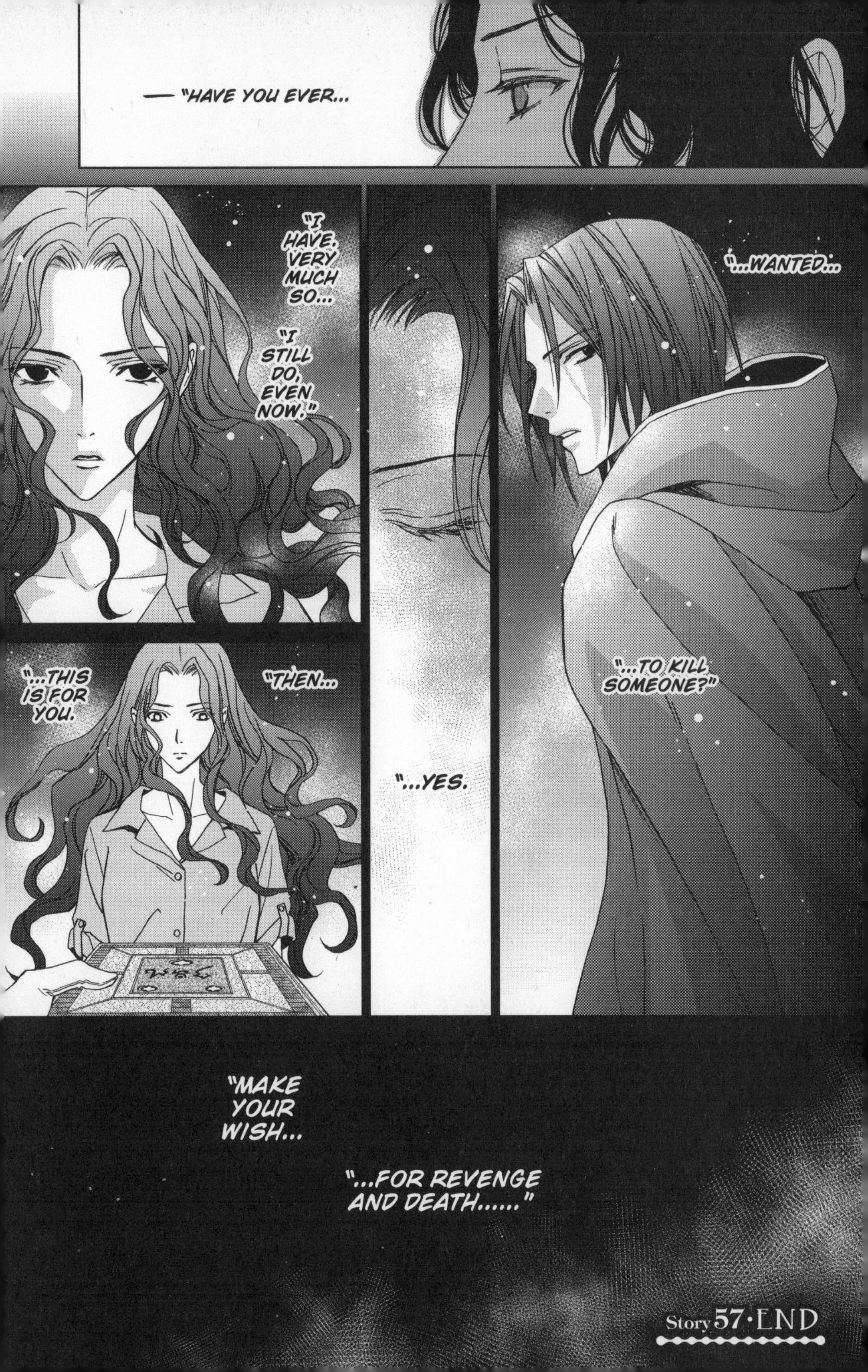
— "HAVE YOU EVER...
"...WANTED...
"...TO KILL SOMEONE?"
"...YES.
"I HAVE. VERY MUCH SO...
"I STILL DO, EVEN NOW."
"THEN...
"...THIS IS FOR YOU.
"MAKE YOUR WISH...
"...FOR REVENGE AND DEATH......"
Story 57 · END

Story 58

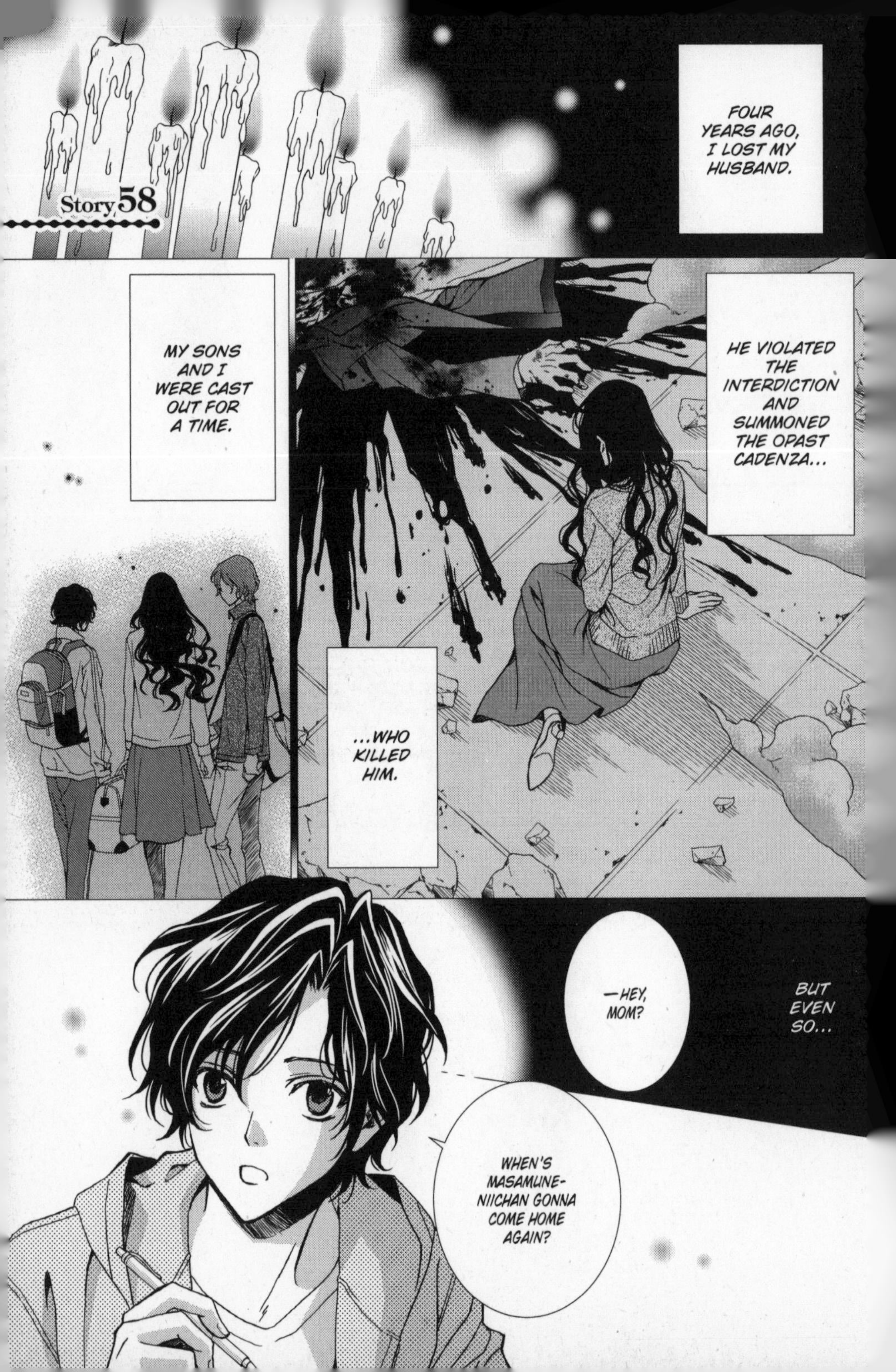
FOUR YEARS AGO, I LOST MY HUSBAND.
HE VIOLATED THE INTERDICTION AND SUMMONED THE OPAST CADENZA...
...WHO KILLED HIM.
MY SONS AND I WERE CAST OUT FOR A TIME.
BUT EVEN SO...
—HEY, MOM?
WHEN'S MASAMUNE-NIICHAN GONNA COME HOME AGAIN?

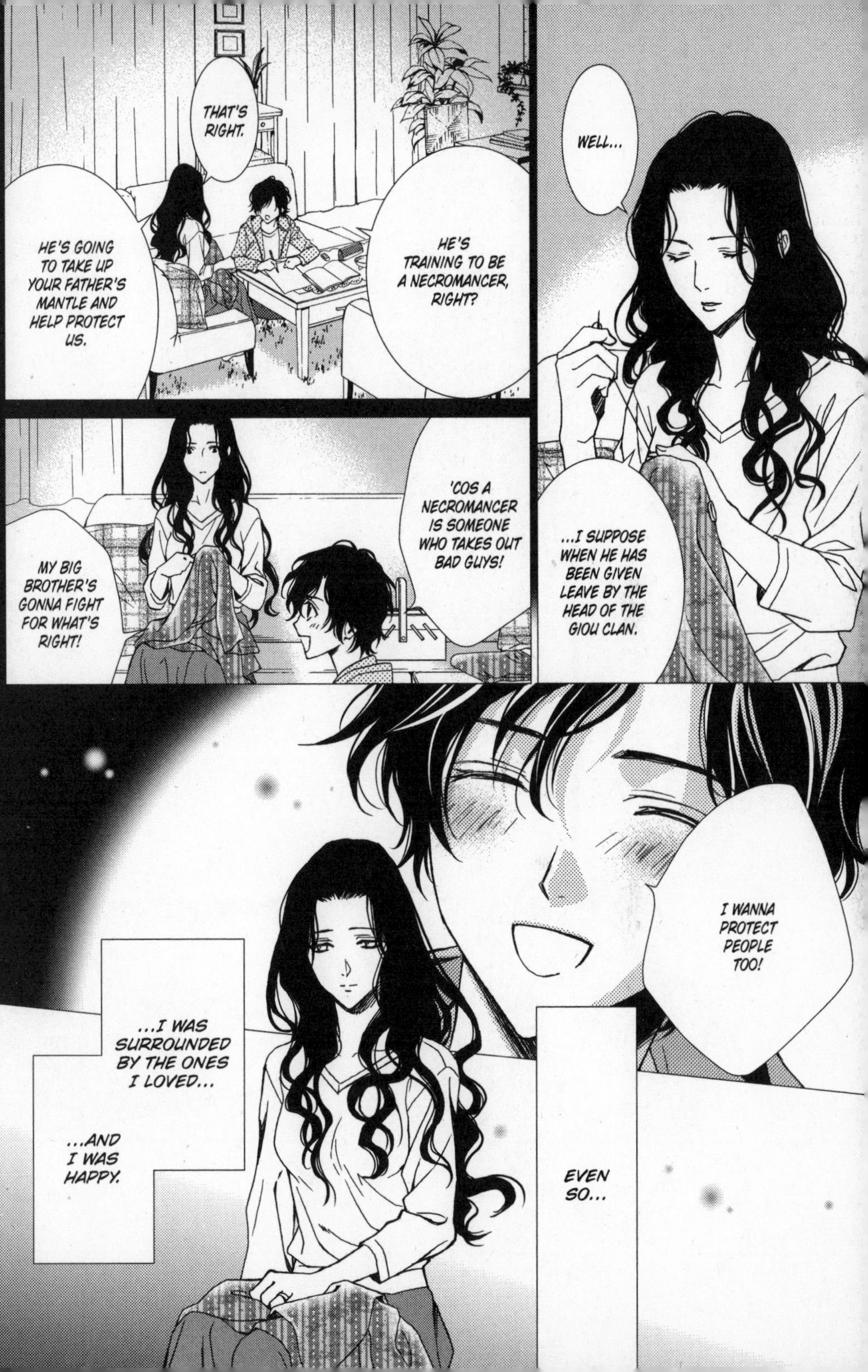
WELL...
...I SUPPOSE WHEN HE HAS BEEN GIVEN LEAVE BY THE HEAD OF THE GIOU CLAN.
HE'S TRAINING TO BE A NECROMANCER, RIGHT?
THAT'S RIGHT.
HE'S GOING TO TAKE UP YOUR FATHER'S MANTLE AND HELP PROTECT US.
'COS A NECROMANCER IS SOMEONE WHO TAKES OUT BAD GUYS!
MY BIG BROTHER'S GONNA FIGHT FOR WHAT'S RIGHT!
I WANNA PROTECT PEOPLE TOO!
EVEN SO...
...I WAS SURROUNDED BY THE ONES I LOVED...
...AND I WAS HAPPY.

Story 58
THE DAY I DIED

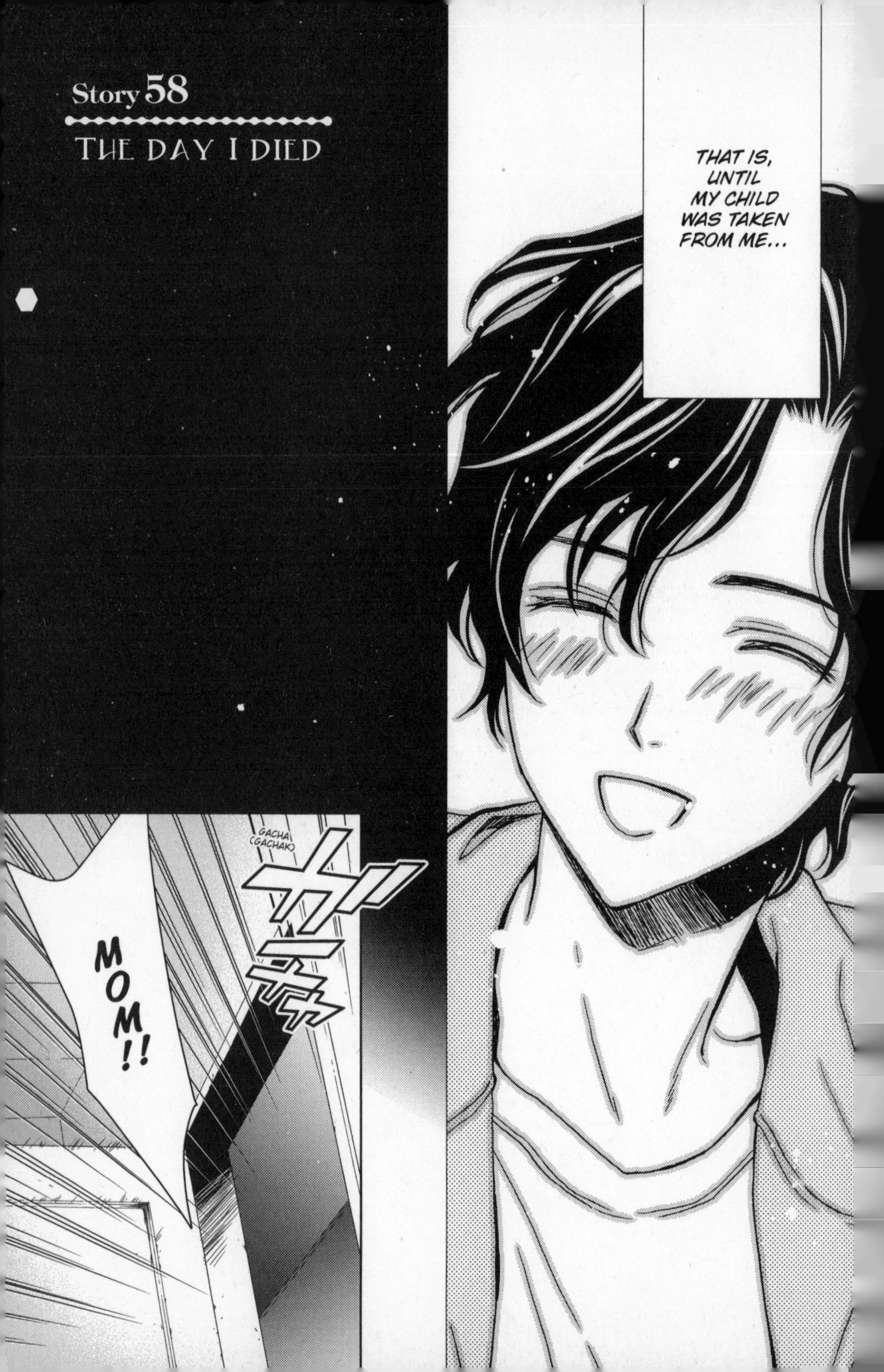
THAT IS, UNTIL MY CHILD WAS TAKEN FROM ME...
GACHA (GACHAK)
MOM!!

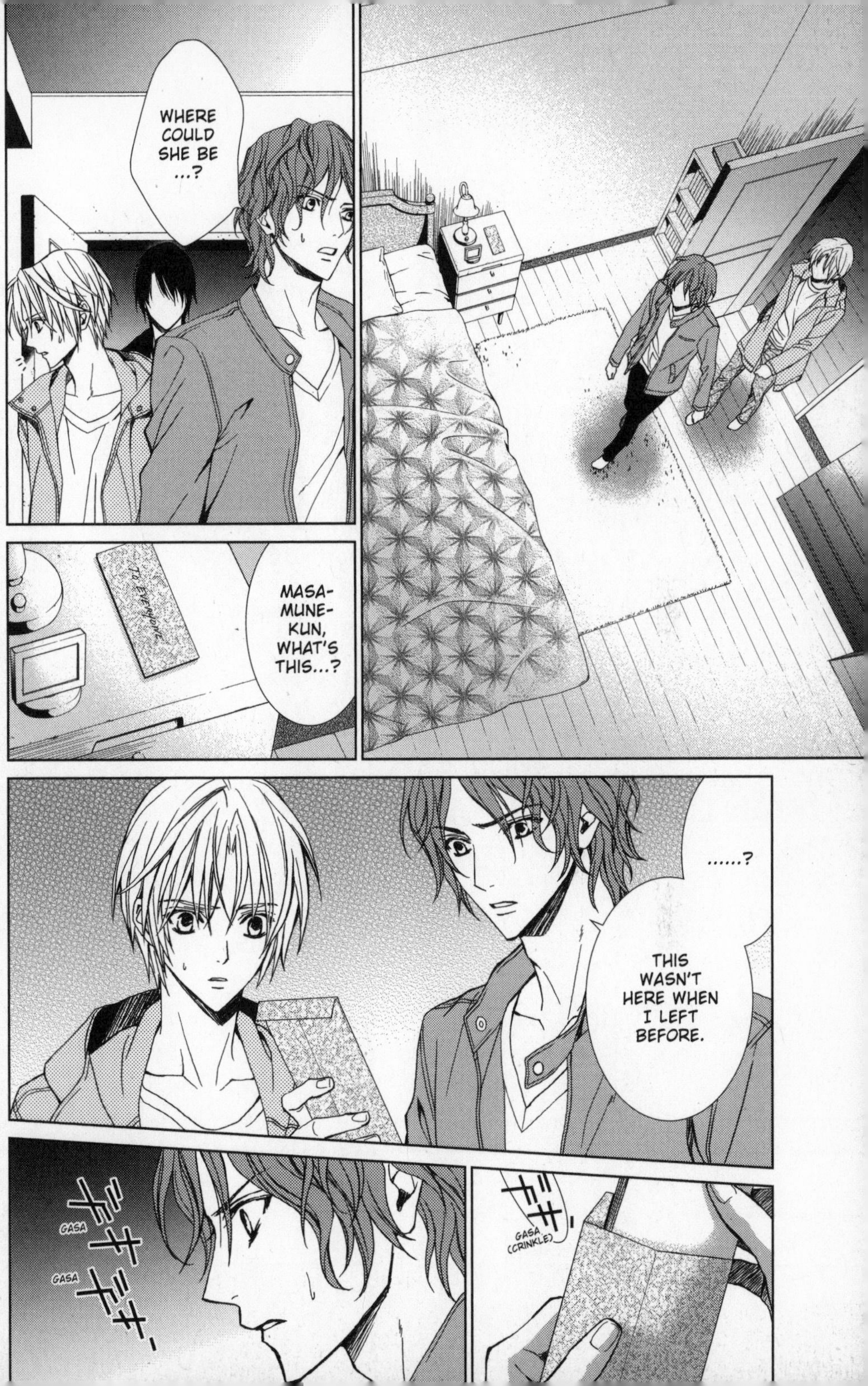
WHERE COULD SHE BE ...?
To Everyone
MASA-MUNE-KUN, WHAT'S THIS...?
......?
THIS WASN'T HERE WHEN I LEFT BEFORE.
GASA (CRINKLE)
GASA
GASA

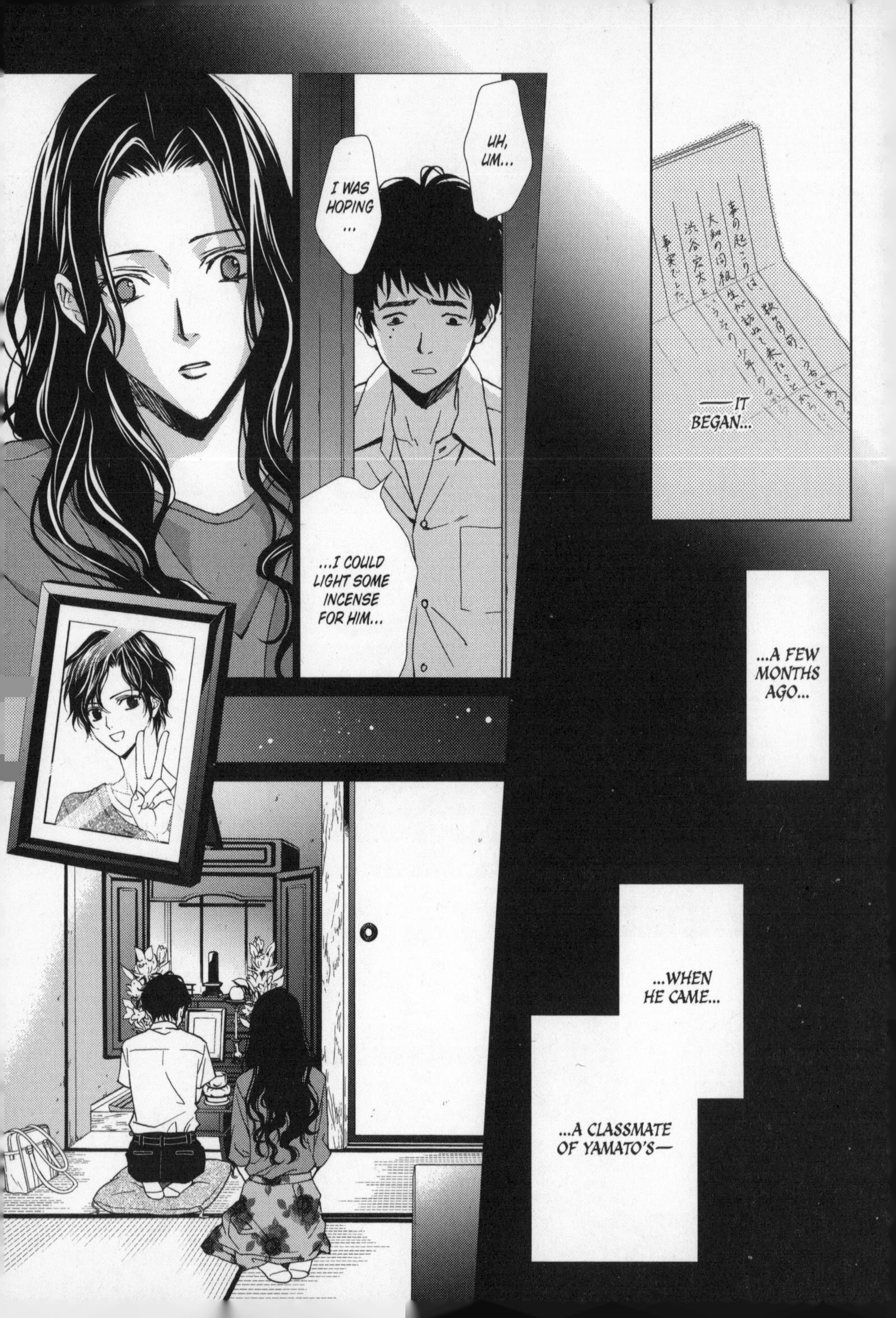

—IT BEGAN...
...A FEW MONTHS AGO...
...WHEN HE CAME...
...A CLASSMATE OF YAMATO'S—
UH, UM...
I WAS HOPING...
...I COULD LIGHT SOME INCENSE FOR HIM...

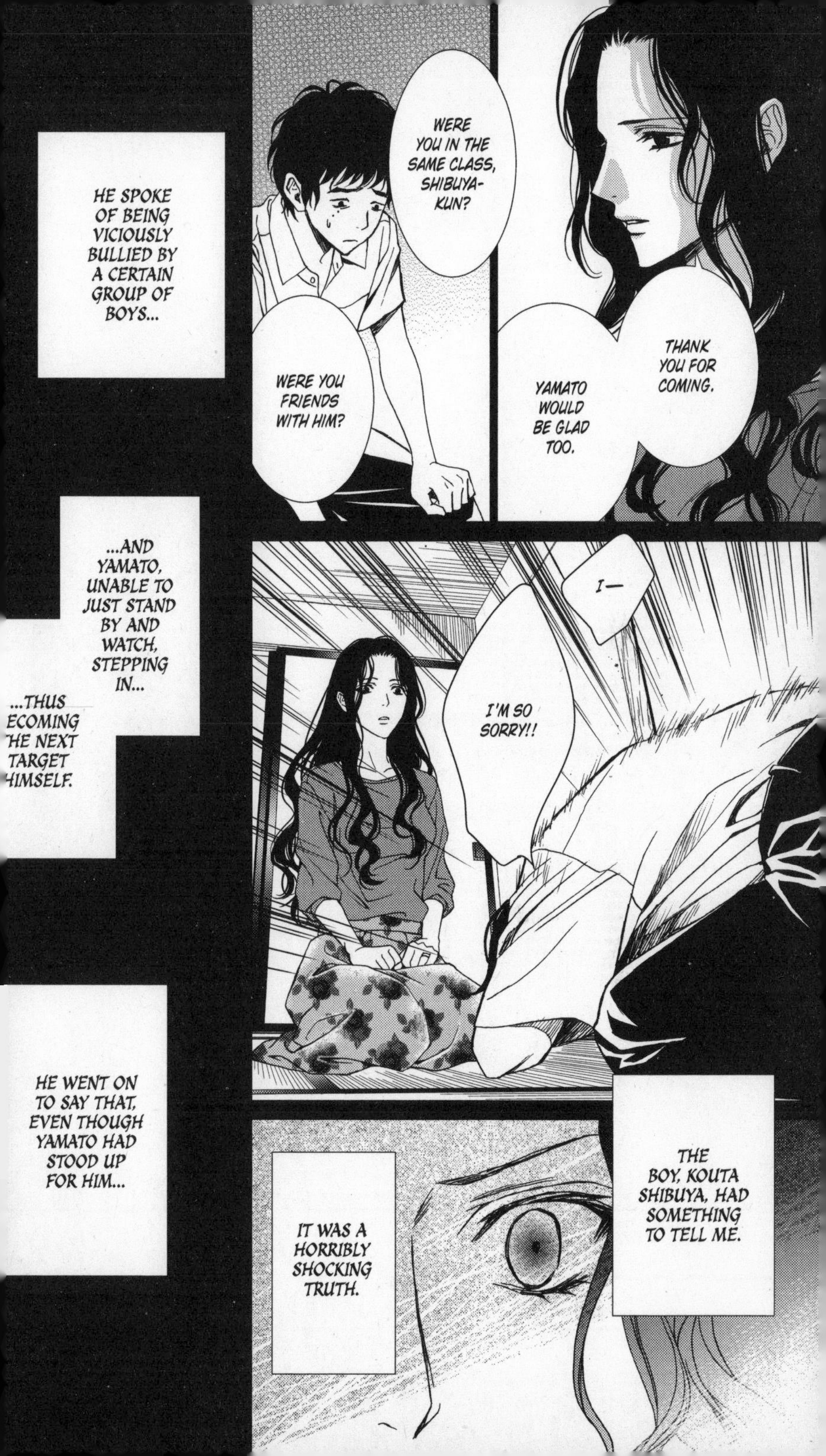
THANK YOU FOR COMING.
YAMATO WOULD BE GLAD TOO.
WERE YOU IN THE SAME CLASS, SHIBUYA-KUN?
WERE YOU FRIENDS WITH HIM?
I—
I'M SO SORRY!!
THE BOY, KOUTA SHIBUYA, HAD SOMETHING TO TELL ME.
IT WAS A HORRIBLY SHOCKING TRUTH.
HE SPOKE OF BEING VICIOUSLY BULLIED BY A CERTAIN GROUP OF BOYS...
...AND YAMATO, UNABLE TO JUST STAND BY AND WATCH, STEPPING IN...
...THUS ECOMING HE NEXT TARGET HIMSELF.
HE WENT ON TO SAY THAT, EVEN THOUGH YAMATO HAD STOOD UP FOR HIM...

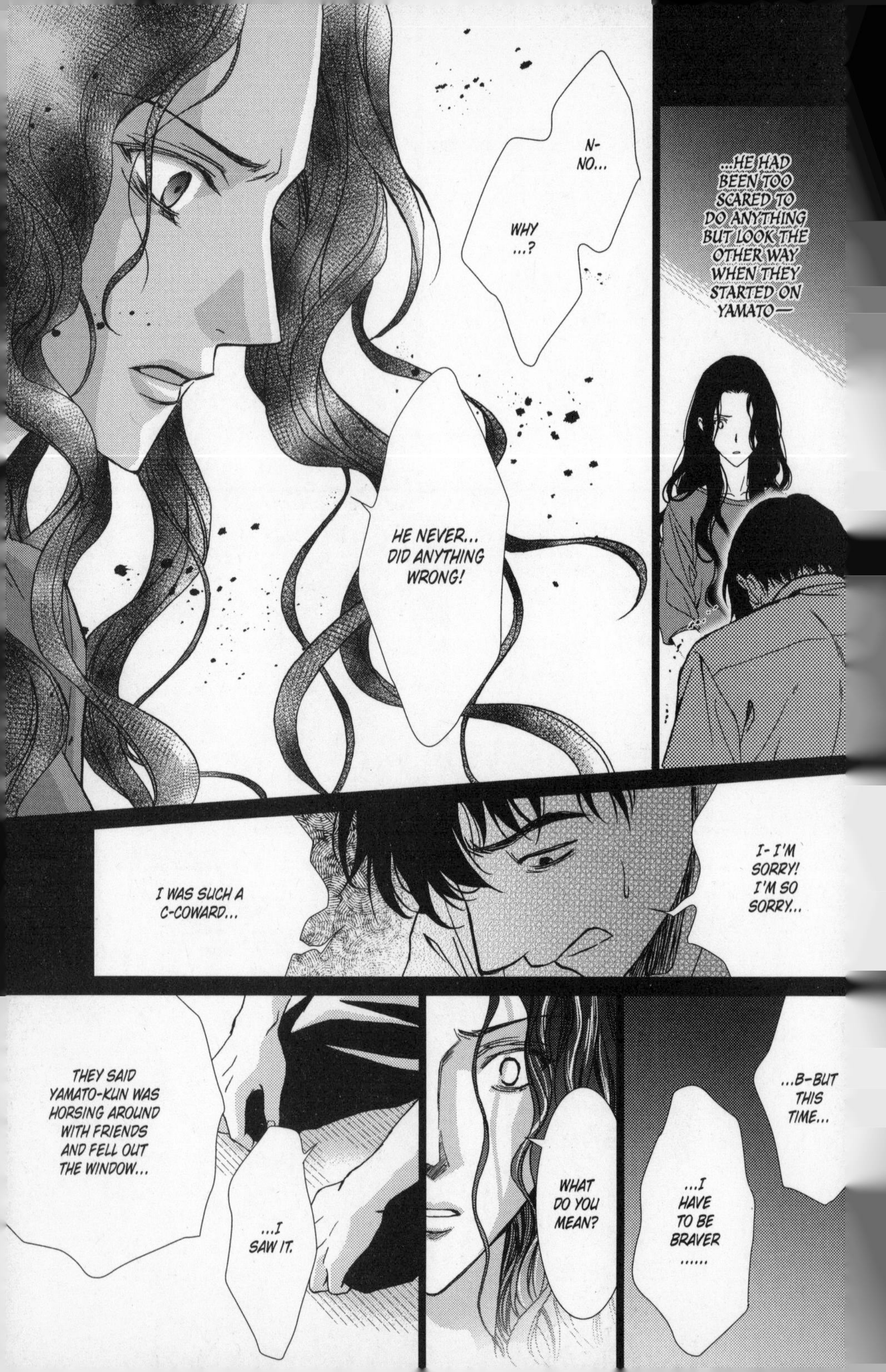
...HE HAD BEEN TOO SCARED TO DO ANYTHING BUT LOOK THE OTHER WAY WHEN THEY STARTED ON YAMATO—
N- NO...
WHY ...?
HE NEVER... DID ANYTHING WRONG!
I- I'M SORRY! I'M SO SORRY...
I WAS SUCH A C-COWARD...
...B-BUT THIS TIME...
...I HAVE TO BE BRAVER ......
WHAT DO YOU MEAN?
THEY SAID YAMATO-KUN WAS HORSING AROUND WITH FRIENDS AND FELL OUT THE WINDOW...
...I SAW IT.

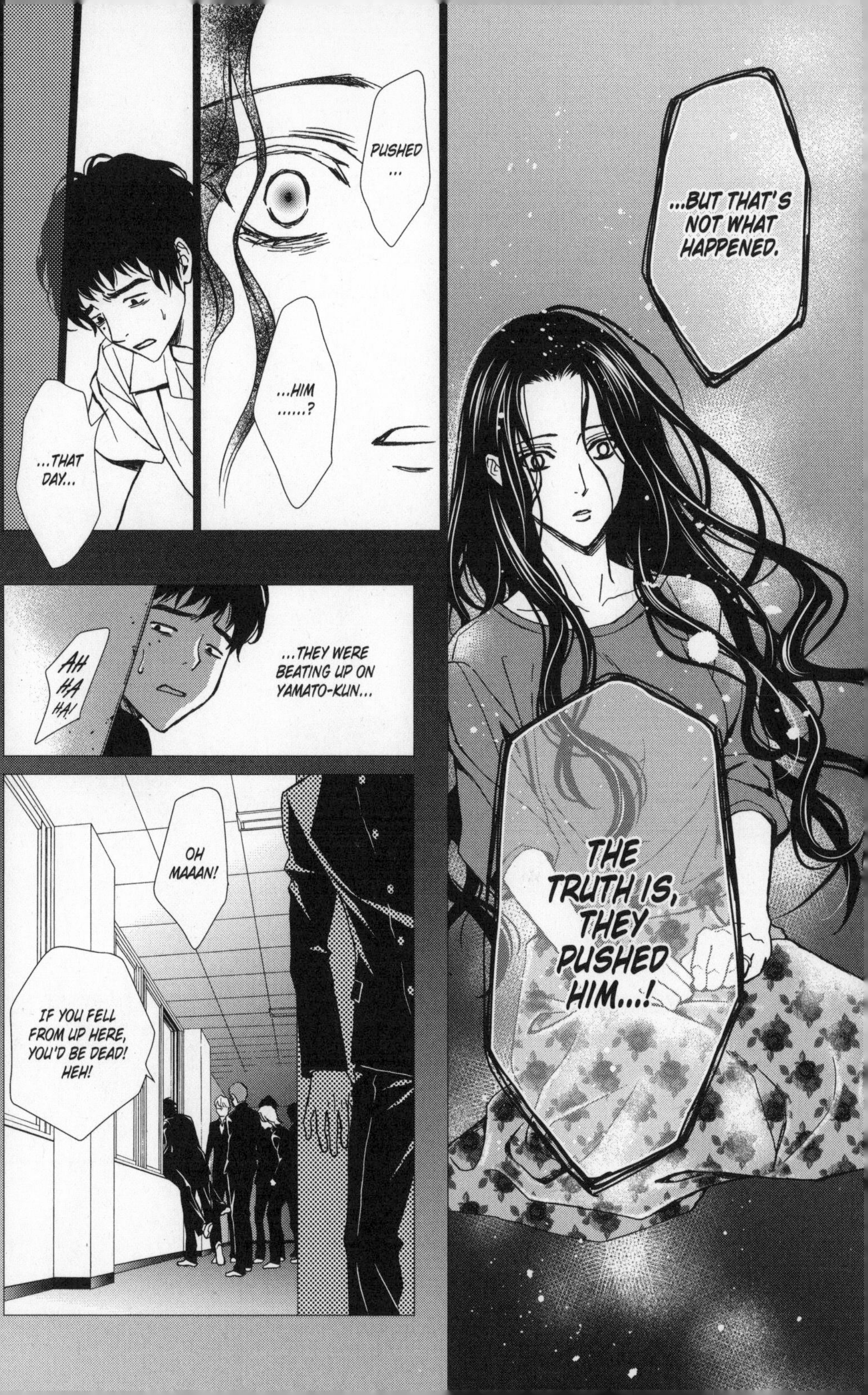
...BUT THAT'S NOT WHAT HAPPENED.
THE TRUTH IS, THEY PUSHED HIM...!
PUSHED ...
...HIM ......?
...THAT DAY...
...THEY WERE BEATING UP ON YAMATO-KUN...
AH HA HA!
OH MAAAN!
IF YOU FELL FROM UP HERE, YOU'D BE DEAD! HEH!

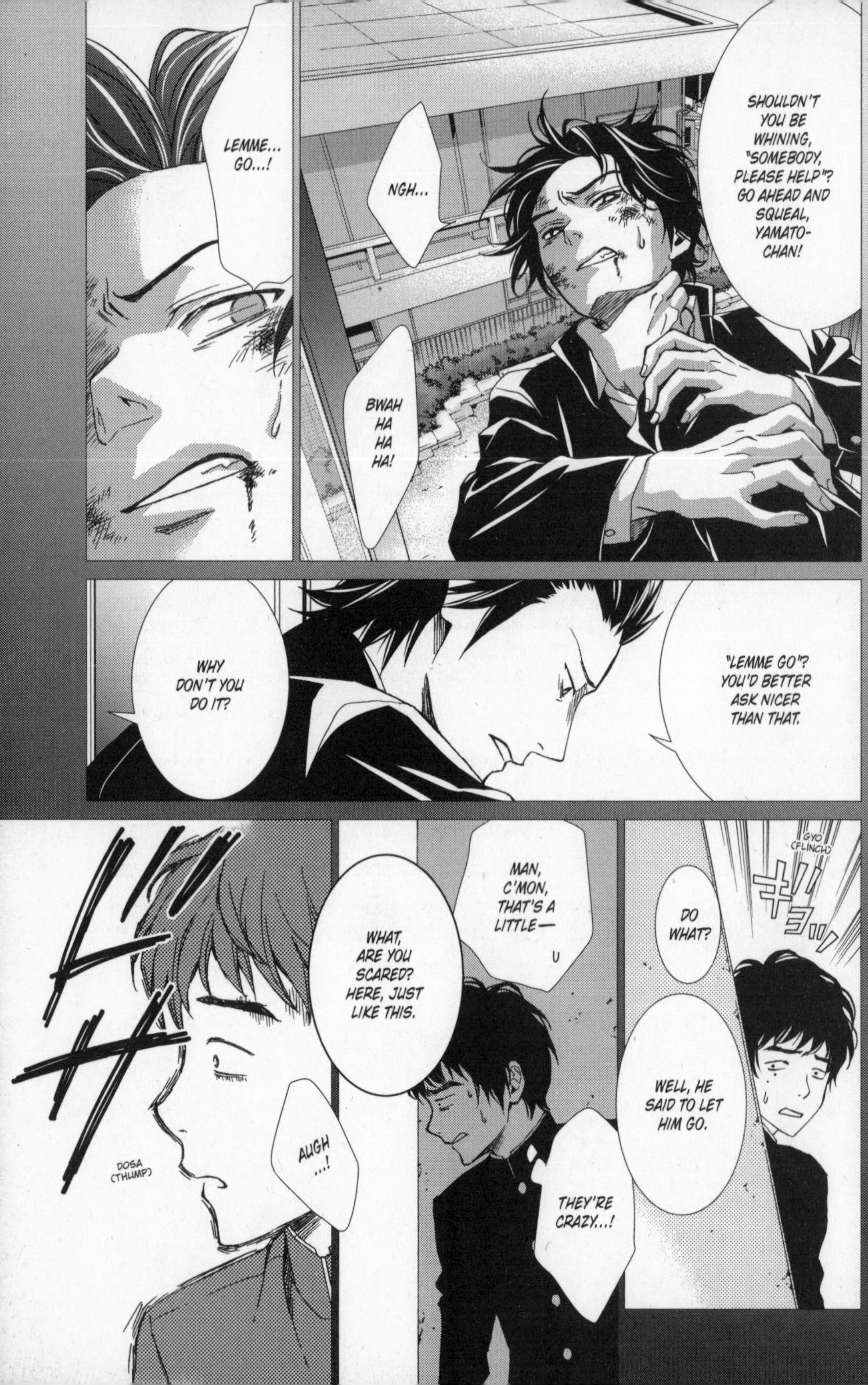
SHOULDN'T YOU BE WHINING, "SOMEBODY, PLEASE HELP"? GO AHEAD AND SQUEAL, YAMATO-CHAN!
NGH...
BWAH HA HA HA!
LEMME... GO...!
"LEMME GO"? YOU'D BETTER ASK NICER THAN THAT.
WHY DON'T YOU DO IT?
GYO (FLINCH)
DO WHAT?
WELL, HE SAID TO LET HIM GO.
MAN, C'MON, THAT'S A LITTLE—
WHAT, ARE YOU SCARED? HERE, JUST LIKE THIS.
THEY'RE CRAZY...!
AUGH...!
DOSA (THUMP)

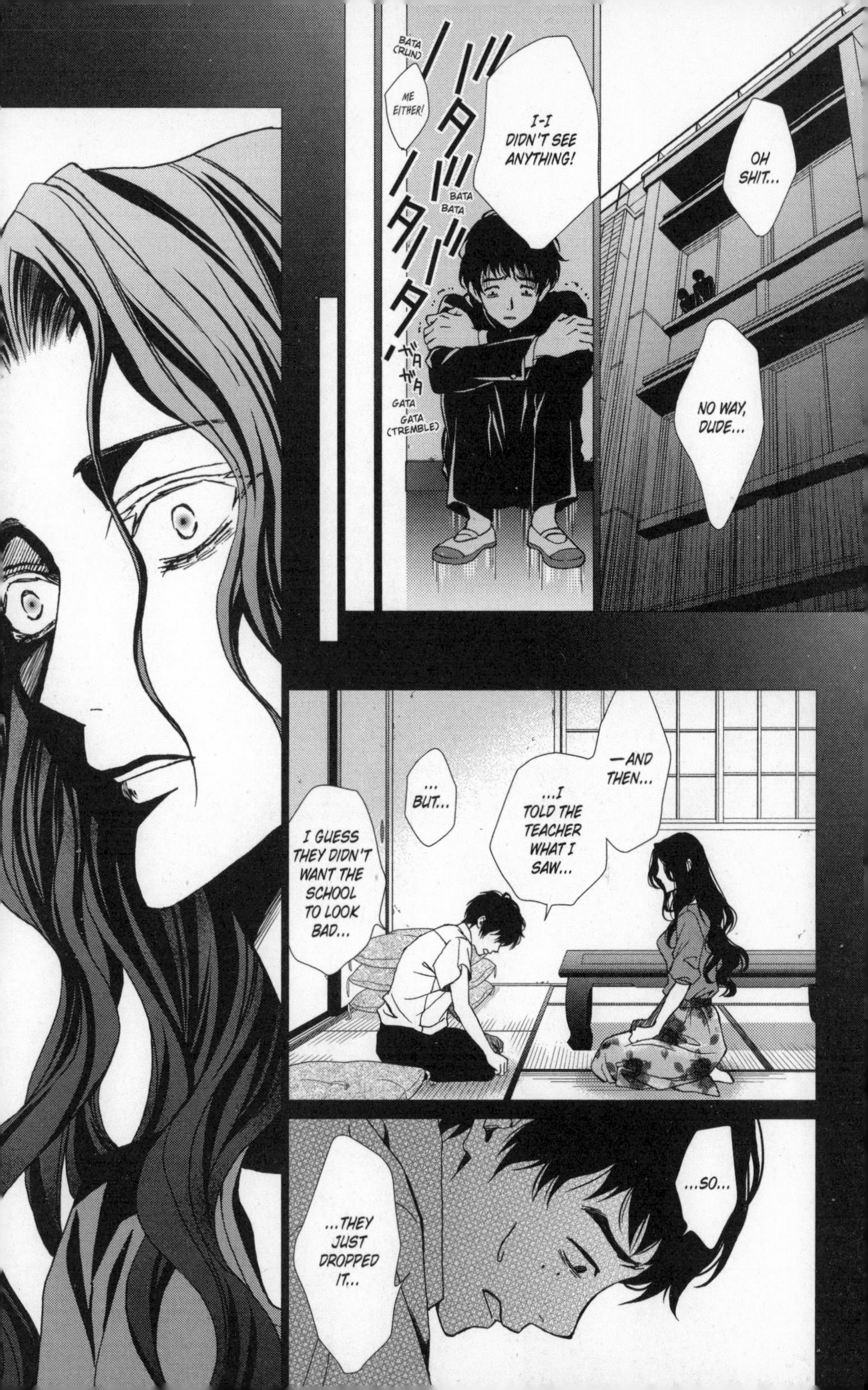
OH SHIT...
NO WAY, DUDE...
I-I DIDN'T SEE ANYTHING!
BATA BATA
BATA (RUN)
ME EITHER!
GATA GATA (TREMBLE)
—AND THEN...
...I TOLD THE TEACHER WHAT I SAW...
... BUT...
I GUESS THEY DIDN'T WANT THE SCHOOL TO LOOK BAD...
...SO...
...THEY JUST DROPPED IT...

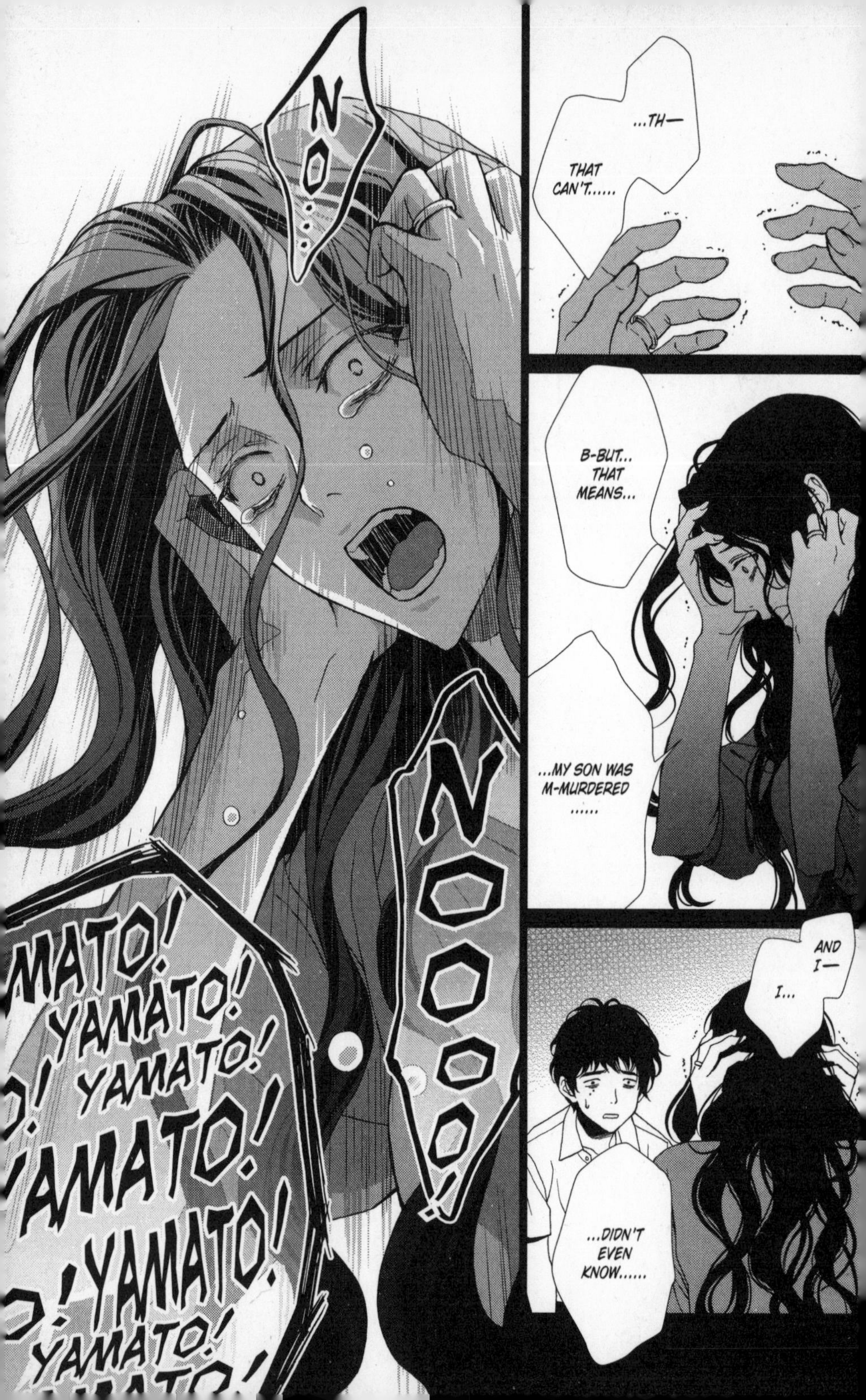
...TH—
THAT CAN'T......
B-BUT... THAT MEANS...
...MY SON WAS M-MURDERED ......
AND I— I...
...DIDN'T EVEN KNOW......
NO...
NOOOOO!
YAMATO! YAMATO! YAMATO! YAMATO! YAMATO!

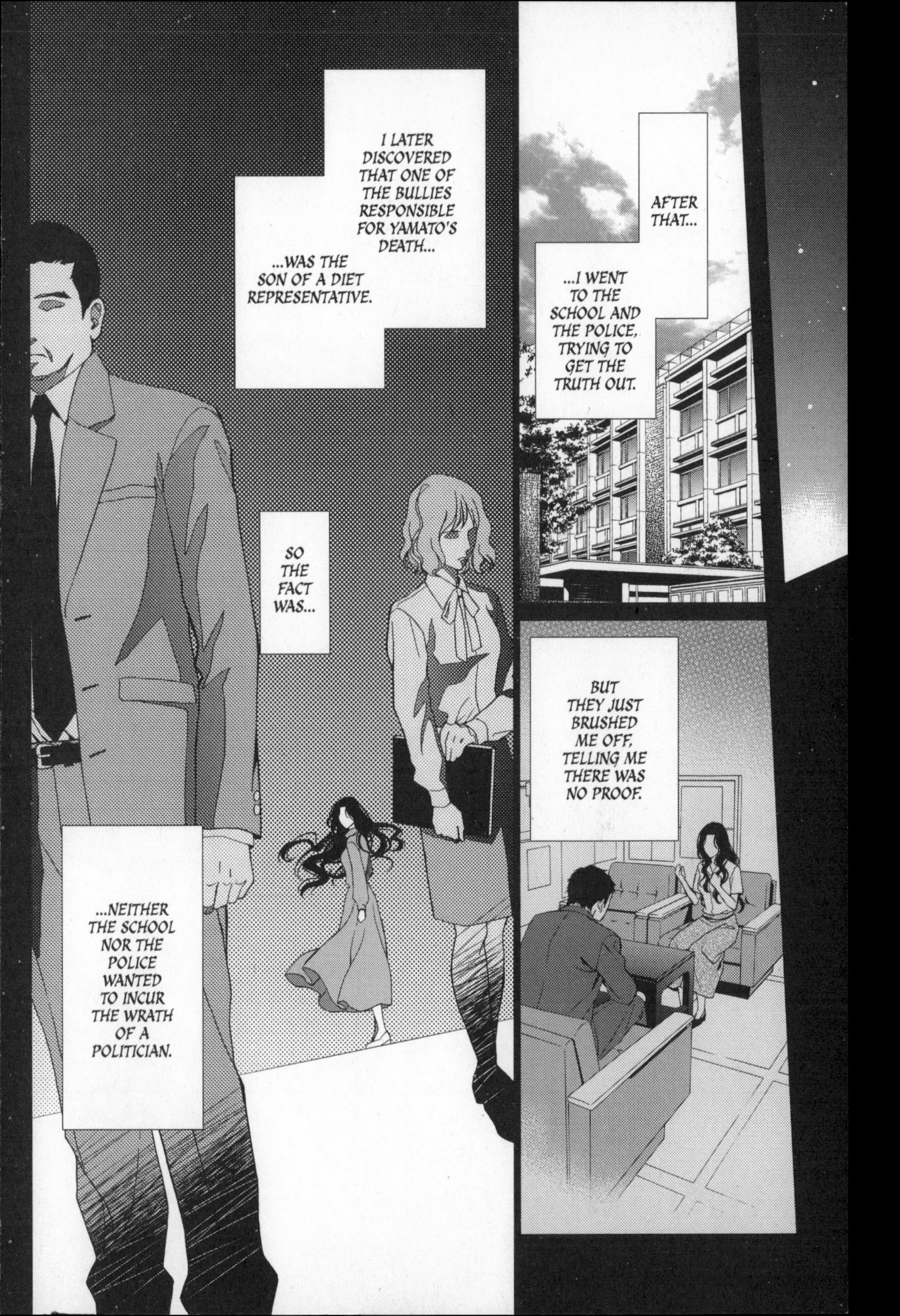
AFTER THAT...
...I WENT TO THE SCHOOL AND THE POLICE, TRYING TO GET THE TRUTH OUT.
BUT THEY JUST BRUSHED ME OFF, TELLING ME THERE WAS NO PROOF.
I LATER DISCOVERED THAT ONE OF THE BULLIES RESPONSIBLE FOR YAMATO'S DEATH...
...WAS THE SON OF A DIET REPRESENTATIVE.
SO THE FACT WAS...
...NEITHER THE SCHOOL NOR THE POLICE WANTED TO INCUR THE WRATH OF A POLITICIAN.

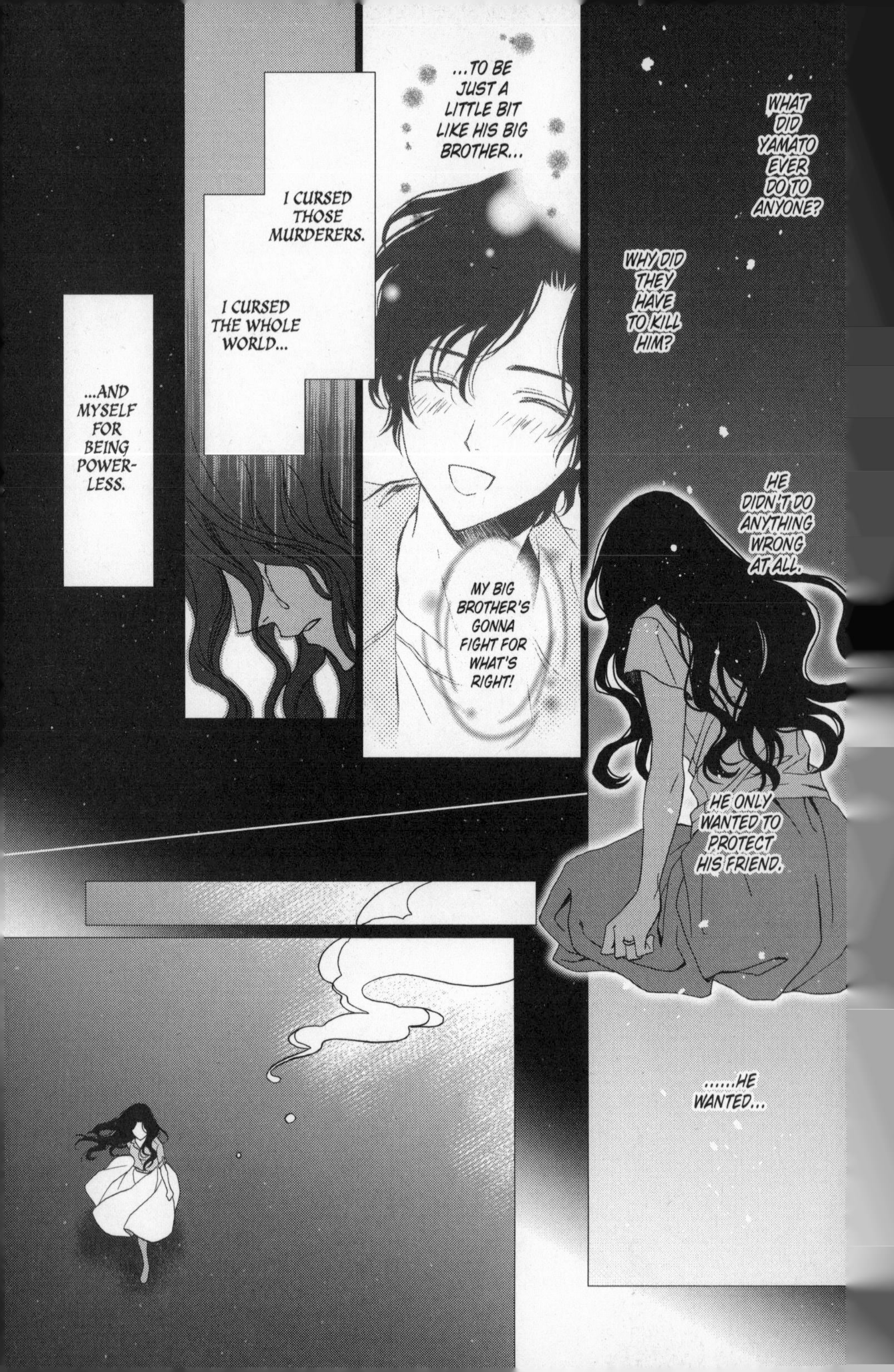
WHAT DID YAMATO EVER DO TO ANYONE?
WHY DID THEY HAVE TO KILL HIM?
HE DIDN'T DO ANYTHING WRONG AT ALL.
HE ONLY WANTED TO PROTECT HIS FRIEND.
......HE WANTED...
...TO BE JUST A LITTLE BIT LIKE HIS BIG BROTHER...
MY BIG BROTHER'S GONNA FIGHT FOR WHAT'S RIGHT!
I CURSED THOSE MURDERERS.
I CURSED THE WHOLE WORLD...
...AND MYSELF FOR BEING POWER-LESS.

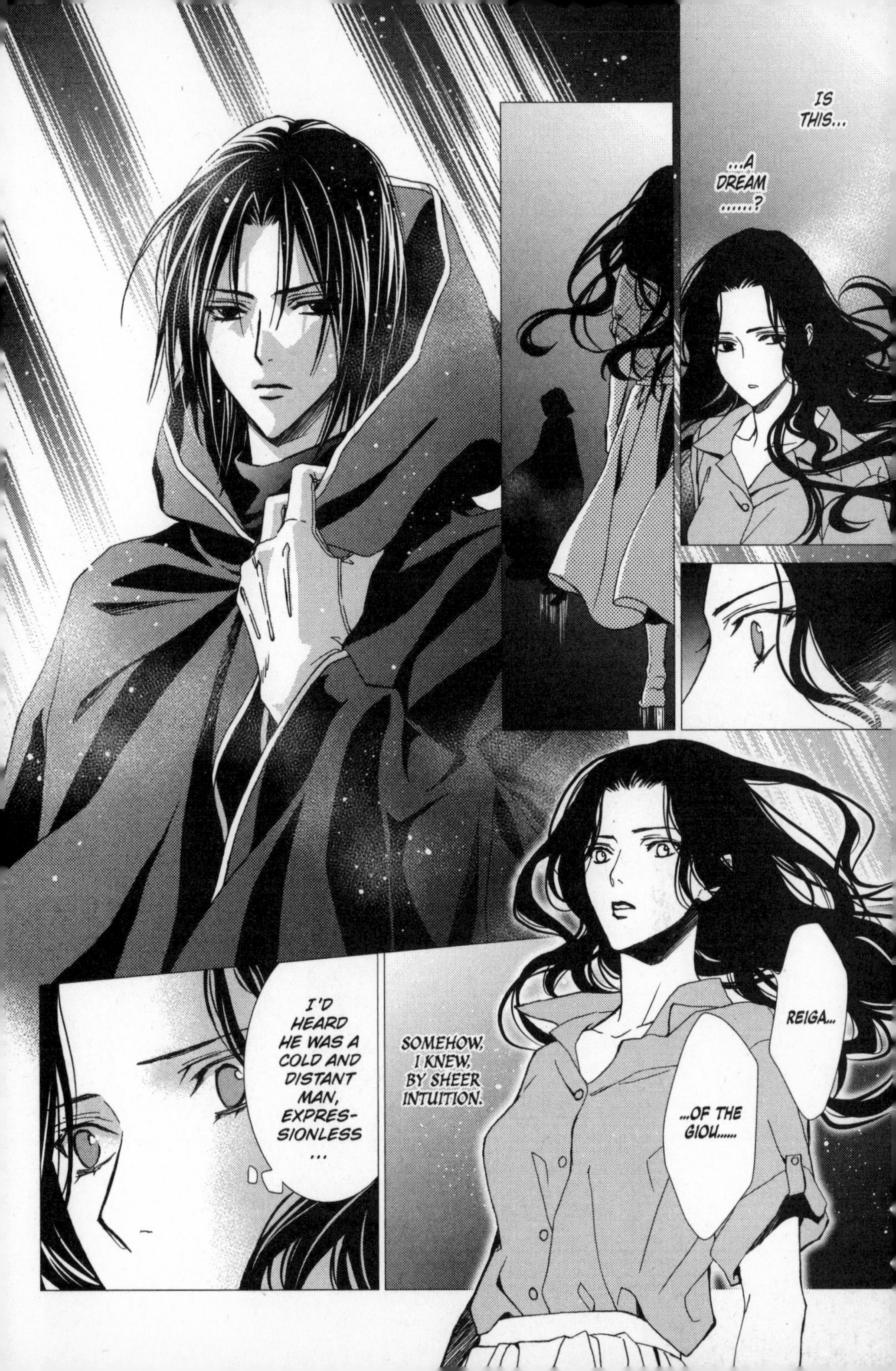
IS THIS...
...A DREAM ......?
REIGA...
...OF THE GIOU......
SOMEHOW, I KNEW, BY SHEER INTUITION.
I'D HEARD HE WAS A COLD AND DISTANT MAN, EXPRES-SIONLESS...

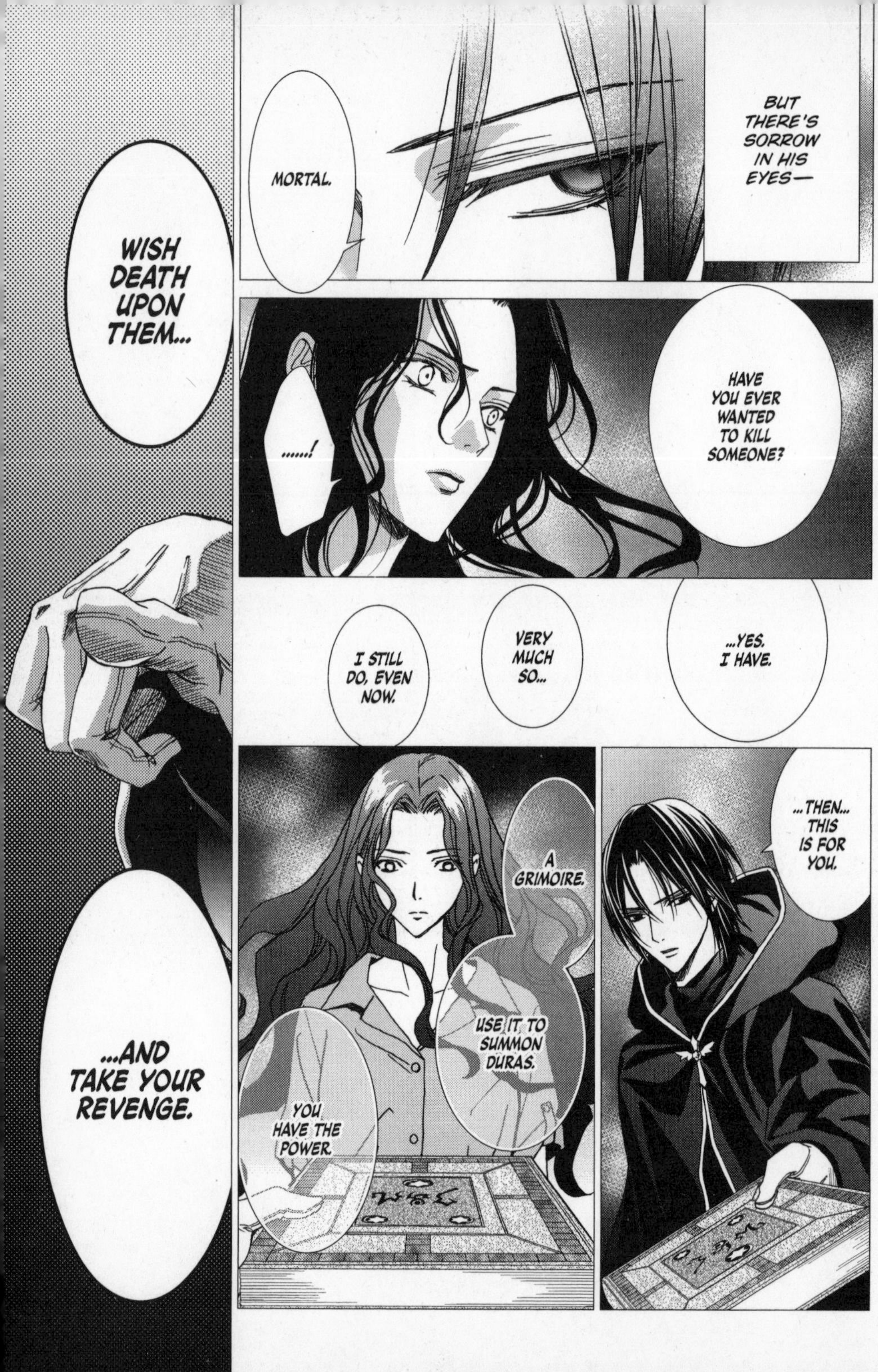
BUT THERE'S SORROW IN HIS EYES—
MORTAL.
HAVE YOU EVER WANTED TO KILL SOMEONE?
......!
...YES. I HAVE.
VERY MUCH SO...
I STILL DO, EVEN NOW.
...THEN... THIS IS FOR YOU.
A GRIMOIRE.
USE IT TO SUMMON DURAS.
YOU HAVE THE POWER.
WISH DEATH UPON THEM...
...AND TAKE YOUR REVENGE.

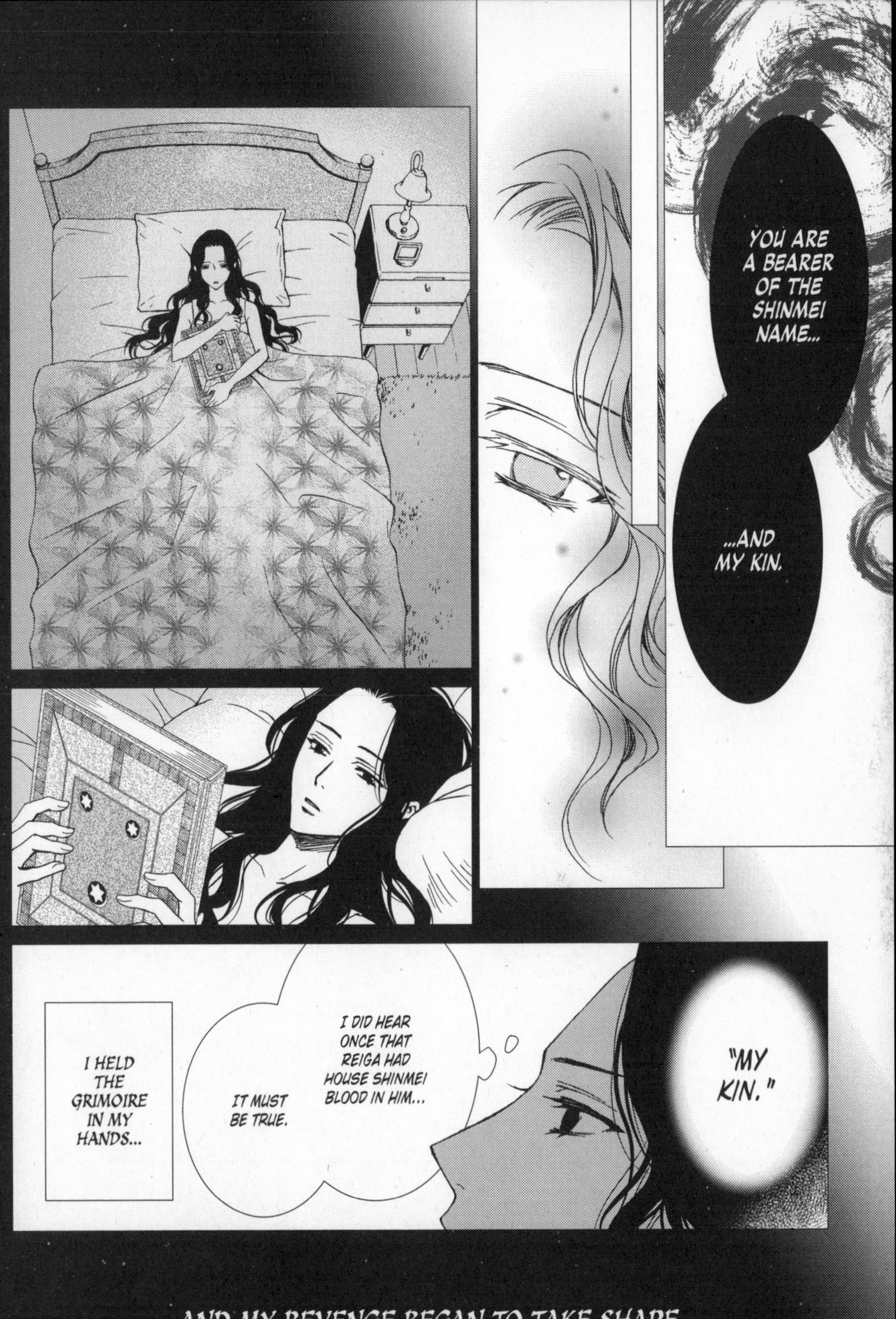

YOU ARE A BEARER OF THE SHINMEI NAME...
...AND MY KIN.
"MY KIN."
I DID HEAR ONCE THAT REIGA HAD HOUSE SHINMEI BLOOD IN HIM...
IT MUST BE TRUE.
I HELD THE GRIMOIRE IN MY HANDS...
...AND MY REVENGE BEGAN TO TAKE SHAPE.

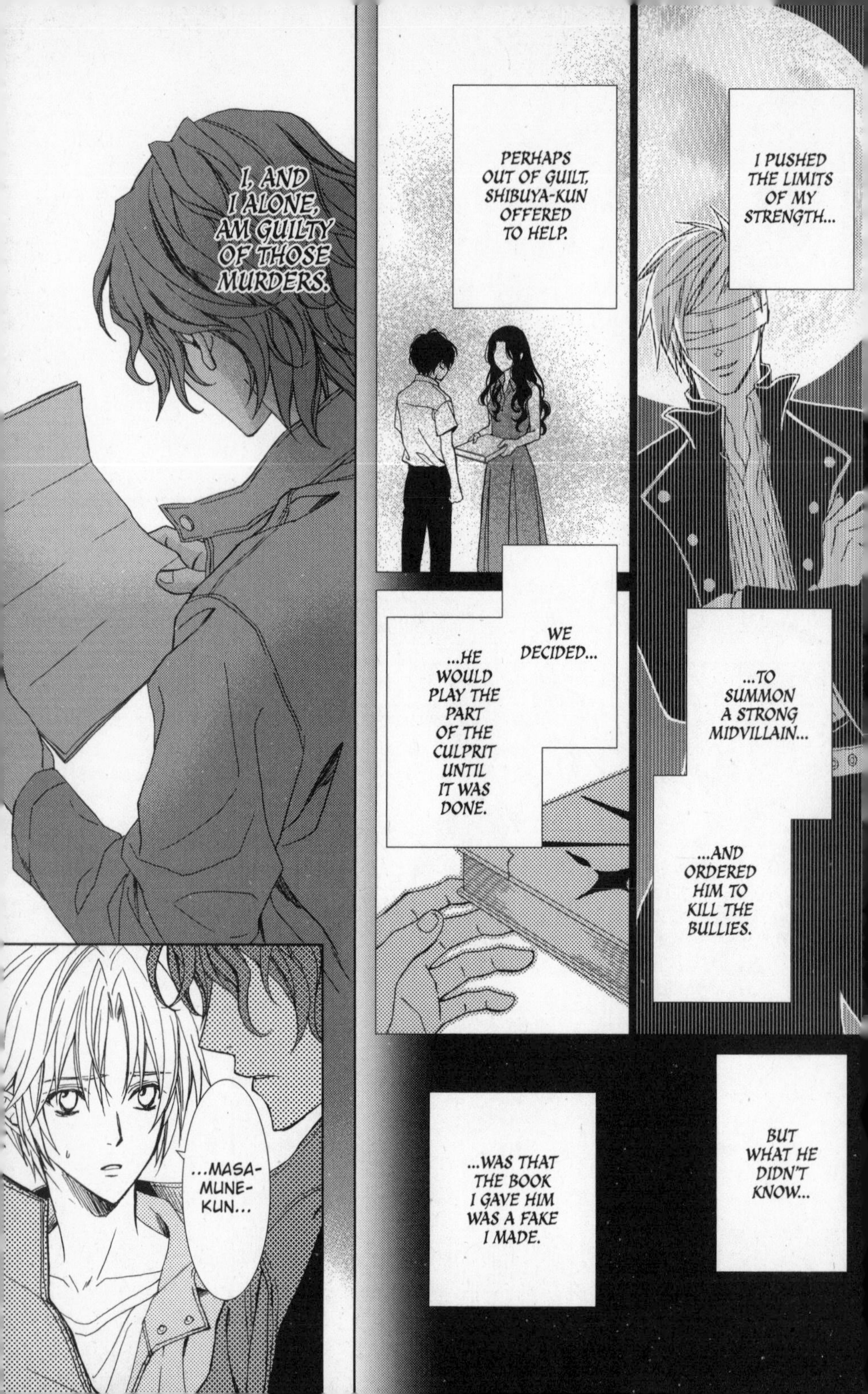
I PUSHED THE LIMITS OF MY STRENGTH...
...TO SUMMON A STRONG MIDVILLAIN...
...AND ORDERED HIM TO KILL THE BULLIES.
PERHAPS OUT OF GUILT, SHIBUYA-KUN OFFERED TO HELP.
WE DECIDED...
...HE WOULD PLAY THE PART OF THE CULPRIT UNTIL IT WAS DONE.
BUT WHAT HE DIDN'T KNOW...
...WAS THAT THE BOOK I GAVE HIM WAS A FAKE I MADE.
I, AND I ALONE, AM GUILTY OF THOSE MURDERS.
...MASAMUNE-KUN...

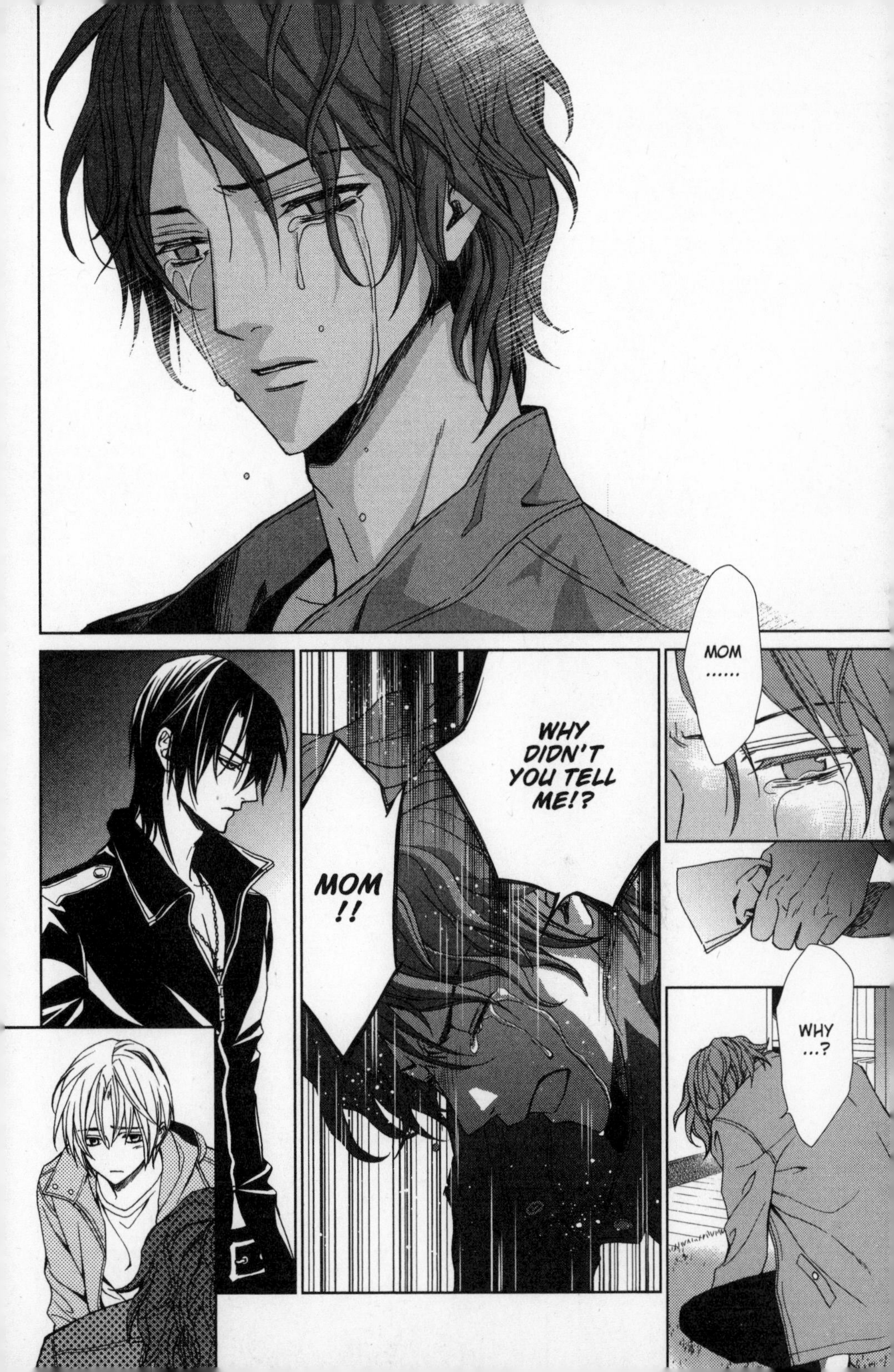
MOM ......
WHY ...?
WHY DIDN'T YOU TELL ME!?
MOM !!

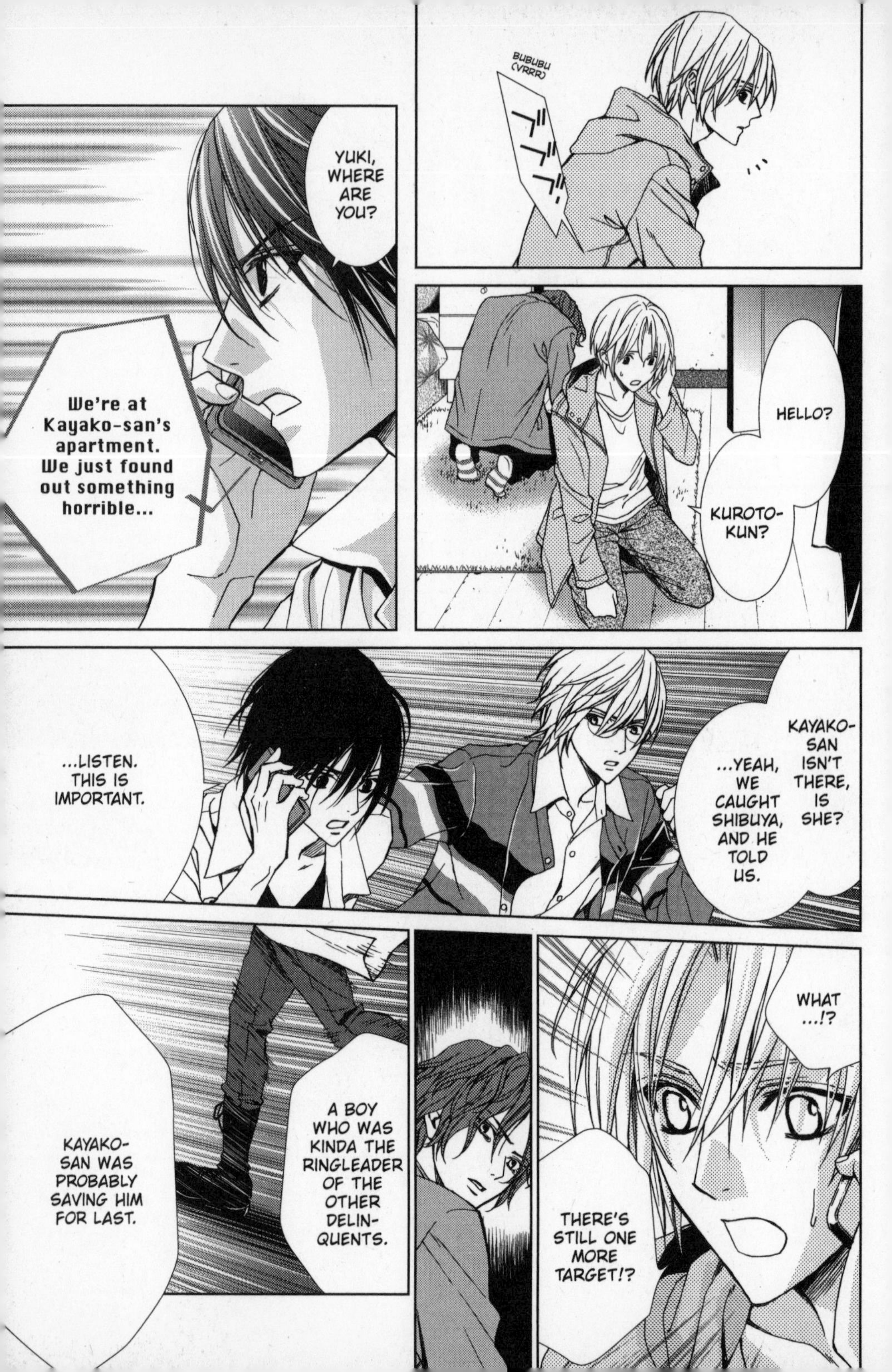
BUBUBU (VRRR)
...
HELLO?
KUROTO-KUN?
YUKI, WHERE ARE YOU?
We're at Kayako-san's apartment. We just found out something horrible...
KAYAKO-SAN ISN'T THERE, IS SHE?
...YEAH, WE CAUGHT SHIBUYA, AND HE TOLD US.
...LISTEN. THIS IS IMPORTANT.
WHAT ...!?
THERE'S STILL ONE MORE TARGET!?
A BOY WHO WAS KINDA THE RINGLEADER OF THE OTHER DELIN-QUENTS.
KAYAKO-SAN WAS PROBABLY SAVING HIM FOR LAST.

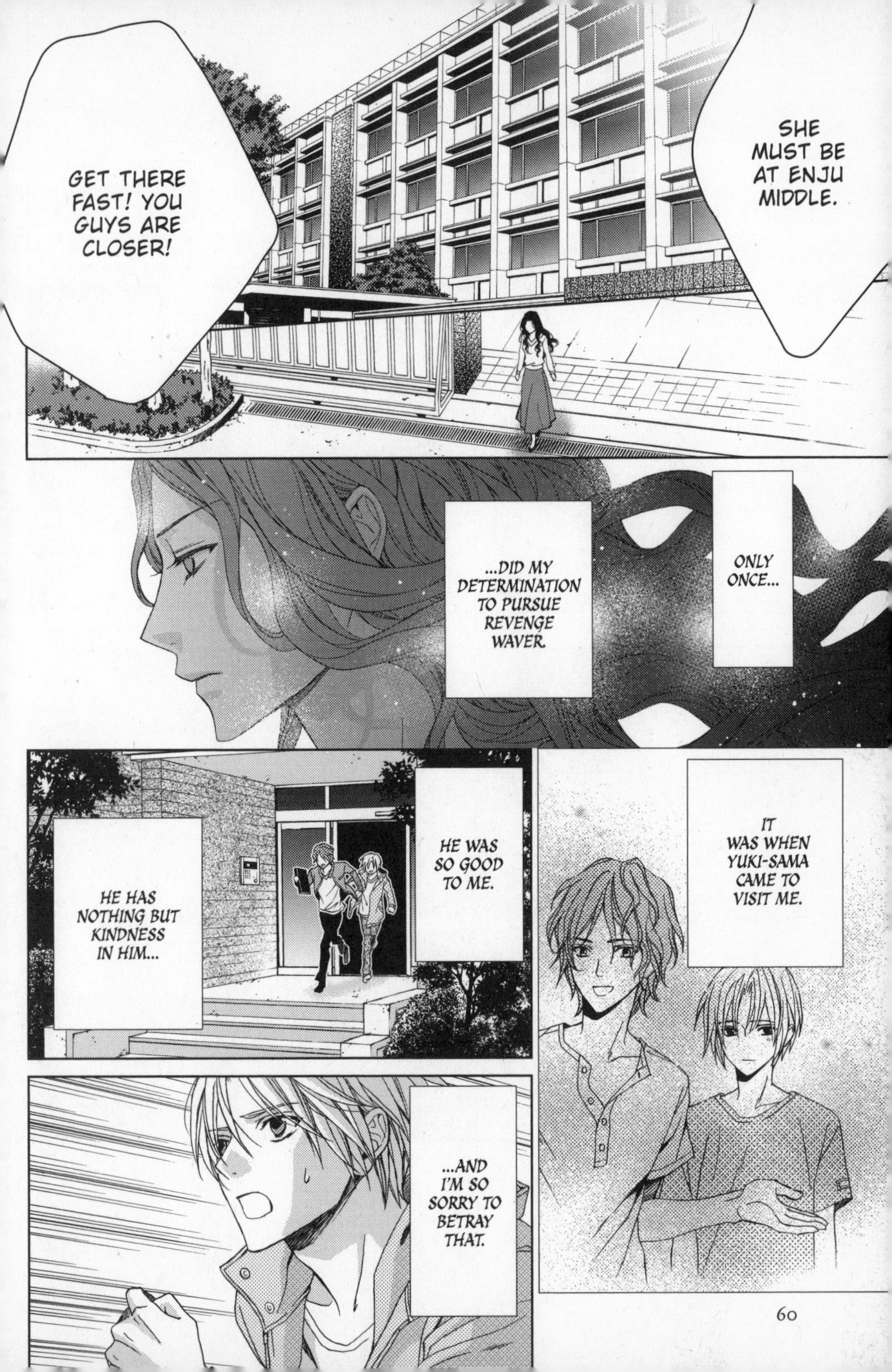
SHE MUST BE AT ENJU MIDDLE.
GET THERE FAST! YOU GUYS ARE CLOSER!
ONLY ONCE...
...DID MY DETERMINATION TO PURSUE REVENGE WAVER.
IT WAS WHEN YUKI-SAMA CAME TO VISIT ME.
HE WAS SO GOOD TO ME.
HE HAS NOTHING BUT KINDNESS IN HIM...
...AND I'M SO SORRY TO BETRAY THAT.

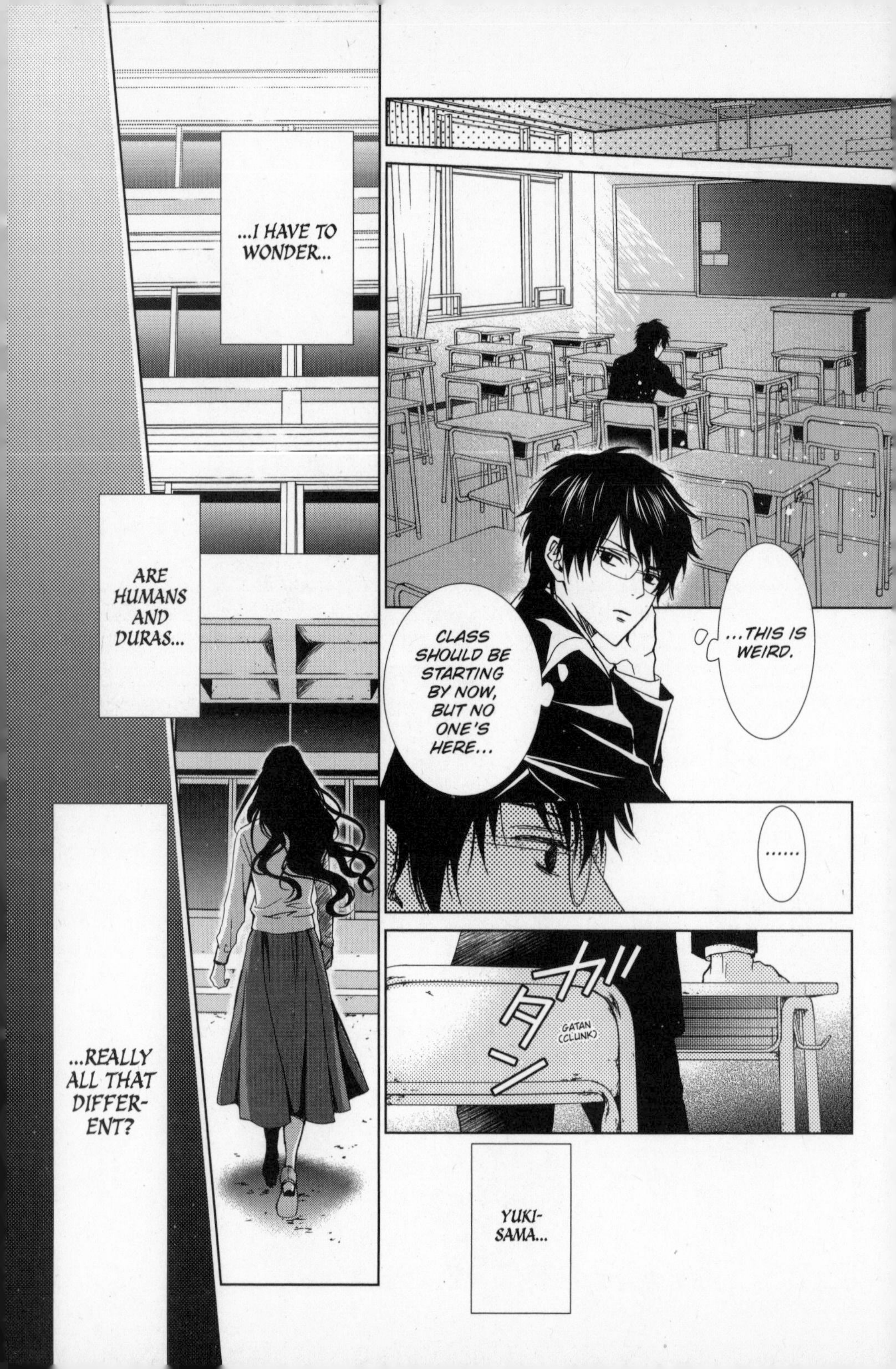
...THIS IS WEIRD.
CLASS SHOULD BE STARTING BY NOW, BUT NO ONE'S HERE...
......
GATAN (CLUNK)
YUKI-SAMA...
...I HAVE TO WONDER...
ARE HUMANS AND DURAS...
...REALLY ALL THAT DIFFER-ENT?

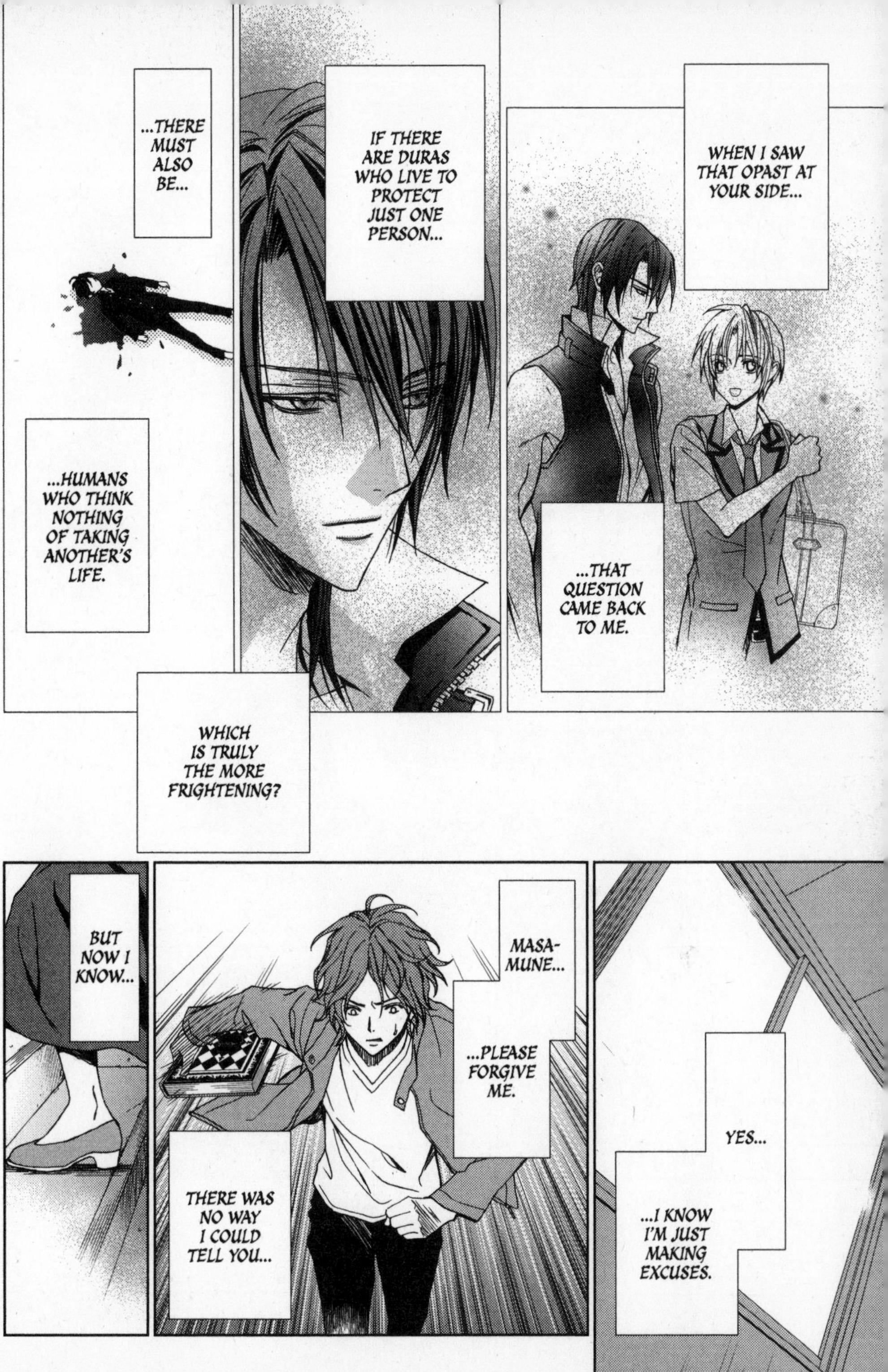
WHEN I SAW THAT OPAST AT YOUR SIDE...
...THAT QUESTION CAME BACK TO ME.
IF THERE ARE DURAS WHO LIVE TO PROTECT JUST ONE PERSON...
...THERE MUST ALSO BE...
...HUMANS WHO THINK NOTHING OF TAKING ANOTHER'S LIFE.
WHICH IS TRULY THE MORE FRIGHTENING?
YES...
...I KNOW I'M JUST MAKING EXCUSES.
MASA-MUNE...
...PLEASE FORGIVE ME.
THERE WAS NO WAY I COULD TELL YOU...
BUT NOW I KNOW...

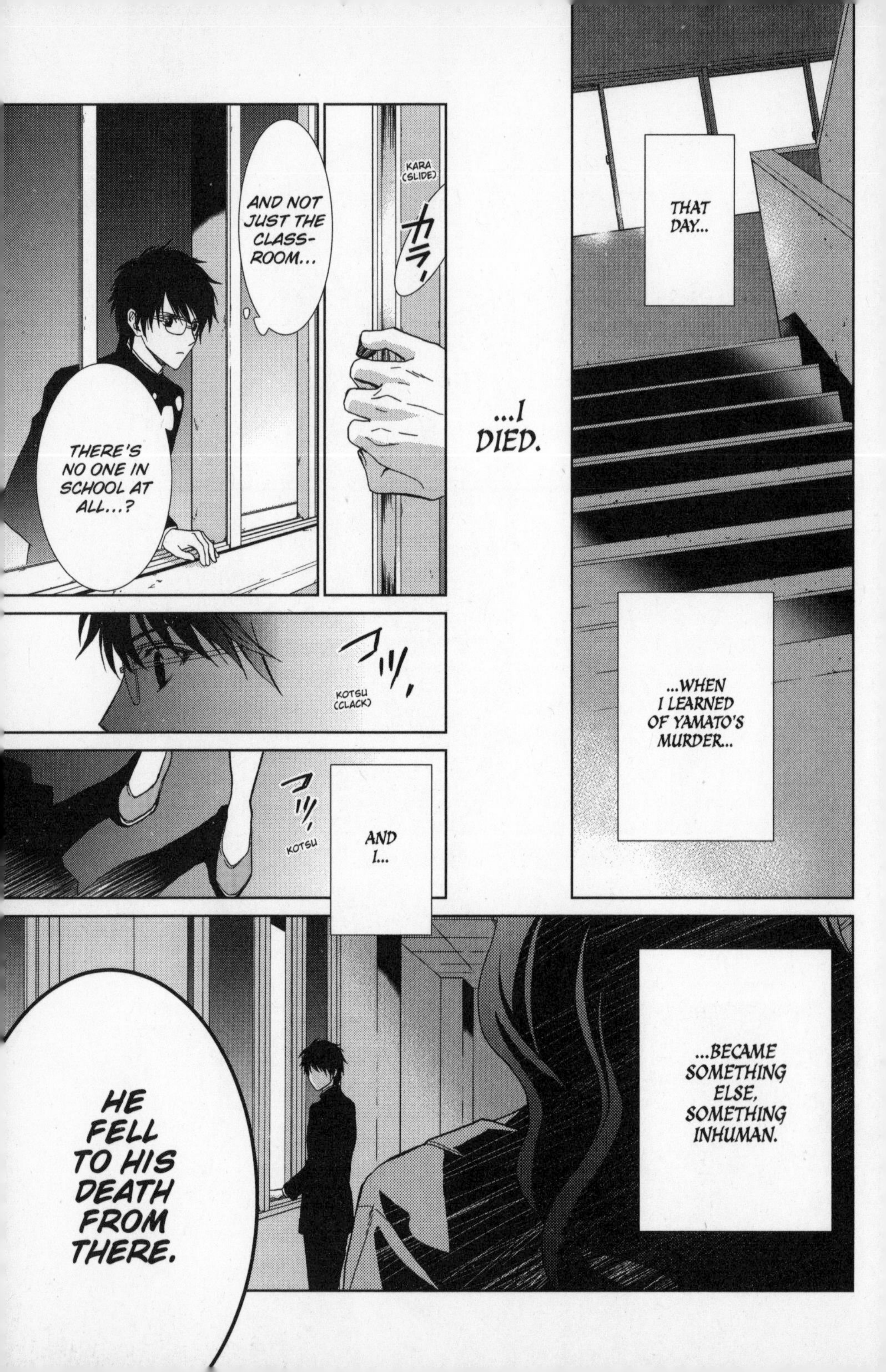

THAT DAY...
...WHEN I LEARNED OF YAMATO'S MURDER...
...I DIED.
KARA (SLIDE)
カラ
AND NOT JUST THE CLASSROOM...
THERE'S NO ONE IN SCHOOL AT ALL...?
コツ
KOTSU (CLACK)
AND I...
コツ
KOTSU
...BECAME SOMETHING ELSE, SOMETHING INHUMAN.
HE FELL TO HIS DEATH FROM THERE.

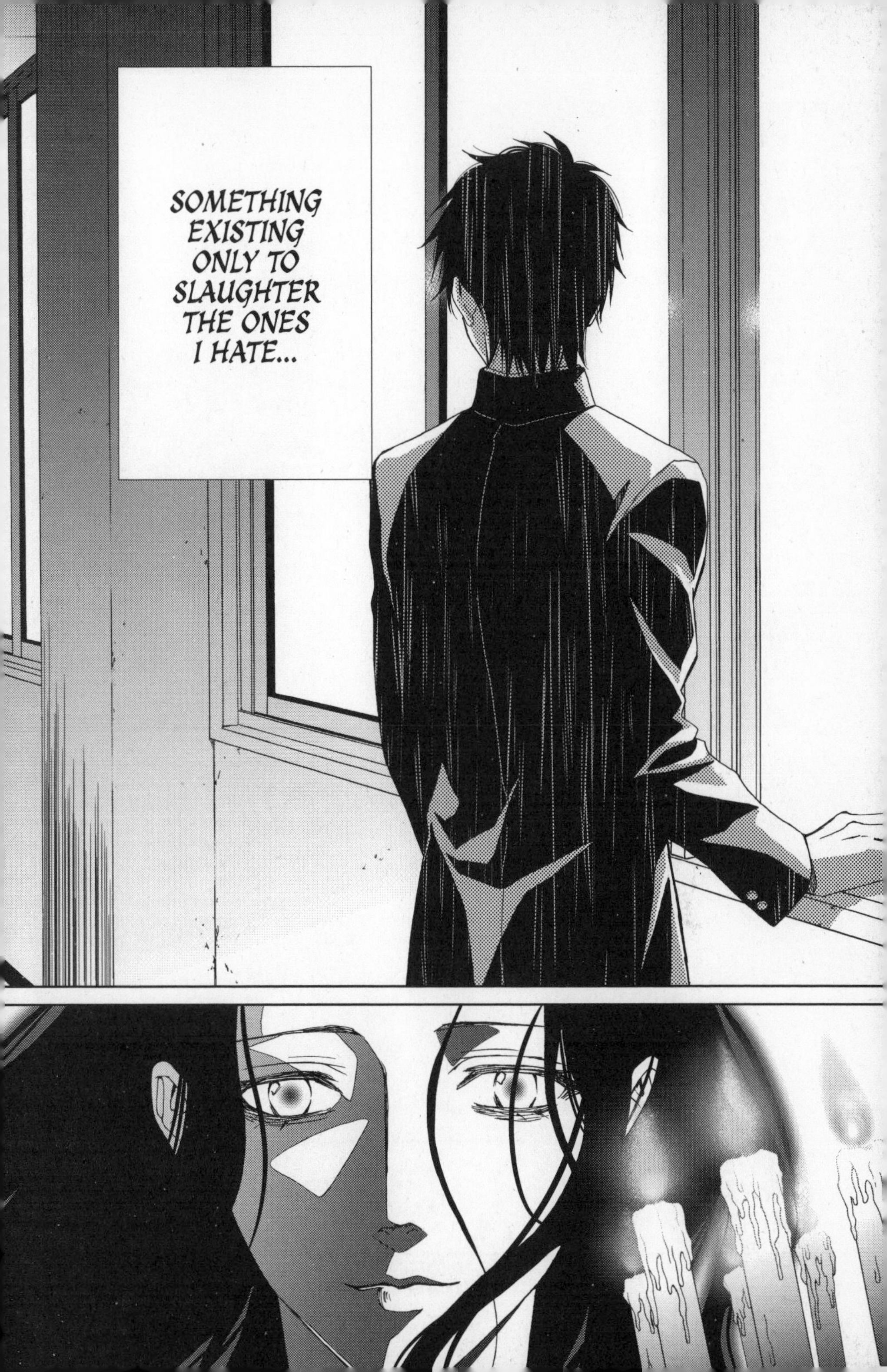
SOMETHING EXISTING ONLY TO SLAUGHTER THE ONES I HATE...

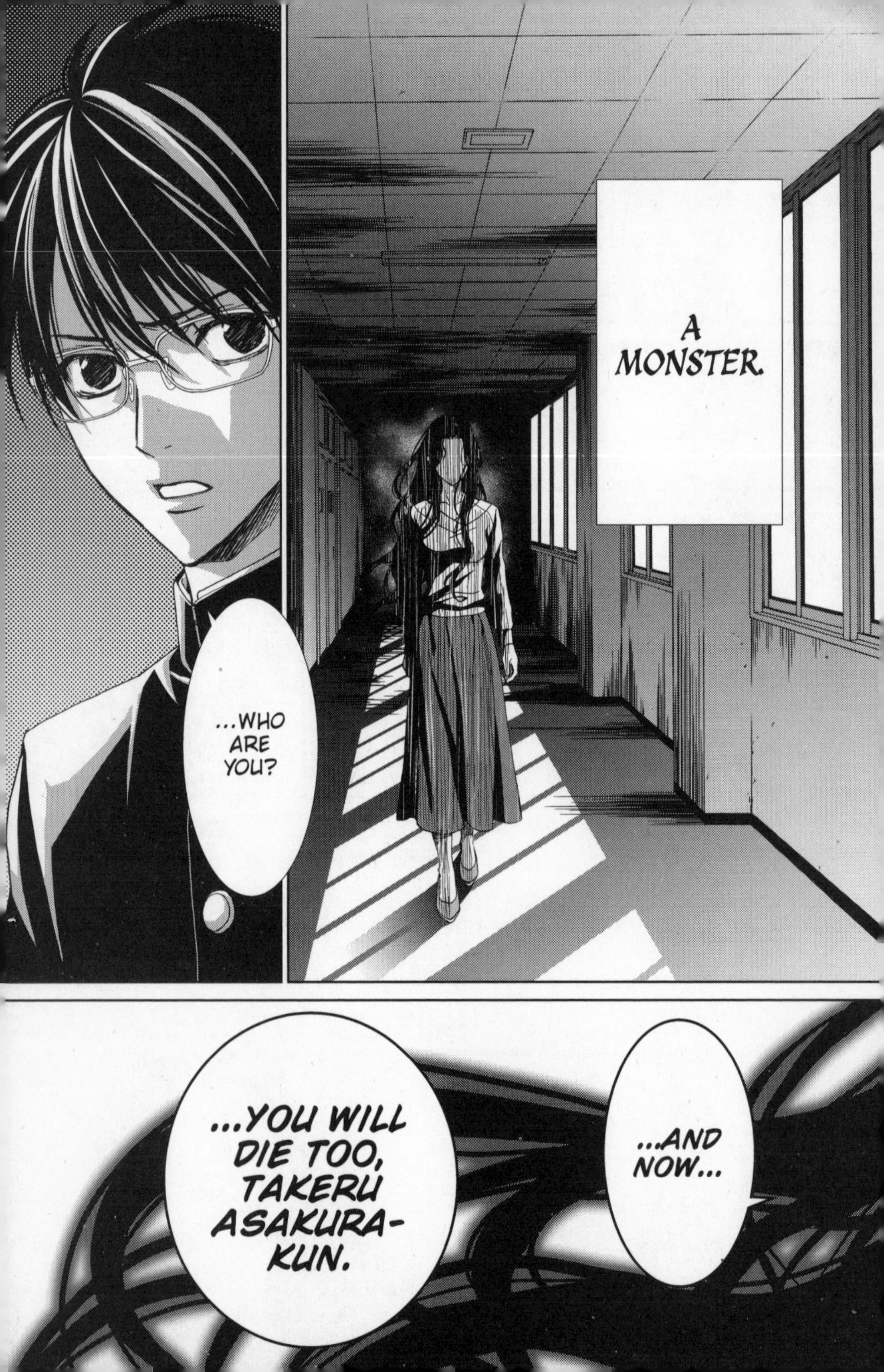
A MONSTER.
...WHO ARE YOU?
...AND NOW...
...YOU WILL DIE TOO, TAKERU ASAKURA-KUN.

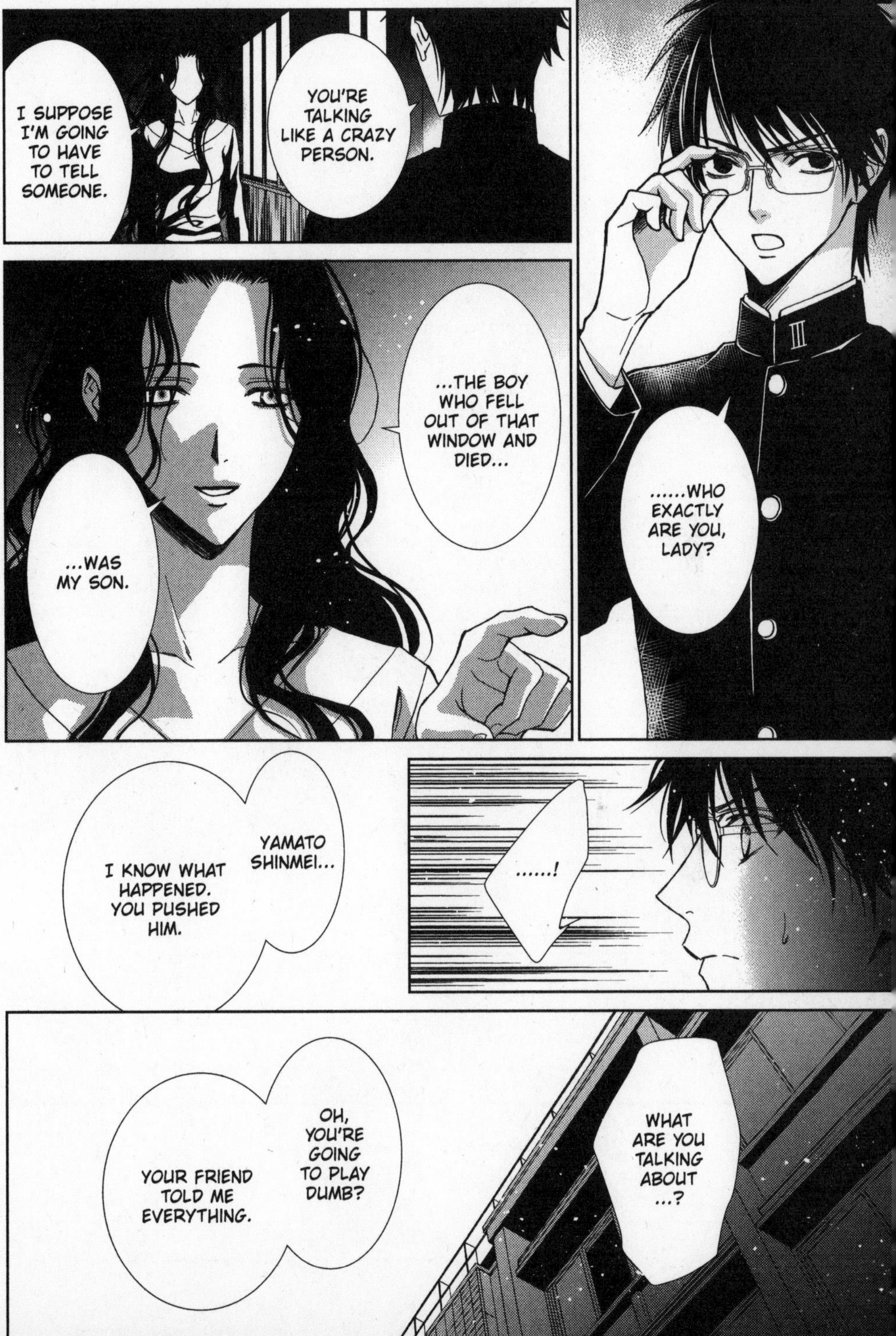
......WHO EXACTLY ARE YOU, LADY?
YOU'RE TALKING LIKE A CRAZY PERSON.
I SUPPOSE I'M GOING TO HAVE TO TELL SOMEONE.
...THE BOY WHO FELL OUT OF THAT WINDOW AND DIED...
...WAS MY SON.
......!
YAMATO SHINMEI...
I KNOW WHAT HAPPENED. YOU PUSHED HIM.
WHAT ARE YOU TALKING ABOUT ...?
OH, YOU'RE GOING TO PLAY DUMB?
YOUR FRIEND TOLD ME EVERYTHING.

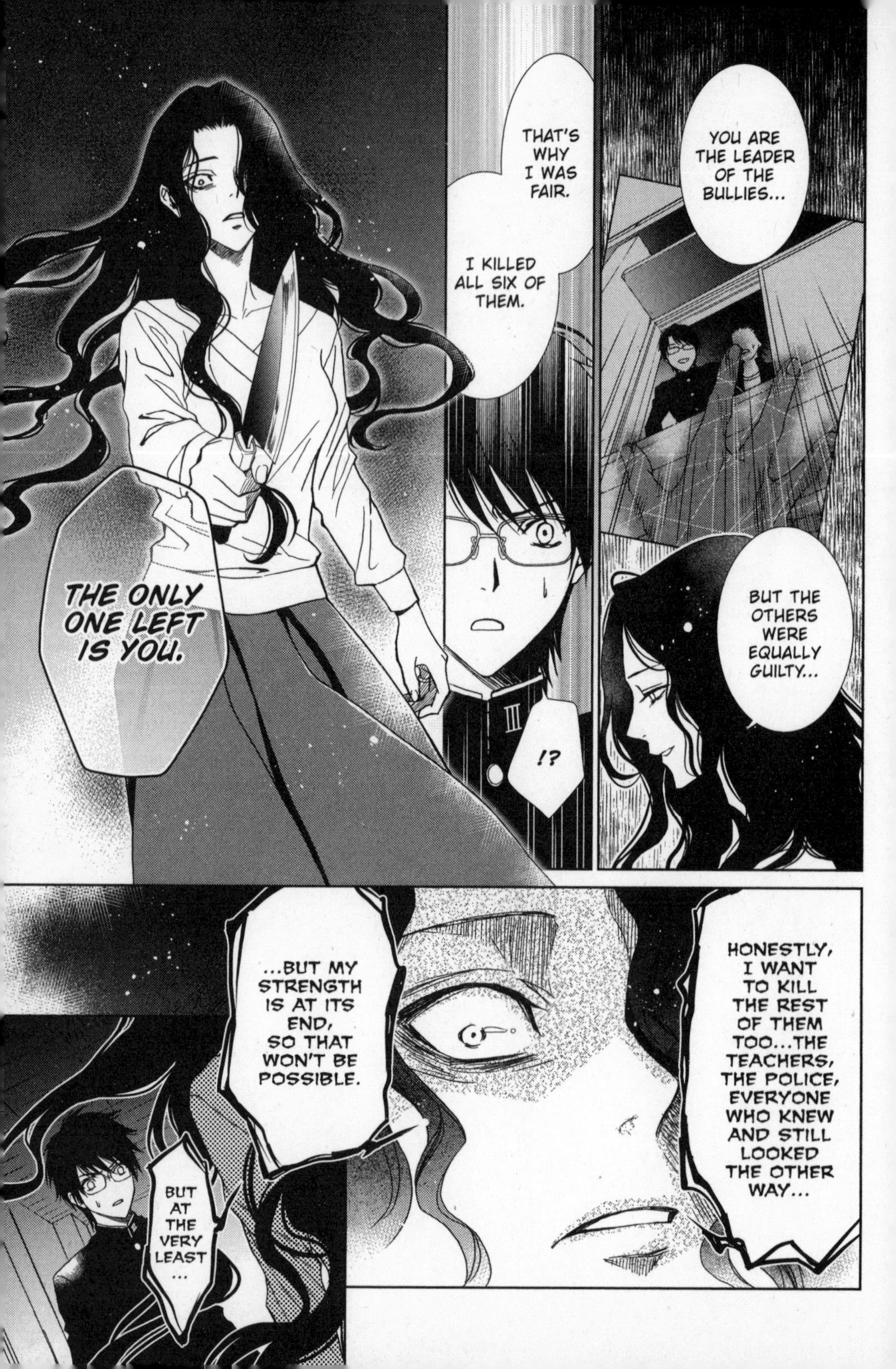
YOU ARE THE LEADER OF THE BULLIES...
BUT THE OTHERS WERE EQUALLY GUILTY...
THAT'S WHY I WAS FAIR.
I KILLED ALL SIX OF THEM.
!?
THE ONLY ONE LEFT IS YOU.
HONESTLY, I WANT TO KILL THE REST OF THEM TOO...THE TEACHERS, THE POLICE, EVERYONE WHO KNEW AND STILL LOOKED THE OTHER WAY...
...BUT MY STRENGTH IS AT ITS END, SO THAT WON'T BE POSSIBLE.
BUT AT THE VERY LEAST...

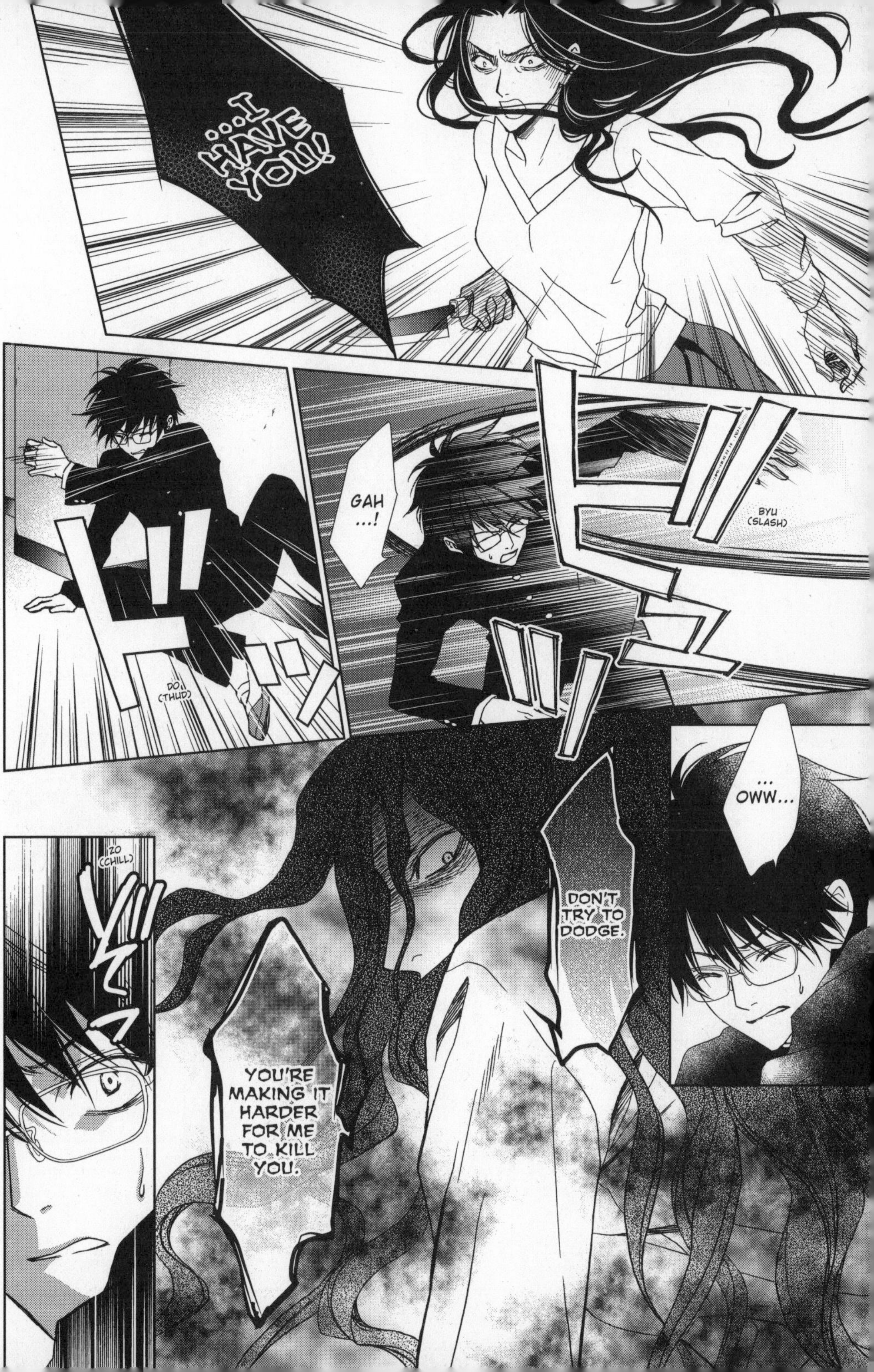
...I HAVE YOU!
BYU (SLASH)
GAH ...!
DO (THUD)
... OWW...
DON'T TRY TO DODGE.
YOU'RE MAKING IT HARDER FOR ME TO KILL YOU.
ZO (CHILL)

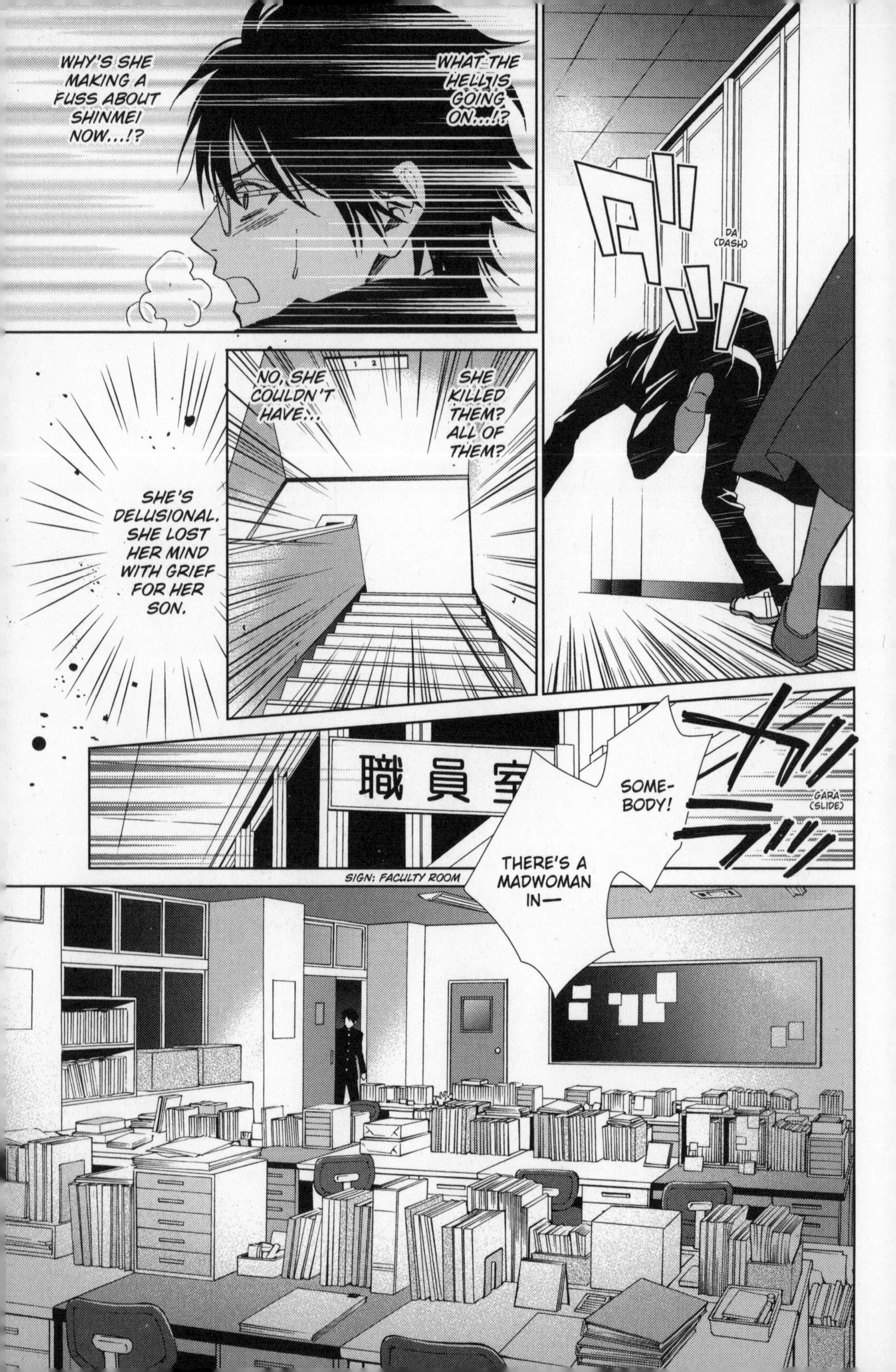
DA
(DASH)
WHAT THE HELL IS GOING ON...!?
WHY'S SHE MAKING A FUSS ABOUT SHINMEI NOW...!?
SHE KILLED THEM? ALL OF THEM?
NO, SHE COULDN'T HAVE...
SHE'S DELUSIONAL. SHE LOST HER MIND WITH GRIEF FOR HER SON.
GARA
(SLIDE)
SOME-BODY!
THERE'S A MADWOMAN IN—
職員室
SIGN: FACULTY ROOM

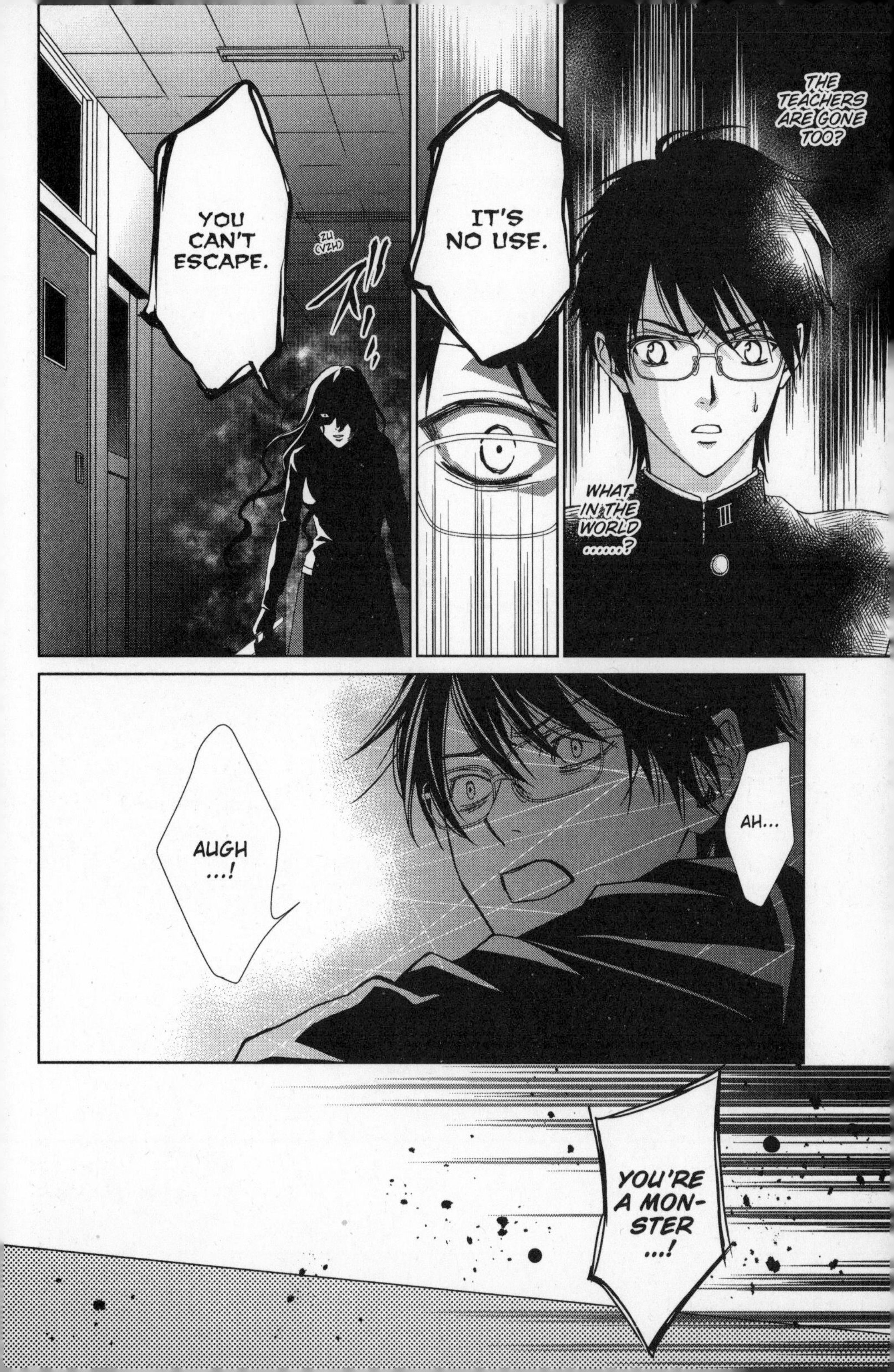
THE TEACHERS ARE GONE TOO?
WHAT IN THE WORLD ......?
IT'S NO USE.
YOU CAN'T ESCAPE.
ZU (VZH)
AH...
AUGH ...!
YOU'RE A MON-STER ...!

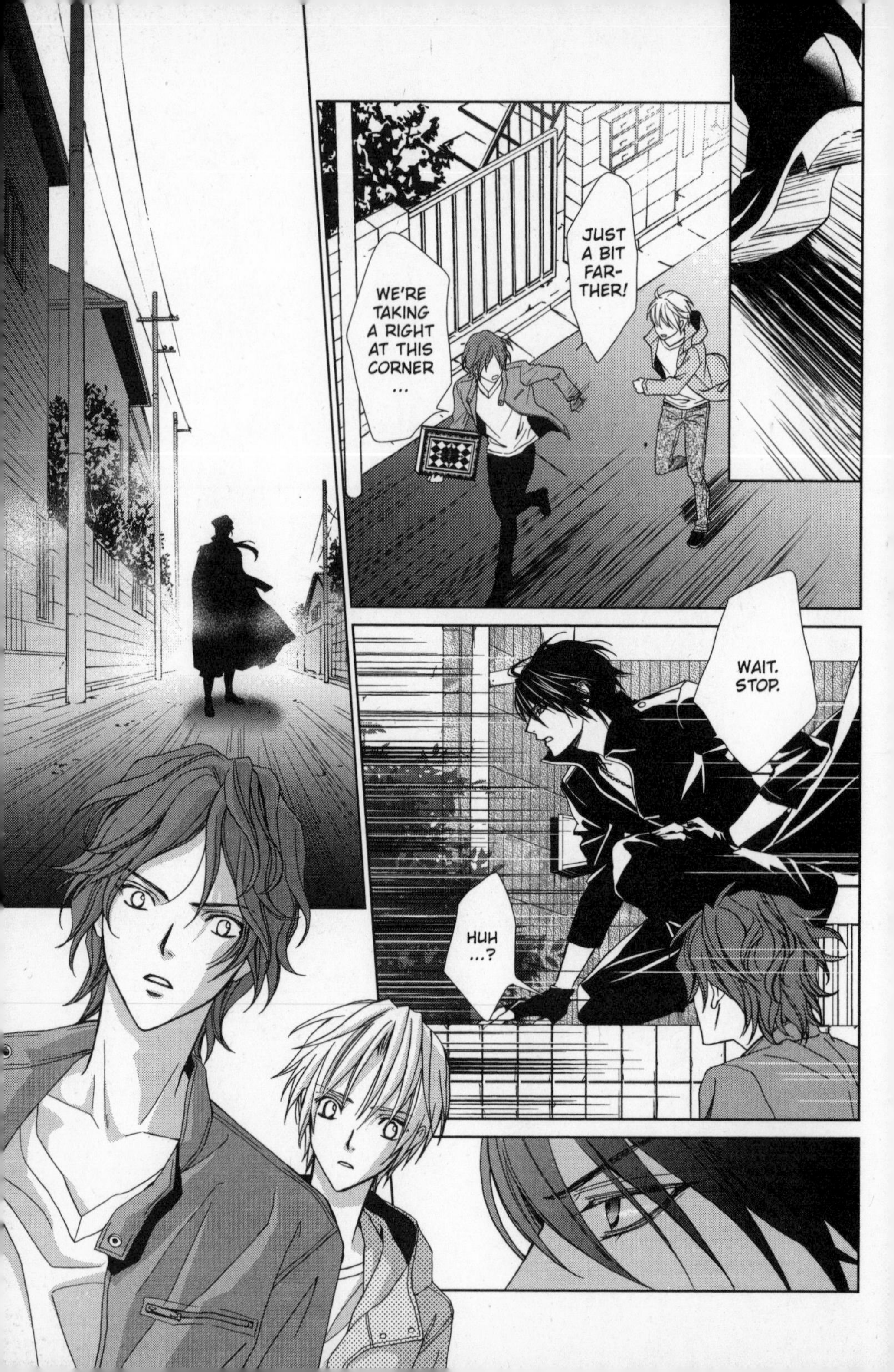
JUST A BIT FAR-THER!
WE'RE TAKING A RIGHT AT THIS CORNER ...
WAIT. STOP.
HUH ...?

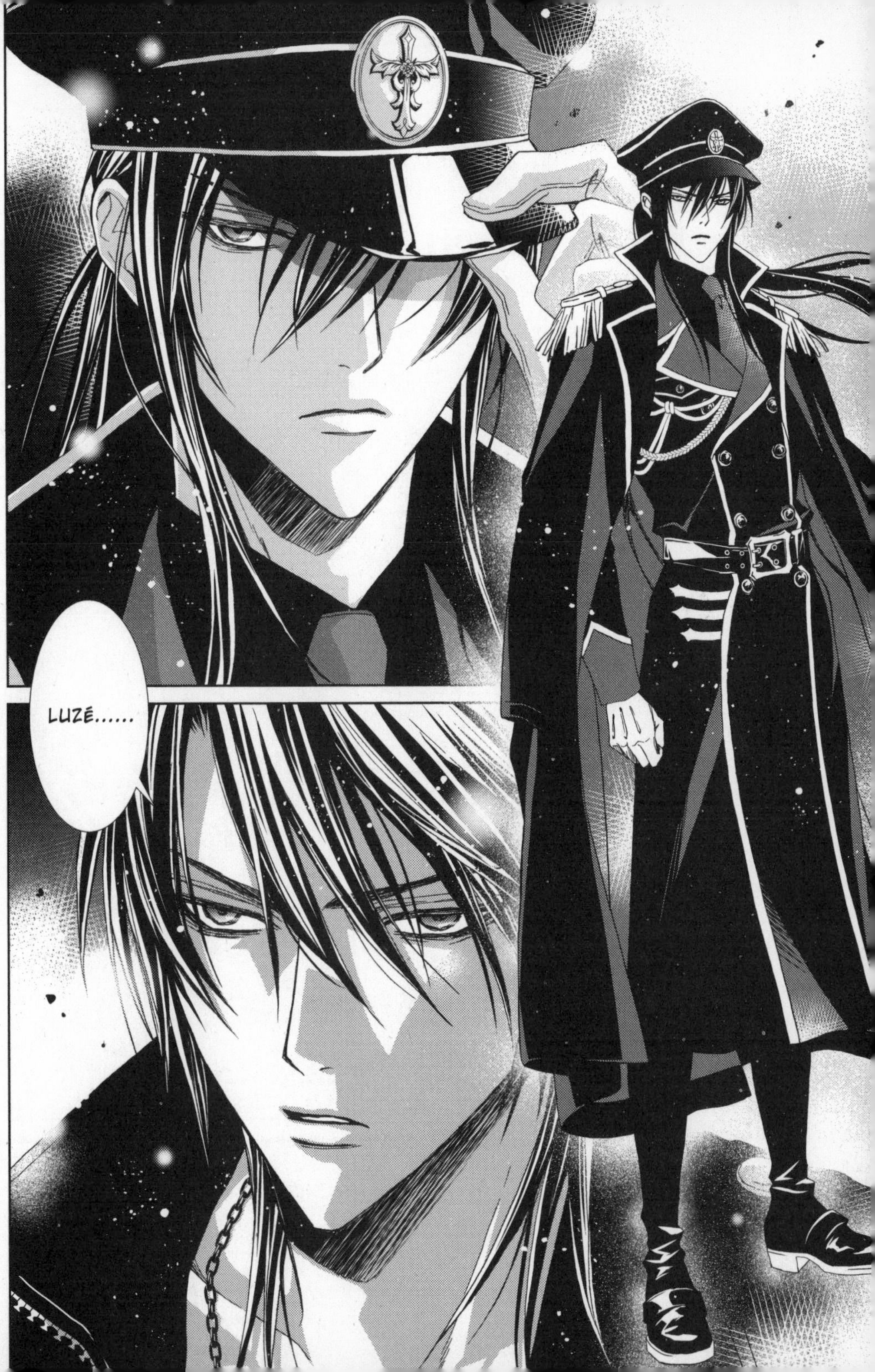
LUZÉ......

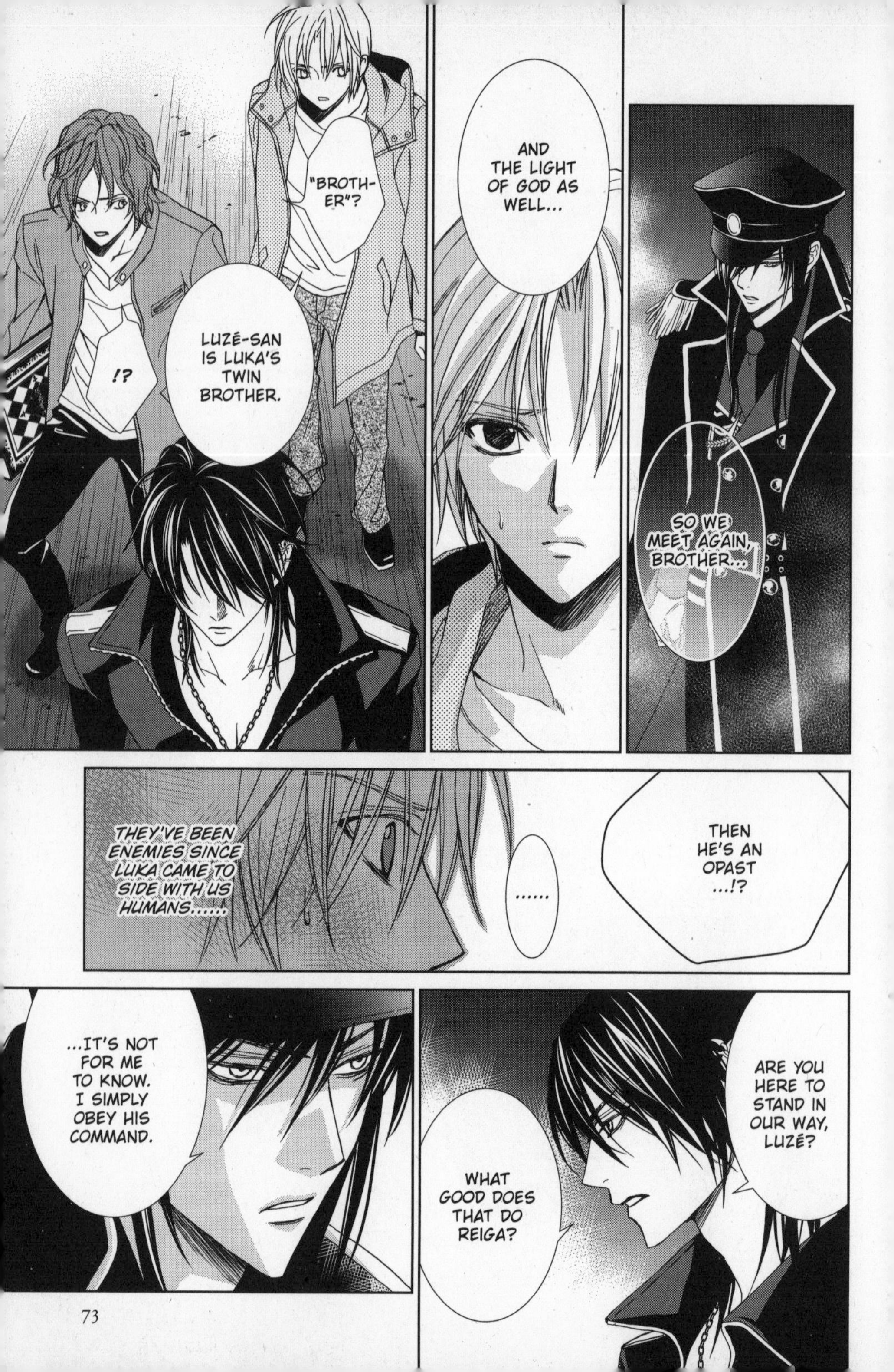
SO WE MEET AGAIN, BROTHER...
AND THE LIGHT OF GOD AS WELL...
"BROTHER-ER"?
LUZÉ-SAN IS LUKA'S TWIN BROTHER.
!?
THEN HE'S AN OPAST ...!?
......
THEY'VE BEEN ENEMIES SINCE LUKA CAME TO SIDE WITH US HUMANS......
ARE YOU HERE TO STAND IN OUR WAY, LUZÉ?
WHAT GOOD DOES THAT DO REIGA?
...IT'S NOT FOR ME TO KNOW. I SIMPLY OBEY HIS COMMAND.

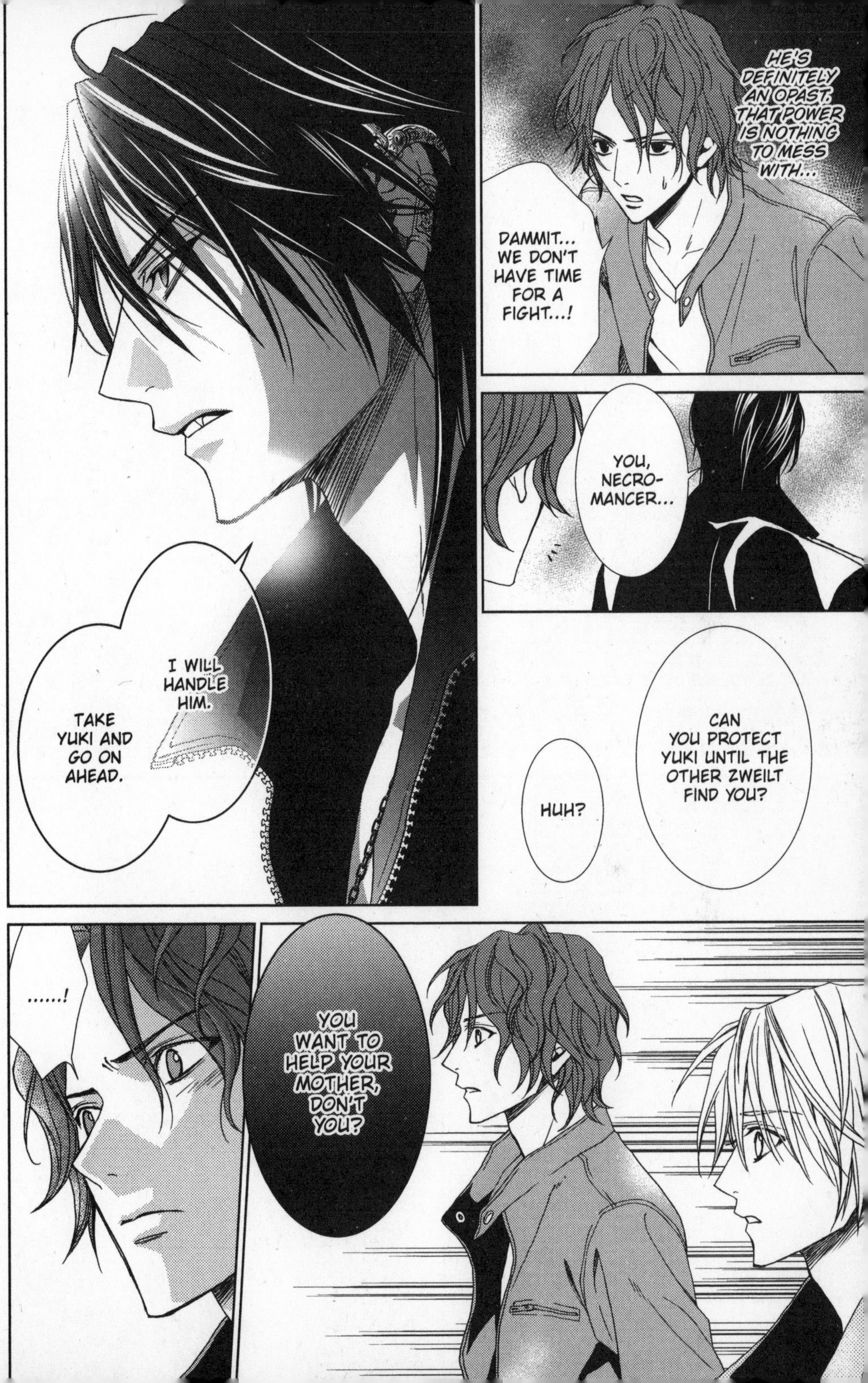

HE'S DEFINITELY AN OPAST. THAT POWER IS NOTHING TO MESS WITH...
DAMMIT... WE DON'T HAVE TIME FOR A FIGHT...!
YOU, NECRO-MANCER...
CAN YOU PROTECT YUKI UNTIL THE OTHER ZWEILT FIND YOU?
HUH?
I WILL HANDLE HIM.
TAKE YUKI AND GO ON AHEAD.
YOU WANT TO HELP YOUR MOTHER, DON'T YOU?
......!

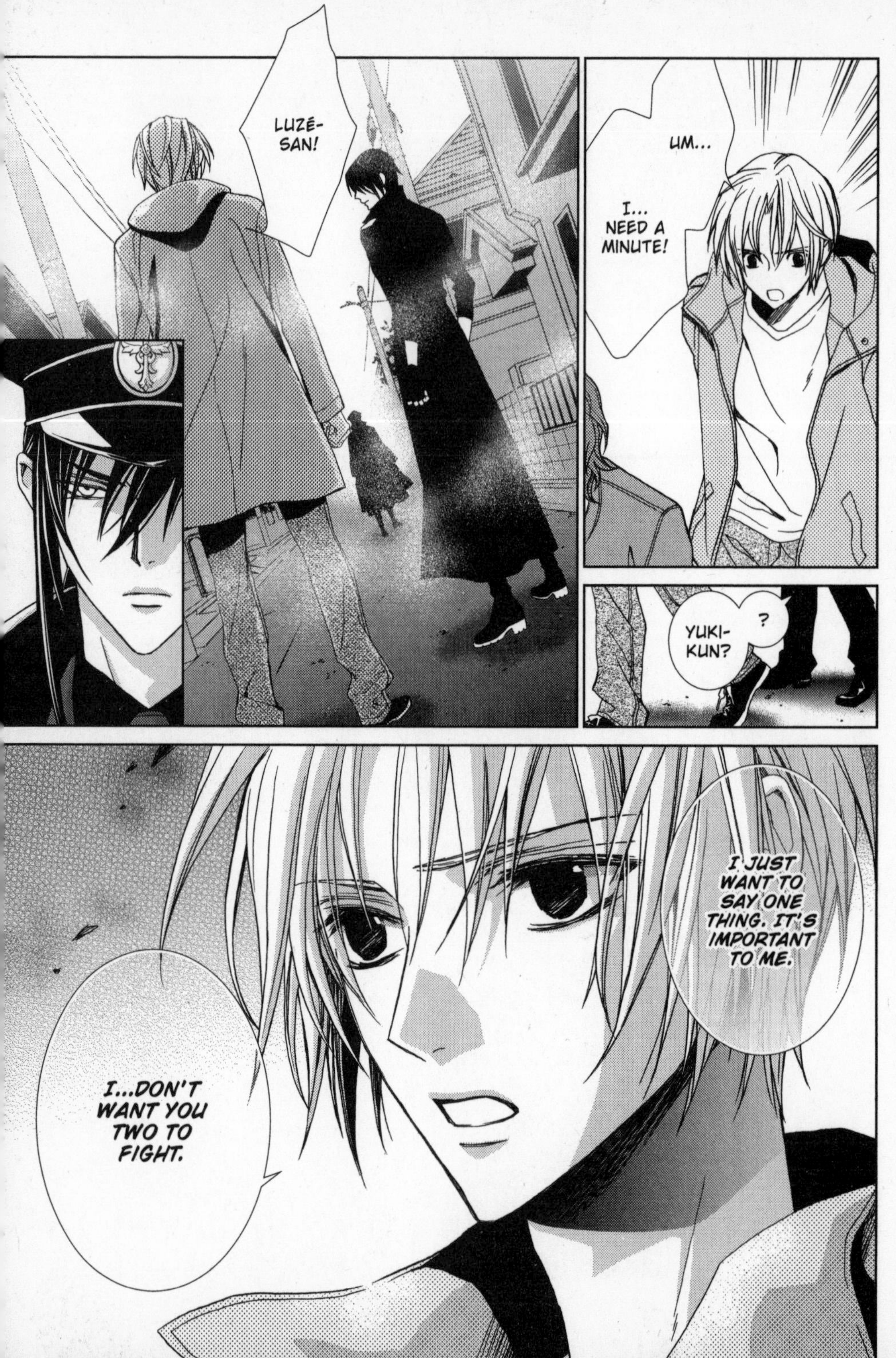
UM...
I... NEED A MINUTE!
?
YUKI-KUN?
LUZÉ-SAN!
I JUST WANT TO SAY ONE THING. IT'S IMPORTANT TO ME.
I...DON'T WANT YOU TWO TO FIGHT.

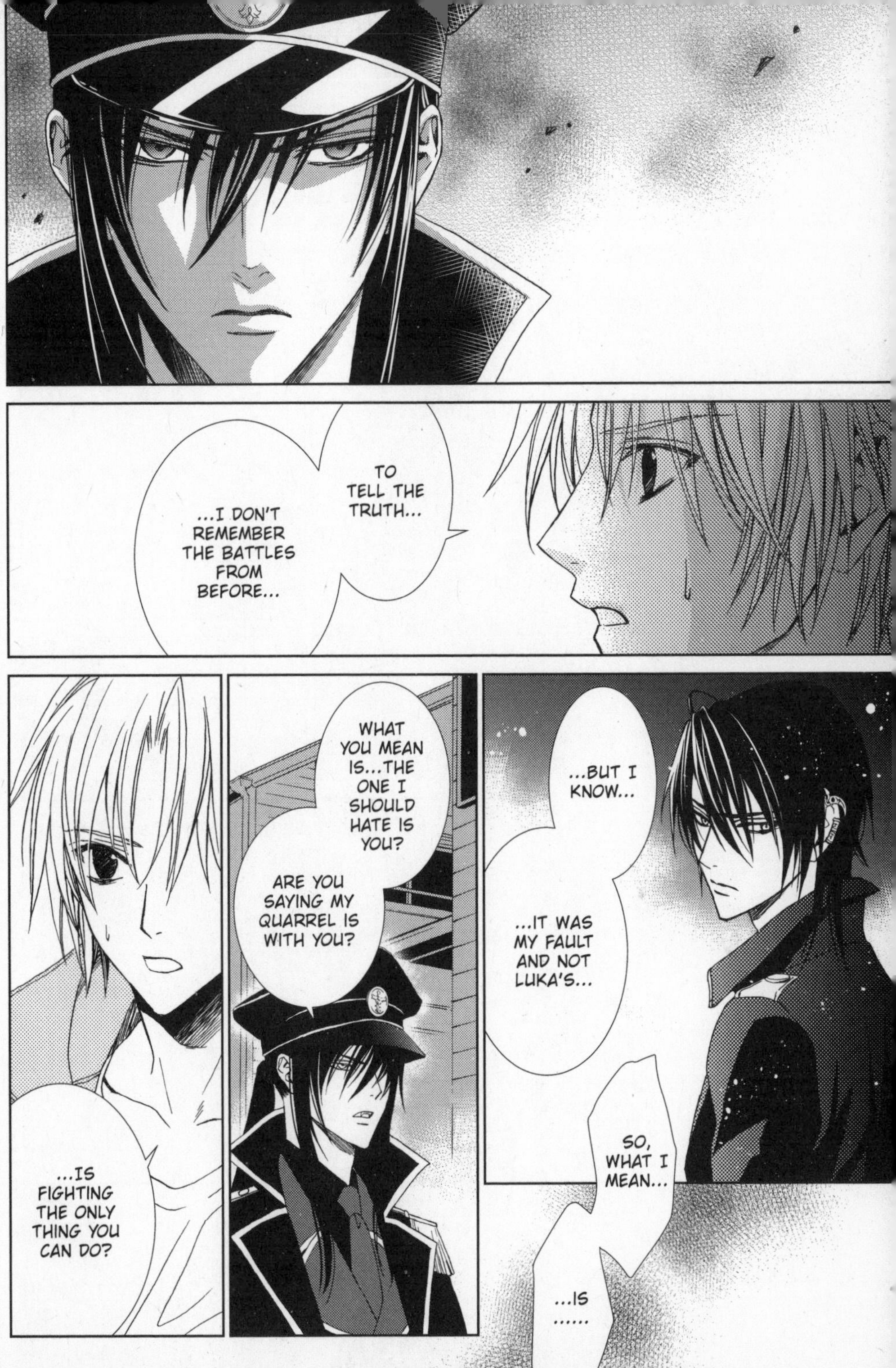
TO TELL THE TRUTH...
...I DON'T REMEMBER THE BATTLES FROM BEFORE...
...BUT I KNOW...
...IT WAS MY FAULT AND NOT LUKA'S...
SO, WHAT I MEAN...
...IS ......
WHAT YOU MEAN IS...THE ONE I SHOULD HATE IS YOU?
ARE YOU SAYING MY QUARREL IS WITH YOU?
...IS FIGHTING THE ONLY THING YOU CAN DO?

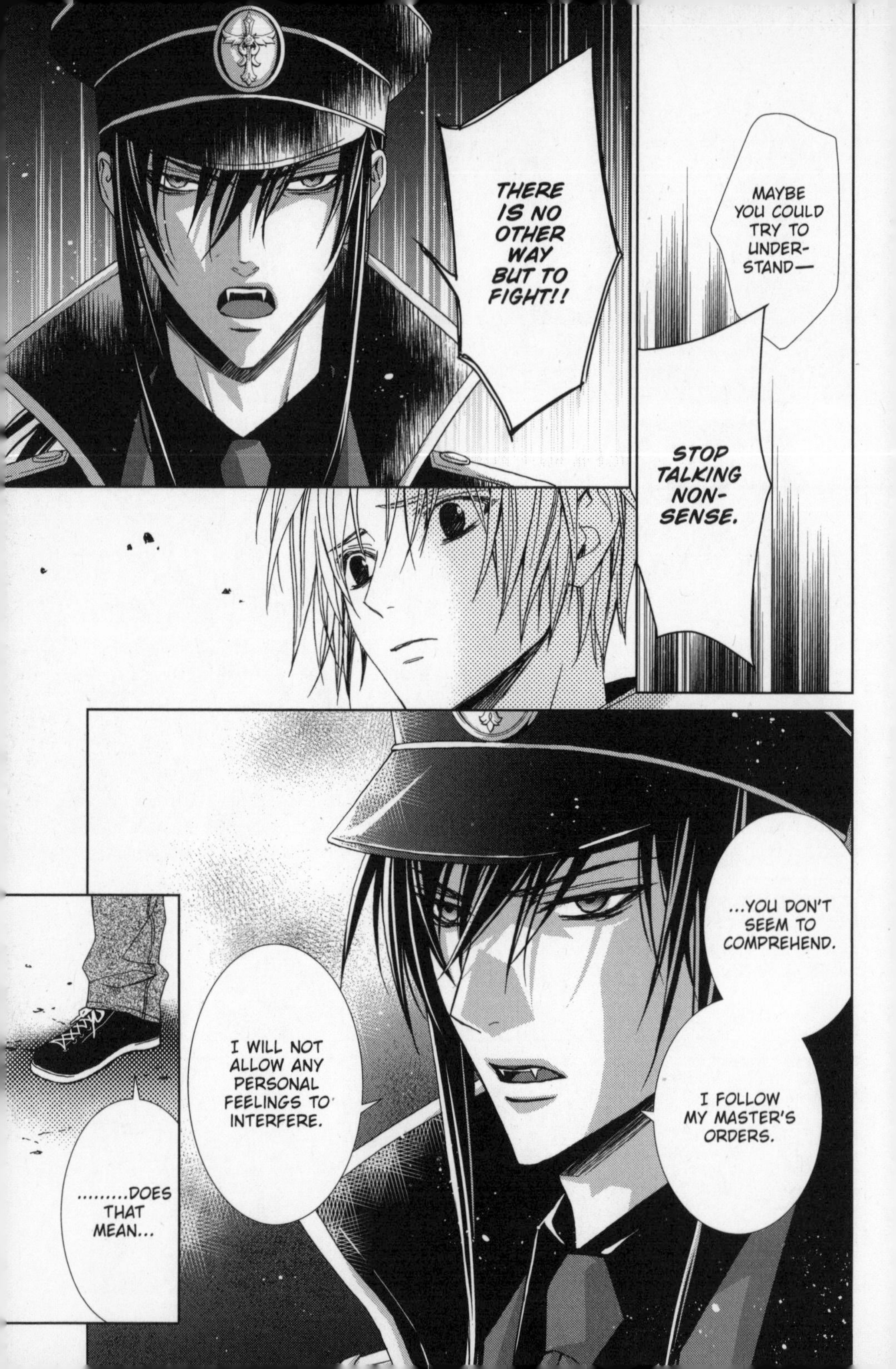
MAYBE YOU COULD TRY TO UNDER-STAND—
STOP TALKING NON-SENSE.
THERE IS NO OTHER WAY BUT TO FIGHT!!
...YOU DON'T SEEM TO COMPREHEND.
I FOLLOW MY MASTER'S ORDERS.
I WILL NOT ALLOW ANY PERSONAL FEELINGS TO INTERFERE.
.........DOES THAT MEAN...

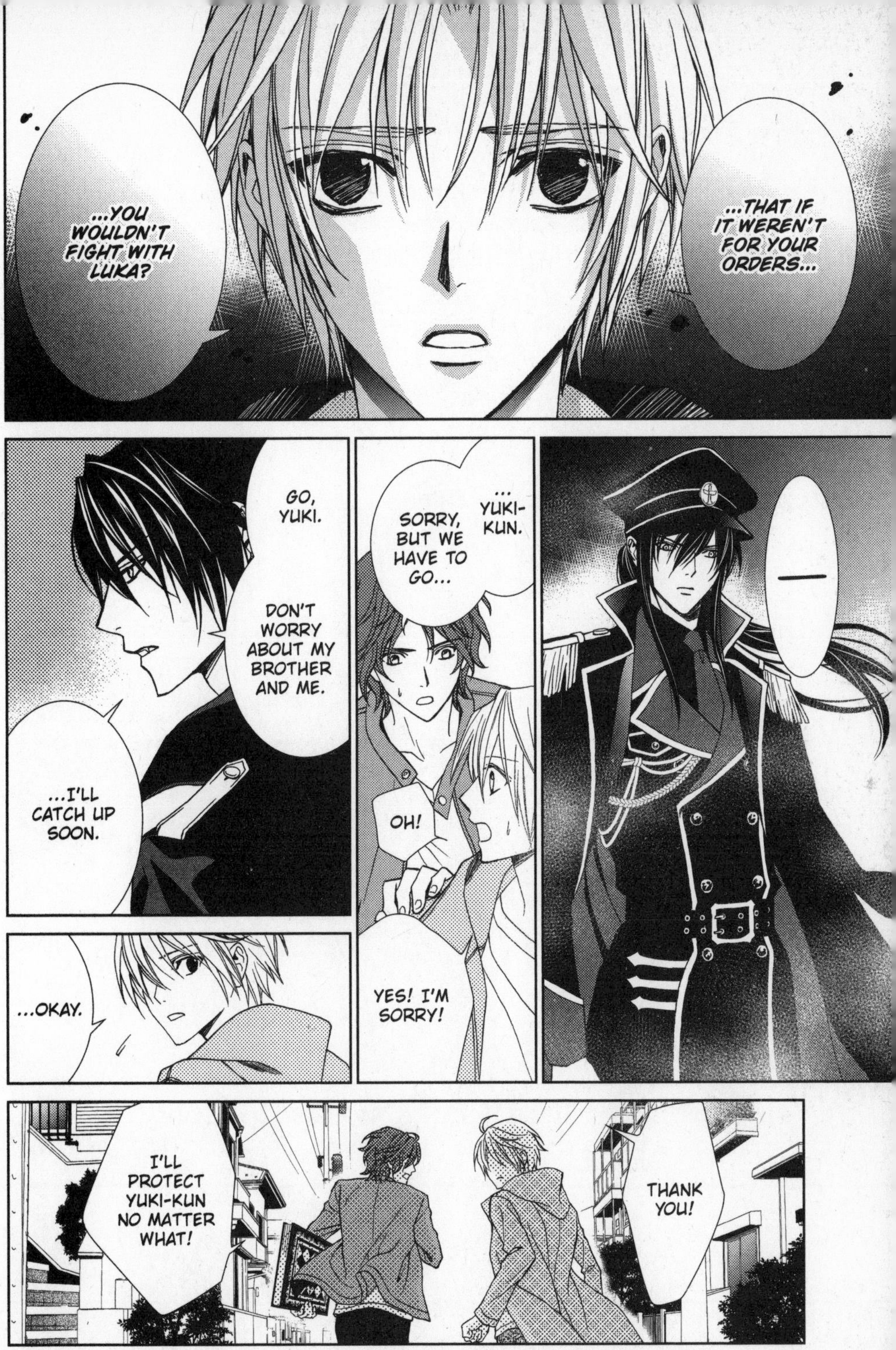
...THAT IF IT WEREN'T FOR YOUR ORDERS...
...YOU WOULDN'T FIGHT WITH LUKA?
—
...YUKI-KUN.
SORRY, BUT WE HAVE TO GO...
OH!
YES! I'M SORRY!
GO, YUKI.
DON'T WORRY ABOUT MY BROTHER AND ME.
...I'LL CATCH UP SOON.
...OKAY.
THANK YOU!
I'LL PROTECT YUKI-KUN NO MATTER WHAT!

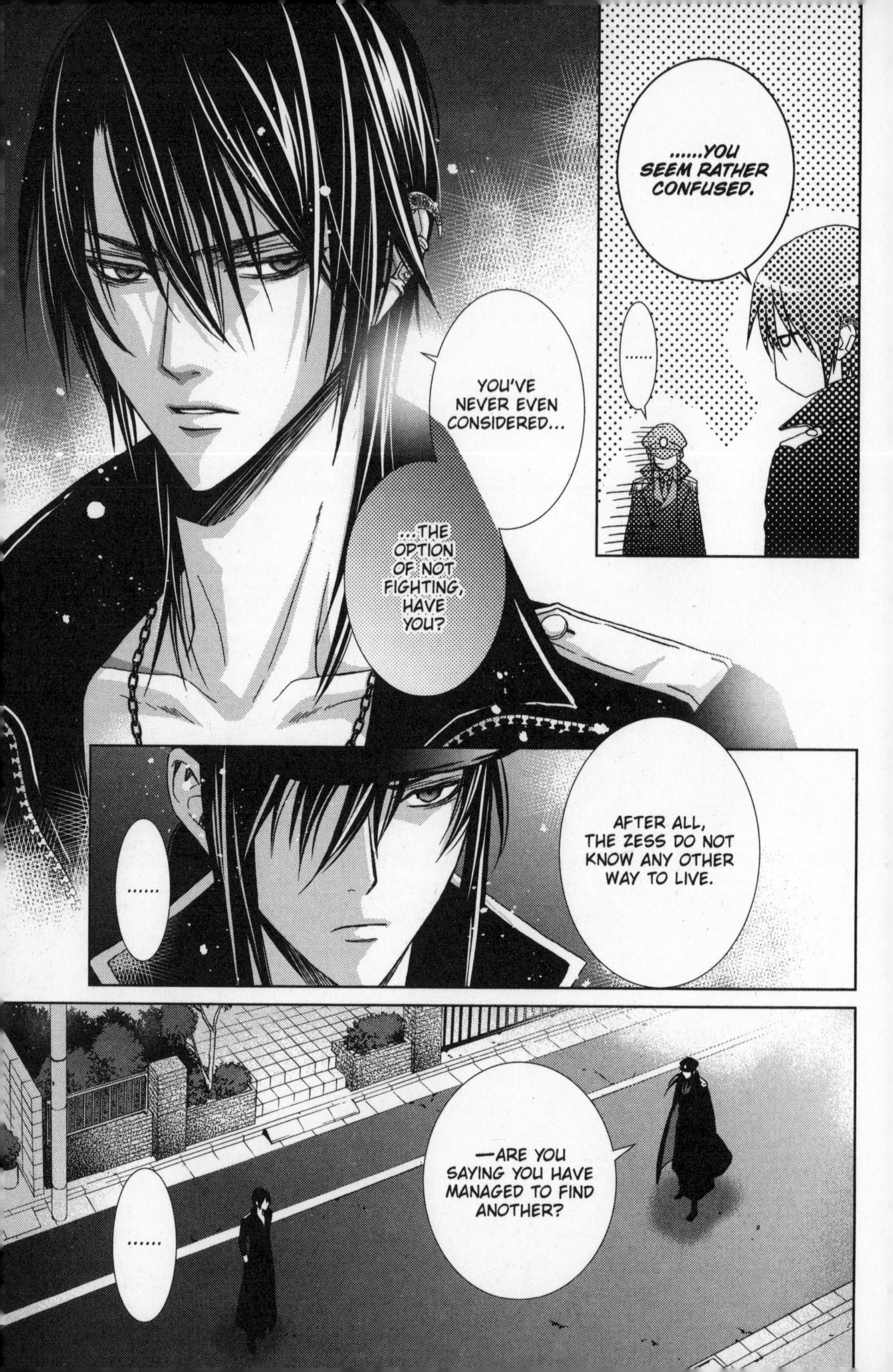
......YOU SEEM RATHER CONFUSED.
......
YOU'VE NEVER EVEN CONSIDERED...
...THE OPTION OF NOT FIGHTING, HAVE YOU?
AFTER ALL, THE ZESS DO NOT KNOW ANY OTHER WAY TO LIVE.
......
—ARE YOU SAYING YOU HAVE MANAGED TO FIND ANOTHER?
......

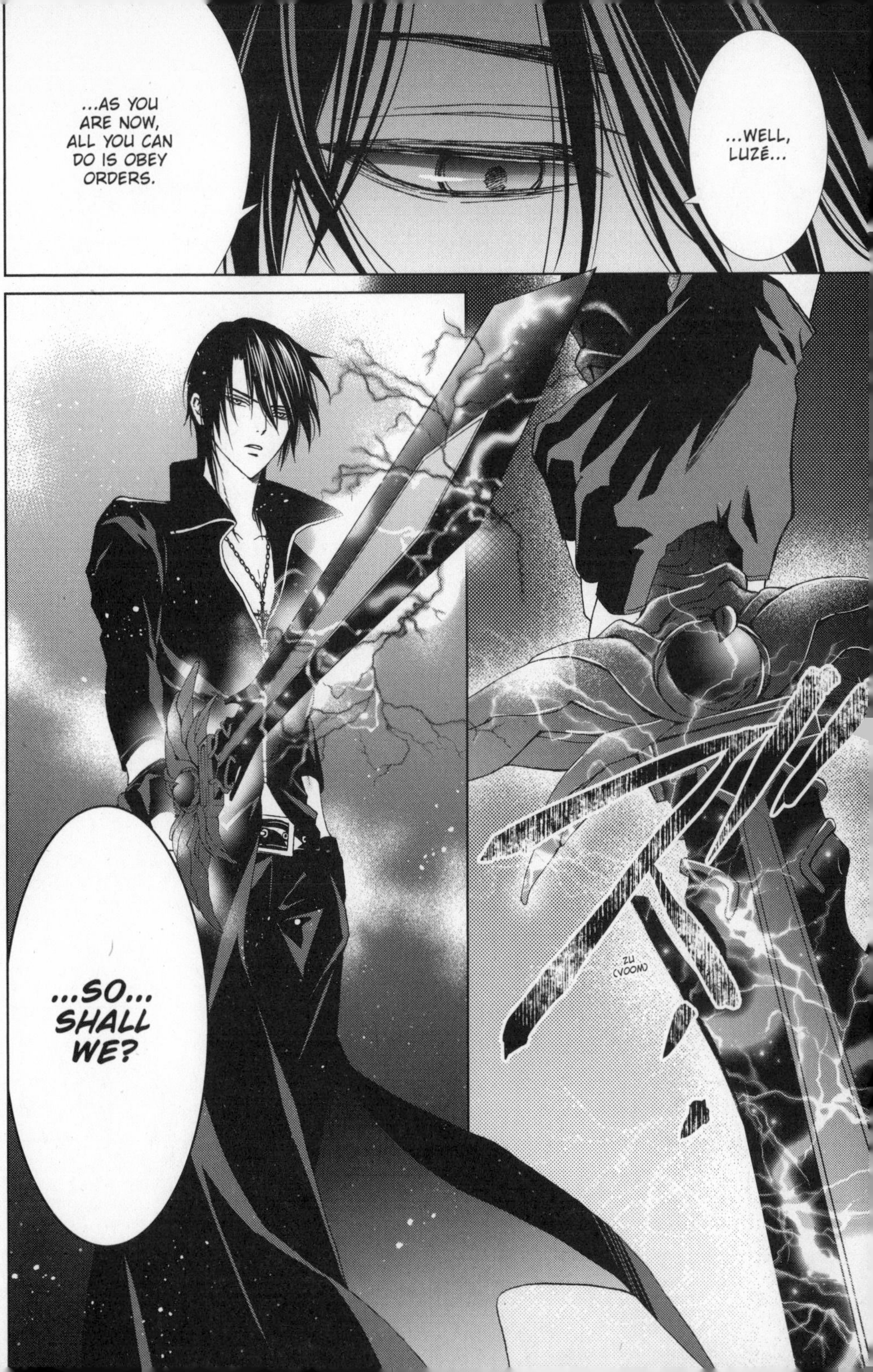
...WELL, LUZÉ...
...AS YOU ARE NOW, ALL YOU CAN DO IS OBEY ORDERS.
ZU (VOOM)
...SO... SHALL WE?

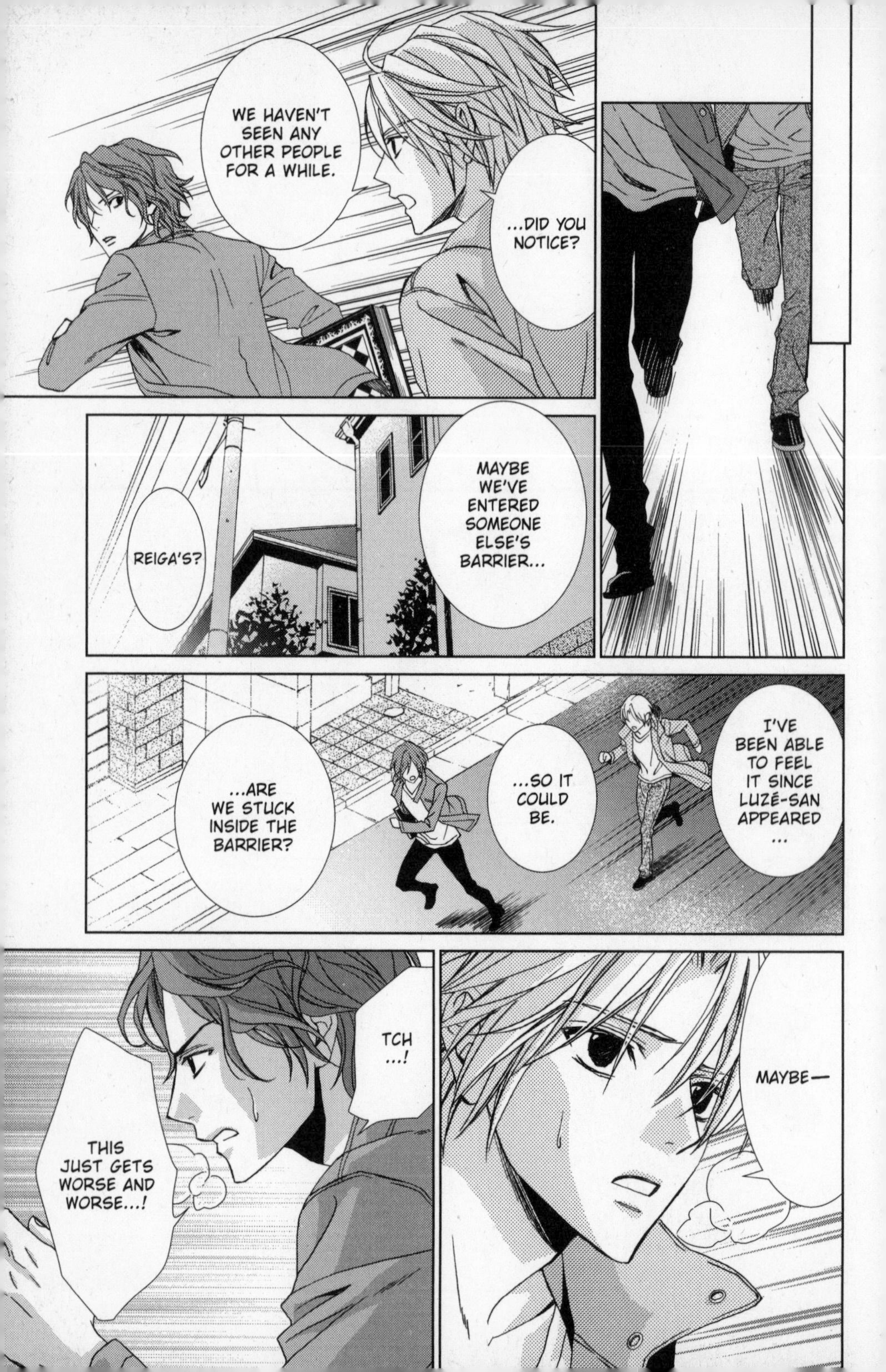
...DID YOU NOTICE?
WE HAVEN'T SEEN ANY OTHER PEOPLE FOR A WHILE.
MAYBE WE'VE ENTERED SOMEONE ELSE'S BARRIER...
REIGA'S?
I'VE BEEN ABLE TO FEEL IT SINCE LUZÉ-SAN APPEARED...
...SO IT COULD BE.
...ARE WE STUCK INSIDE THE BARRIER?
MAYBE—
TCH...!
THIS JUST GETS WORSE AND WORSE...!

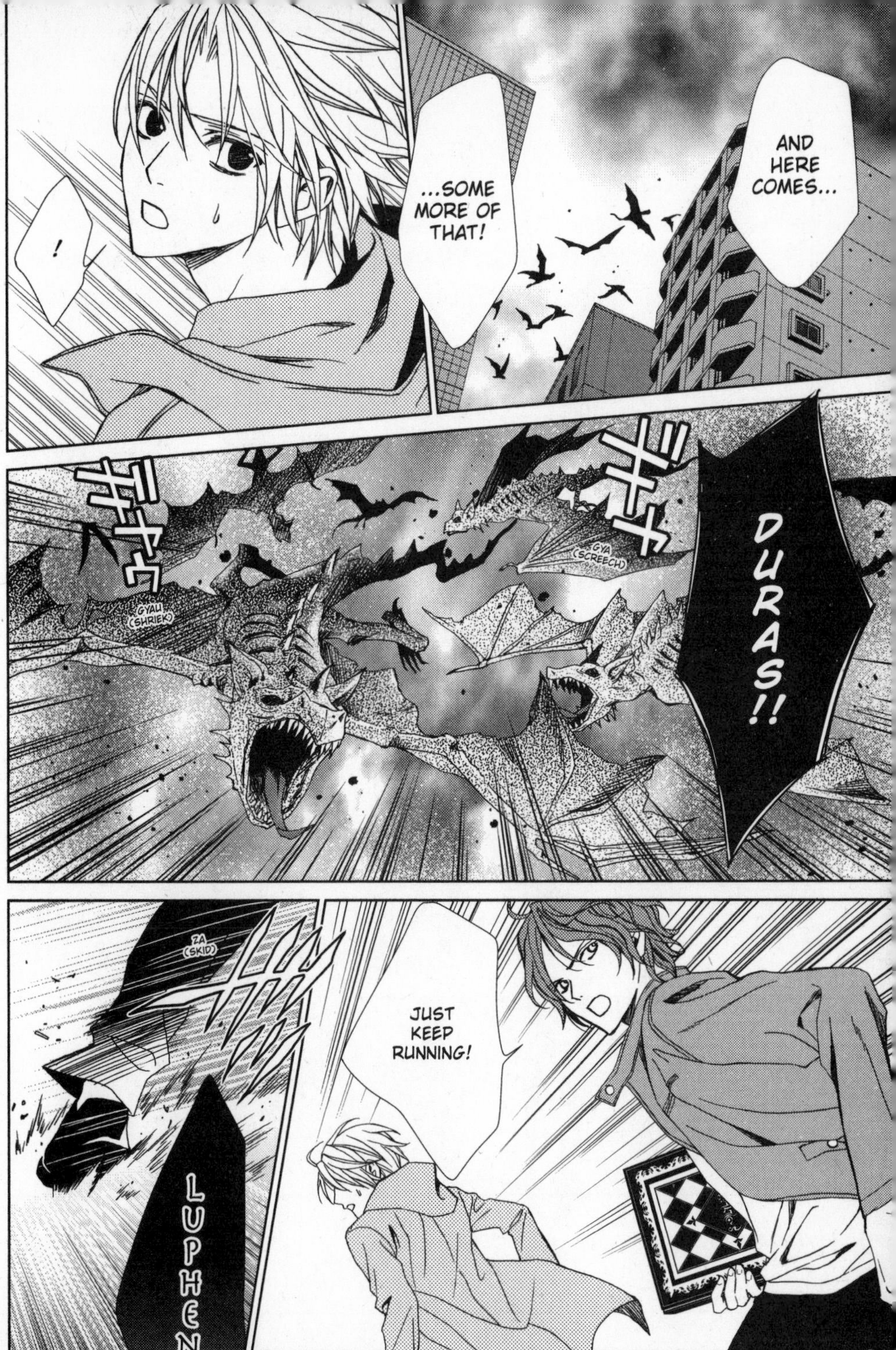
AND HERE COMES...
...SOME MORE OF THAT!
!
DURAS!!
GYA (SCREECH)
GYAU (SHRIEK)
JUST KEEP RUNNING!
ZA (SKID)
LUPHEN!

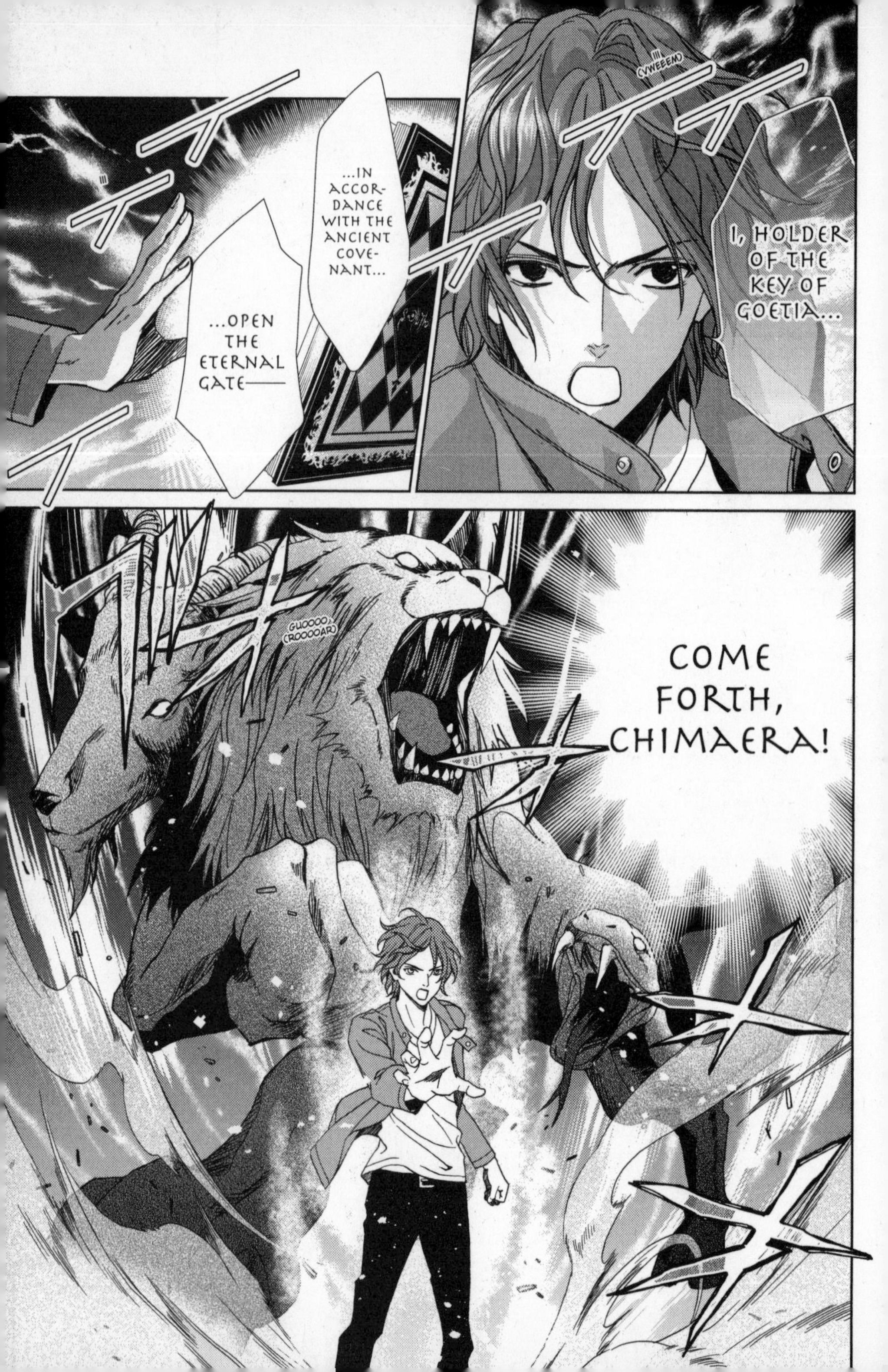
(VWEEEM)
I, HOLDER OF THE KEY OF GOETIA...
...IN ACCORDANCE WITH THE ANCIENT COVENANT...
...OPEN THE ETERNAL GATE——
COME FORTH, CHIMAERA!
GUOOOO (ROOOOAR)

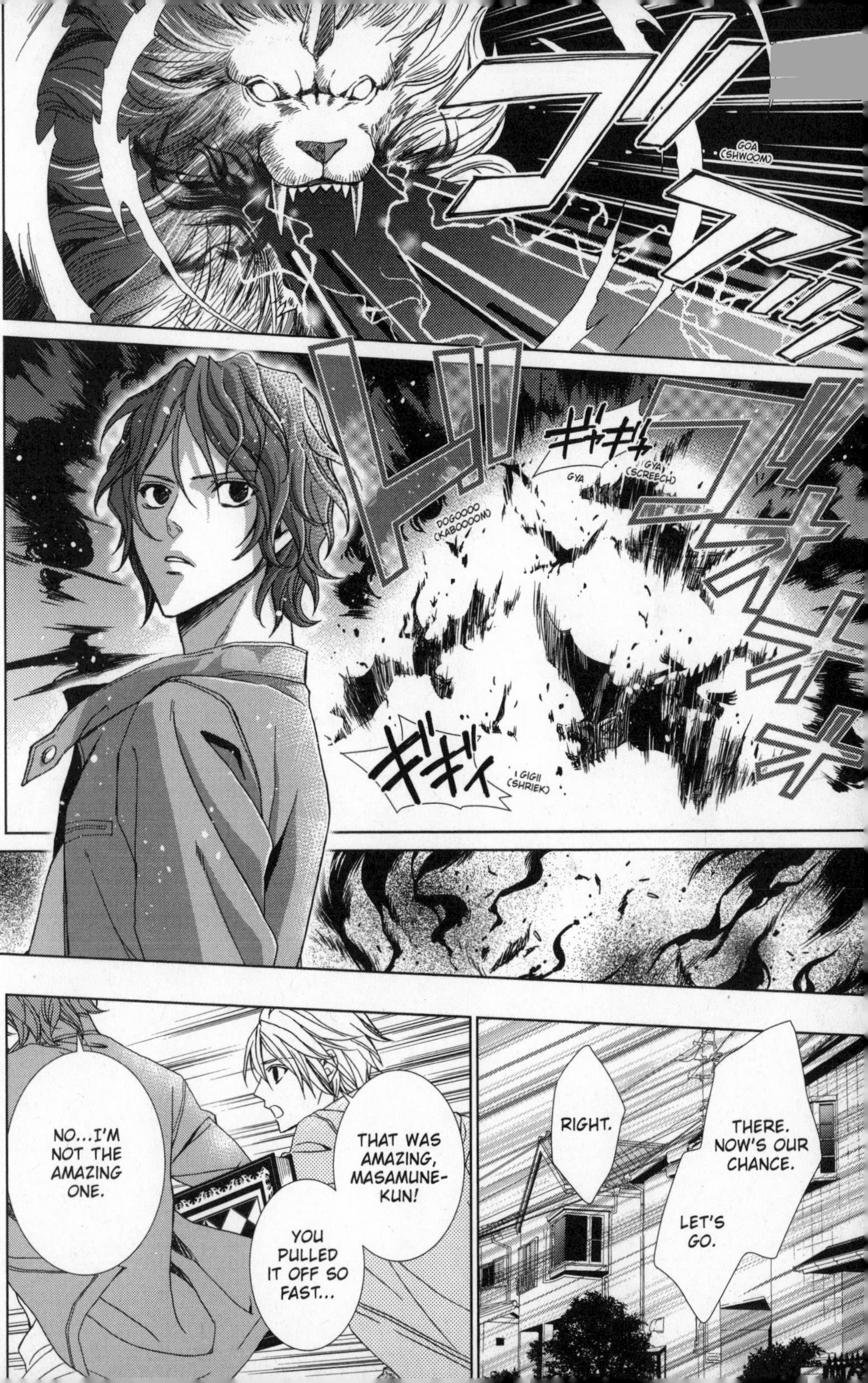
GOA (SHWOOM)
GYA GYA (SCREECH)
DOGOOOO (KABOOOOM)
GIGII (SHRIEK)
THERE. NOW'S OUR CHANCE.
LET'S GO.
RIGHT.
THAT WAS AMAZING, MASAMUNE-KUN!
YOU PULLED IT OFF SO FAST...
NO...I'M NOT THE AMAZING ONE.

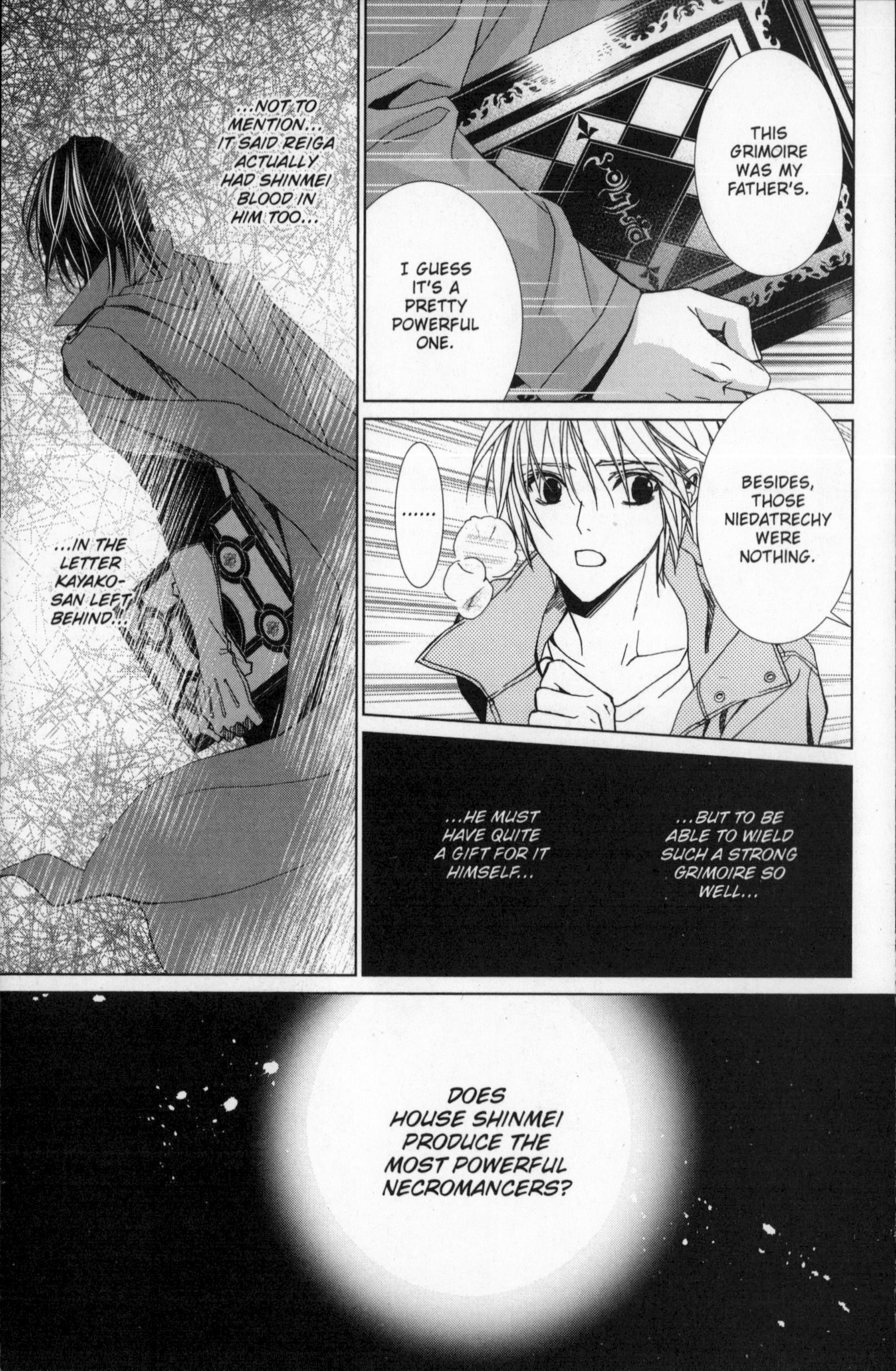
THIS GRIMOIRE WAS MY FATHER'S.
I GUESS IT'S A PRETTY POWERFUL ONE.
BESIDES, THOSE NIEDATRECHY WERE NOTHING.
......
...BUT TO BE ABLE TO WIELD SUCH A STRONG GRIMOIRE SO WELL...
...HE MUST HAVE QUITE A GIFT FOR IT HIMSELF...
...NOT TO MENTION... IT SAID REIGA ACTUALLY HAD SHINMEI BLOOD IN HIM TOO...
...IN THE LETTER KAYAKO-SAN LEFT BEHIND...
DOES HOUSE SHINMEI PRODUCE THE MOST POWERFUL NECROMANCERS?

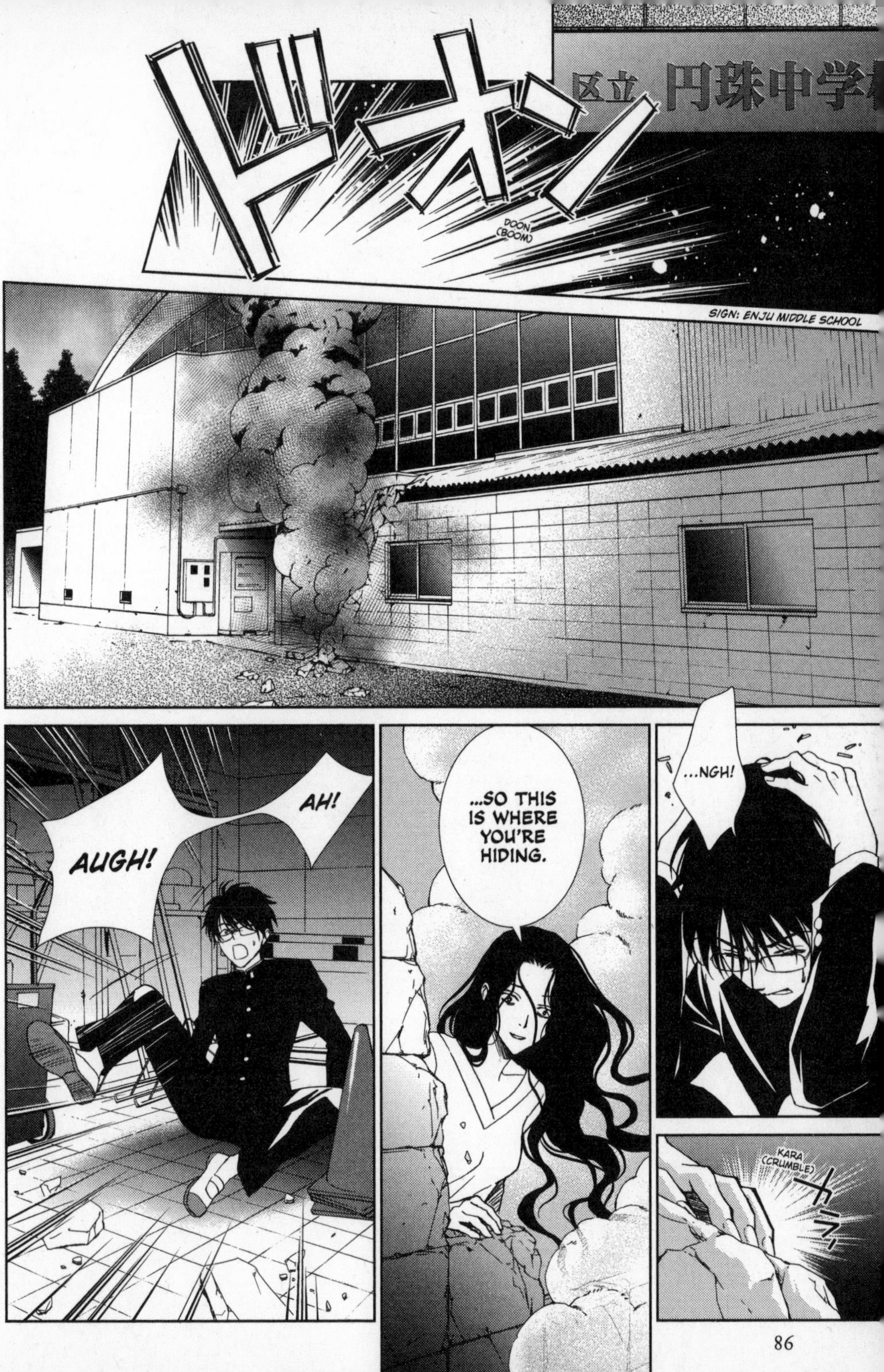
区立 円珠中学
ドーン
DOON (BOOM)
SIGN: ENJU MIDDLE SCHOOL
...NGH!
KARA (CRUMBLE)
...SO THIS IS WHERE YOU'RE HIDING.
AH!
AUGH!

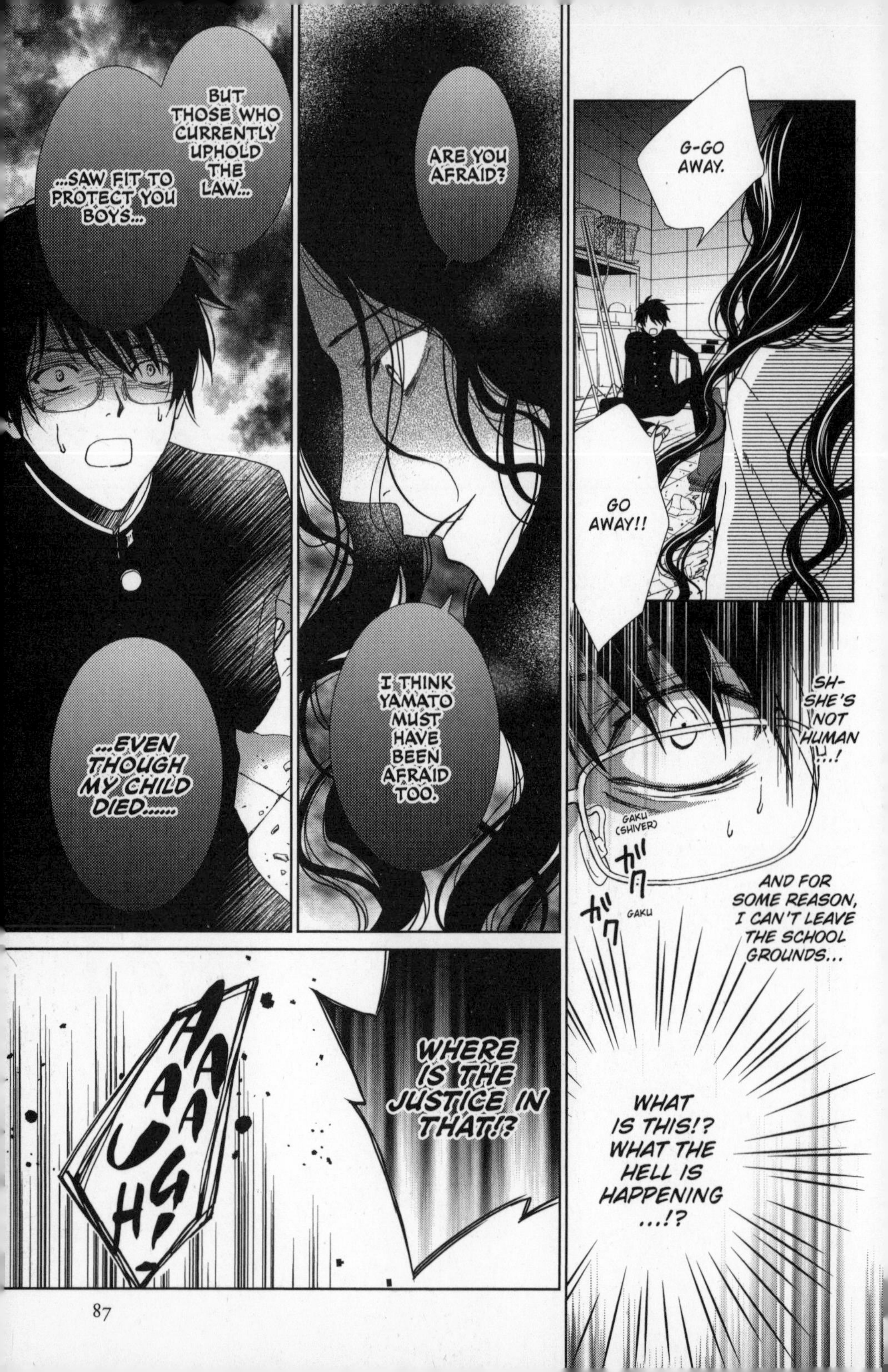
G-GO AWAY.
GO AWAY!!
SH-SHE'S NOT HUMAN...!
GAKU (SHIVER)
GAKU
AND FOR SOME REASON, I CAN'T LEAVE THE SCHOOL GROUNDS...
ARE YOU AFRAID?
I THINK YAMATO MUST HAVE BEEN AFRAID TOO.
BUT THOSE WHO CURRENTLY UPHOLD THE LAW...
...SAW FIT TO PROTECT YOU BOYS...
...EVEN THOUGH MY CHILD DIED......
WHAT IS THIS!? WHAT THE HELL IS HAPPENING ...!?
WHERE IS THE JUSTICE IN THAT!?
HAAAAUGH!

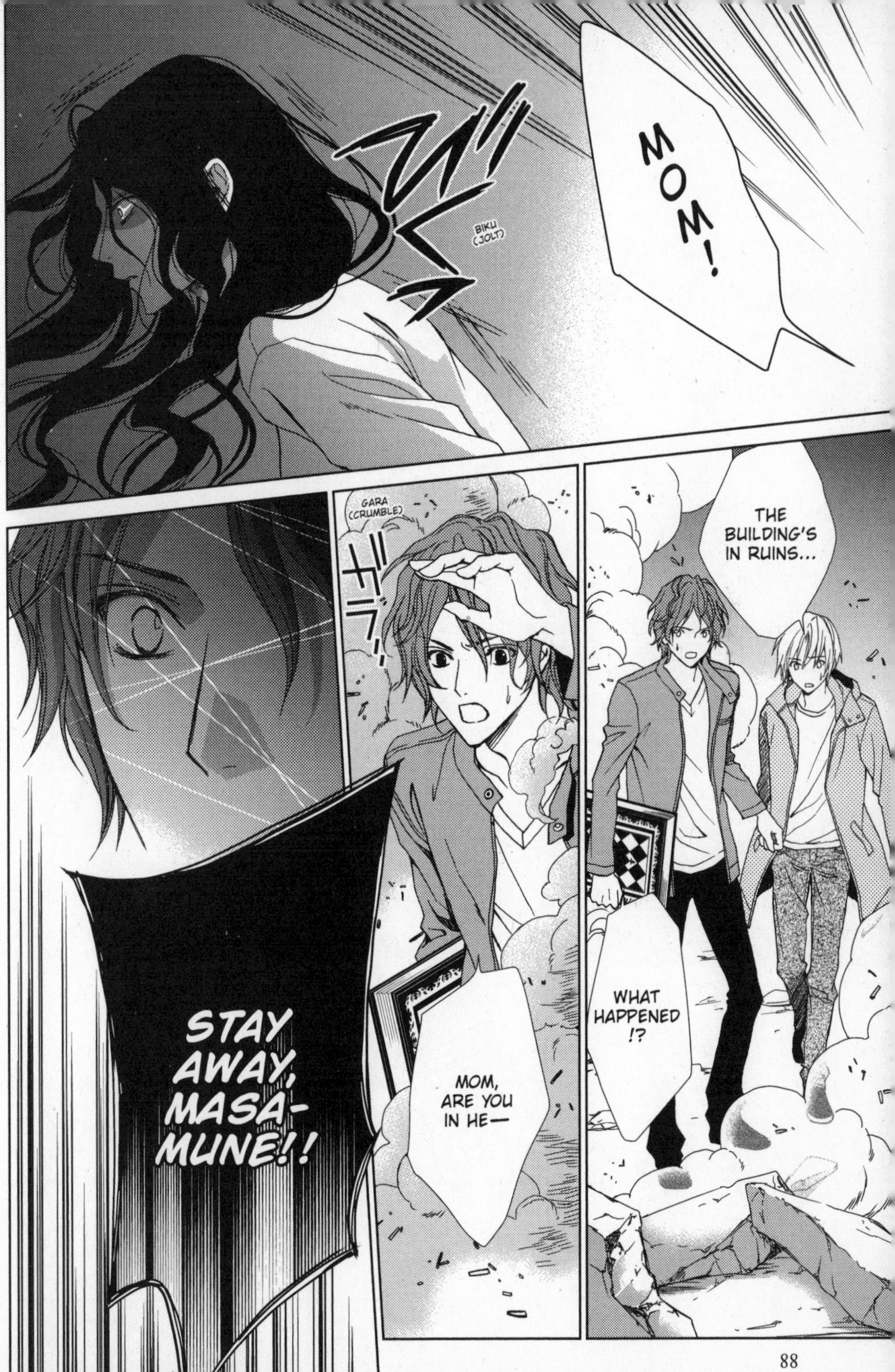
MOM!
BIKU (JOLT)
THE BUILDING'S IN RUINS...
WHAT HAPPENED !?
GARA (CRUMBLE)
MOM, ARE YOU IN HE—
STAY AWAY, MASA-MUNE!!

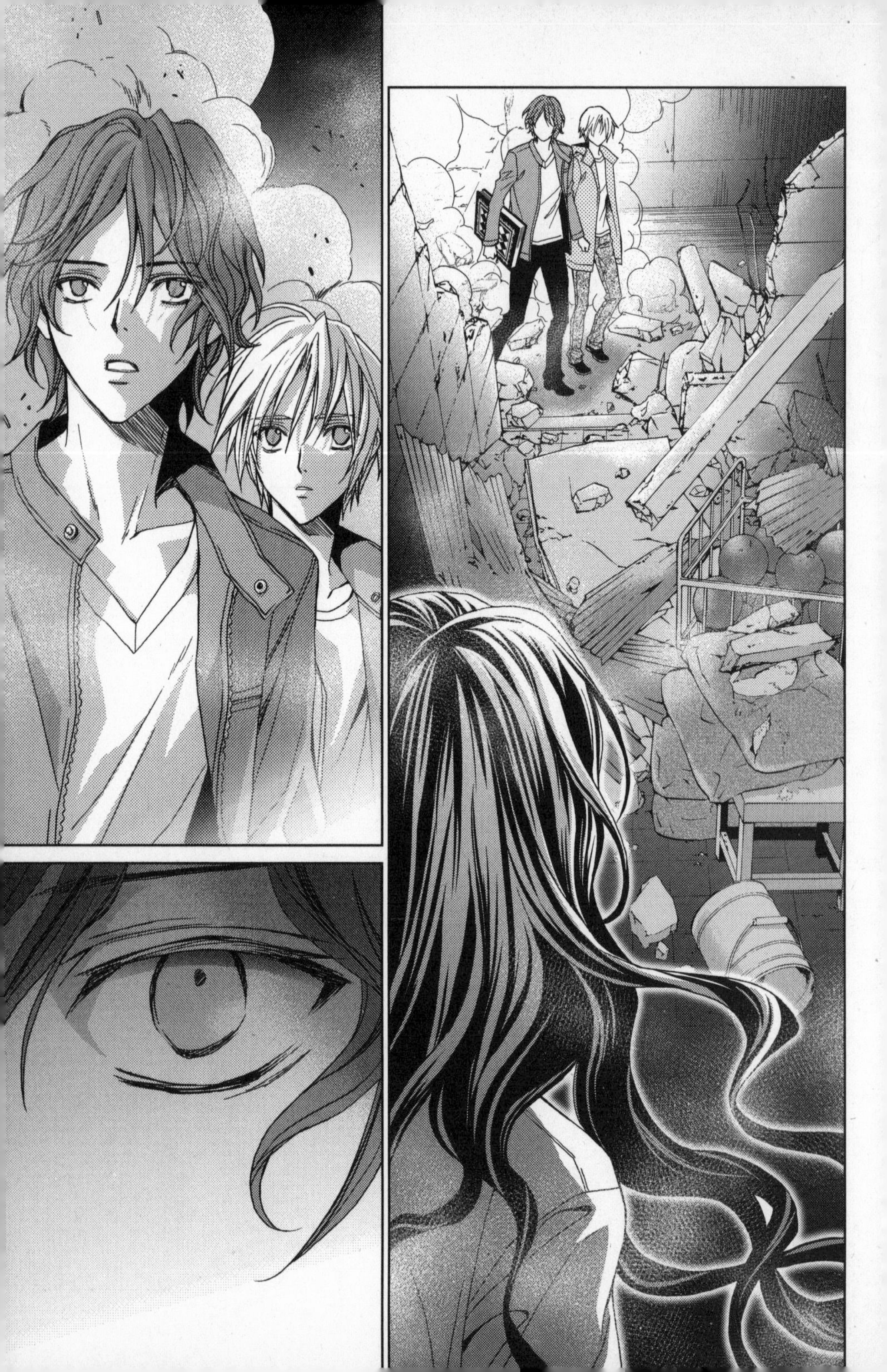

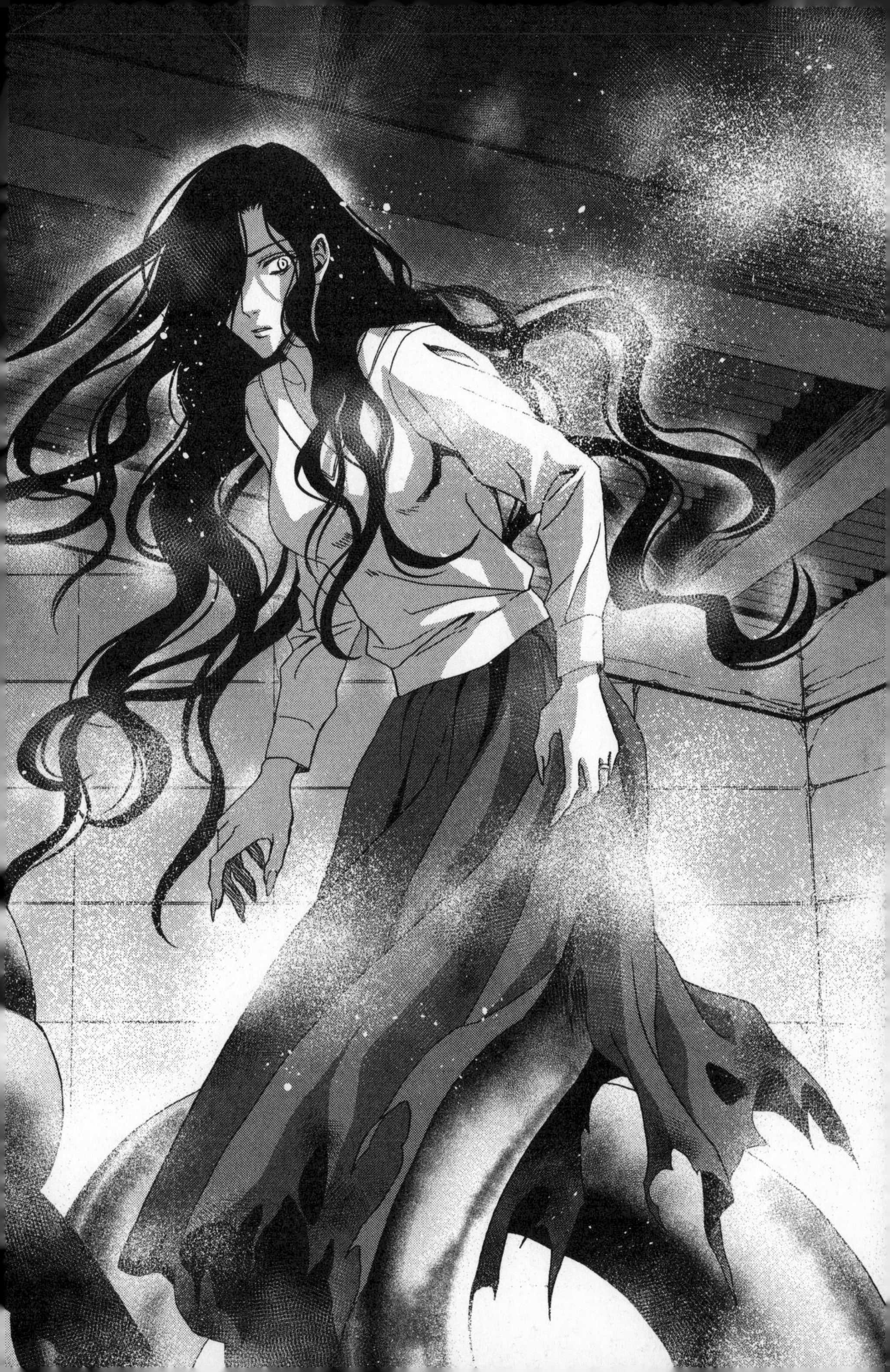

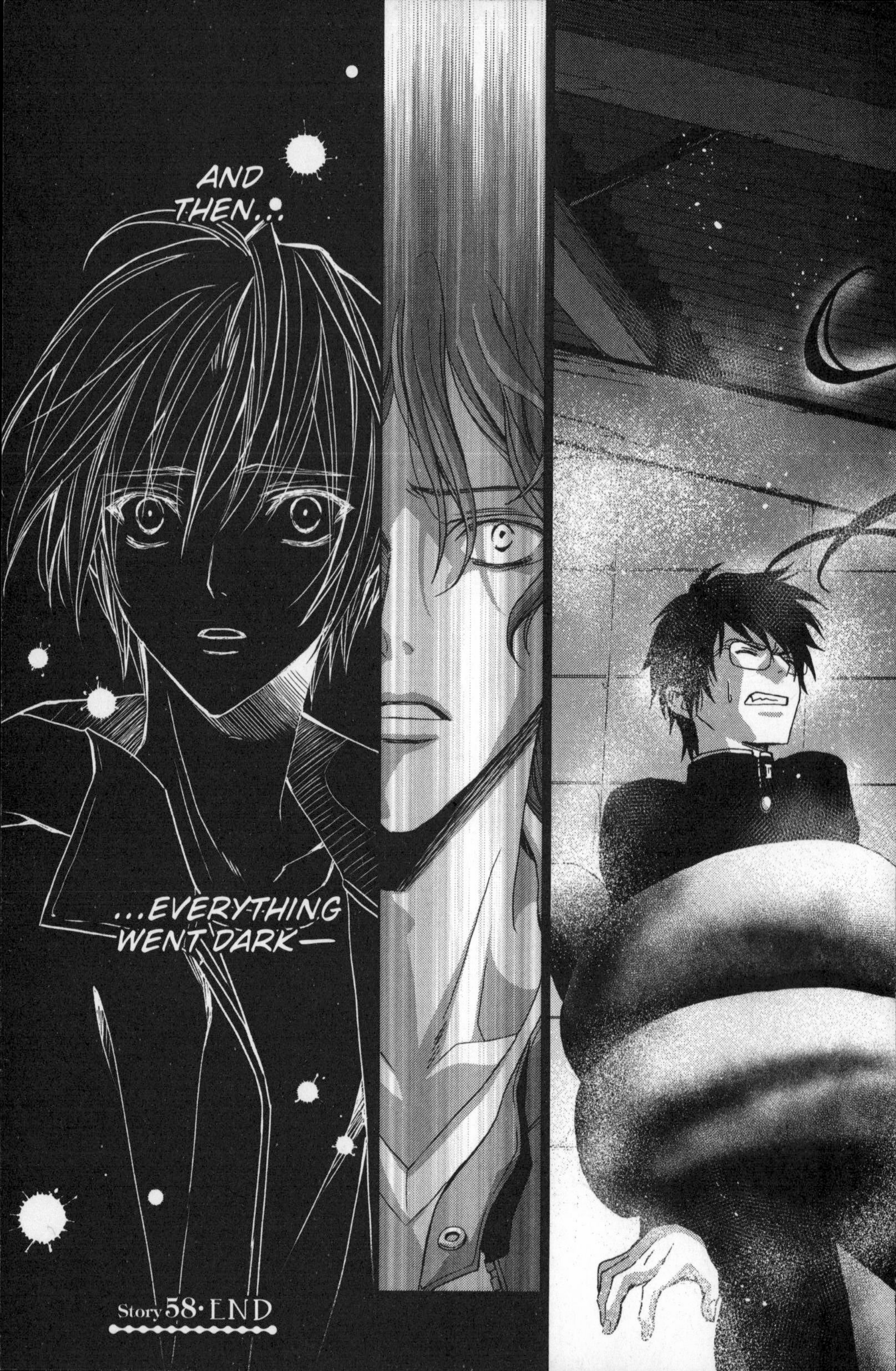
AND THEN...
...EVERYTHING WENT DARK—
Story 58 • END

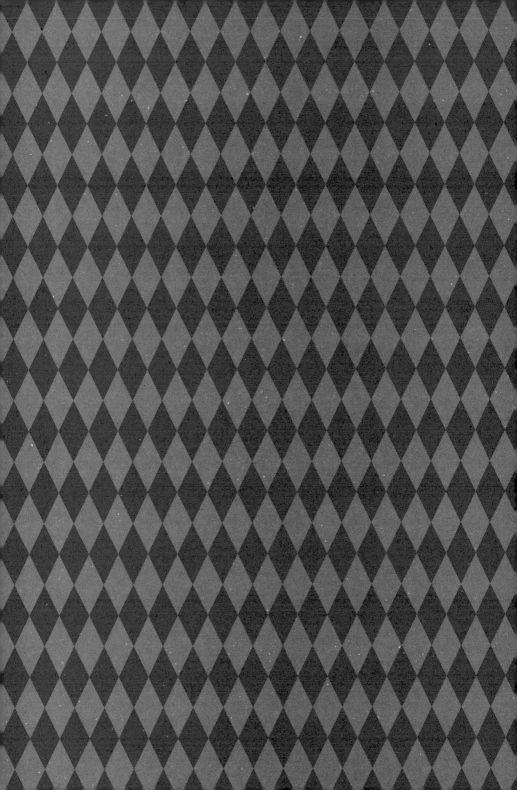

Story 59

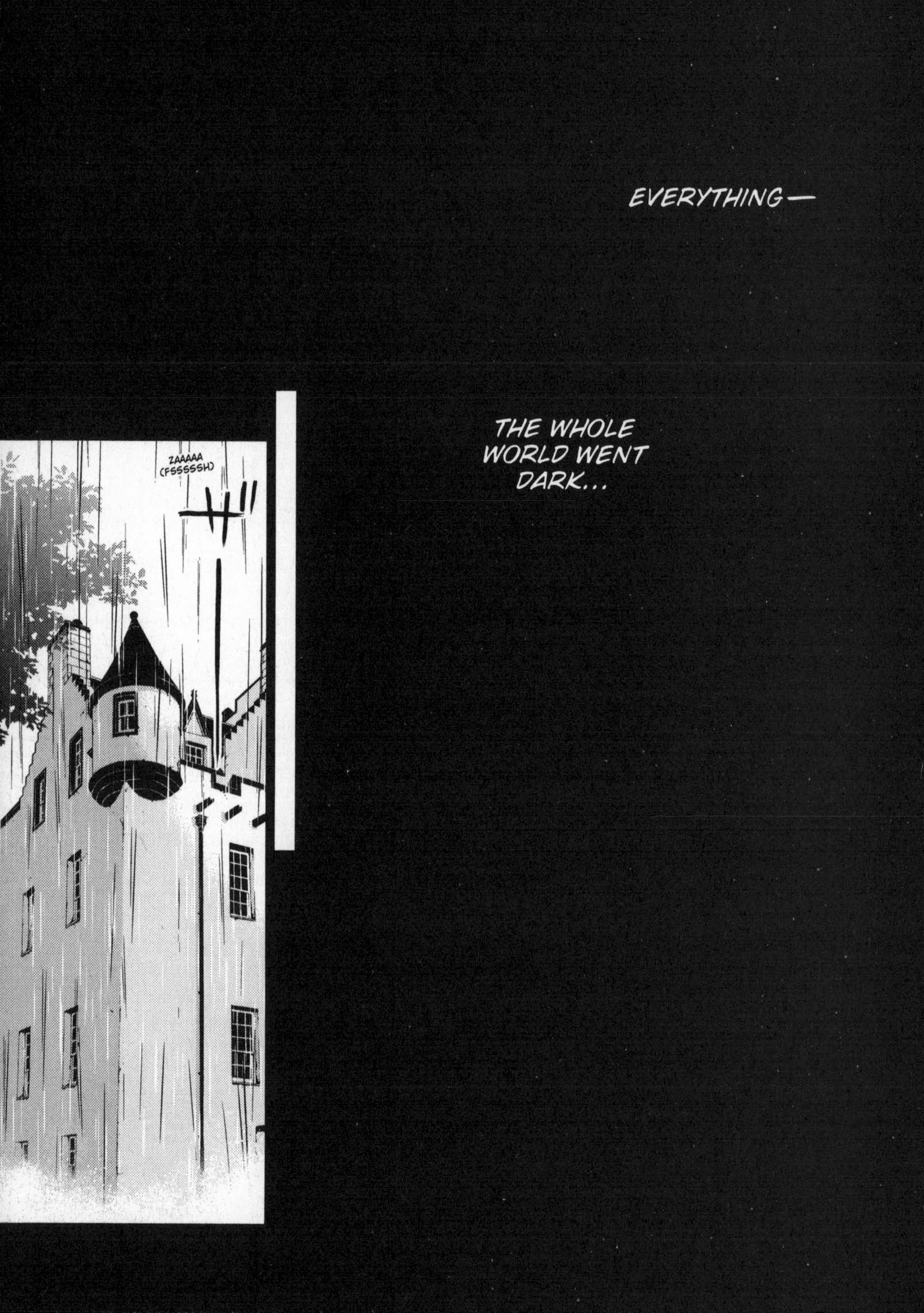
EVERYTHING—
THE WHOLE WORLD WENT DARK...
ZAAAAA (FSSSSSH)

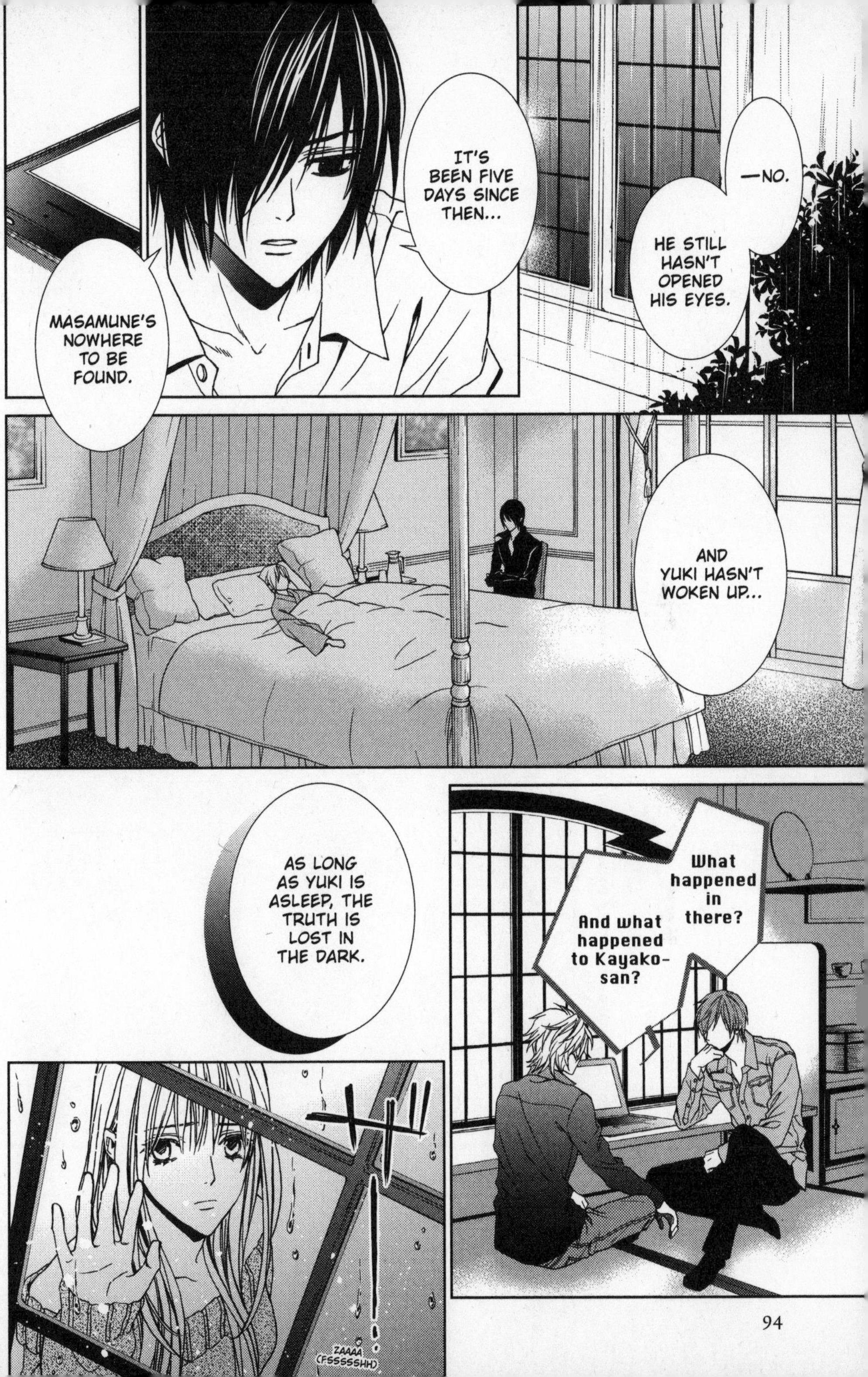
—NO.
HE STILL HASN'T OPENED HIS EYES.
IT'S BEEN FIVE DAYS SINCE THEN...
MASAMUNE'S NOWHERE TO BE FOUND.
AND YUKI HASN'T WOKEN UP...
What happened in there?
And what happened to Kayako-san?
AS LONG AS YUKI IS ASLEEP, THE TRUTH IS LOST IN THE DARK.
ZAAAA (FSSSSSHH)

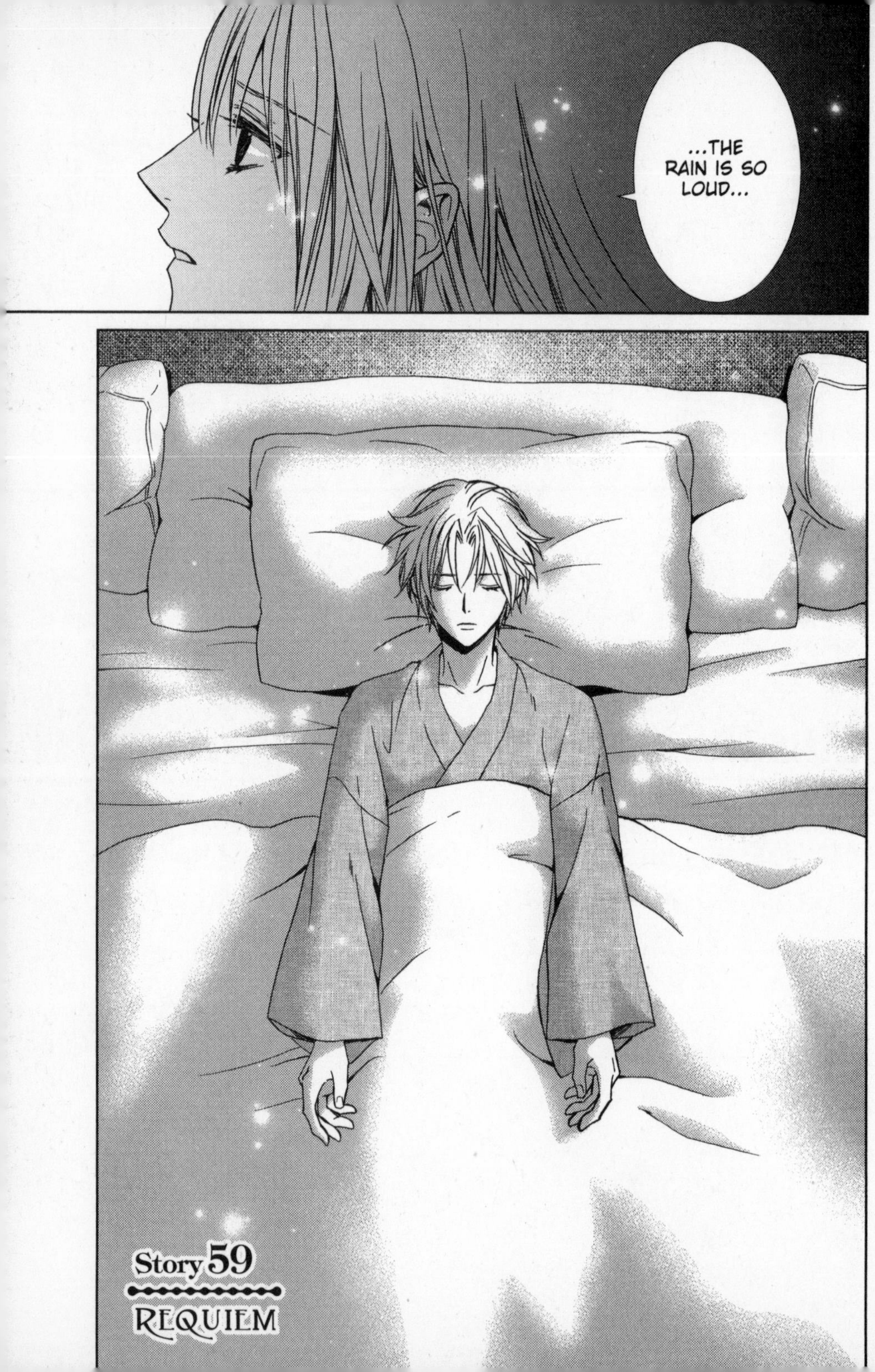
...THE RAIN IS SO LOUD...
Story 59
REQUIEM

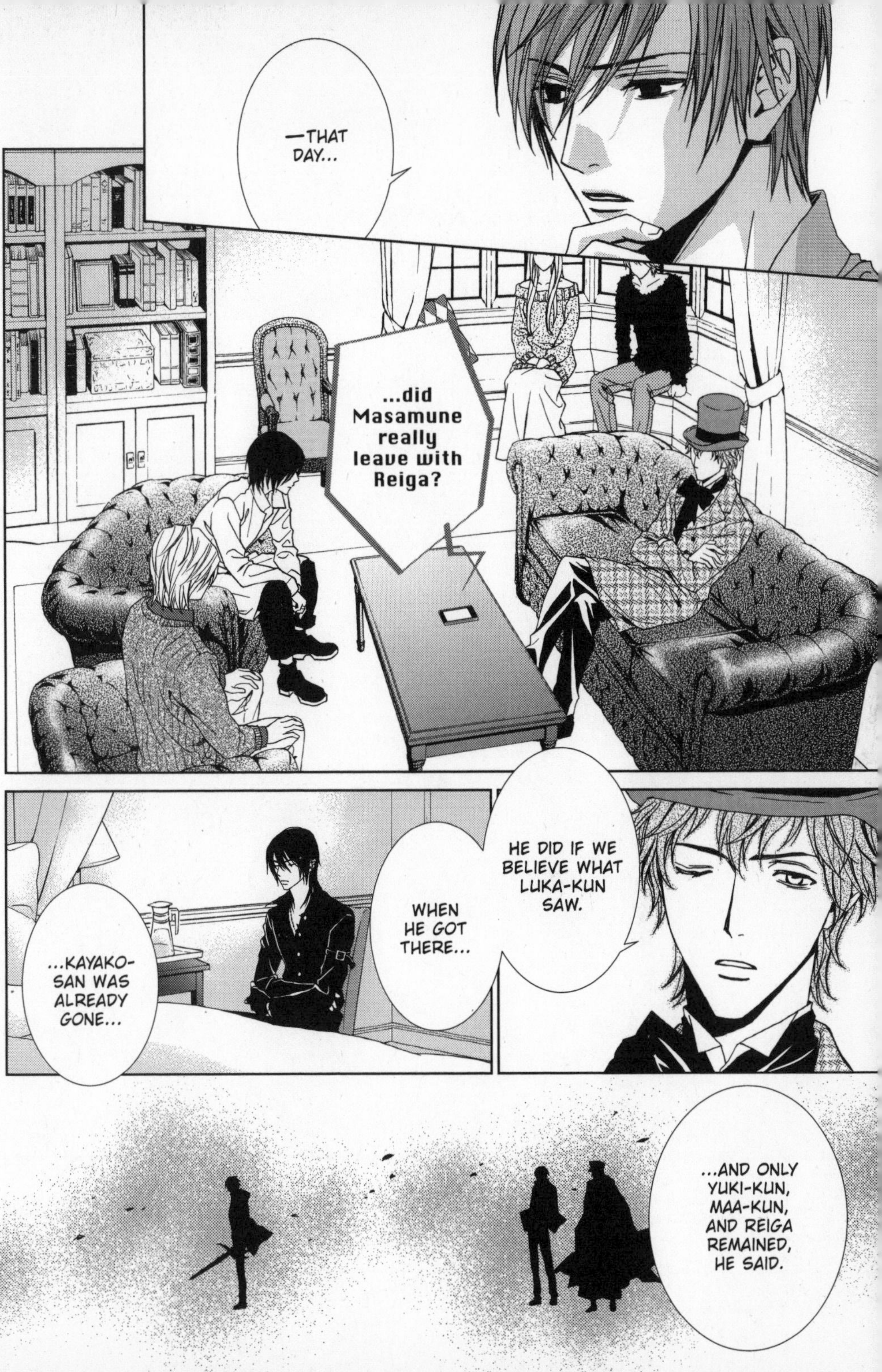
—THAT DAY...
...did Masamune really leave with Reiga?
HE DID IF WE BELIEVE WHAT LUKA-KUN SAW.
WHEN HE GOT THERE...
...KAYAKO-SAN WAS ALREADY GONE...
...AND ONLY YUKI-KUN, MAA-KUN, AND REIGA REMAINED, HE SAID.

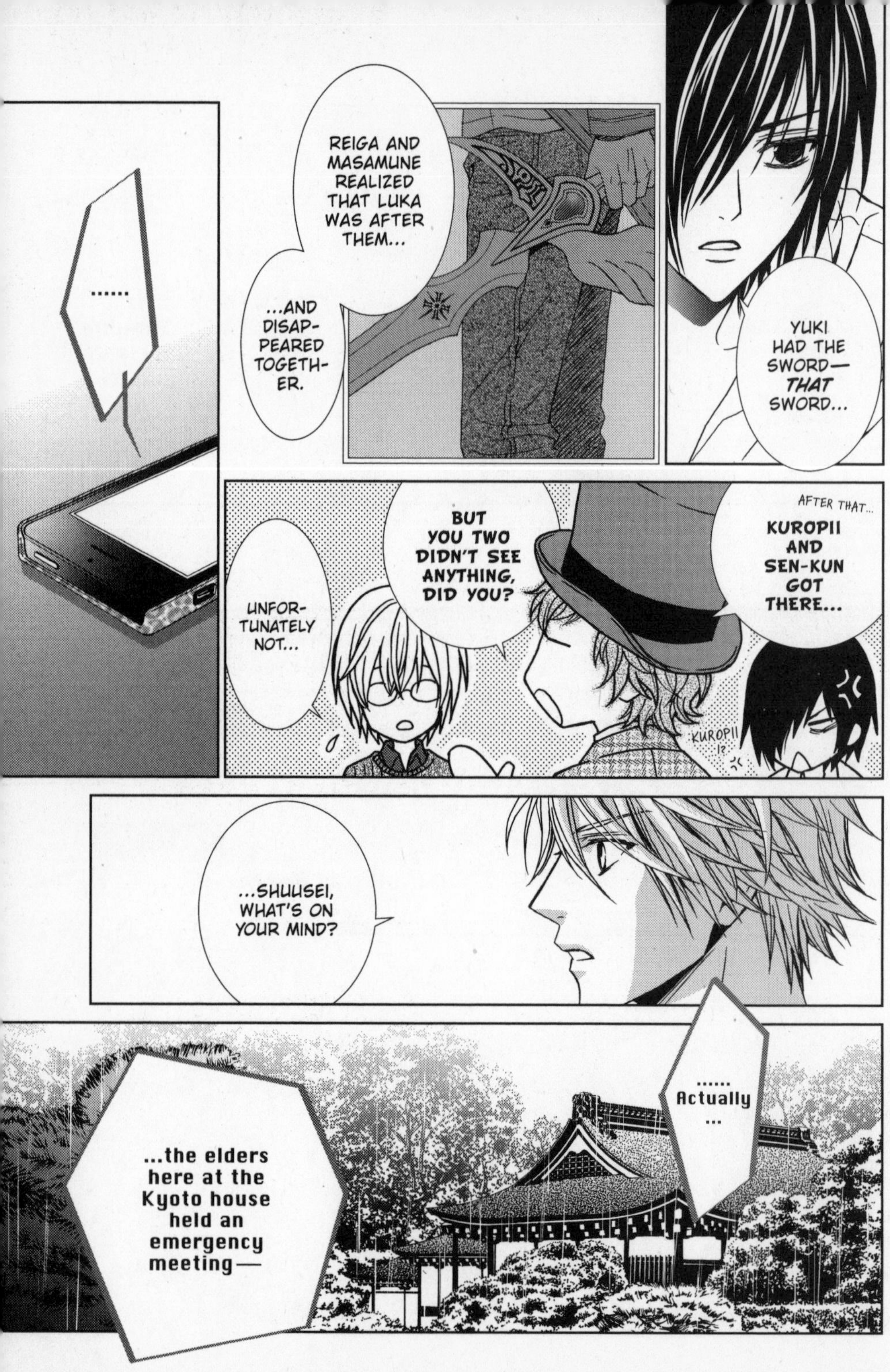
YUKI HAD THE SWORD—*THAT* SWORD...
REIGA AND MASAMUNE REALIZED THAT LUKA WAS AFTER THEM...
...AND DISAPPEARED TOGETHER.
AFTER THAT...
KUROPII AND SEN-KUN GOT THERE...
KUROPII!?
BUT YOU TWO DIDN'T SEE ANYTHING, DID YOU?
UNFORTUNATELY NOT...
......
...SHUUSEI, WHAT'S ON YOUR MIND?
......Actually...
...the elders here at the Kyoto house held an emergency meeting—

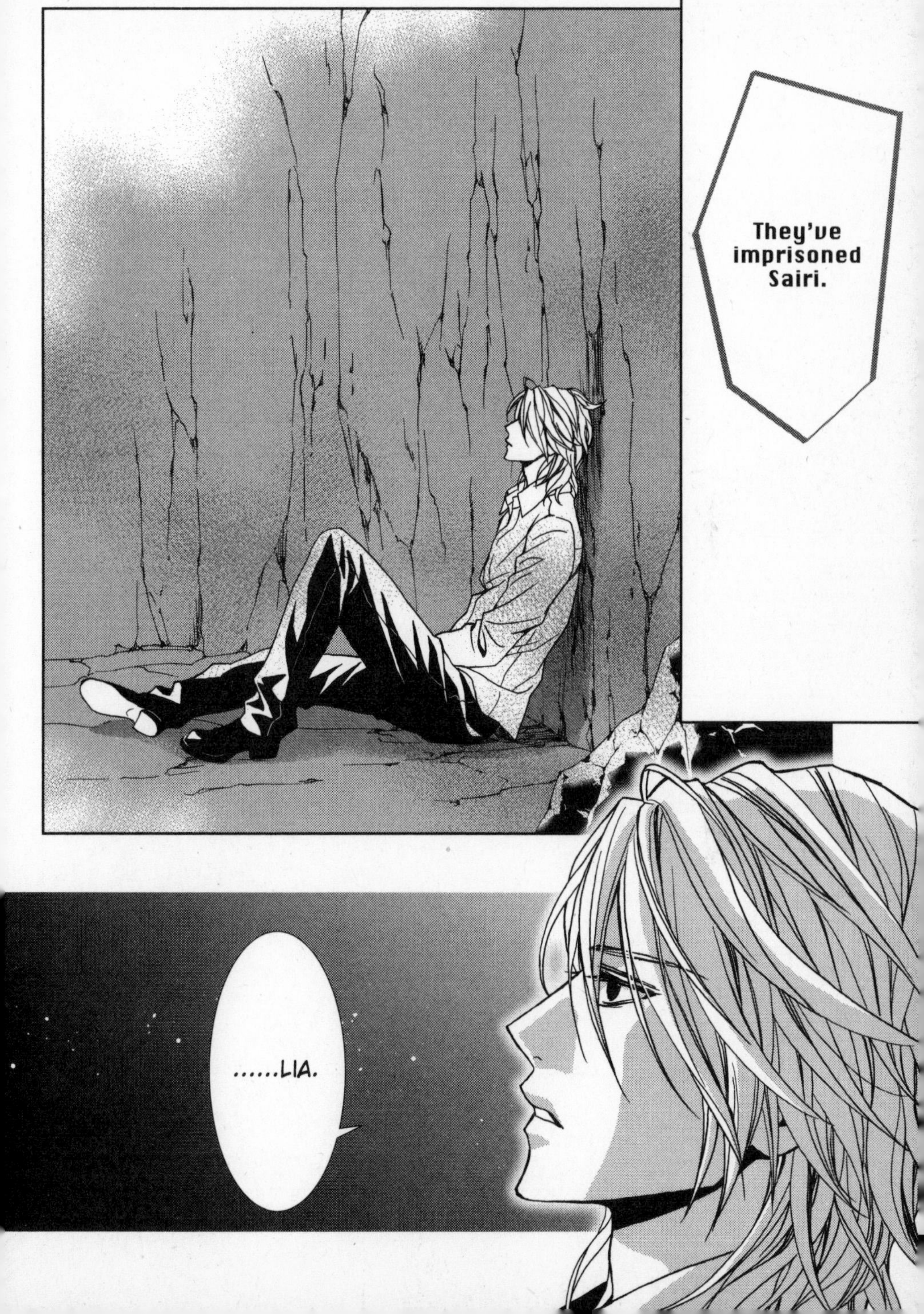
They've imprisoned Sairi.
......LIA.

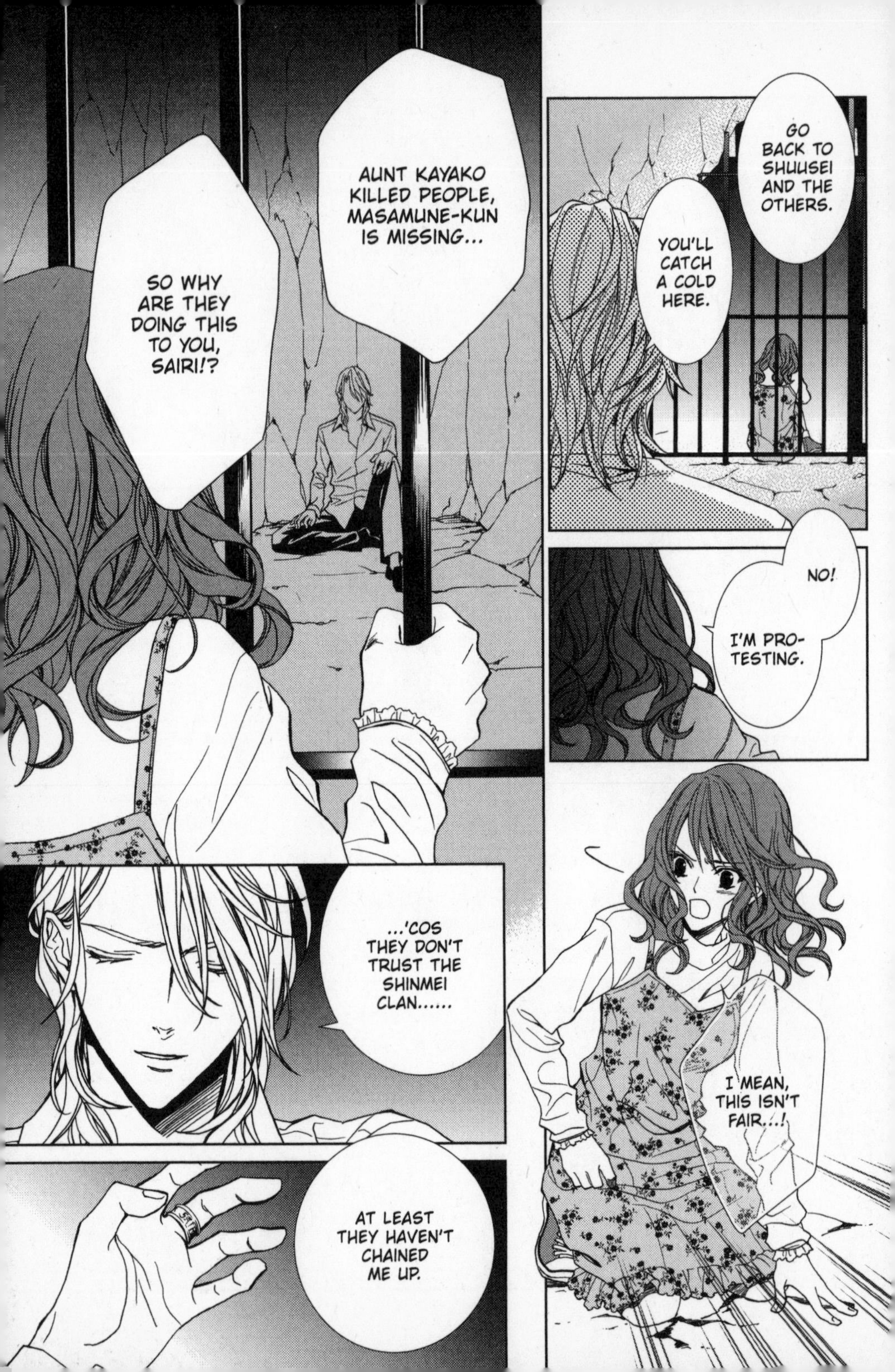
GO BACK TO SHUUSEI AND THE OTHERS.
YOU'LL CATCH A COLD HERE.
NO!
I'M PRO-TESTING.
AUNT KAYAKO KILLED PEOPLE, MASAMUNE-KUN IS MISSING...
SO WHY ARE THEY DOING THIS TO YOU, SAIRI!?
I MEAN, THIS ISN'T FAIR...!
...'COS THEY DON'T TRUST THE SHINMEI CLAN......
AT LEAST THEY HAVEN'T CHAINED ME UP.

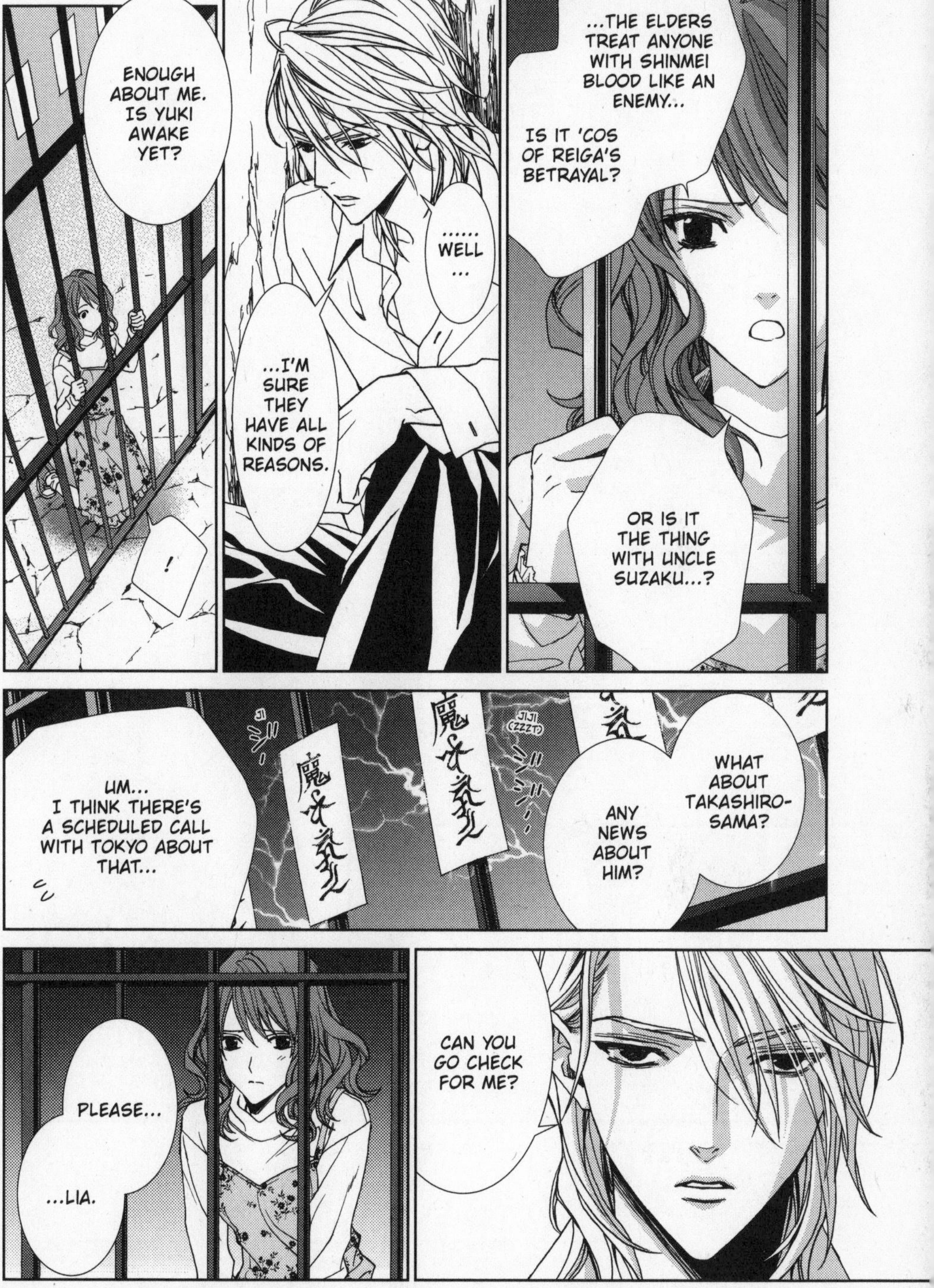
...THE ELDERS TREAT ANYONE WITH SHINMEI BLOOD LIKE AN ENEMY...
IS IT 'COS OF REIGA'S BETRAYAL?
OR IS IT THE THING WITH UNCLE SUZAKU...?
......WELL...
...I'M SURE THEY HAVE ALL KINDS OF REASONS.
ENOUGH ABOUT ME. IS YUKI AWAKE YET?
!
WHAT ABOUT TAKASHIRO-SAMA?
ANY NEWS ABOUT HIM?
JIJI (ZZZT)
JI
UM... I THINK THERE'S A SCHEDULED CALL WITH TOKYO ABOUT THAT...
CAN YOU GO CHECK FOR ME?
PLEASE...
...LIA.

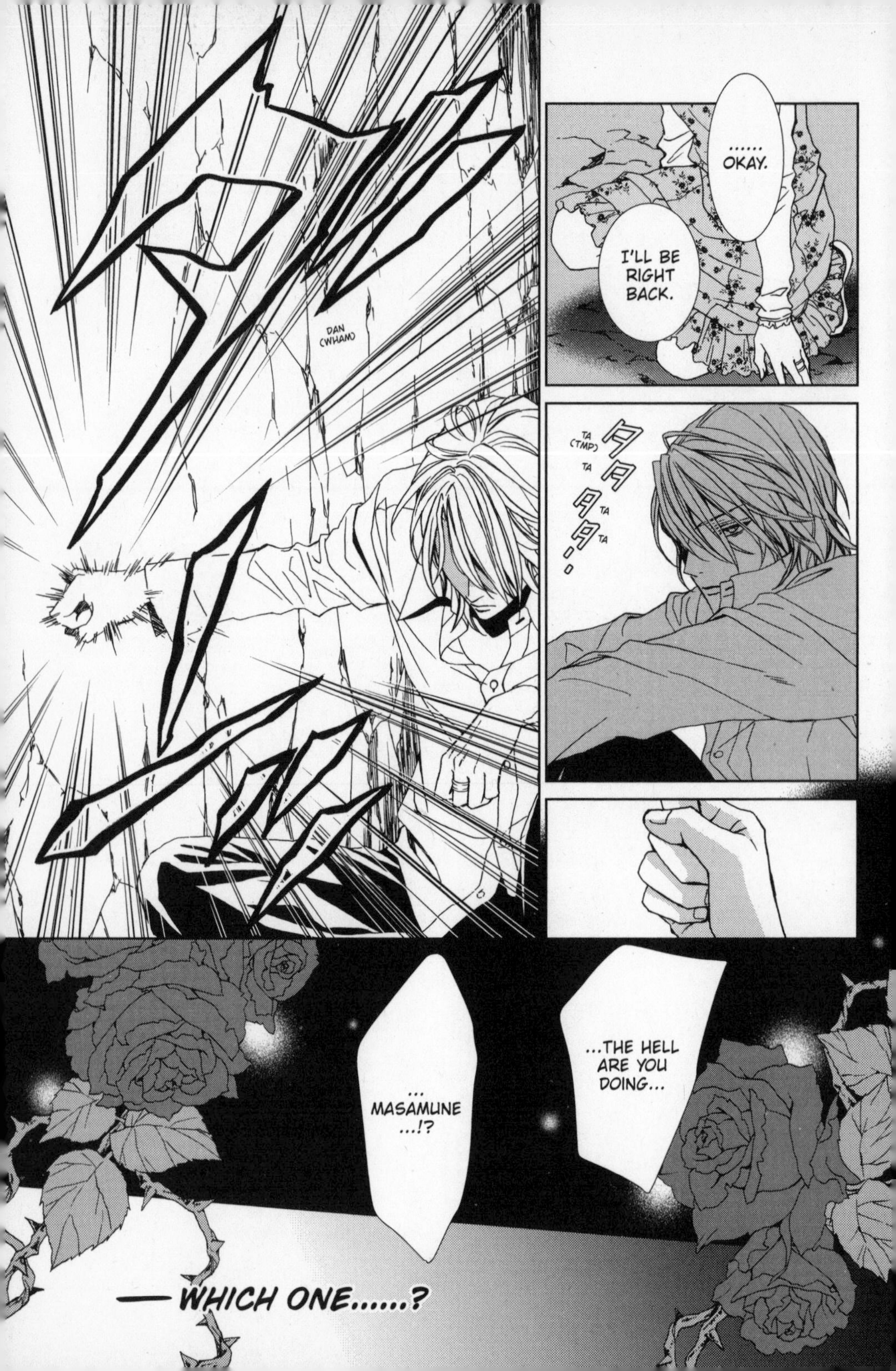

......OKAY.
I'LL BE RIGHT BACK.
TA (TMP) TA TA TA
DAN (WHAM)
...THE HELL ARE YOU DOING...
...MASAMUNE...!?
—WHICH ONE......?

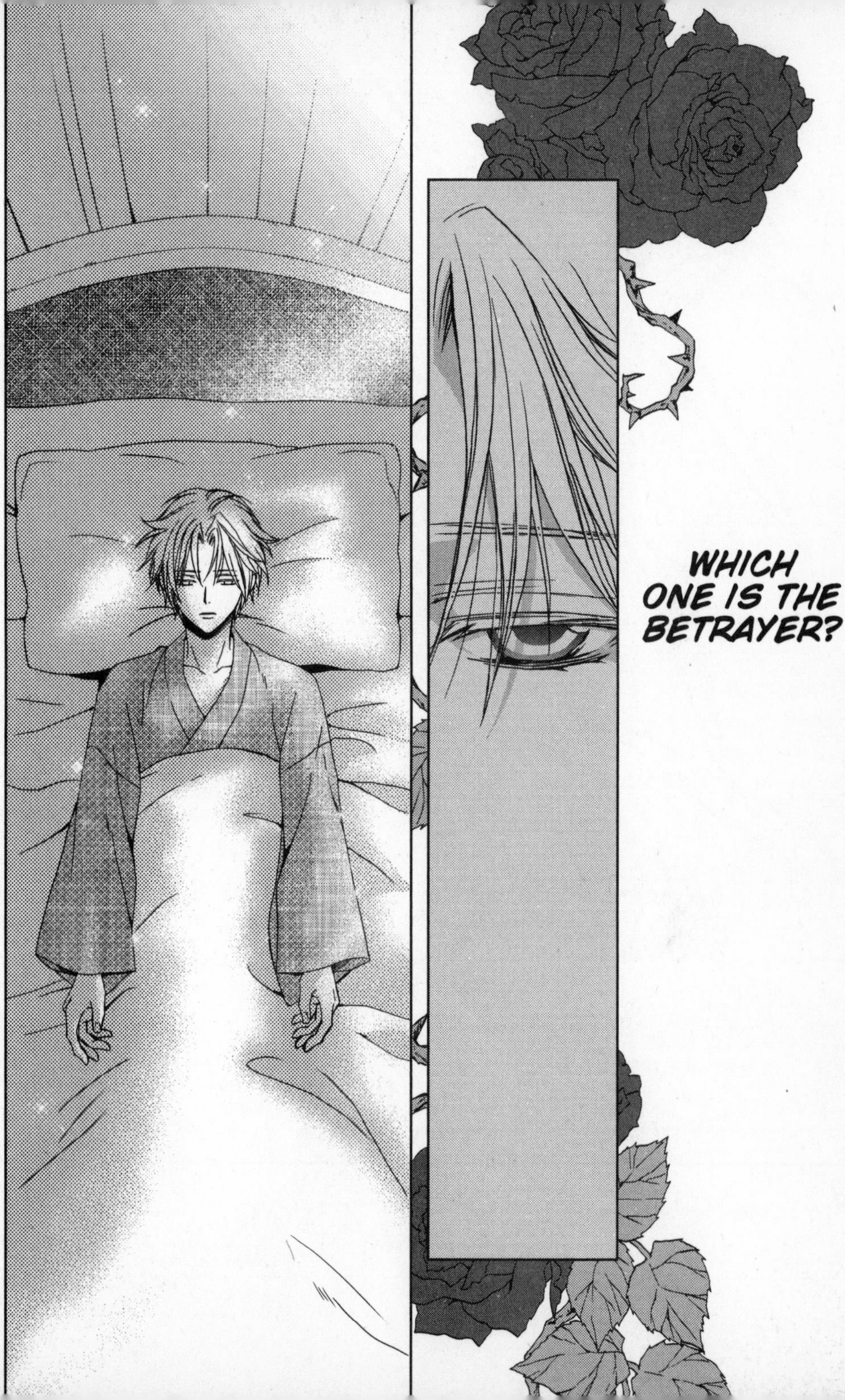
WHICH ONE IS THE BETRAYER?

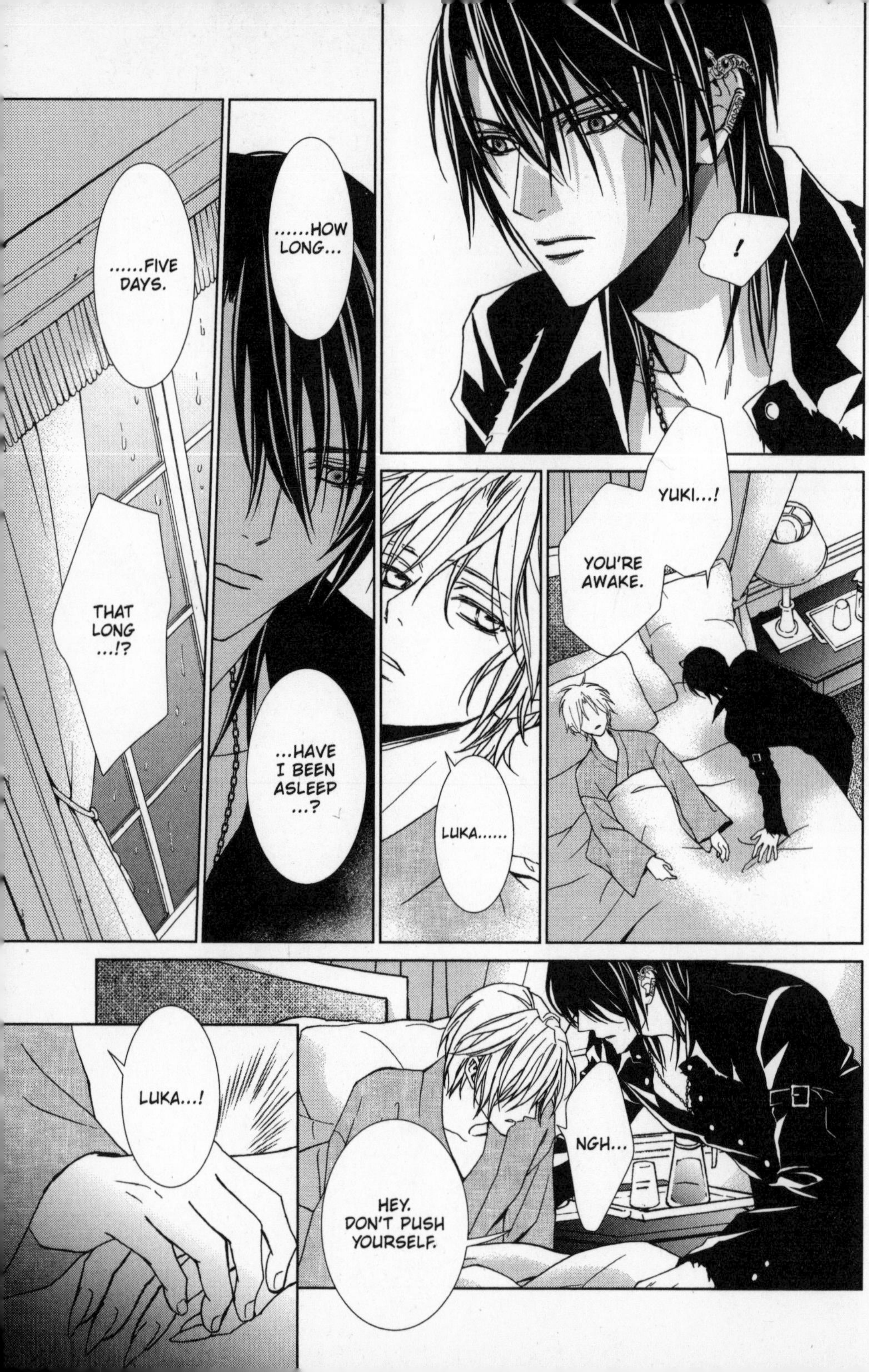
!
YUKI...!
YOU'RE AWAKE.
LUKA......
......HOW LONG...
...HAVE I BEEN ASLEEP ...?
......FIVE DAYS.
THAT LONG ...!?
NGH...
HEY. DON'T PUSH YOURSELF.
LUKA...!

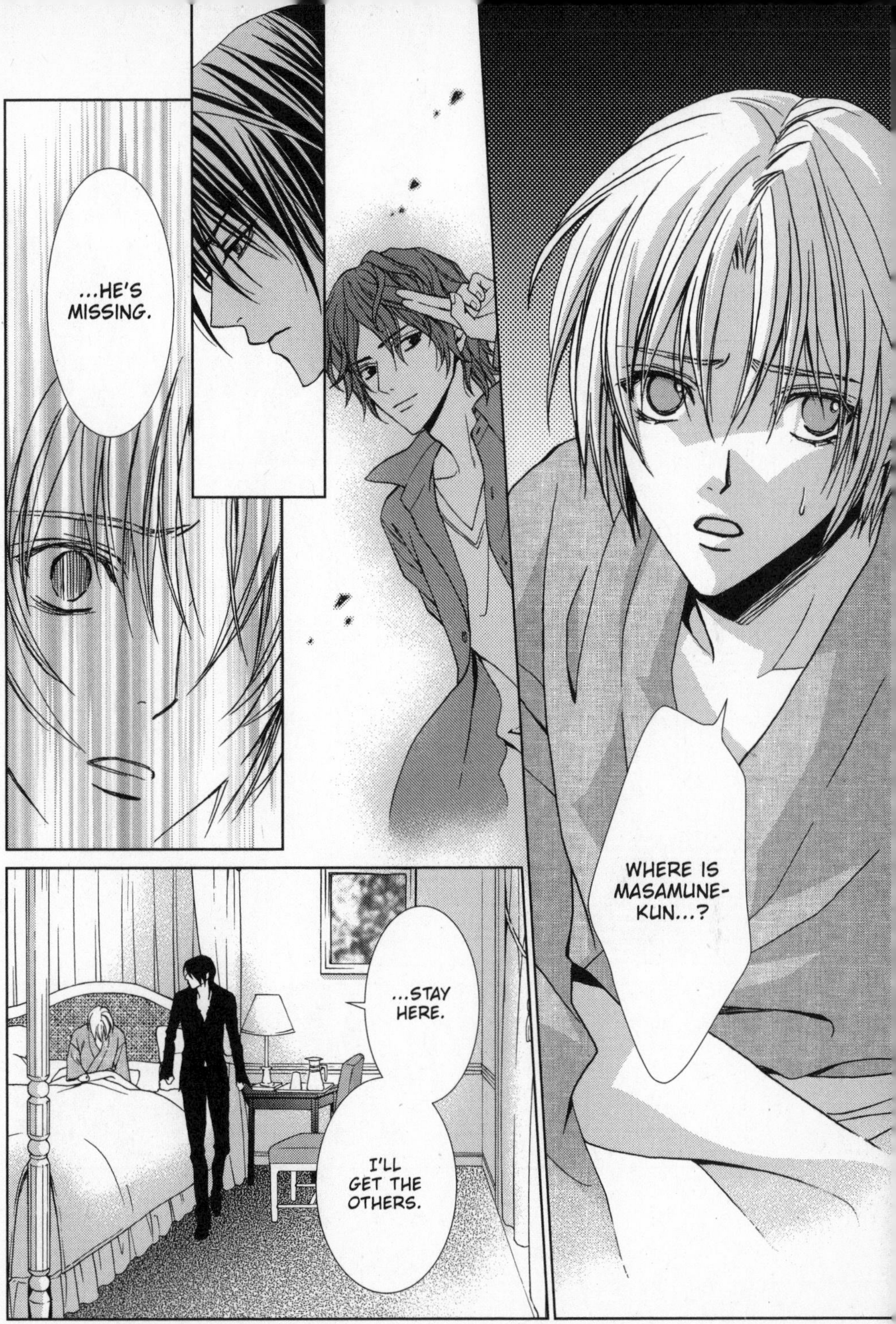
WHERE IS MASAMUNE-KUN...?
...HE'S MISSING.
...STAY HERE.
I'LL GET THE OTHERS.

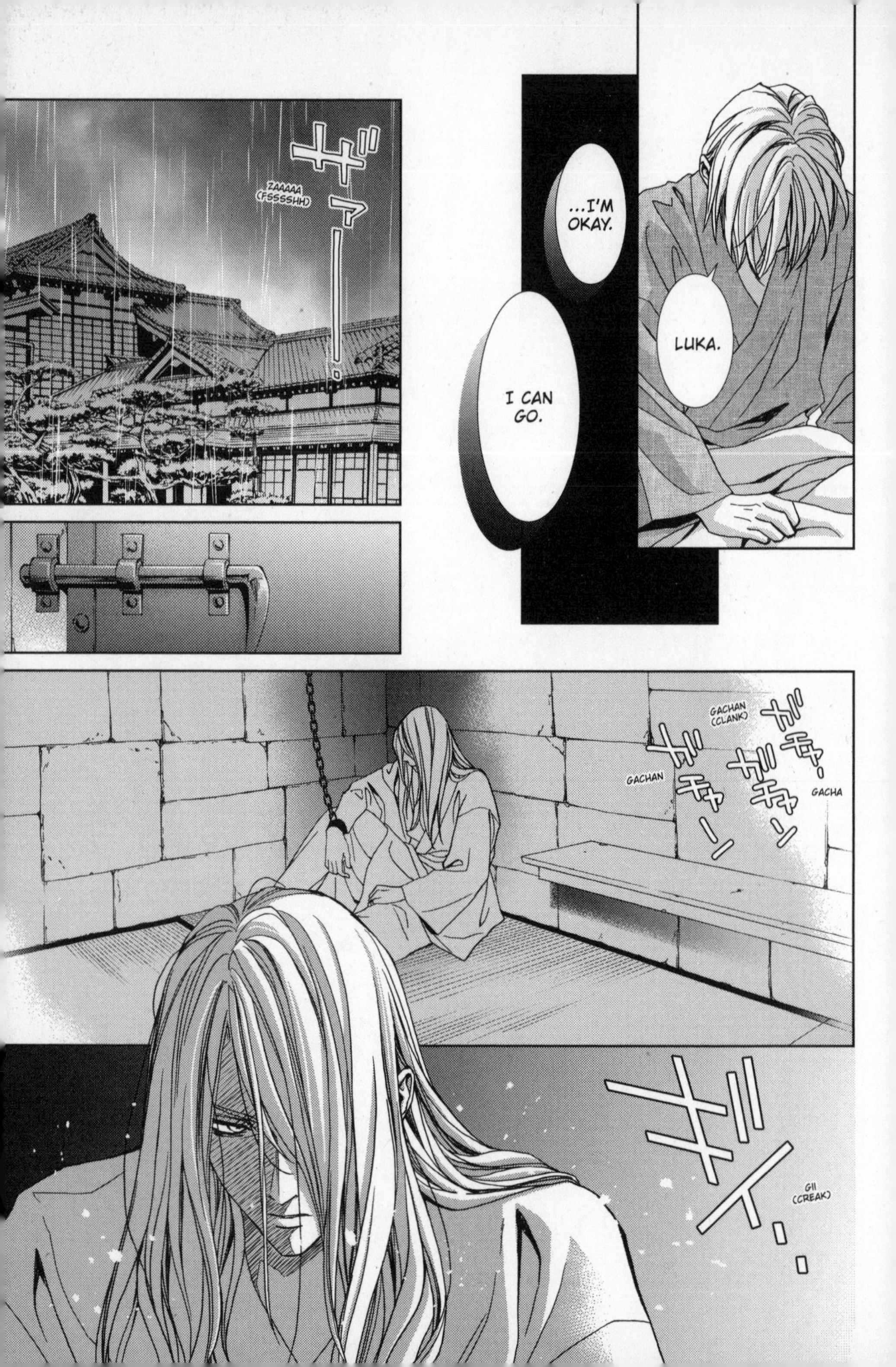
LUKA.
...I'M OKAY.
I CAN GO.
ZAAAAA (FSSSSHH)
GACHA
GACHAN (CLANK)
GACHAN
GII (CREAK)

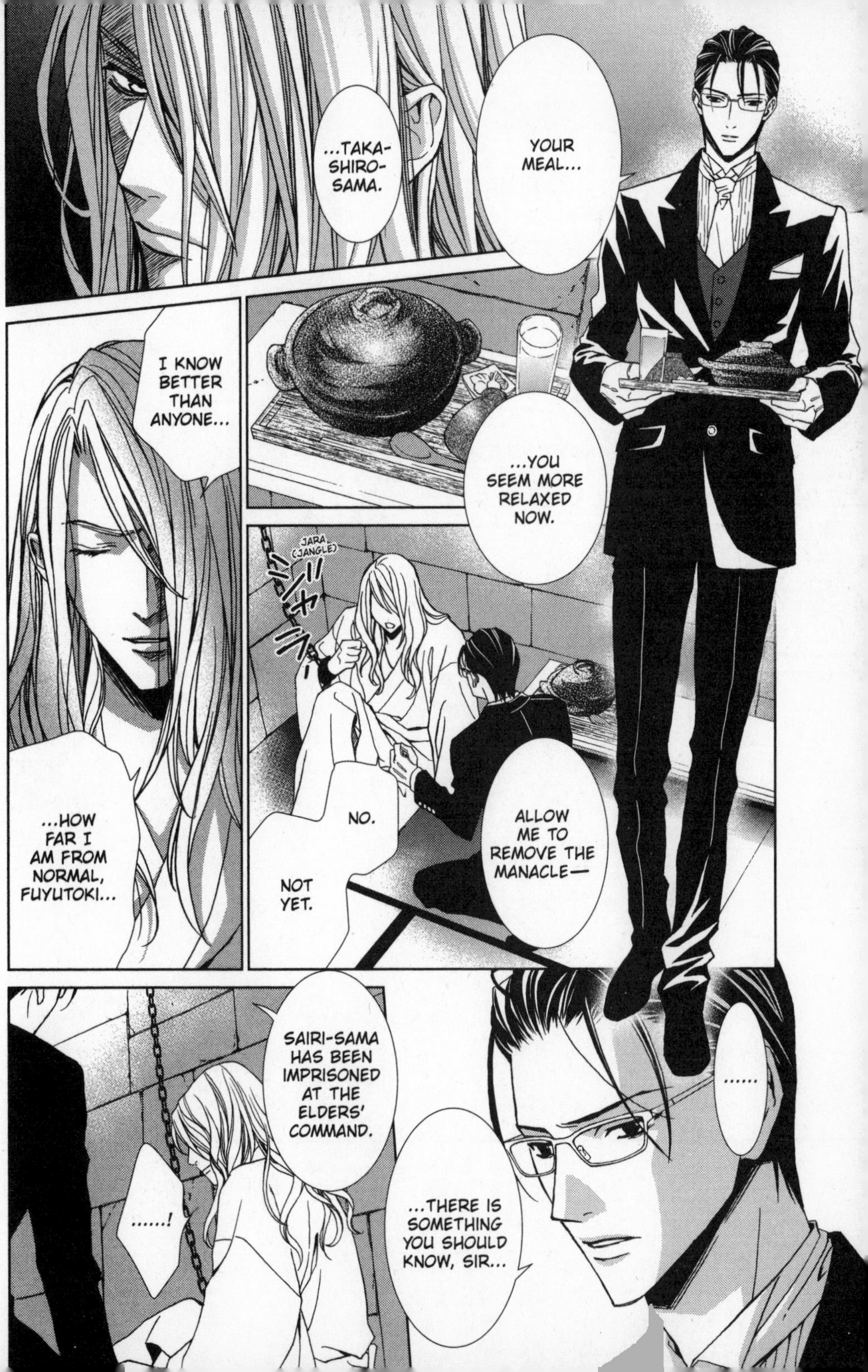
YOUR MEAL...
...TAKA-SHIRO-SAMA.
...YOU SEEM MORE RELAXED NOW.
JARA (JANGLE)
ALLOW ME TO REMOVE THE MANACLE—
NO.
NOT YET.
I KNOW BETTER THAN ANYONE...
...HOW FAR I AM FROM NORMAL, FUYUTOKI...
......
...THERE IS SOMETHING YOU SHOULD KNOW, SIR...
SAIRI-SAMA HAS BEEN IMPRISONED AT THE ELDERS' COMMAND.
......!

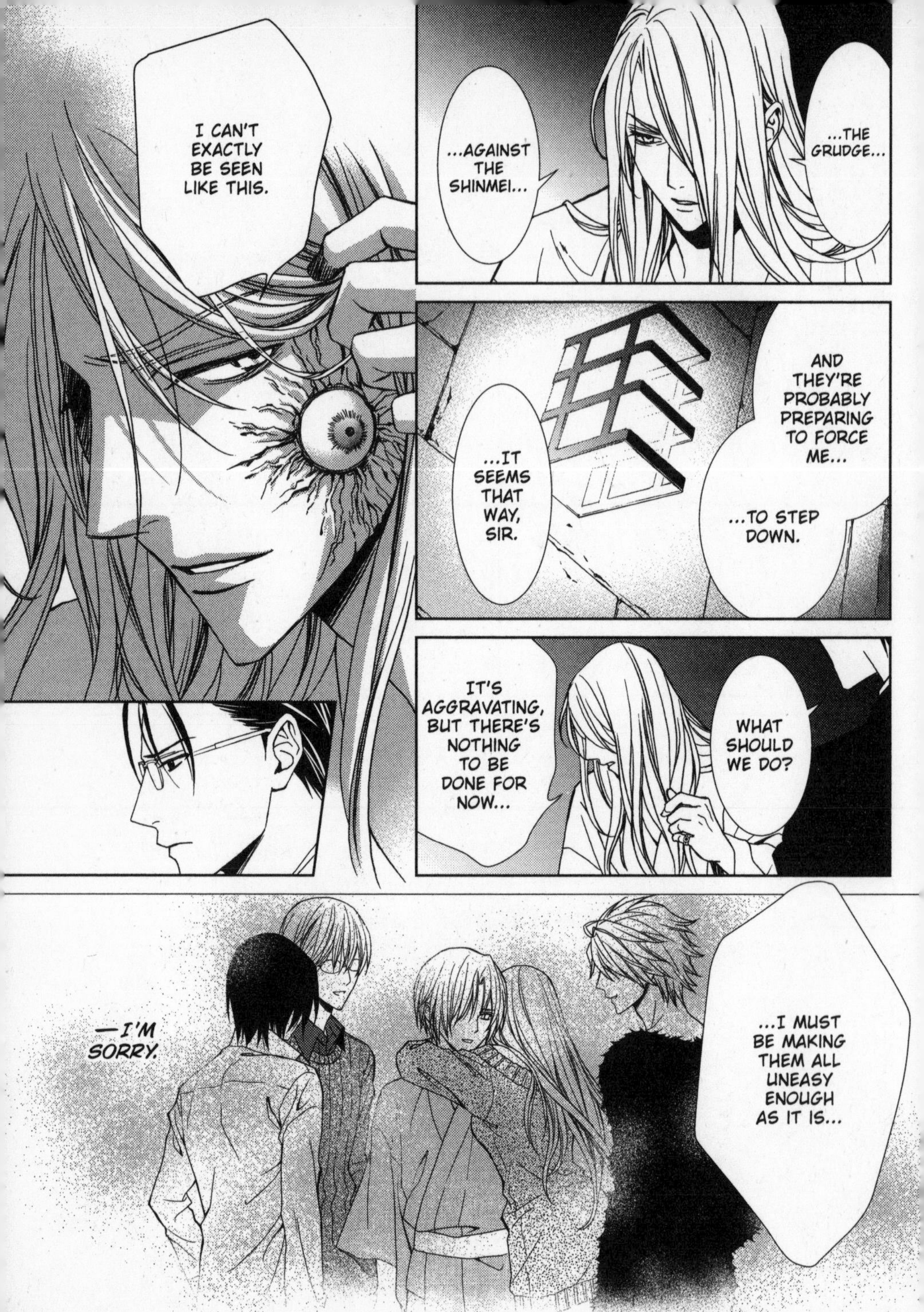

...THE GRUDGE...
...AGAINST THE SHINMEI...
AND THEY'RE PROBABLY PREPARING TO FORCE ME...
...TO STEP DOWN.
...IT SEEMS THAT WAY, SIR.
WHAT SHOULD WE DO?
IT'S AGGRAVATING, BUT THERE'S NOTHING TO BE DONE FOR NOW...
I CAN'T EXACTLY BE SEEN LIKE THIS.
...I MUST BE MAKING THEM ALL UNEASY ENOUGH AS IT IS...
—I'M SORRY.

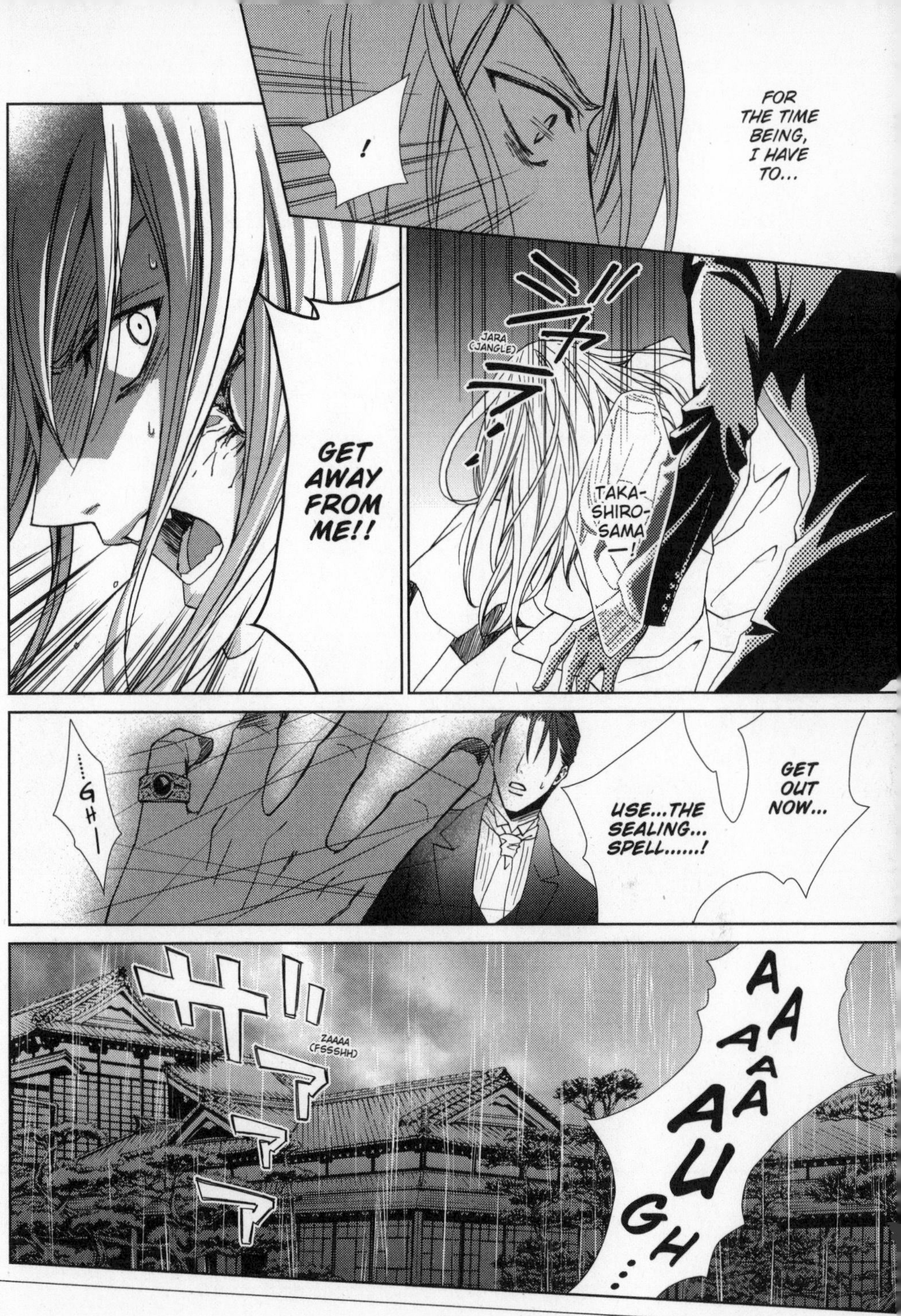
FOR THE TIME BEING, I HAVE TO...
!
JARA (JANGLE)
TAKA-SHIRO-SAMA—!
GET AWAY FROM ME!!
GET OUT NOW...
USE...THE SEALING... SPELL......!
......GH!
AAAAAAUGH...
ZAAAA (FSSSHH)

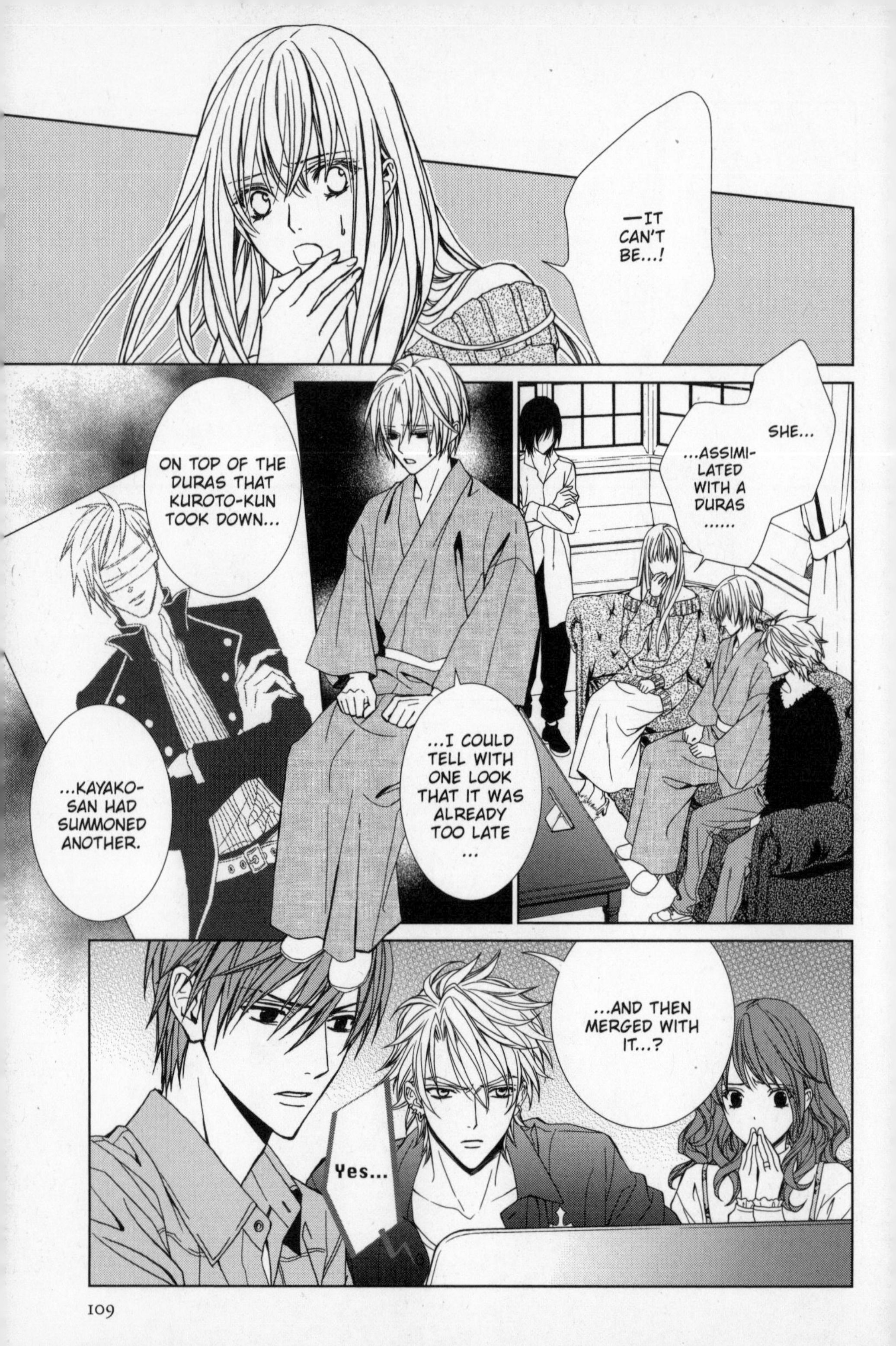
—IT CAN'T BE...!
SHE... ...ASSIMILATED WITH A DURAS ......
...I COULD TELL WITH ONE LOOK THAT IT WAS ALREADY TOO LATE ...
ON TOP OF THE DURAS THAT KUROTO-KUN TOOK DOWN...
...KAYAKO-SAN HAD SUMMONED ANOTHER.
...AND THEN MERGED WITH IT...?
Yes...

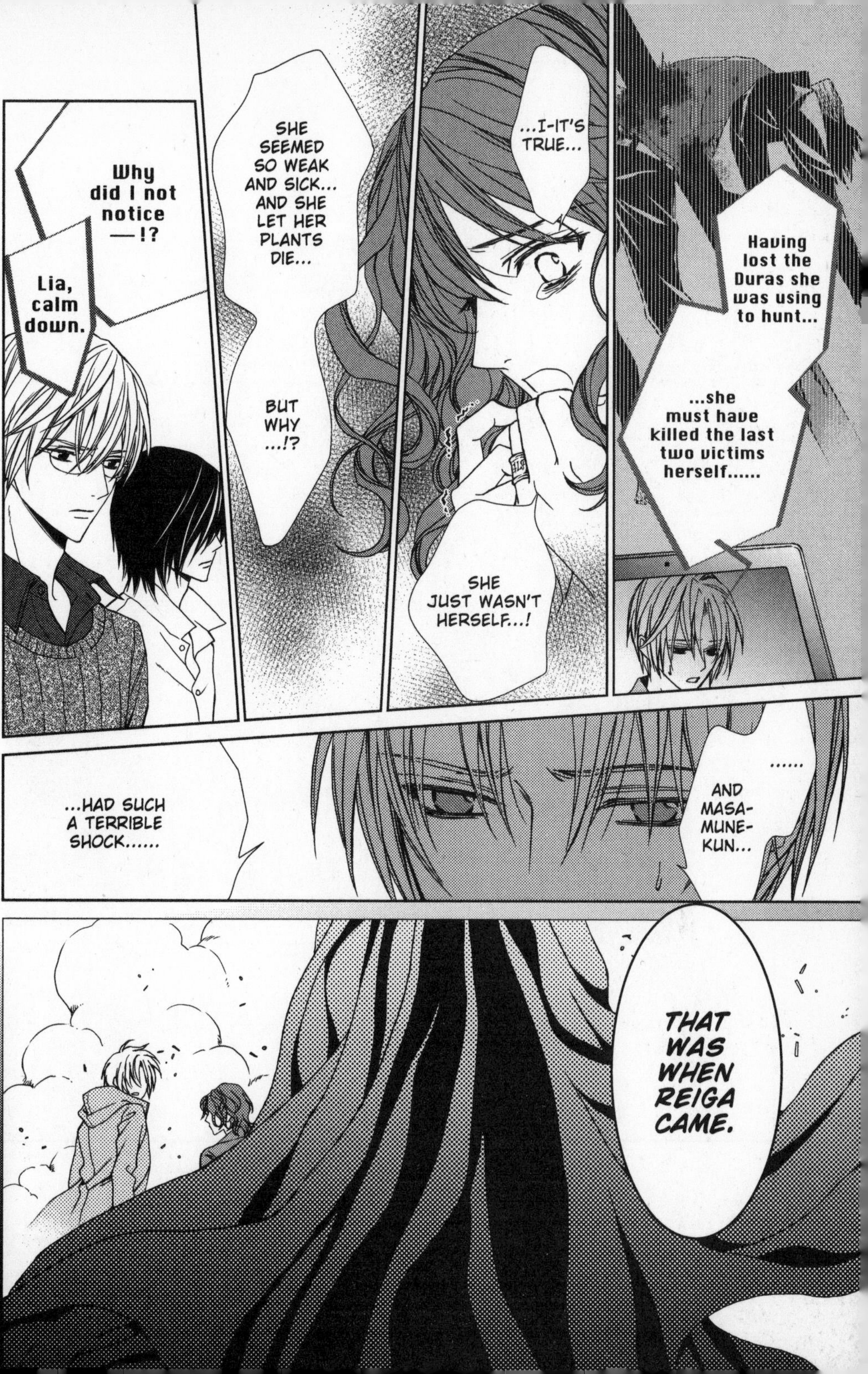
Having lost the Duras she was using to hunt...
...she must have killed the last two victims herself......
...I-IT'S TRUE...
SHE JUST WASN'T HERSELF...!
SHE SEEMED SO WEAK AND SICK... AND SHE LET HER PLANTS DIE...
BUT WHY ...!?
Why did I not notice—!?
Lia, calm down.
......
AND MASA-MUNE-KUN...
...HAD SUCH A TERRIBLE SHOCK......
THAT WAS WHEN REIGA CAME.

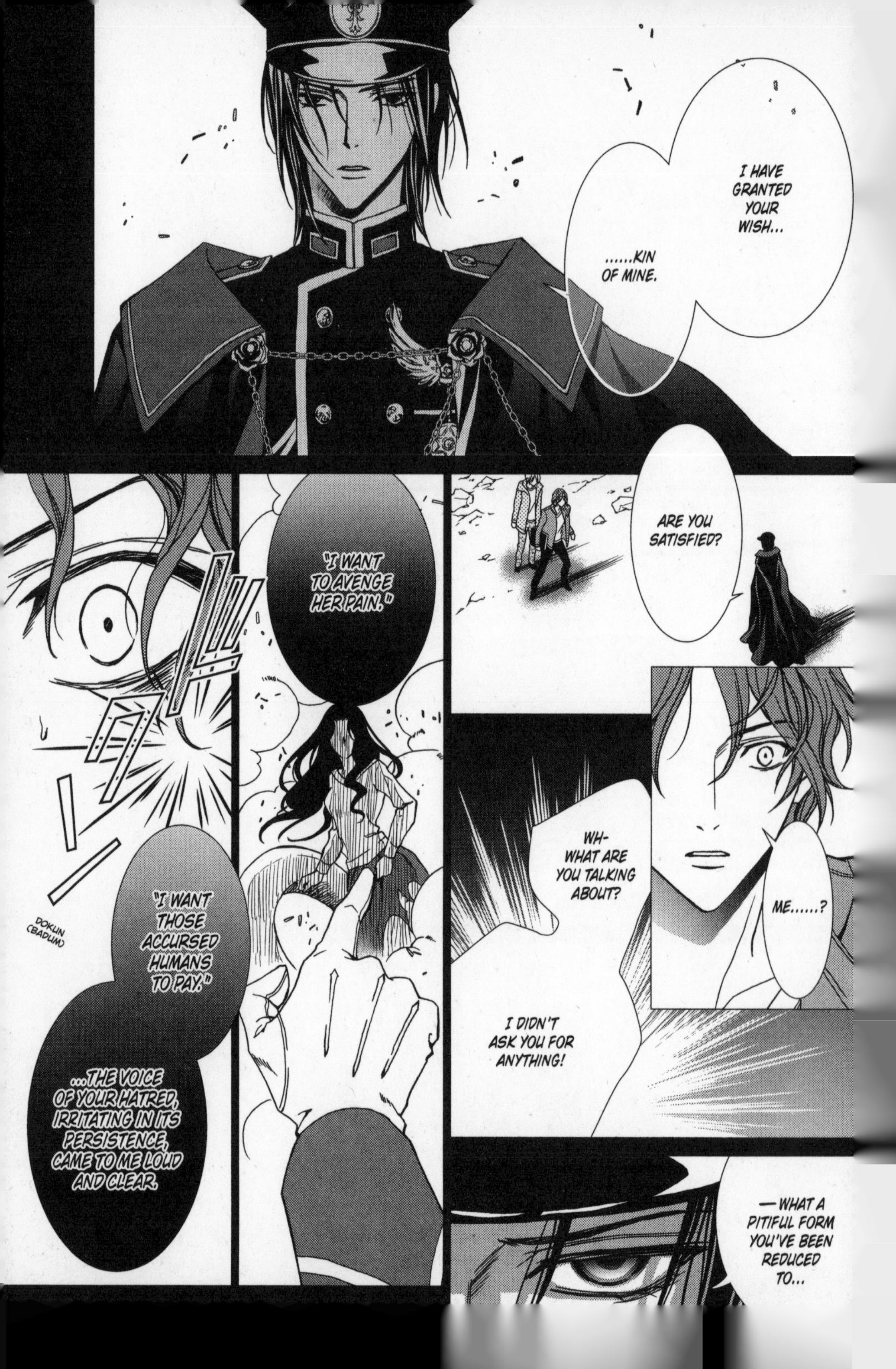
I HAVE GRANTED YOUR WISH...
......KIN OF MINE.
ARE YOU SATISFIED?
ME......?
WH- WHAT ARE YOU TALKING ABOUT?
I DIDN'T ASK YOU FOR ANYTHING!
—WHAT A PITIFUL FORM YOU'VE BEEN REDUCED TO...
"I WANT TO AVENGE HER PAIN."
"I WANT THOSE ACCURSED HUMANS TO PAY."
...THE VOICE OF YOUR HATRED, IRRITATING IN ITS PERSISTENCE, CAME TO ME LOUD AND CLEAR.
DOKUN (BADUM)

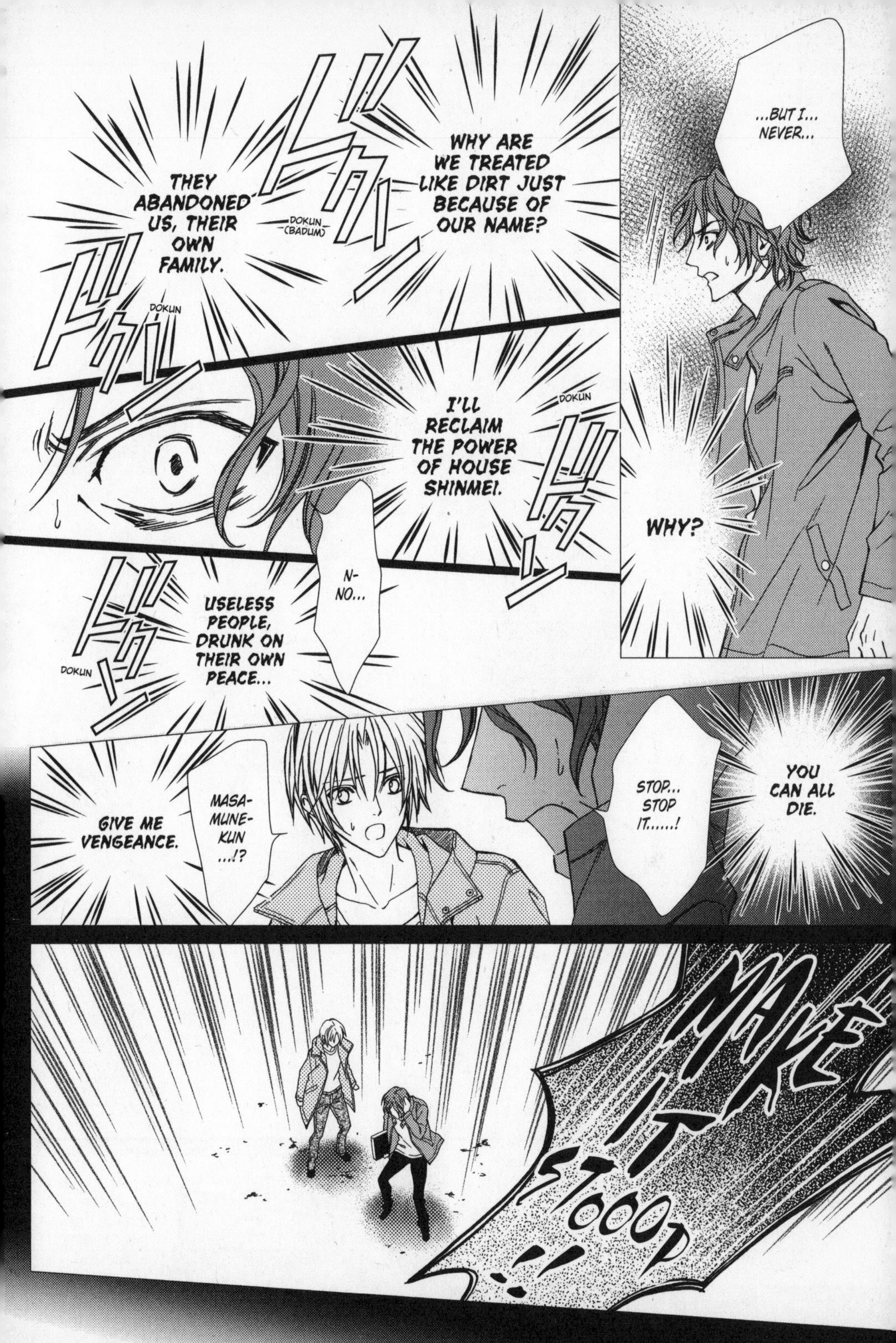
...BUT I... NEVER...
WHY?
WHY ARE WE TREATED LIKE DIRT JUST BECAUSE OF OUR NAME?
DOKUN (BADUM)
THEY ABANDONED US, THEIR OWN FAMILY.
DOKUN
DOKUN
I'LL RECLAIM THE POWER OF HOUSE SHINMEI.
N-NO...
USELESS PEOPLE, DRUNK ON THEIR OWN PEACE...
DOKUN
YOU CAN ALL DIE.
STOP... STOP IT......!
MASA-MUNE-KUN ...!?
GIVE ME VENGEANCE.
MAKE IT STOOOP!!

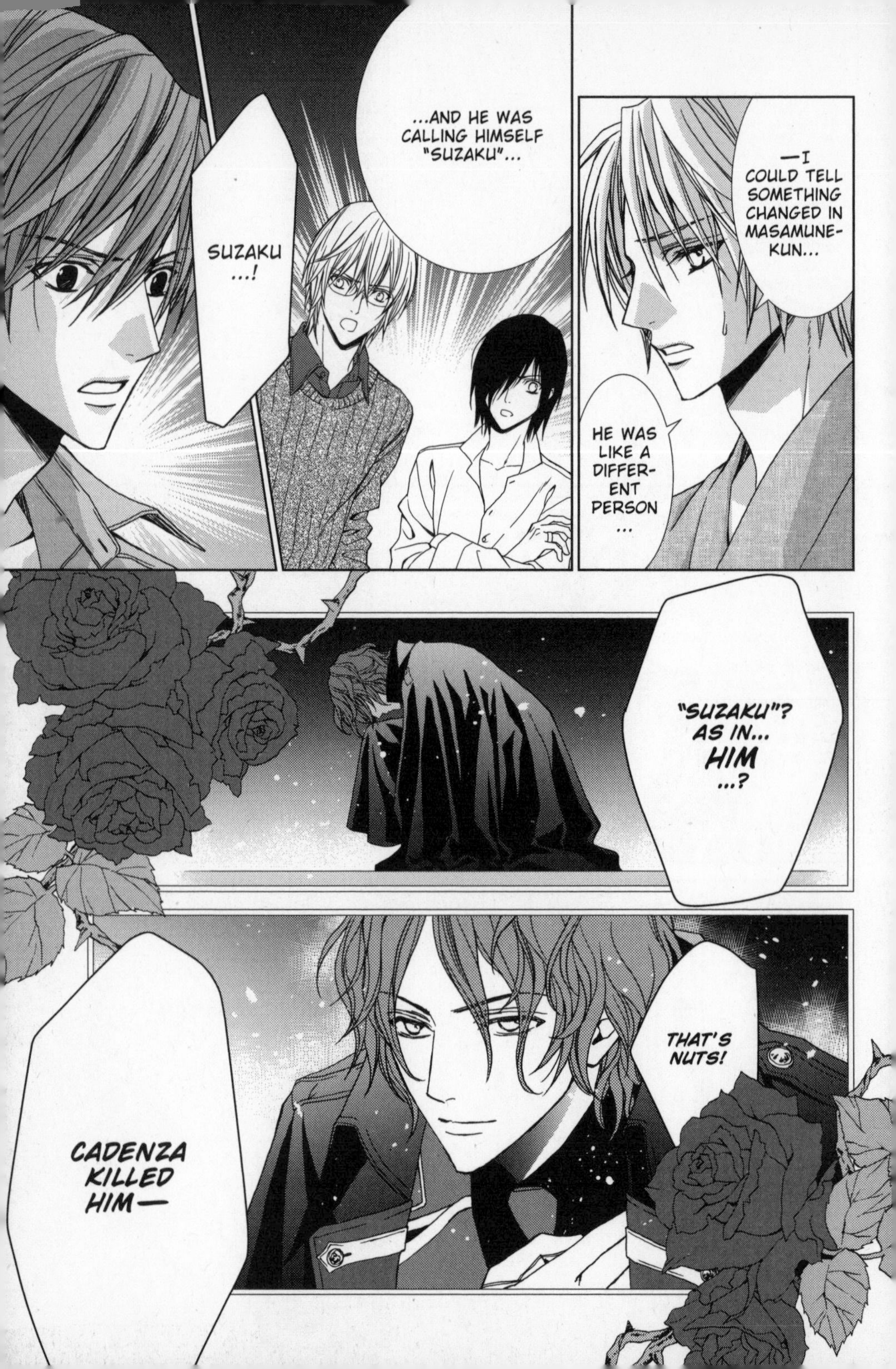
—I COULD TELL SOMETHING CHANGED IN MASAMUNE-KUN...
HE WAS LIKE A DIFFERENT PERSON ...
...AND HE WAS CALLING HIMSELF "SUZAKU"...
SUZAKU ...!
"SUZAKU"? AS IN... HIM ...?
THAT'S NUTS!
CADENZA KILLED HIM—

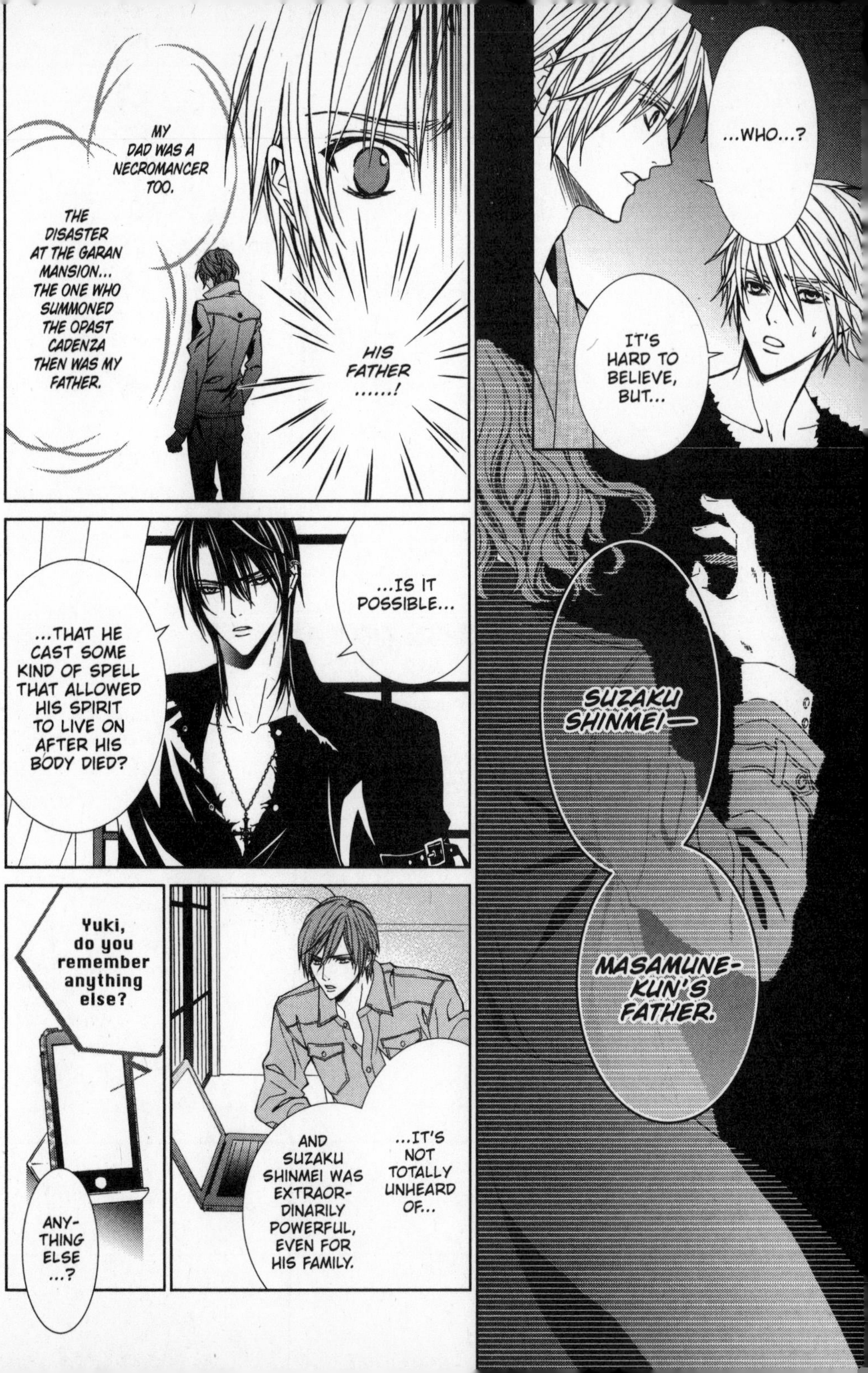
...WHO...?
IT'S HARD TO BELIEVE, BUT...
SUZAKU SHINMEI—
MASAMUNE-KUN'S FATHER.
MY DAD WAS A NECROMANCER TOO.
THE DISASTER AT THE GARAN MANSION... THE ONE WHO SUMMONED THE OPAST CADENZA THEN WAS MY FATHER.
HIS FATHER ......!
...IS IT POSSIBLE...
...THAT HE CAST SOME KIND OF SPELL THAT ALLOWED HIS SPIRIT TO LIVE ON AFTER HIS BODY DIED?
...IT'S NOT TOTALLY UNHEARD OF...
AND SUZAKU SHINMEI WAS EXTRAOR-DINARILY POWERFUL, EVEN FOR HIS FAMILY.
Yuki, do you remember anything else?
ANY-THING ELSE ...?

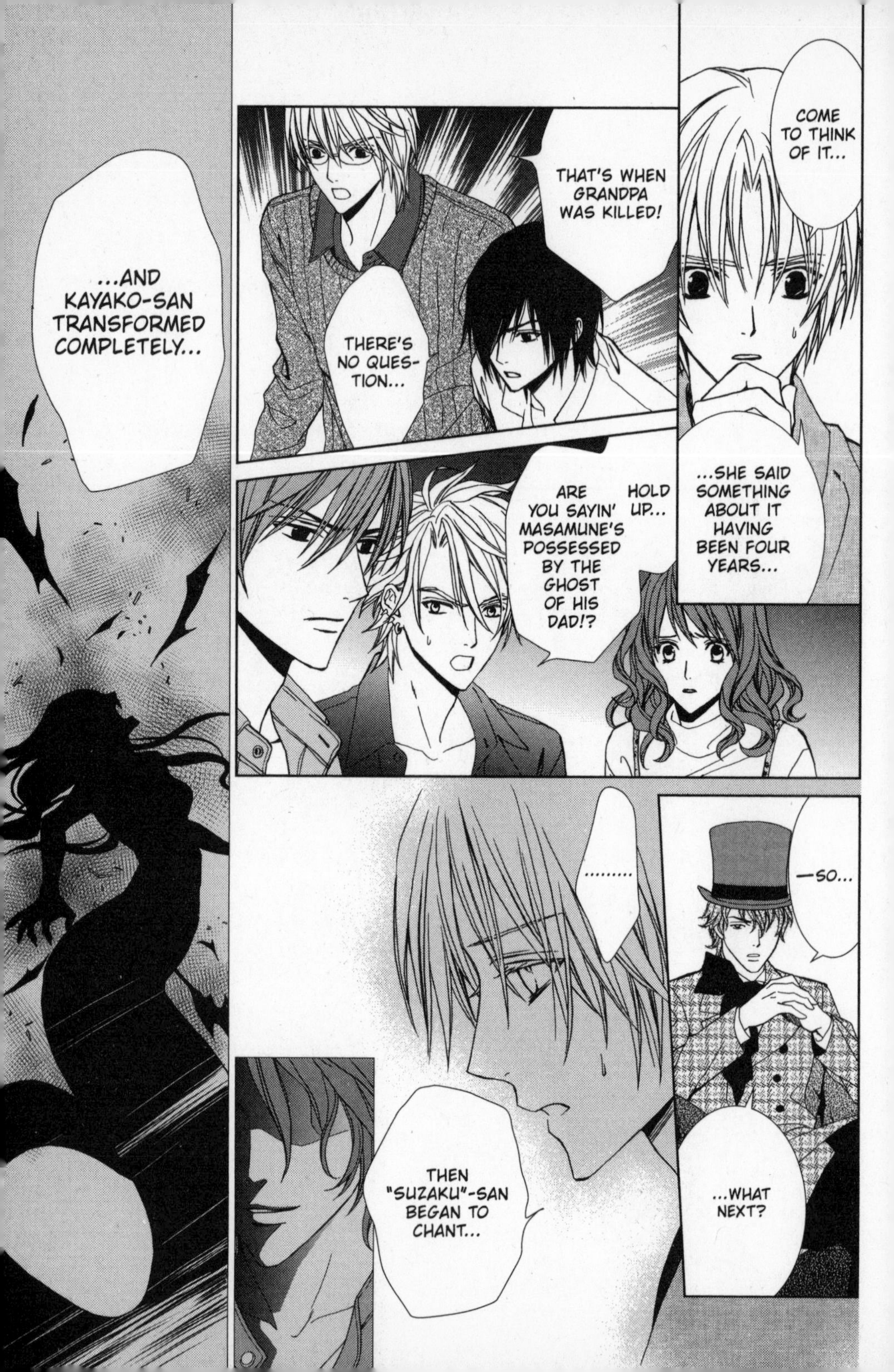
COME TO THINK OF IT...
...SHE SAID SOMETHING ABOUT IT HAVING BEEN FOUR YEARS...
THAT'S WHEN GRANDPA WAS KILLED!
THERE'S NO QUES-TION...
HOLD UP...
ARE YOU SAYIN' MASAMUNE'S POSSESSED BY THE GHOST OF HIS DAD!?
—SO...
...WHAT NEXT?
....
THEN "SUZAKU"-SAN BEGAN TO CHANT...
...AND KAYAKO-SAN TRANSFORMED COMPLETELY...

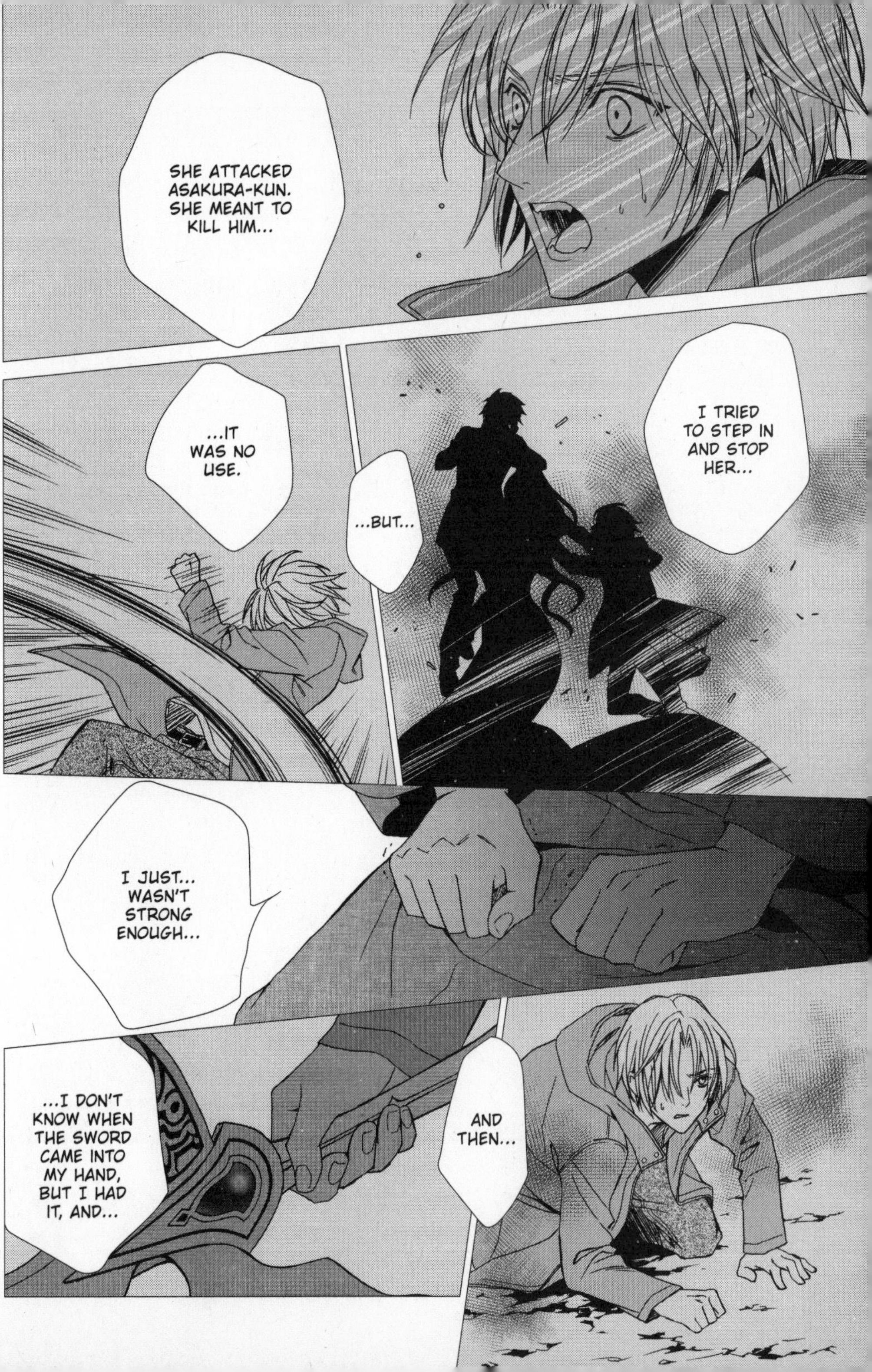
SHE ATTACKED ASAKURA-KUN. SHE MEANT TO KILL HIM...
I TRIED TO STEP IN AND STOP HER...
...BUT...
...IT WAS NO USE.
I JUST... WASN'T STRONG ENOUGH...
AND THEN...
...I DON'T KNOW WHEN THE SWORD CAME INTO MY HAND, BUT I HAD IT, AND...

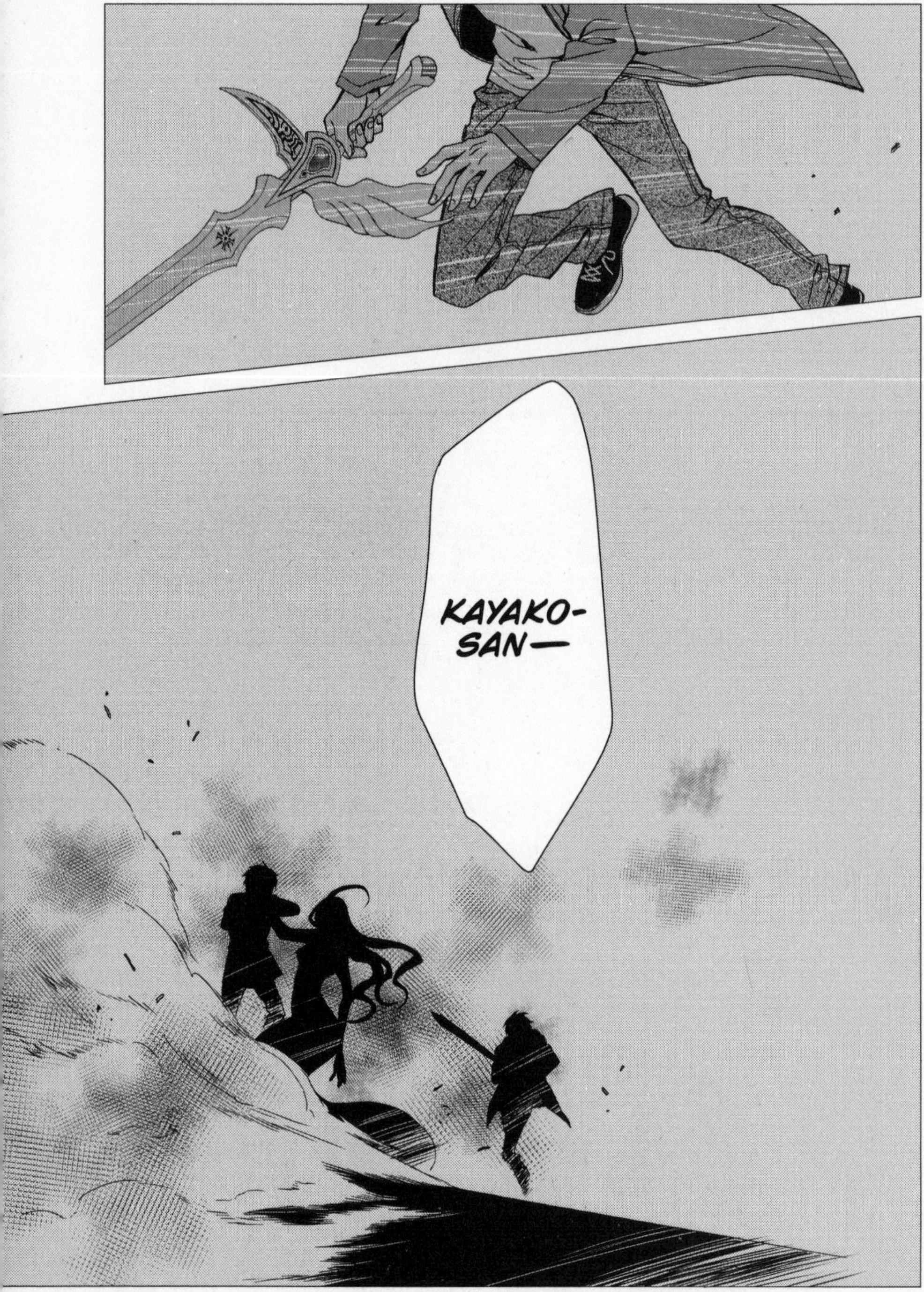
KAYAKO-SAN—

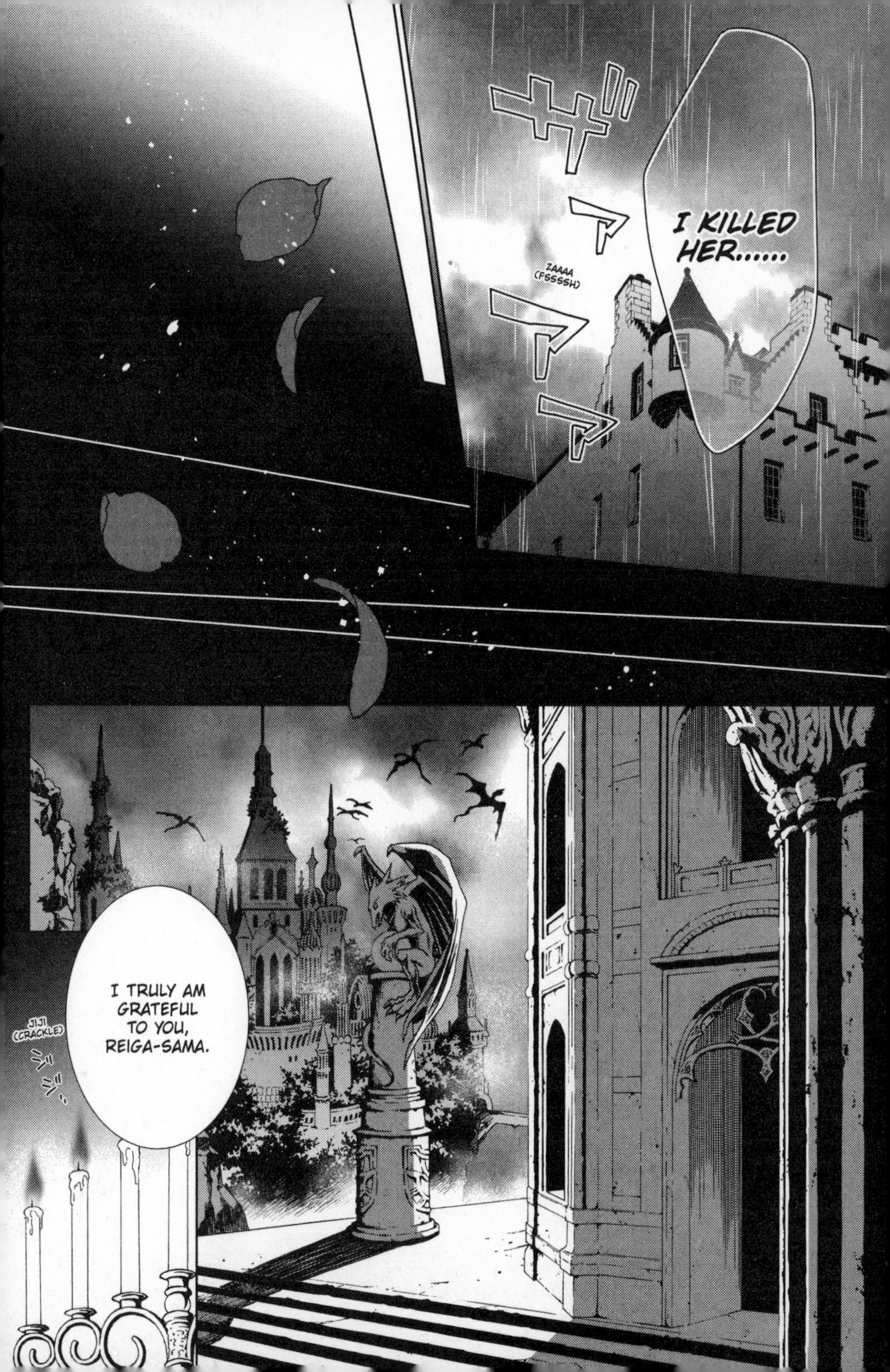
I KILLED HER......
ザァァァ
ZAAAA (FSSSSH)
I TRULY AM GRATEFUL TO YOU, REIGA-SAMA.
ジジ…
JIJI (CRACKLE)

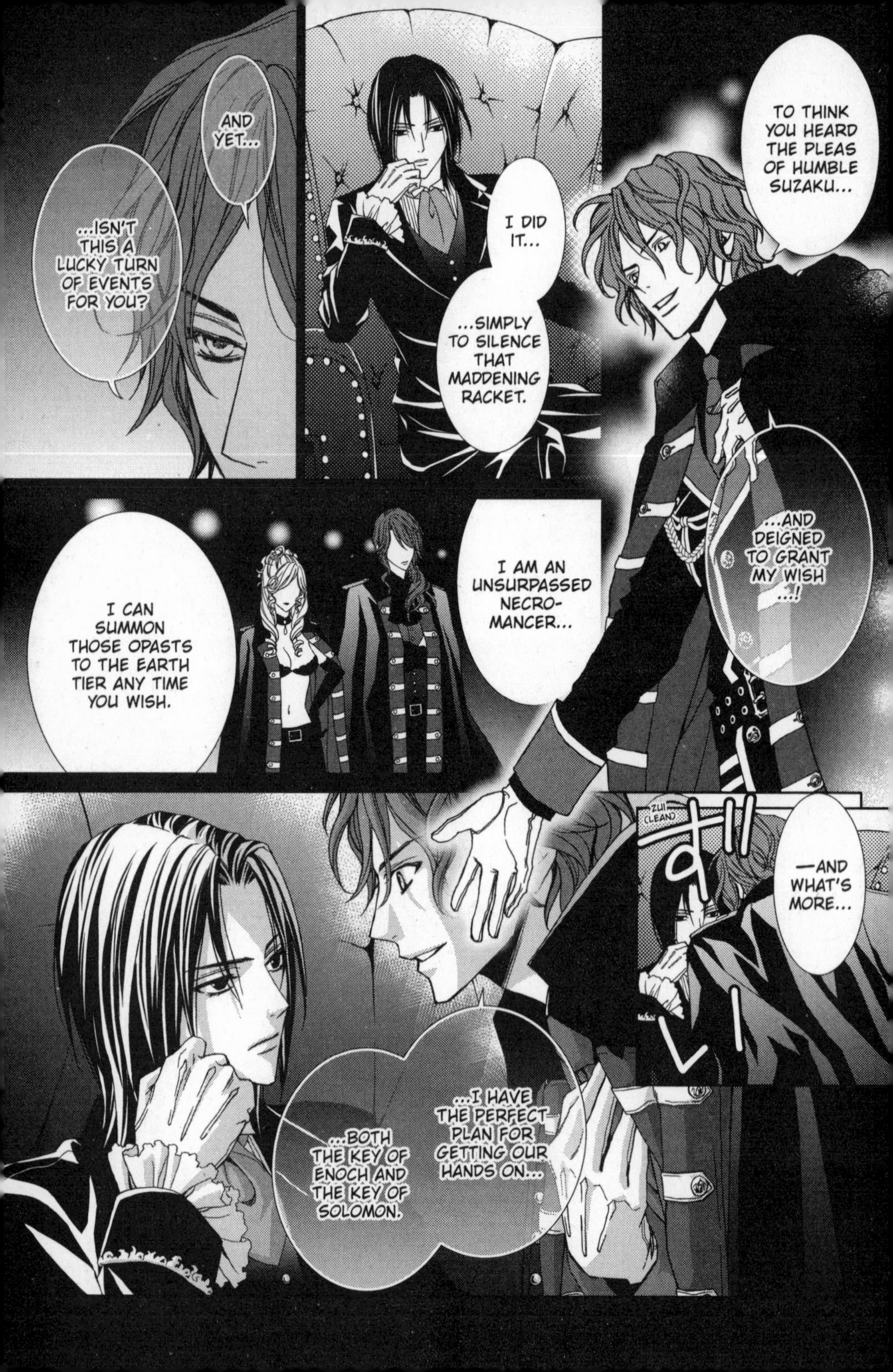
TO THINK YOU HEARD THE PLEAS OF HUMBLE SUZAKU...
...AND DEIGNED TO GRANT MY WISH ...!
I DID IT...
...SIMPLY TO SILENCE THAT MADDENING RACKET.
AND YET...
...ISN'T THIS A LUCKY TURN OF EVENTS FOR YOU?
I AM AN UNSURPASSED NECRO-MANCER...
I CAN SUMMON THOSE OPASTS TO THE EARTH TIER ANY TIME YOU WISH.
ZUI CLEAN
すっ
—AND WHAT'S MORE...
...I HAVE THE PERFECT PLAN FOR GETTING OUR HANDS ON...
...BOTH THE KEY OF ENOCH AND THE KEY OF SOLOMON.

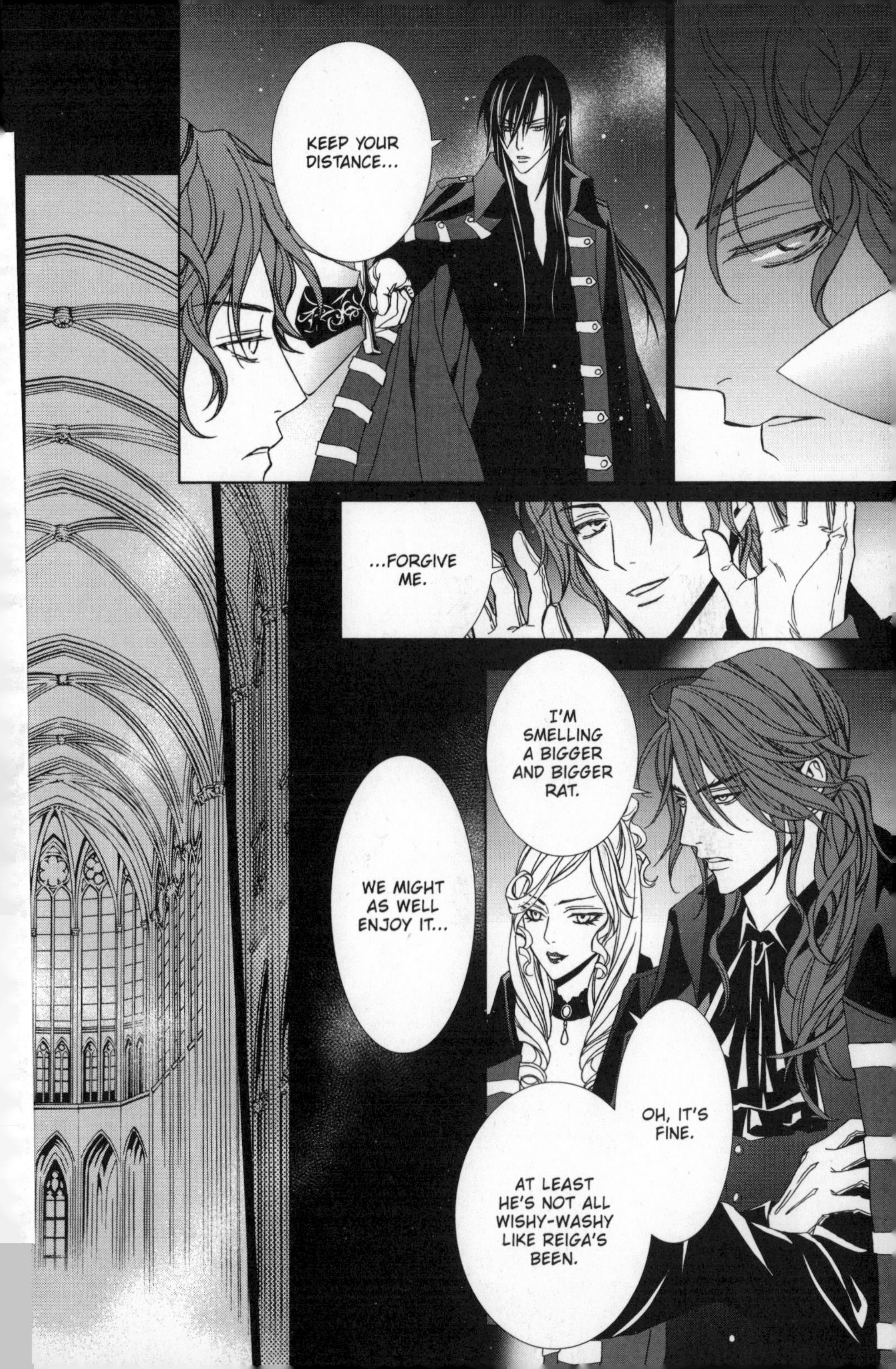
KEEP YOUR DISTANCE...
...FORGIVE ME.
I'M SMELLING A BIGGER AND BIGGER RAT.
WE MIGHT AS WELL ENJOY IT...
OH, IT'S FINE.
AT LEAST HE'S NOT ALL WISHY-WASHY LIKE REIGA'S BEEN.

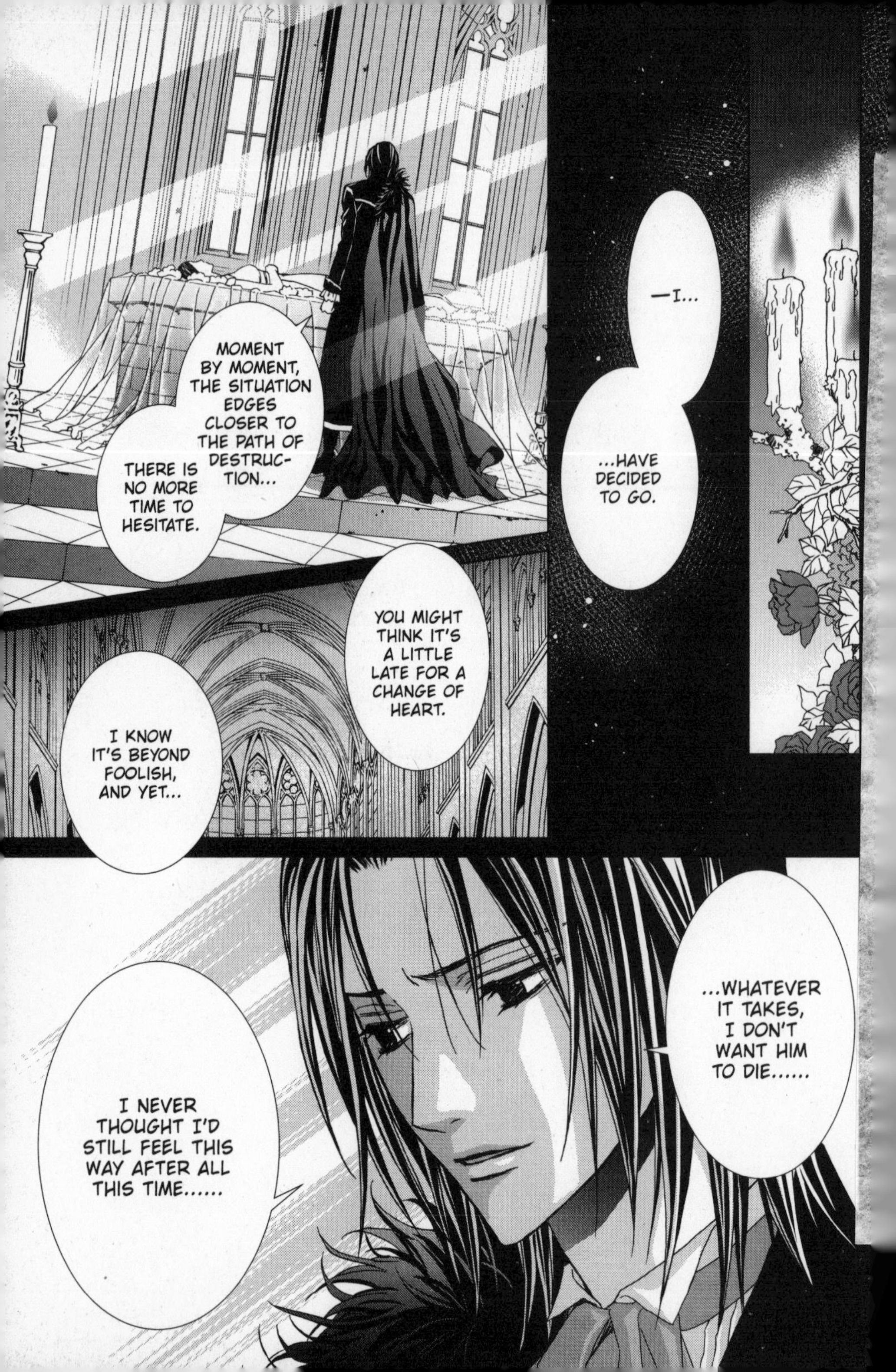
—I...
...HAVE DECIDED TO GO.
MOMENT BY MOMENT, THE SITUATION EDGES CLOSER TO THE PATH OF DESTRUC-TION...
THERE IS NO MORE TIME TO HESITATE.
YOU MIGHT THINK IT'S A LITTLE LATE FOR A CHANGE OF HEART.
I KNOW IT'S BEYOND FOOLISH, AND YET...
...WHATEVER IT TAKES, I DON'T WANT HIM TO DIE......
I NEVER THOUGHT I'D STILL FEEL THIS WAY AFTER ALL THIS TIME......

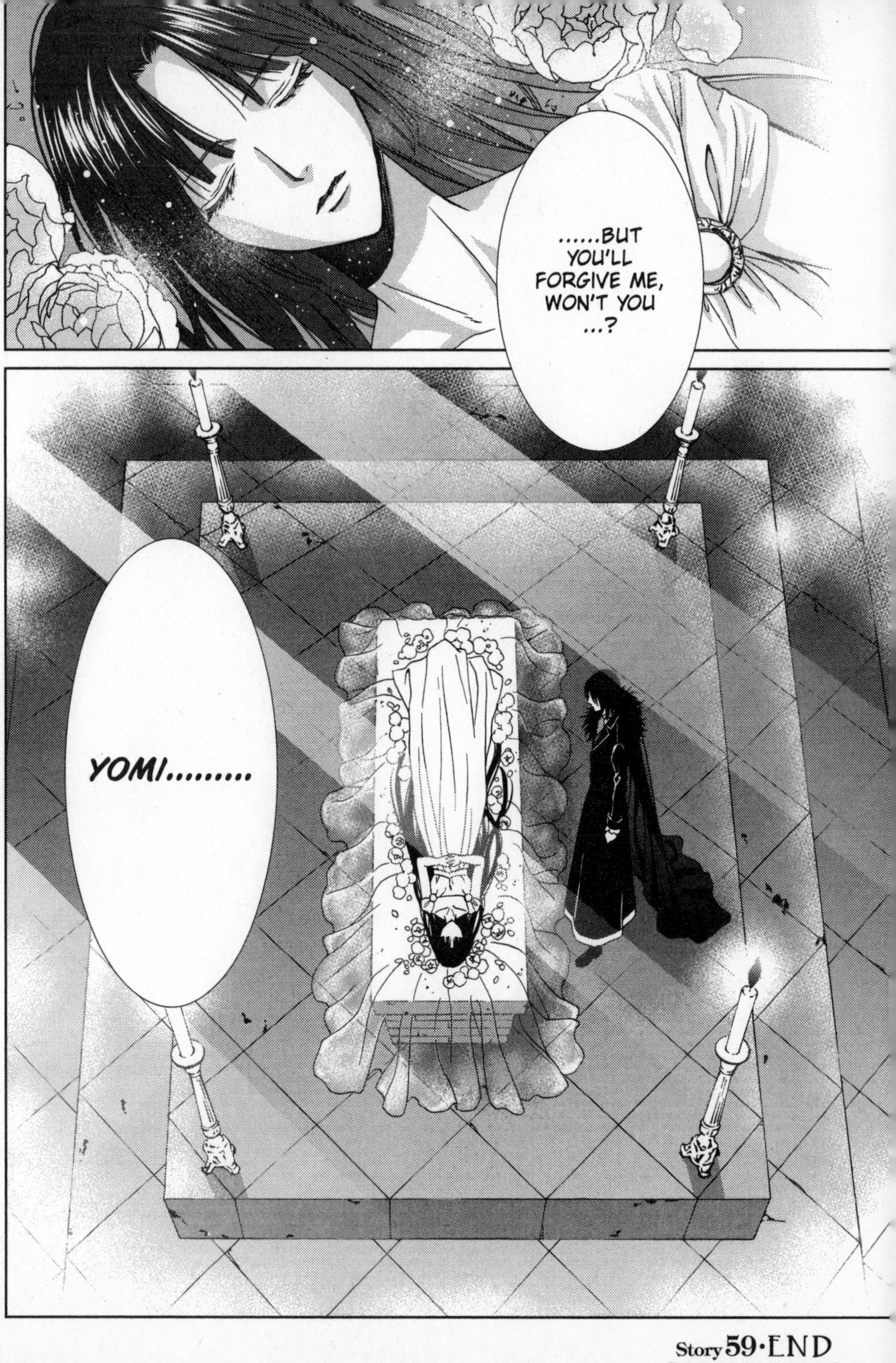
......BUT YOU'LL FORGIVE ME, WON'T YOU ...?
YOMI.........

Story 59·END

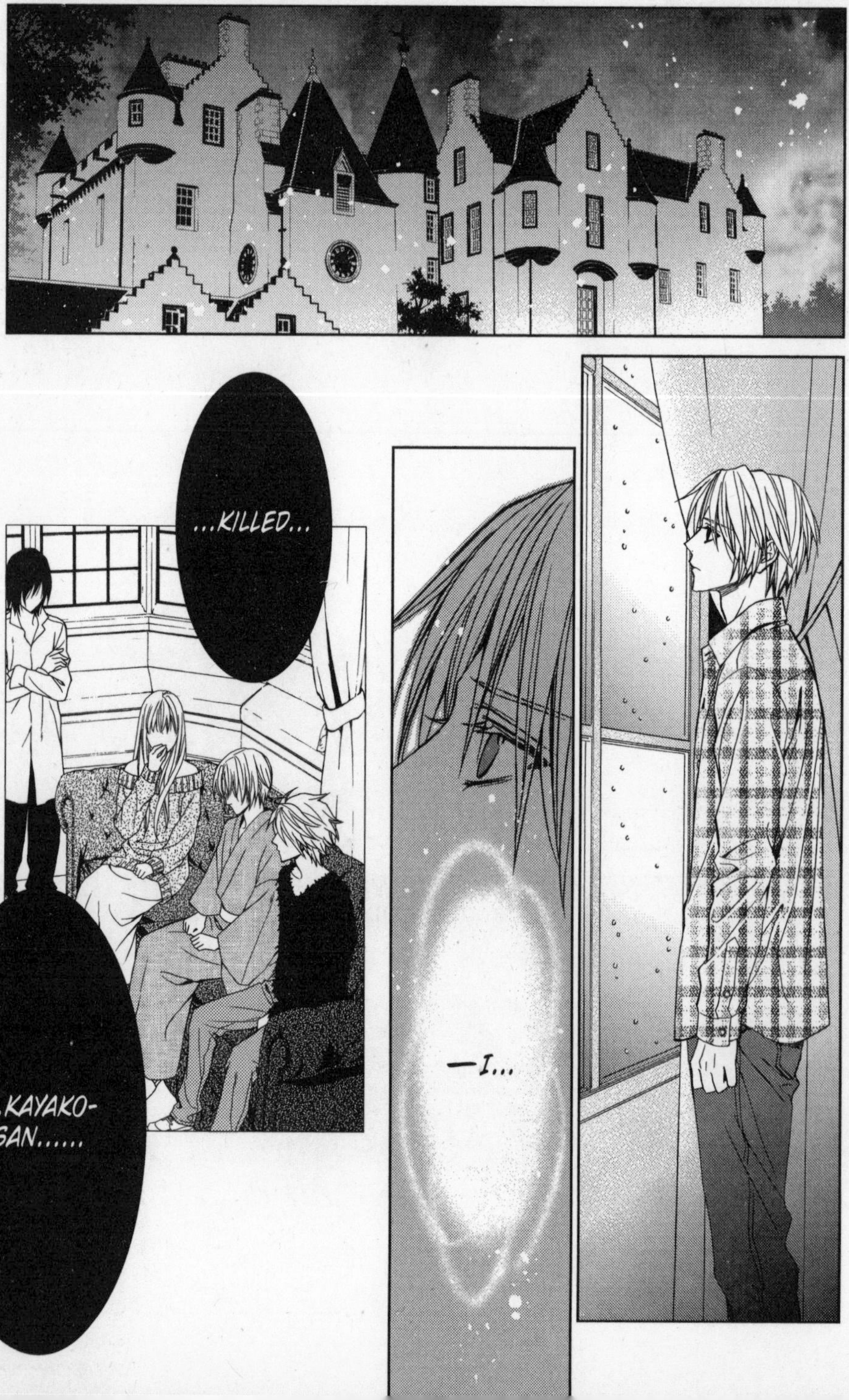
—I...
...KILLED...
...KAYAKO-SAN......

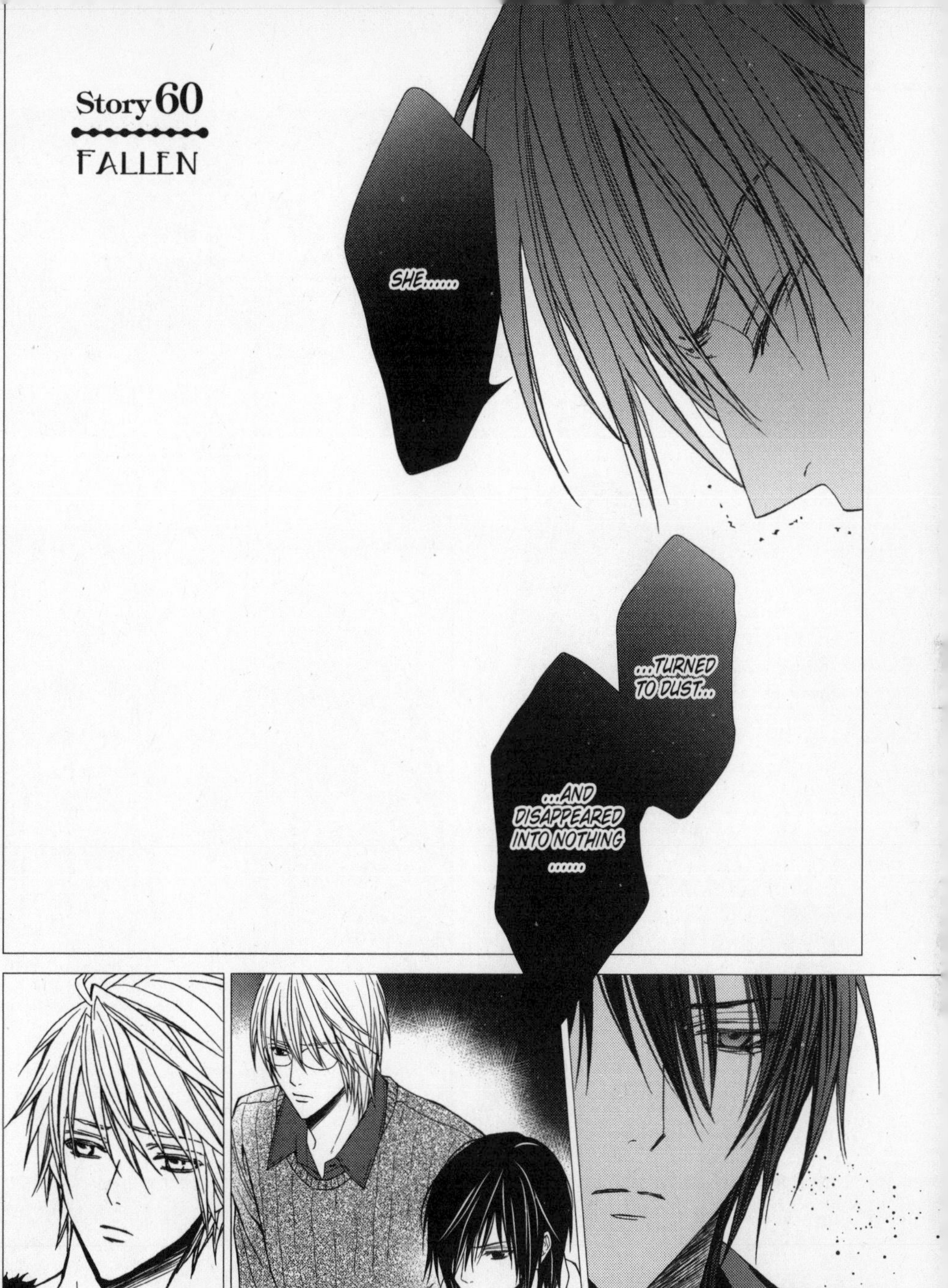
Story 60
FALLEN
SHE......
...TURNED TO DUST...
...AND DISAPPEARED INTO NOTHING ......

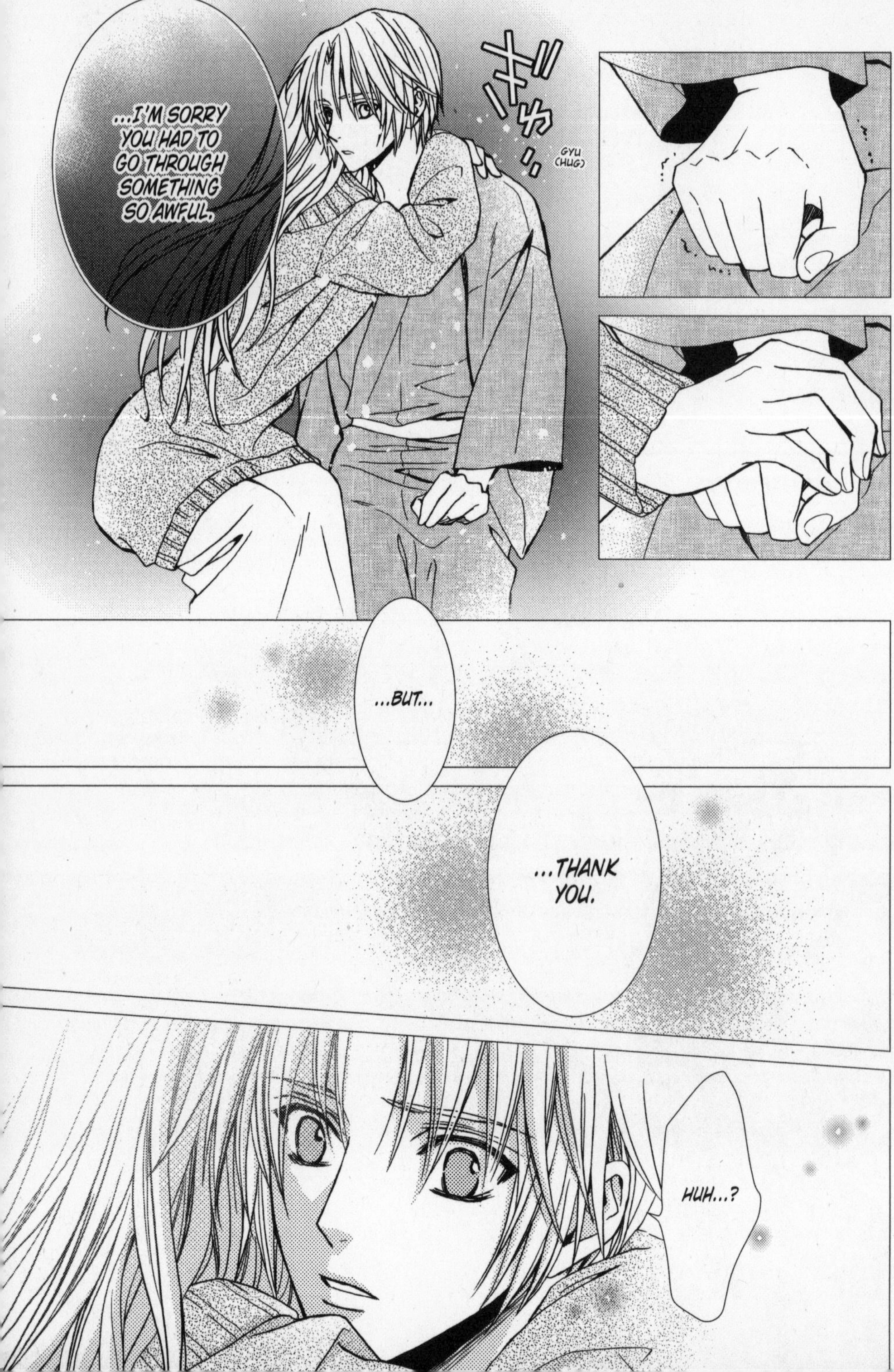
GYU (HUG)
...I'M SORRY YOU HAD TO GO THROUGH SOMETHING SO AWFUL.
...BUT...
...THANK YOU.
HUH...?

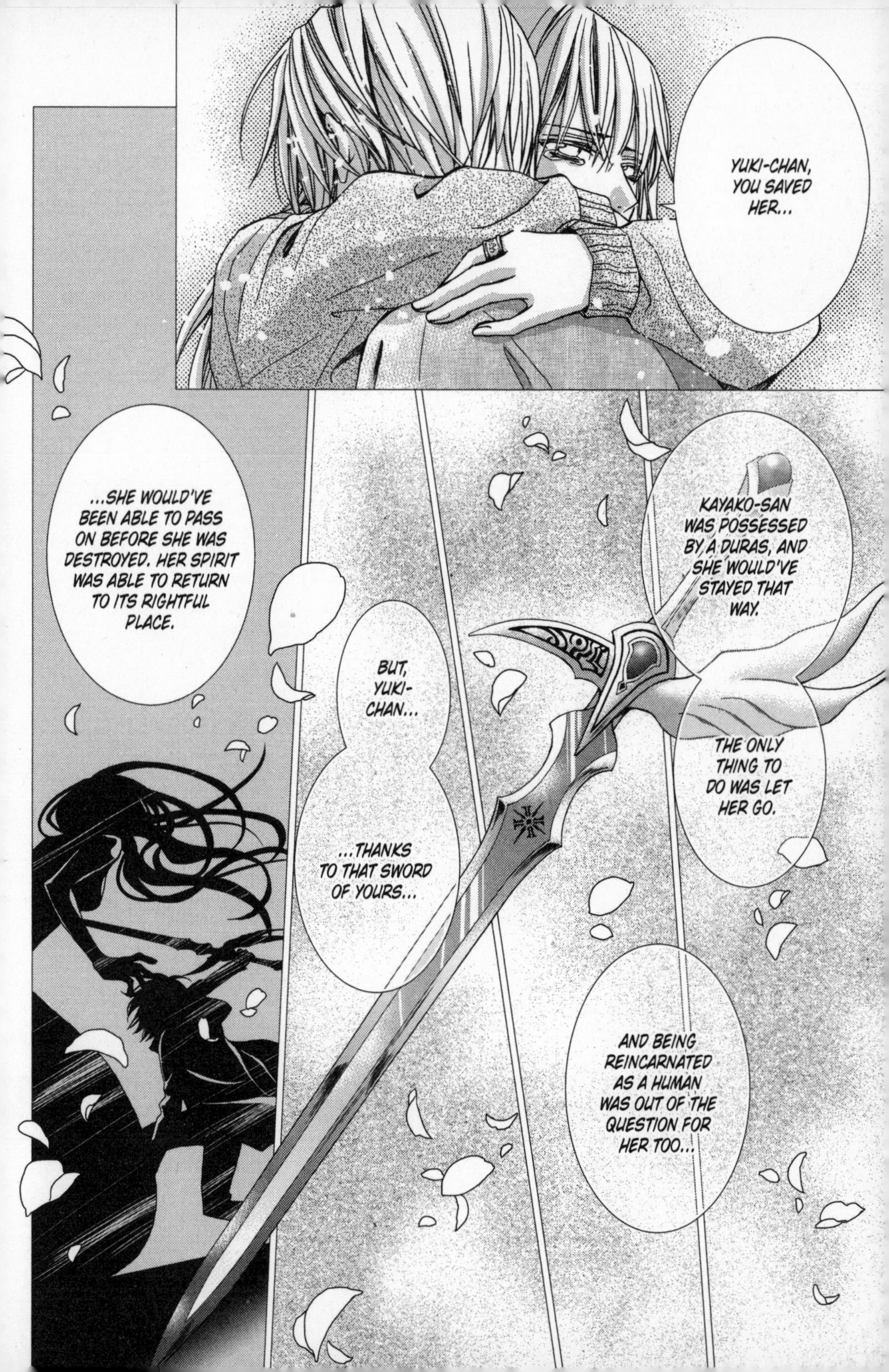
YUKI-CHAN, YOU SAVED HER...
KAYAKO-SAN WAS POSSESSED BY A DURAS, AND SHE WOULD'VE STAYED THAT WAY.
THE ONLY THING TO DO WAS LET HER GO.
AND BEING REINCARNATED AS A HUMAN WAS OUT OF THE QUESTION FOR HER TOO...
BUT, YUKI-CHAN...
...THANKS TO THAT SWORD OF YOURS...
...SHE WOULD'VE BEEN ABLE TO PASS ON BEFORE SHE WAS DESTROYED. HER SPIRIT WAS ABLE TO RETURN TO ITS RIGHTFUL PLACE.

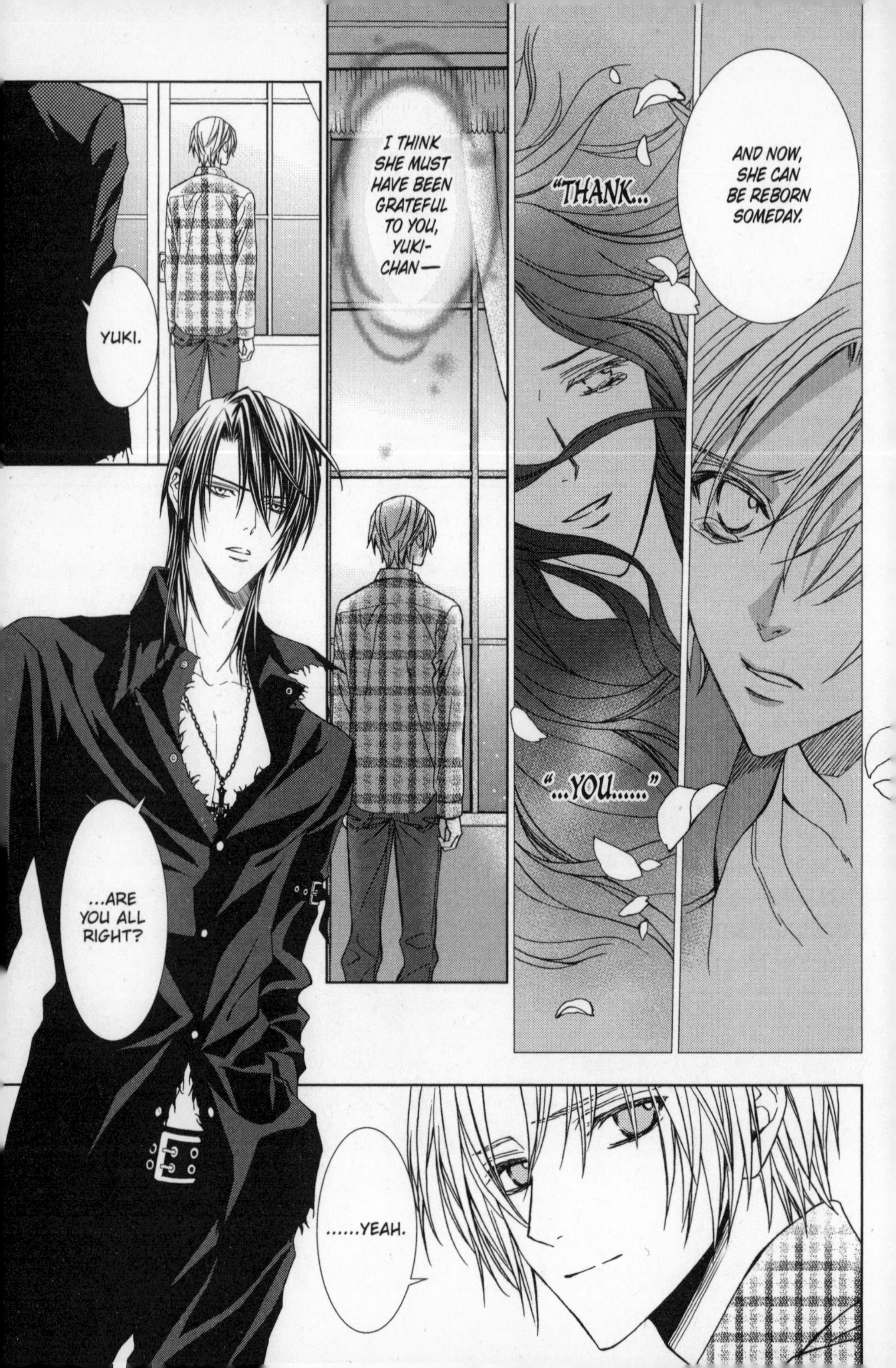
AND NOW, SHE CAN BE REBORN SOMEDAY.
"THANK...
"...YOU......"
I THINK SHE MUST HAVE BEEN GRATEFUL TO YOU, YUKI-CHAN—
YUKI.
...ARE YOU ALL RIGHT?
......YEAH.

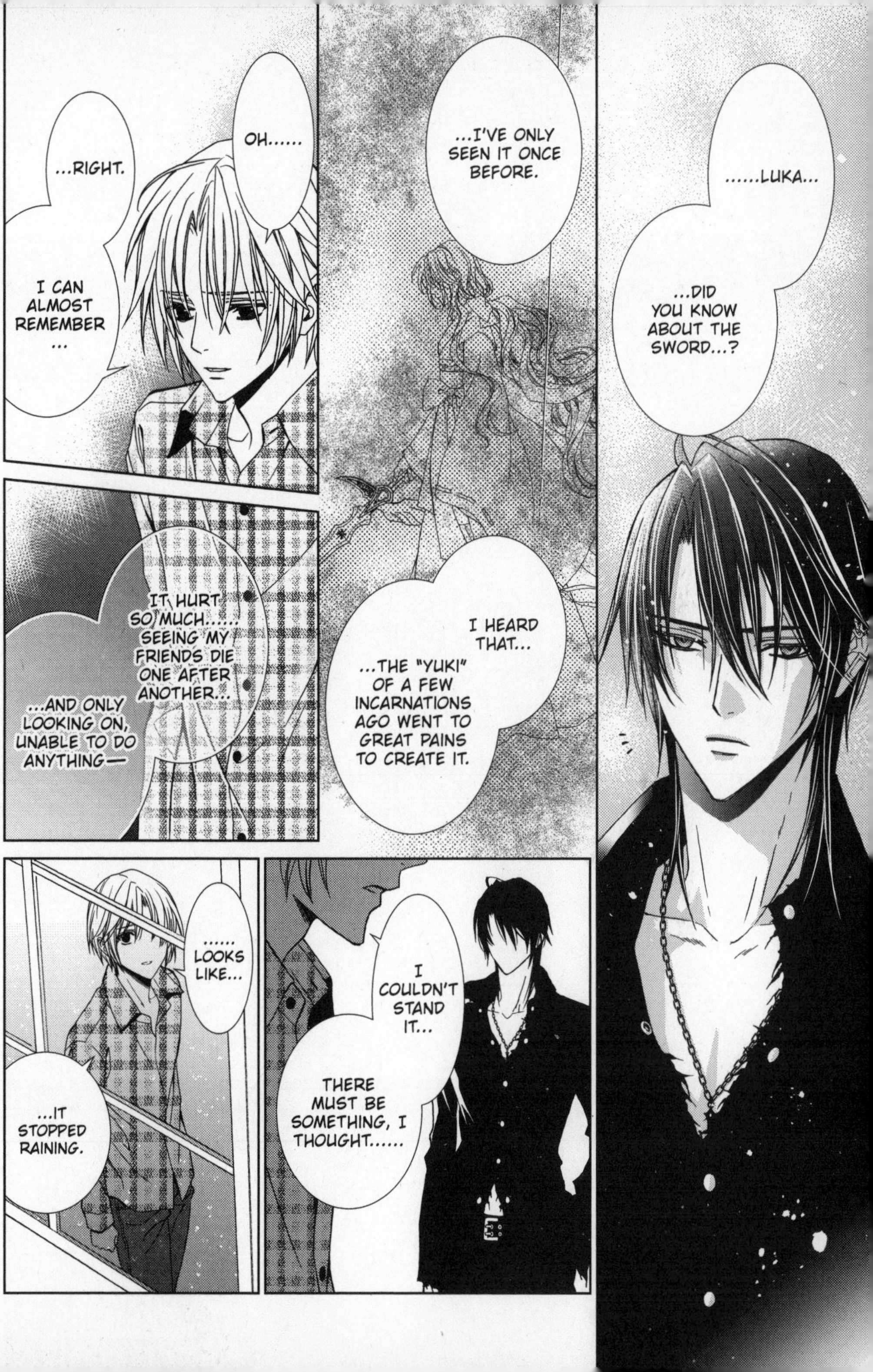
......LUKA...
...DID YOU KNOW ABOUT THE SWORD...?
...I'VE ONLY SEEN IT ONCE BEFORE.
I HEARD THAT...
...THE "YUKI" OF A FEW INCARNATIONS AGO WENT TO GREAT PAINS TO CREATE IT.
OH......
...RIGHT.
I CAN ALMOST REMEMBER...
IT HURT SO MUCH...... SEEING MY FRIENDS DIE ONE AFTER ANOTHER...
...AND ONLY LOOKING ON, UNABLE TO DO ANYTHING—
I COULDN'T STAND IT...
THERE MUST BE SOMETHING, I THOUGHT......
......LOOKS LIKE...
...IT STOPPED RAINING.

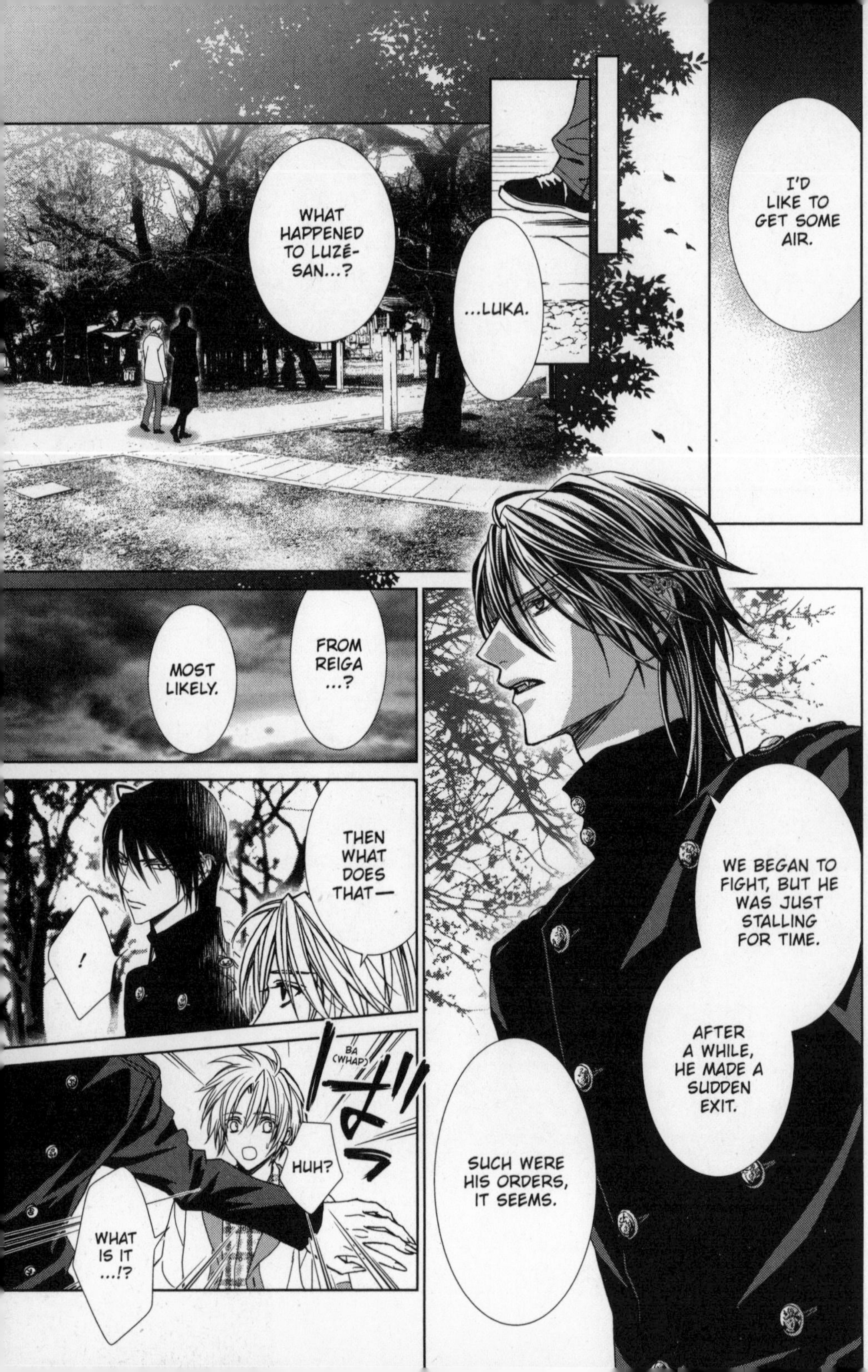
I'D LIKE TO GET SOME AIR.
...LUKA.
WHAT HAPPENED TO LUZÉ-SAN...?
WE BEGAN TO FIGHT, BUT HE WAS JUST STALLING FOR TIME.
AFTER A WHILE, HE MADE A SUDDEN EXIT.
SUCH WERE HIS ORDERS, IT SEEMS.
FROM REIGA...?
MOST LIKELY.
THEN WHAT DOES THAT—
!
BA (WHAP)
HUH?
WHAT IS IT...!?

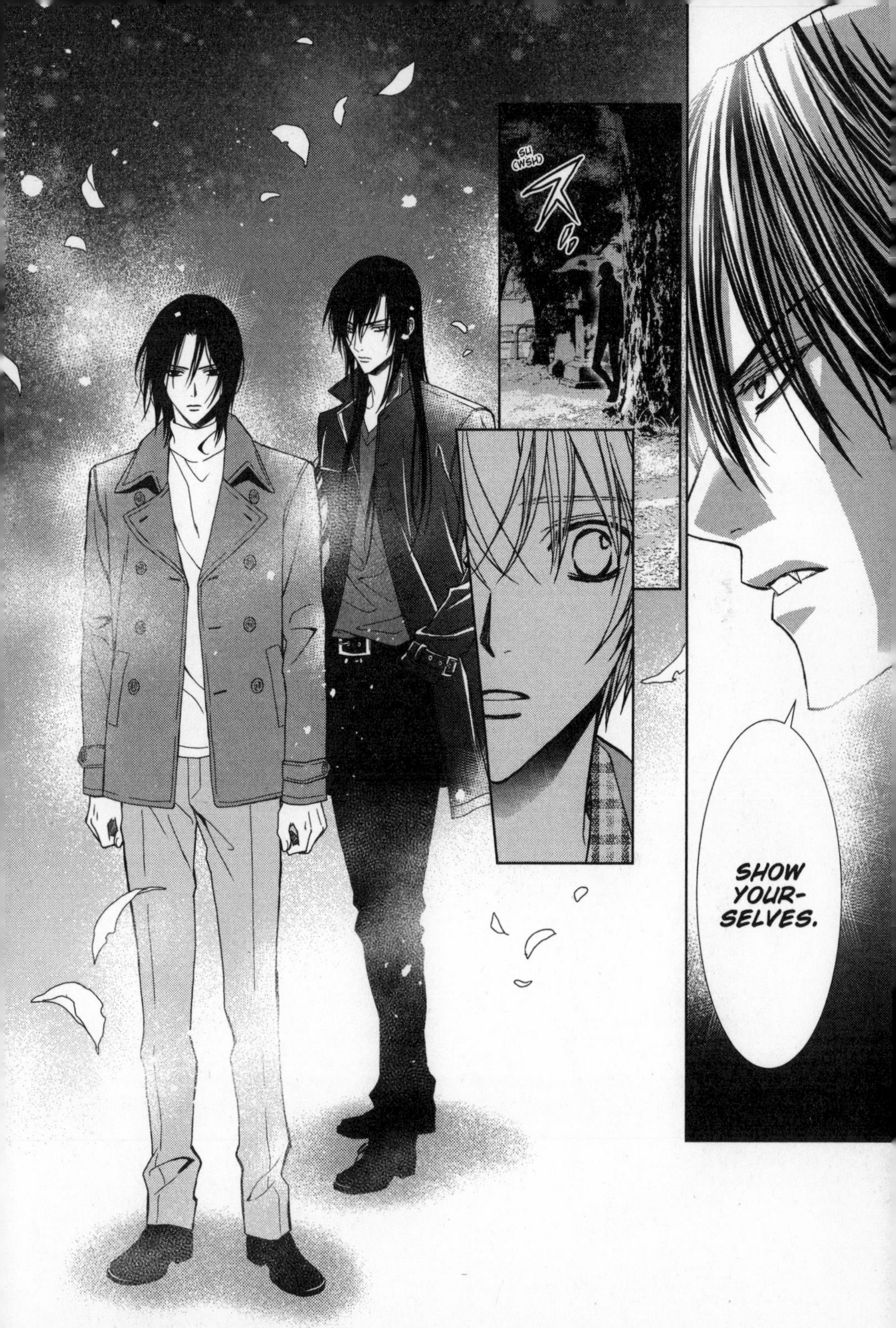
SHOW YOUR-SELVES.
SU (WSH)

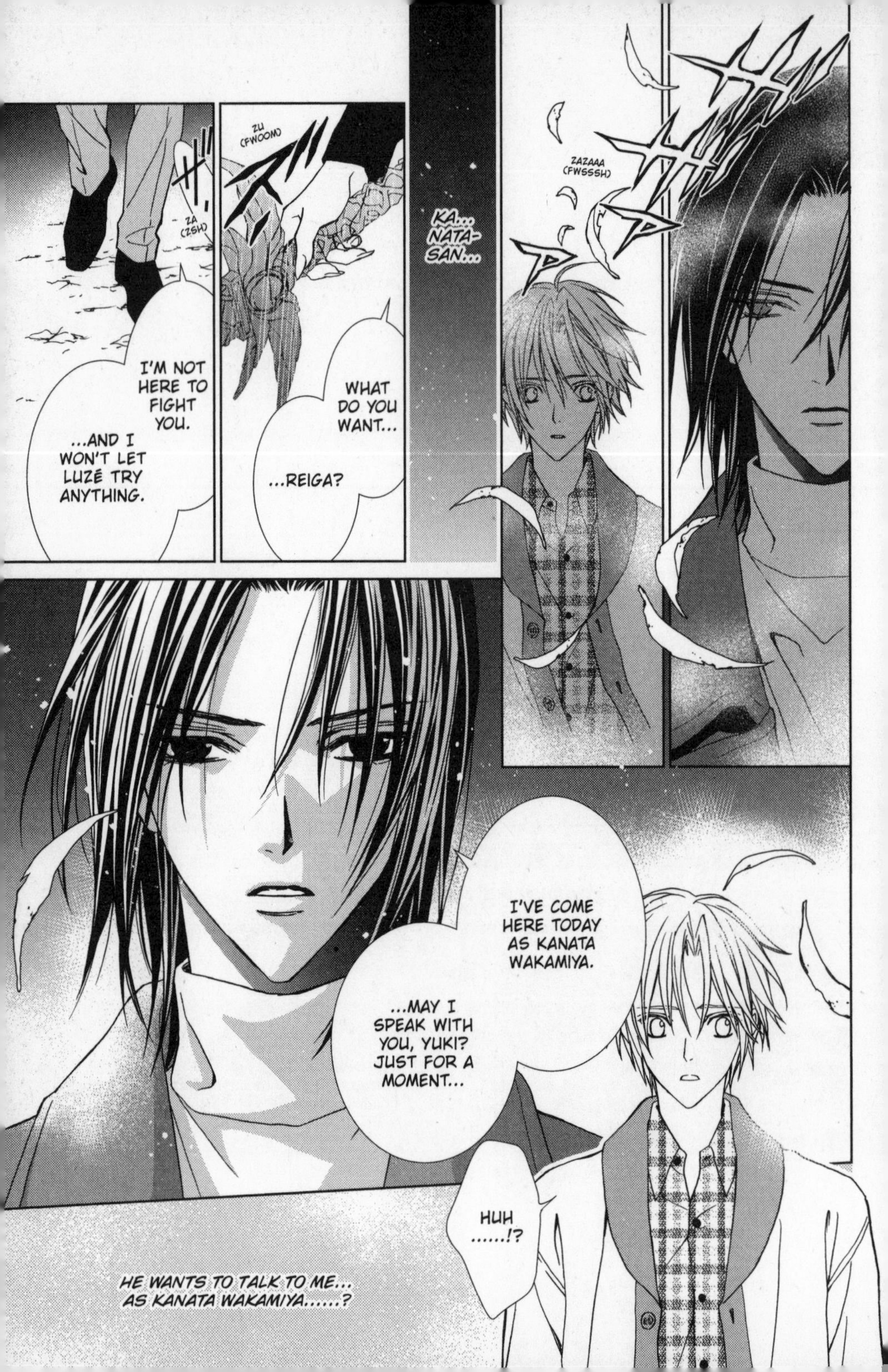
ZAZAAA (FWSSSH)
KA... NATA-SAN...
ZU (FWOOM)
WHAT DO YOU WANT...
...REIGA?
ZA (ZSH)
I'M NOT HERE TO FIGHT YOU.
...AND I WON'T LET LUZÉ TRY ANYTHING.
I'VE COME HERE TODAY AS KANATA WAKAMIYA.
...MAY I SPEAK WITH YOU, YUKI? JUST FOR A MOMENT...
HUH ......!?
HE WANTS TO TALK TO ME... AS KANATA WAKAMIYA......?

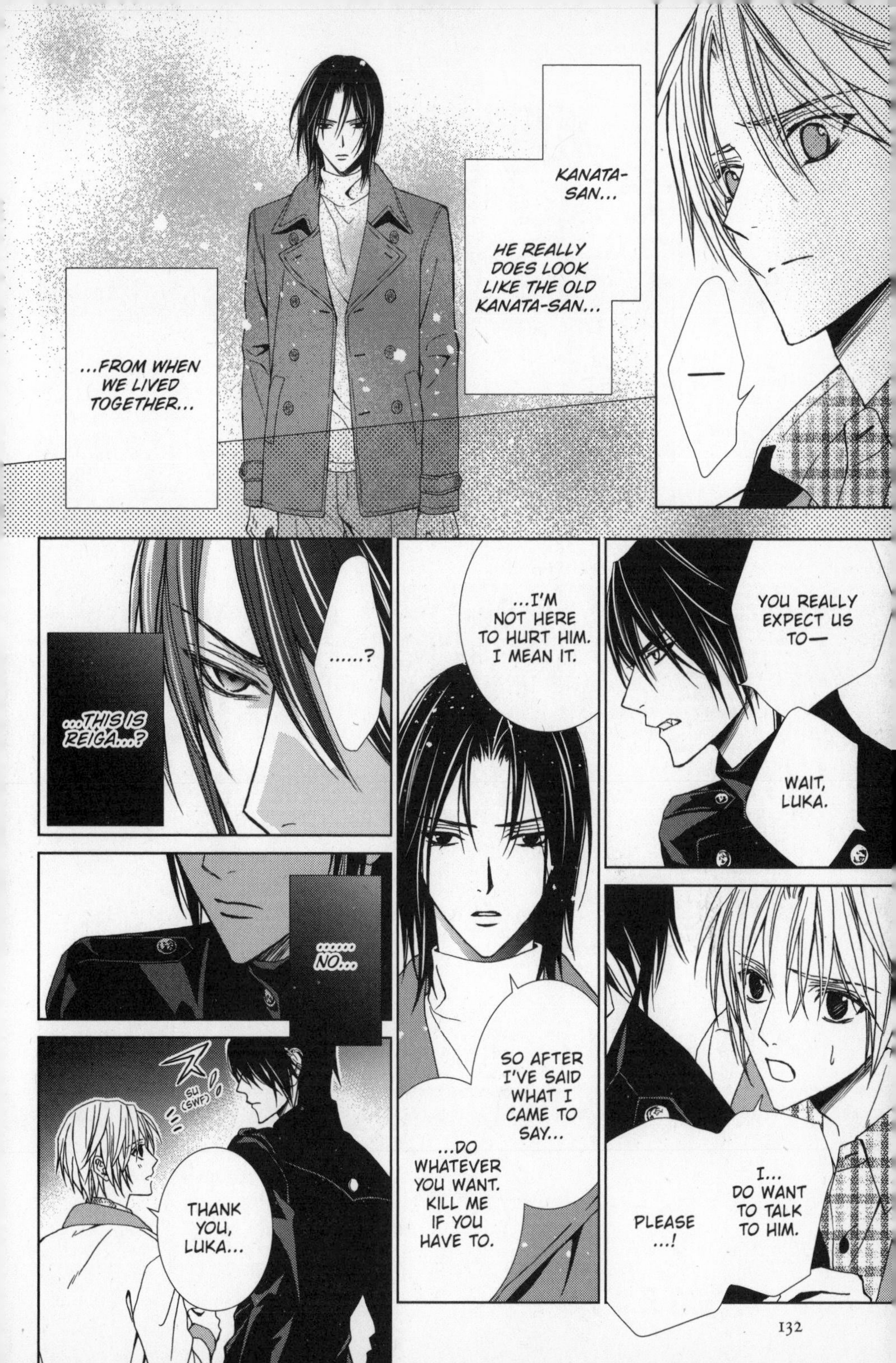

—
KANATA-SAN...
HE REALLY DOES LOOK LIKE THE OLD KANATA-SAN...
...FROM WHEN WE LIVED TOGETHER...
YOU REALLY EXPECT US TO—
WAIT, LUKA.
I... DO WANT TO TALK TO HIM.
PLEASE ...!
...I'M NOT HERE TO HURT HIM. I MEAN IT.
SO AFTER I'VE SAID WHAT I CAME TO SAY...
...DO WHATEVER YOU WANT. KILL ME IF YOU HAVE TO.
......?
...THIS IS REIGA...?
......NO...
ス
SU (SWF)
THANK YOU, LUKA...

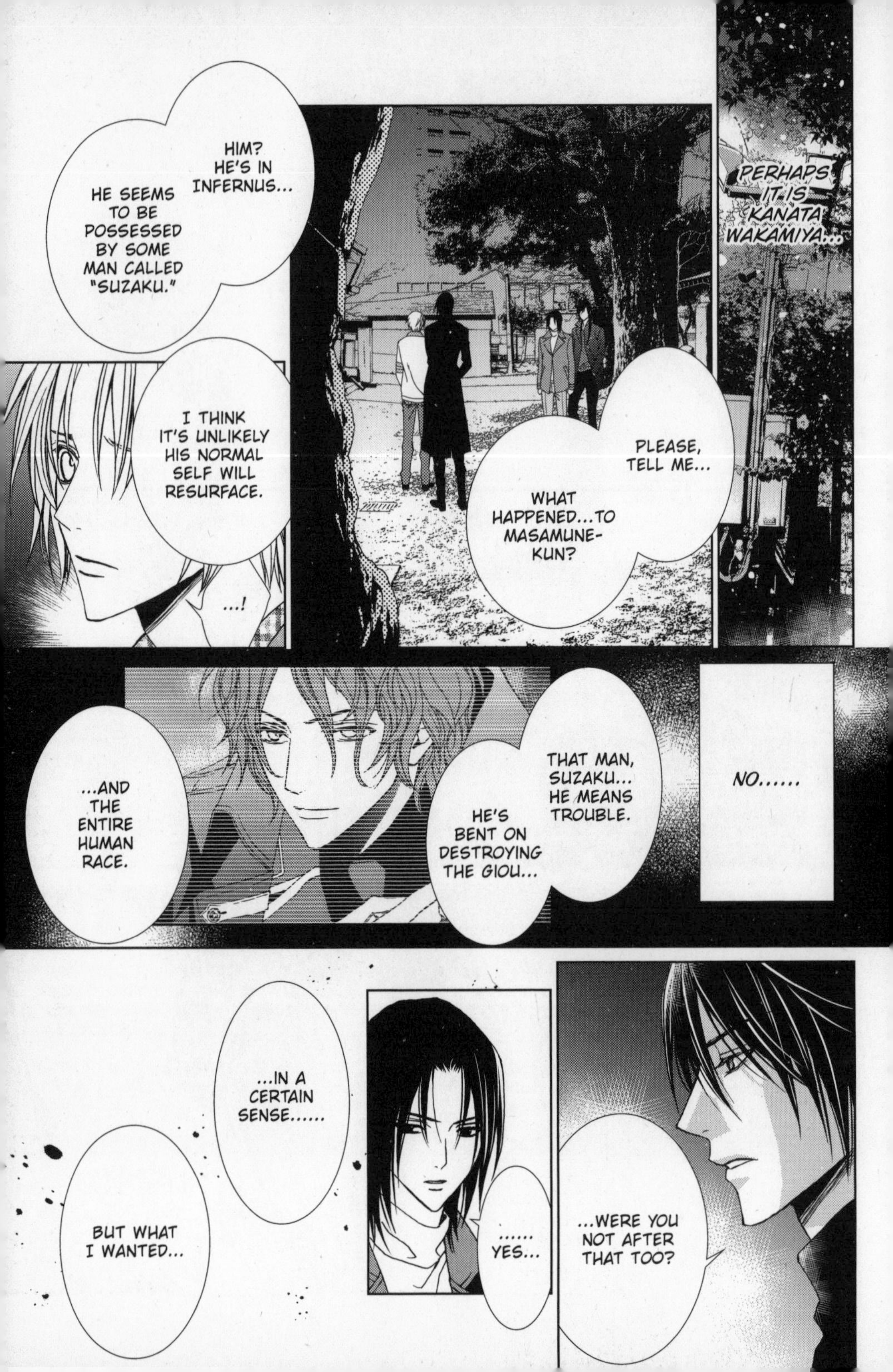
PERHAPS IT IS KANATA WAKAMIYA...
PLEASE, TELL ME...
WHAT HAPPENED...TO MASAMUNE-KUN?
HIM? HE'S IN INFERNUS...
HE SEEMS TO BE POSSESSED BY SOME MAN CALLED "SUZAKU."
I THINK IT'S UNLIKELY HIS NORMAL SELF WILL RESURFACE.
...!
NO......
THAT MAN, SUZAKU... HE MEANS TROUBLE.
HE'S BENT ON DESTROYING THE GIOU...
...AND THE ENTIRE HUMAN RACE.
...WERE YOU NOT AFTER THAT TOO?
......YES...
...IN A CERTAIN SENSE......
BUT WHAT I WANTED...

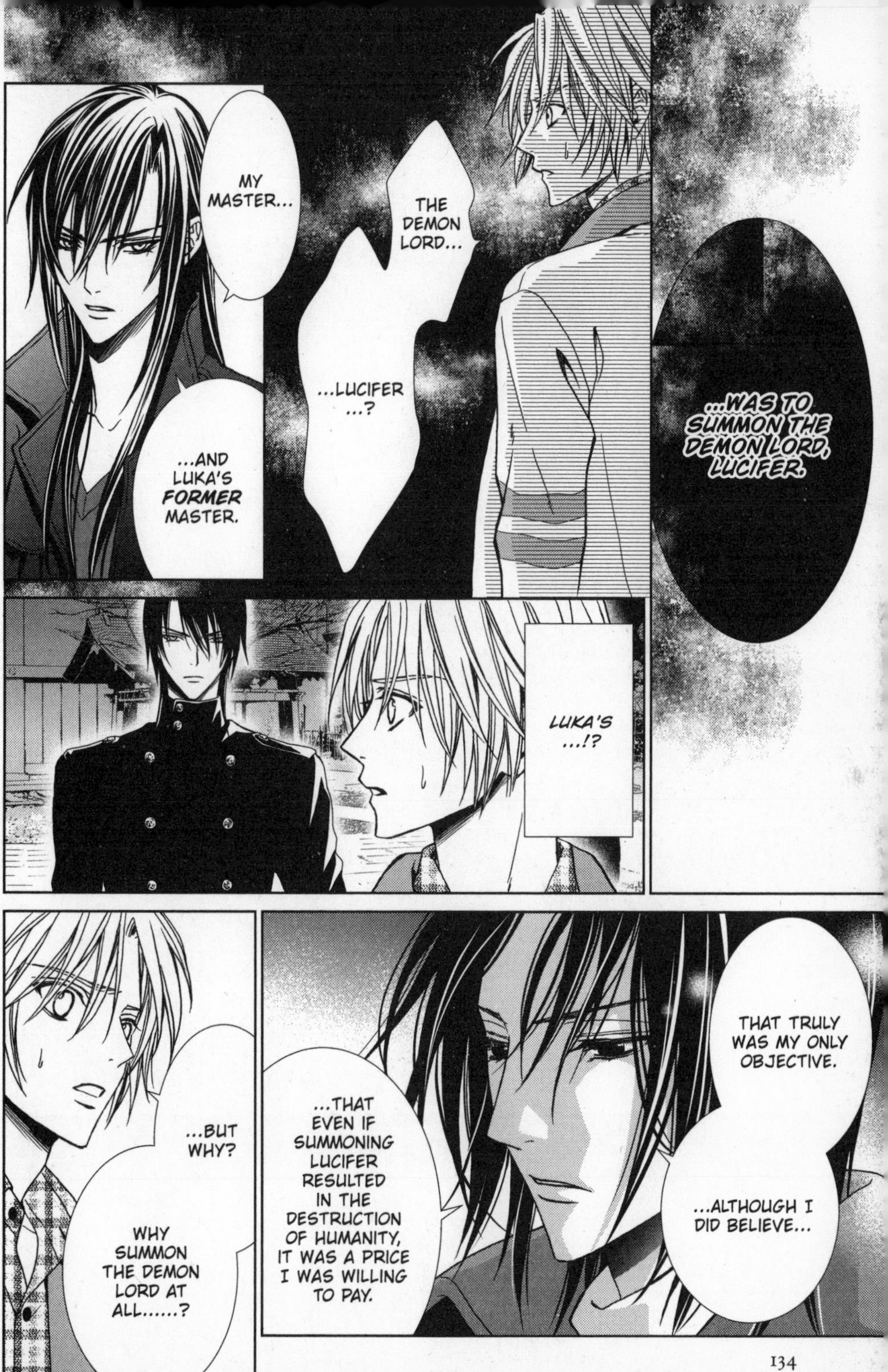
...WAS TO SUMMON THE DEMON LORD, LUCIFER.
THE DEMON LORD...
...LUCIFER...?
MY MASTER...
...AND LUKA'S *FORMER* MASTER.
LUKA'S ...!?
THAT TRULY WAS MY ONLY OBJECTIVE.
...ALTHOUGH I DID BELIEVE...
...THAT EVEN IF SUMMONING LUCIFER RESULTED IN THE DESTRUCTION OF HUMANITY, IT WAS A PRICE I WAS WILLING TO PAY.
...BUT WHY?
WHY SUMMON THE DEMON LORD AT ALL......?

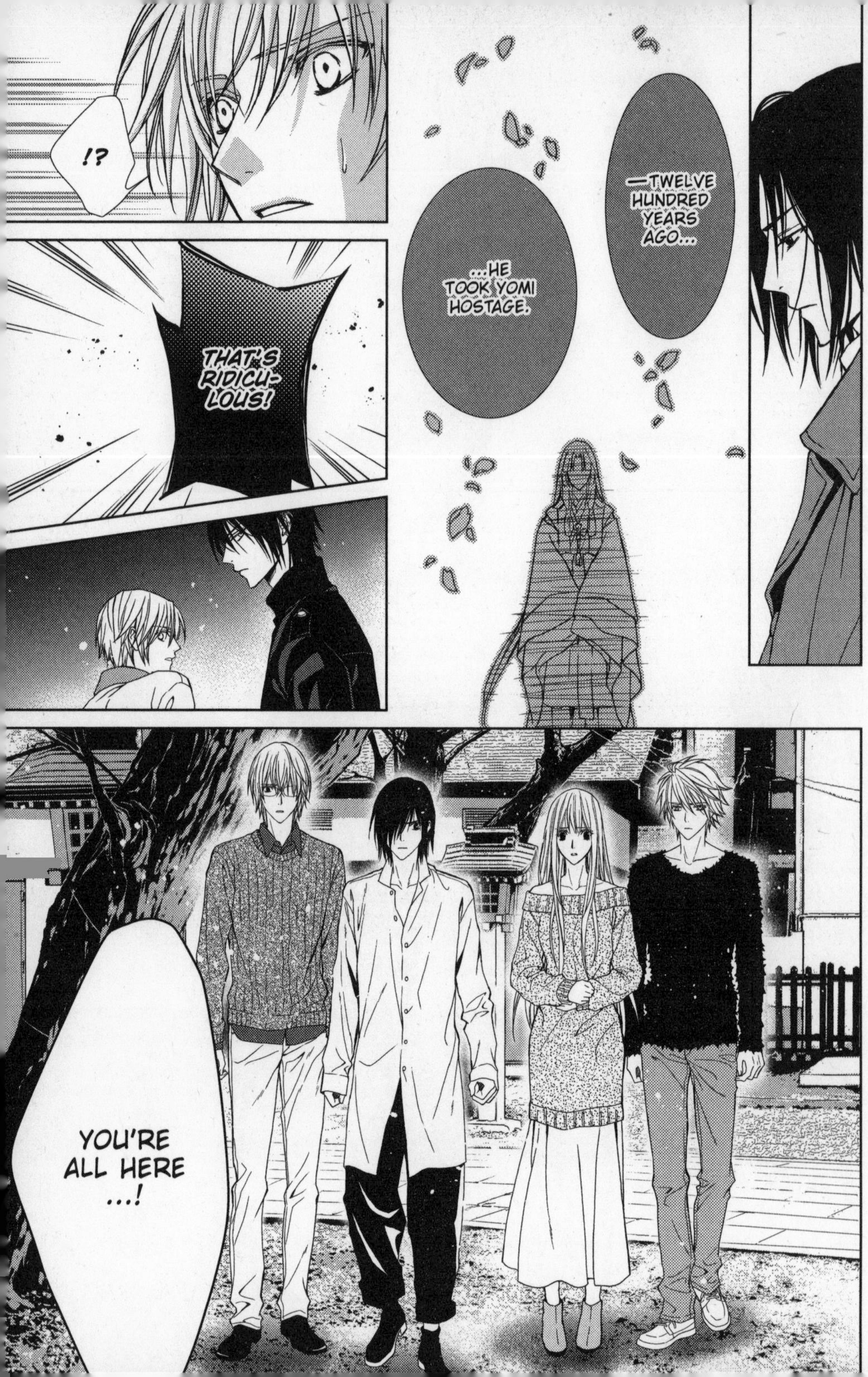
—TWELVE HUNDRED YEARS AGO...
...HE TOOK YOMI HOSTAGE.
!?
THAT'S RIDICU-LOUS!
YOU'RE ALL HERE ...!

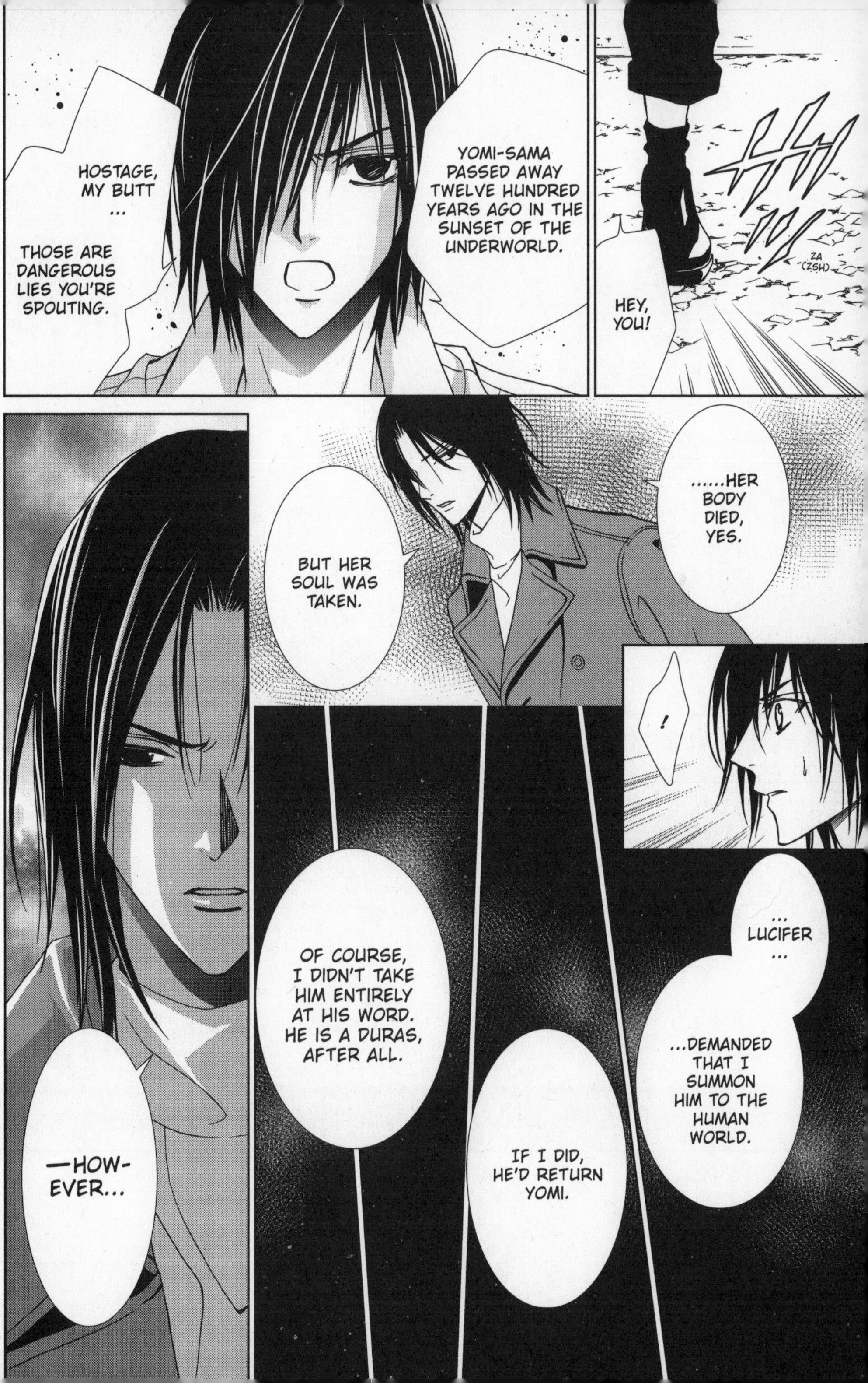

ZA (ZSH)
HEY, YOU!
YOMI-SAMA PASSED AWAY TWELVE HUNDRED YEARS AGO IN THE SUNSET OF THE UNDERWORLD.
HOSTAGE, MY BUTT ...
THOSE ARE DANGEROUS LIES YOU'RE SPOUTING.
......HER BODY DIED, YES.
BUT HER SOUL WAS TAKEN.
!
... LUCIFER ...
...DEMANDED THAT I SUMMON HIM TO THE HUMAN WORLD.
IF I DID, HE'D RETURN YOMI.
OF COURSE, I DIDN'T TAKE HIM ENTIRELY AT HIS WORD. HE IS A DURAS, AFTER ALL.
—HOW-EVER...

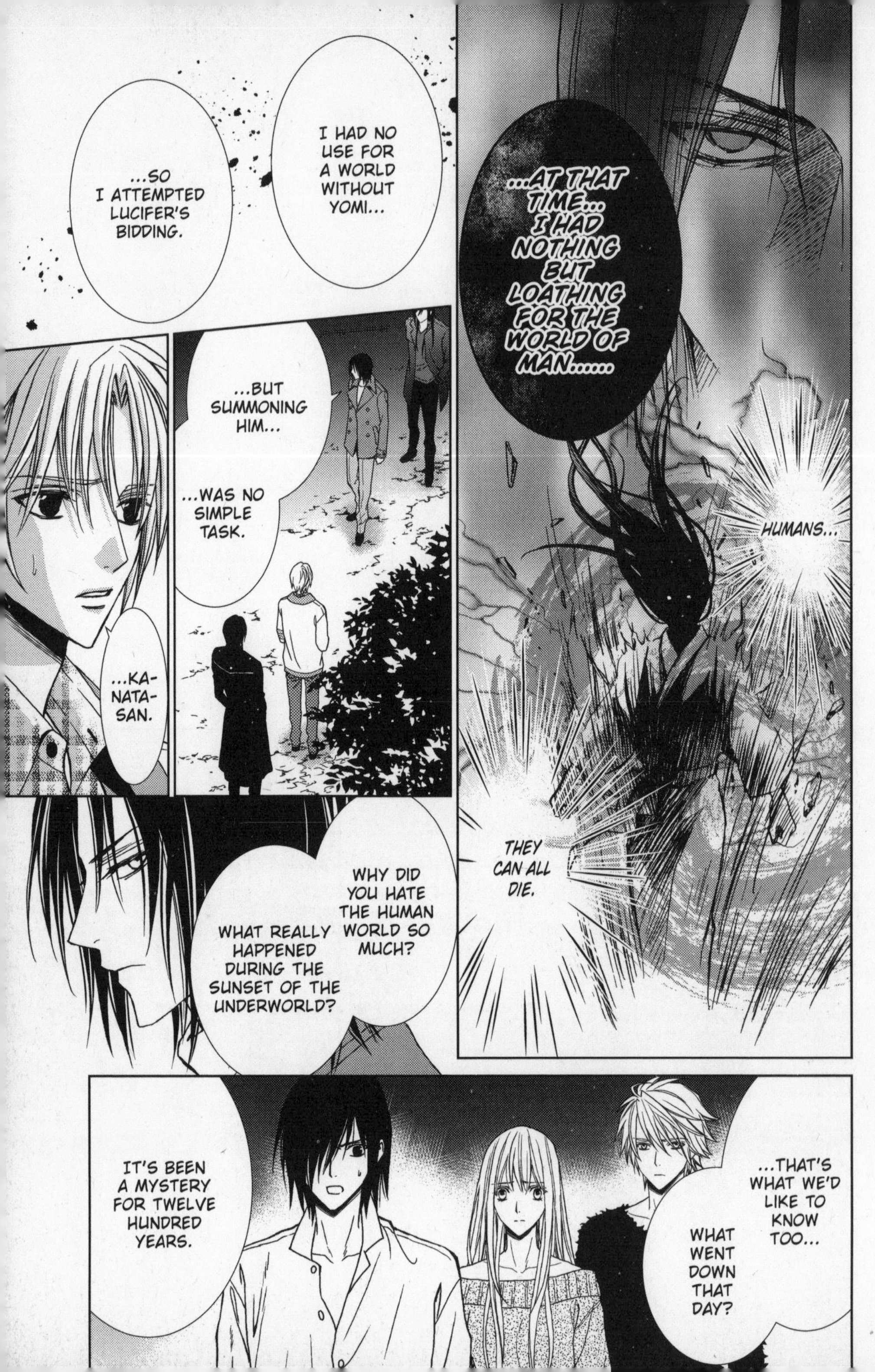
...AT THAT TIME... I HAD NOTHING BUT LOATHING FOR THE WORLD OF MAN......
HUMANS...
THEY CAN ALL DIE.
I HAD NO USE FOR A WORLD WITHOUT YOMI...
...SO I ATTEMPTED LUCIFER'S BIDDING.
...BUT SUMMONING HIM...
...WAS NO SIMPLE TASK.
...KA-NATA-SAN.
WHY DID YOU HATE THE HUMAN WORLD SO MUCH?
WHAT REALLY HAPPENED DURING THE SUNSET OF THE UNDERWORLD?
...THAT'S WHAT WE'D LIKE TO KNOW TOO...
WHAT WENT DOWN THAT DAY?
IT'S BEEN A MYSTERY FOR TWELVE HUNDRED YEARS.

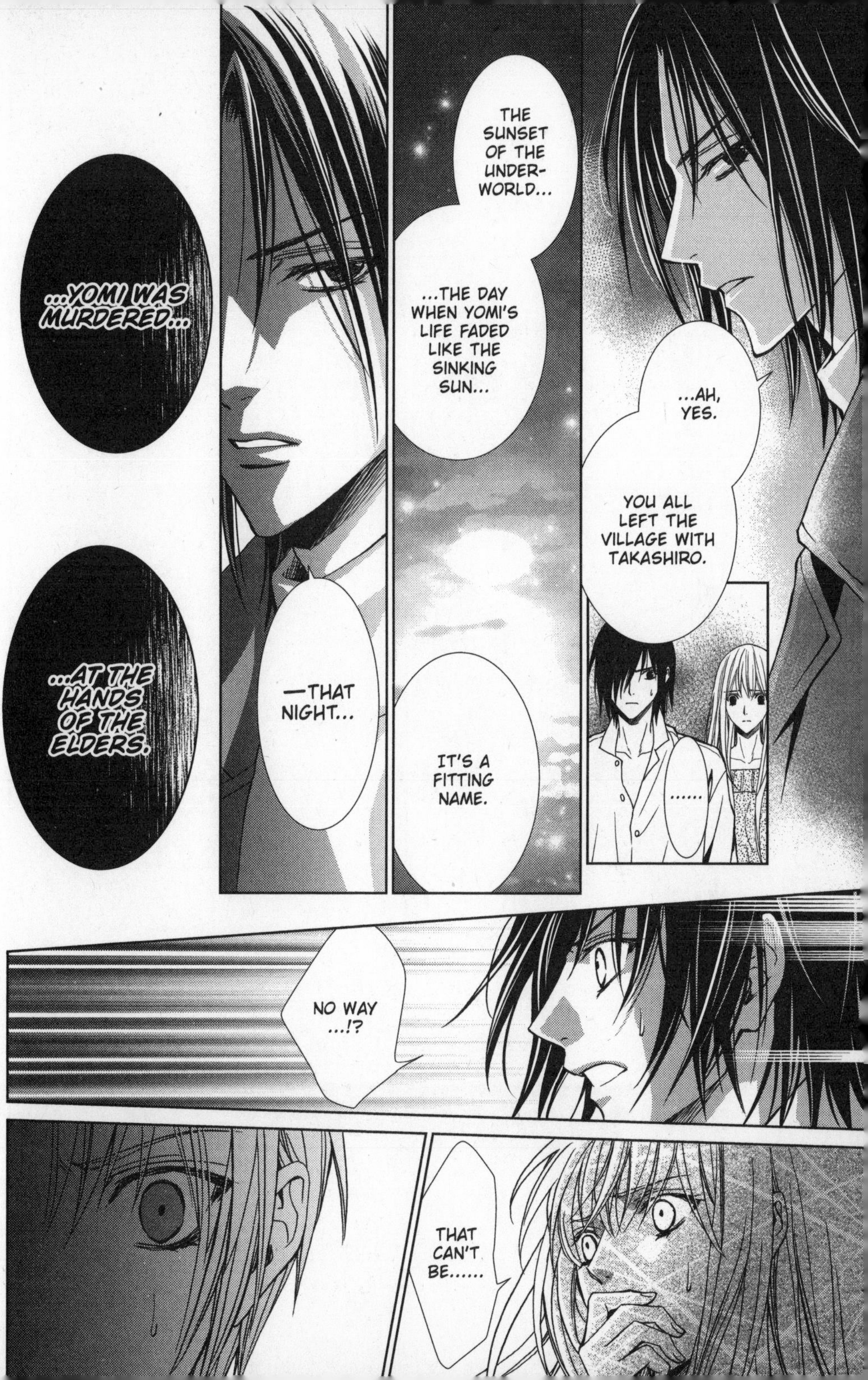
...AH, YES.
YOU ALL LEFT THE VILLAGE WITH TAKASHIRO.
......
THE SUNSET OF THE UNDER-WORLD...
...THE DAY WHEN YOMI'S LIFE FADED LIKE THE SINKING SUN...
IT'S A FITTING NAME.
—THAT NIGHT...
...YOMI WAS MURDERED...
...AT THE HANDS OF THE ELDERS.
NO WAY ...!?
THAT CAN'T BE......

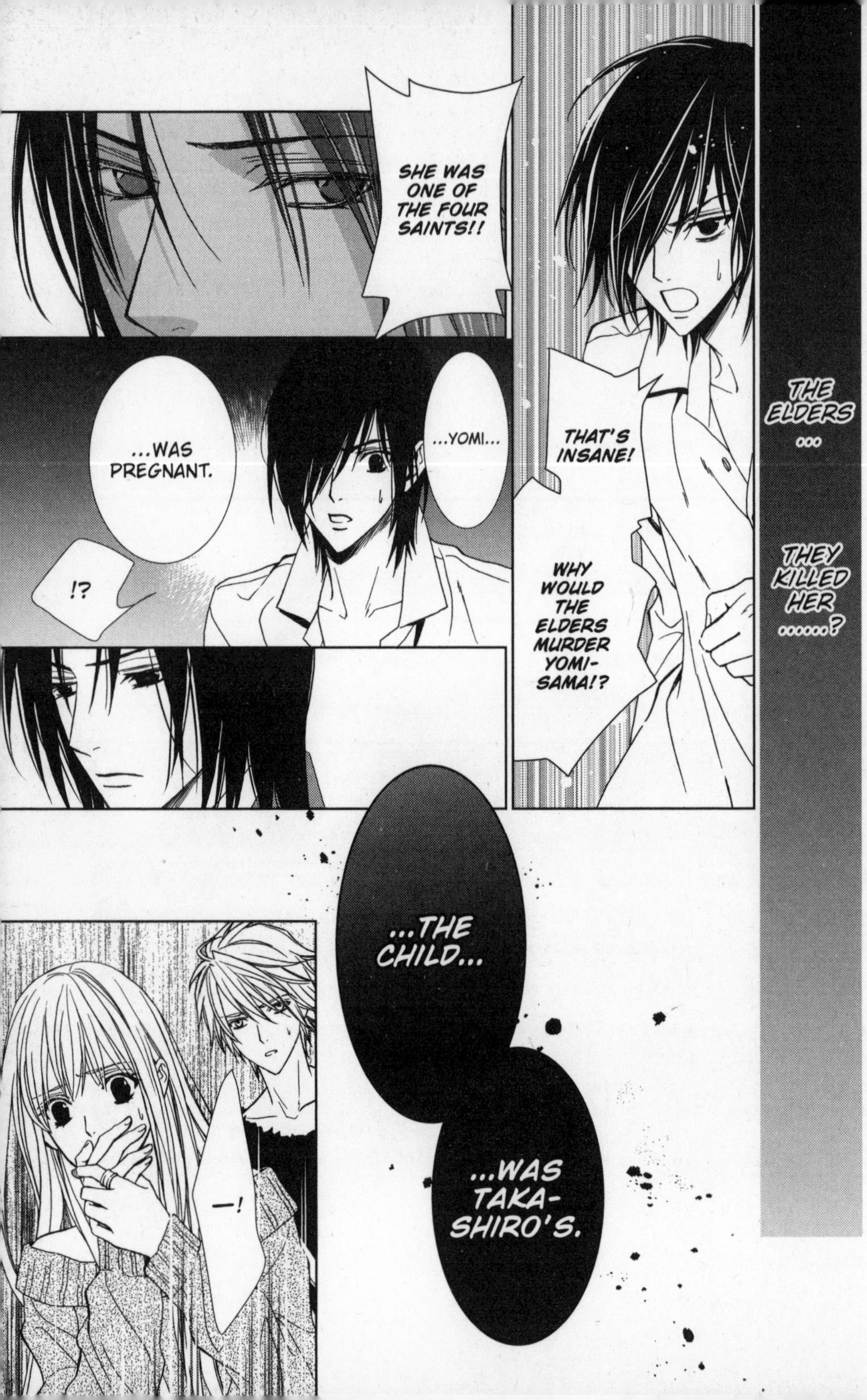

THE ELDERS...
THEY KILLED HER ....?
THAT'S INSANE!
WHY WOULD THE ELDERS MURDER YOMI-SAMA!?
SHE WAS ONE OF THE FOUR SAINTS!!
...YOMI...
...WAS PREGNANT.
!?
...THE CHILD...
...WAS TAKA-SHIRO'S.
—!

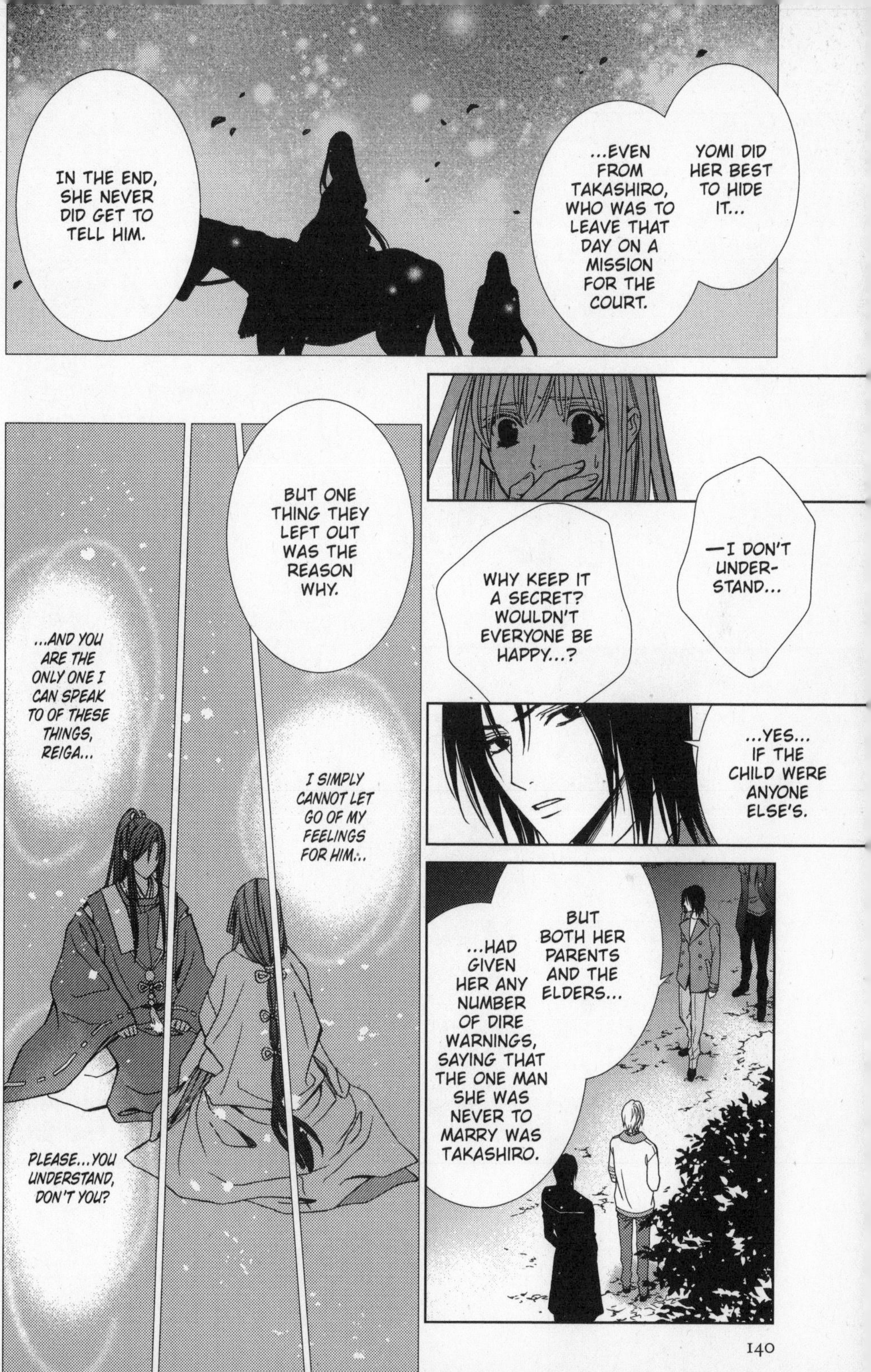
YOMI DID HER BEST TO HIDE IT...
...EVEN FROM TAKASHIRO, WHO WAS TO LEAVE THAT DAY ON A MISSION FOR THE COURT.
IN THE END, SHE NEVER DID GET TO TELL HIM.
—I DON'T UNDER-STAND...
WHY KEEP IT A SECRET? WOULDN'T EVERYONE BE HAPPY...?
...YES... IF THE CHILD WERE ANYONE ELSE'S.
BUT BOTH HER PARENTS AND THE ELDERS...
...HAD GIVEN HER ANY NUMBER OF DIRE WARNINGS, SAYING THAT THE ONE MAN SHE WAS NEVER TO MARRY WAS TAKASHIRO.
BUT ONE THING THEY LEFT OUT WAS THE REASON WHY.
I SIMPLY CANNOT LET GO OF MY FEELINGS FOR HIM...
...AND YOU ARE THE ONLY ONE I CAN SPEAK TO OF THESE THINGS, REIGA...
PLEASE...YOU UNDERSTAND, DON'T YOU?

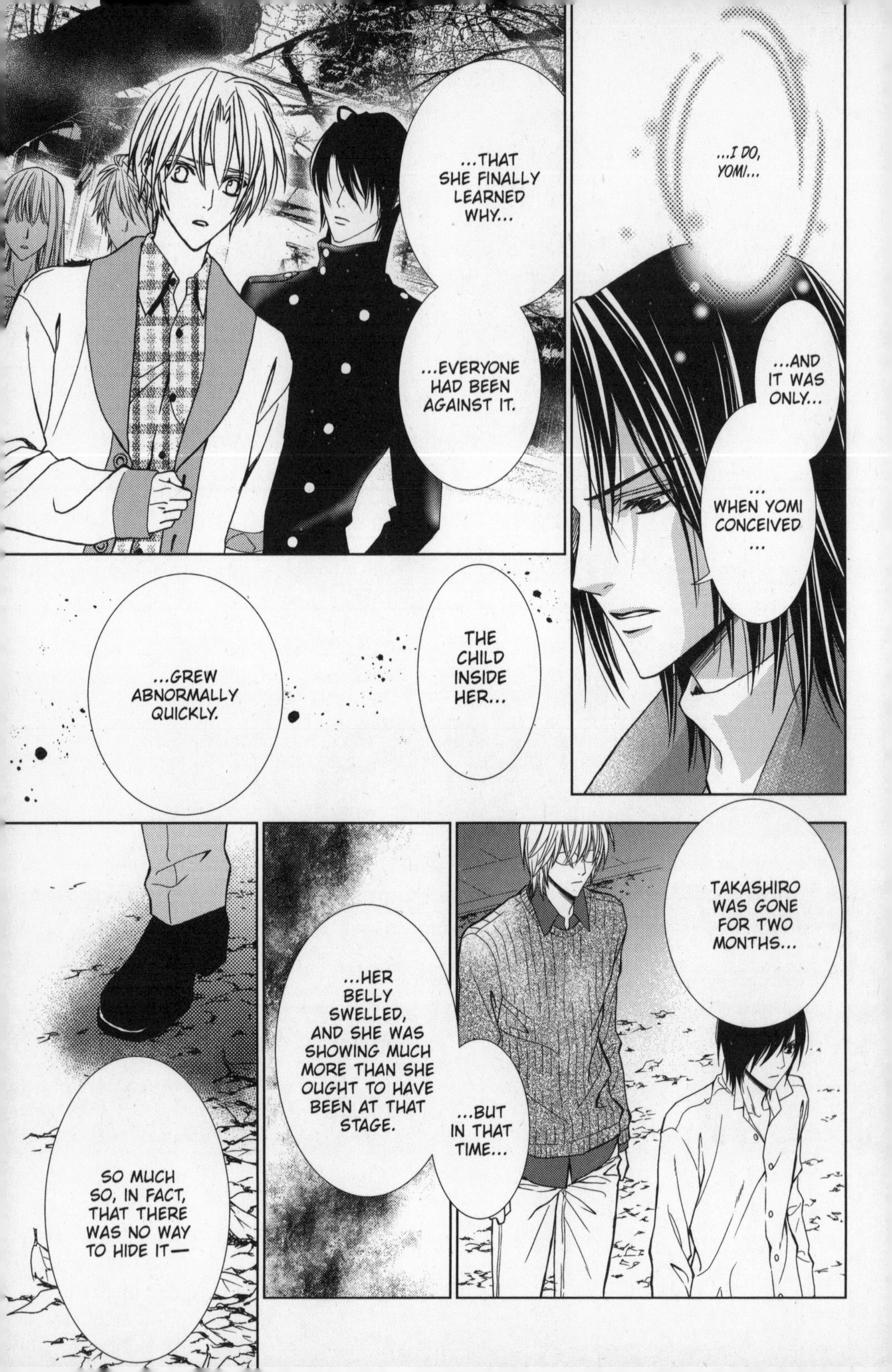
...I DO, YOMI...
...AND IT WAS ONLY...
... WHEN YOMI CONCEIVED ...
...THAT SHE FINALLY LEARNED WHY...
...EVERYONE HAD BEEN AGAINST IT.
THE CHILD INSIDE HER...
...GREW ABNORMALLY QUICKLY.
TAKASHIRO WAS GONE FOR TWO MONTHS...
...BUT IN THAT TIME...
...HER BELLY SWELLED, AND SHE WAS SHOWING MUCH MORE THAN SHE OUGHT TO HAVE BEEN AT THAT STAGE.
SO MUCH SO, IN FACT, THAT THERE WAS NO WAY TO HIDE IT—

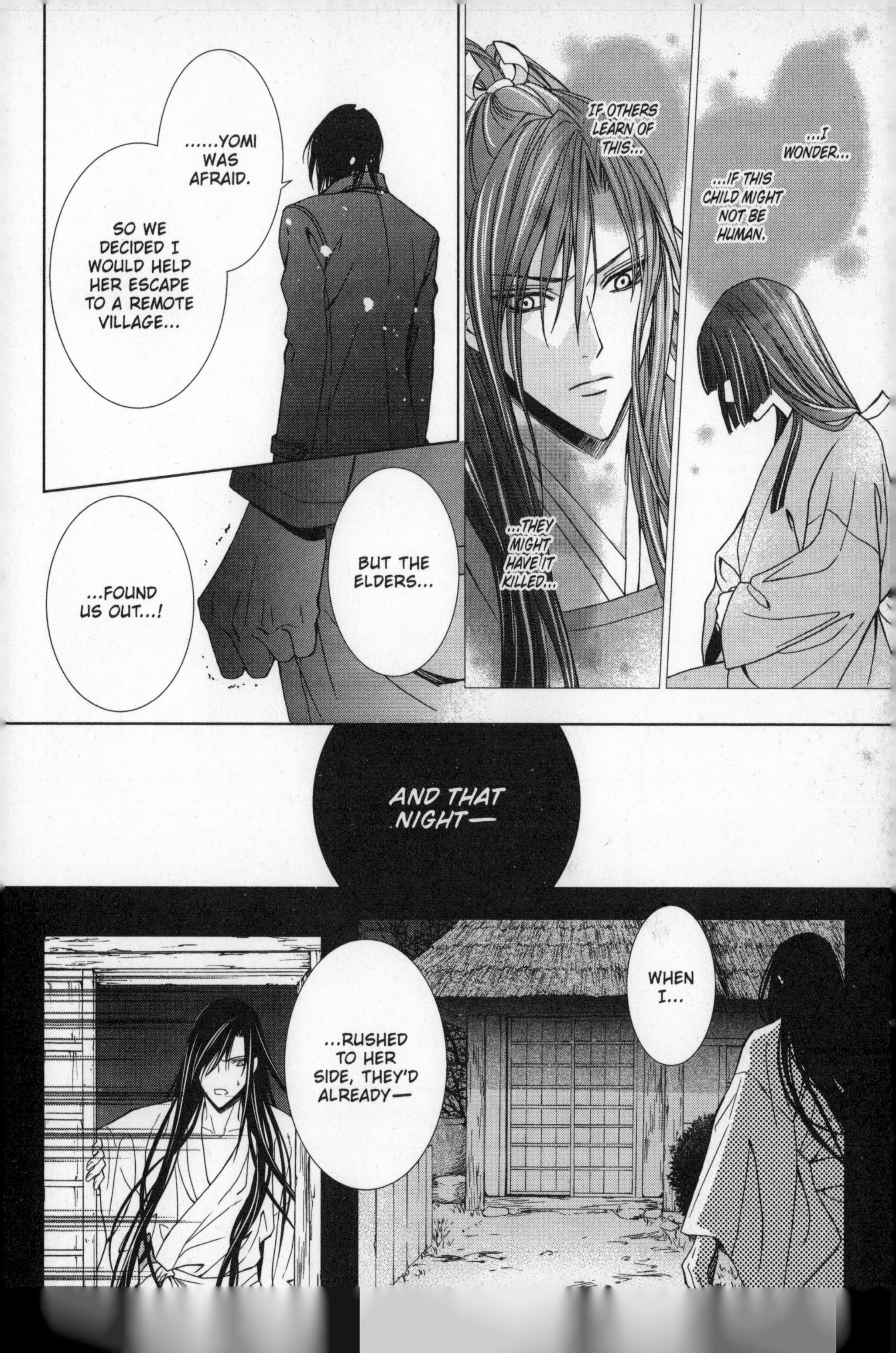
...I WONDER...
...IF THIS CHILD MIGHT NOT BE HUMAN.
IF OTHERS LEARN OF THIS...
...THEY MIGHT HAVE IT KILLED...
......YOMI WAS AFRAID.
SO WE DECIDED I WOULD HELP HER ESCAPE TO A REMOTE VILLAGE...
BUT THE ELDERS...
...FOUND US OUT...!
AND THAT NIGHT—
WHEN I...
...RUSHED TO HER SIDE, THEY'D ALREADY—

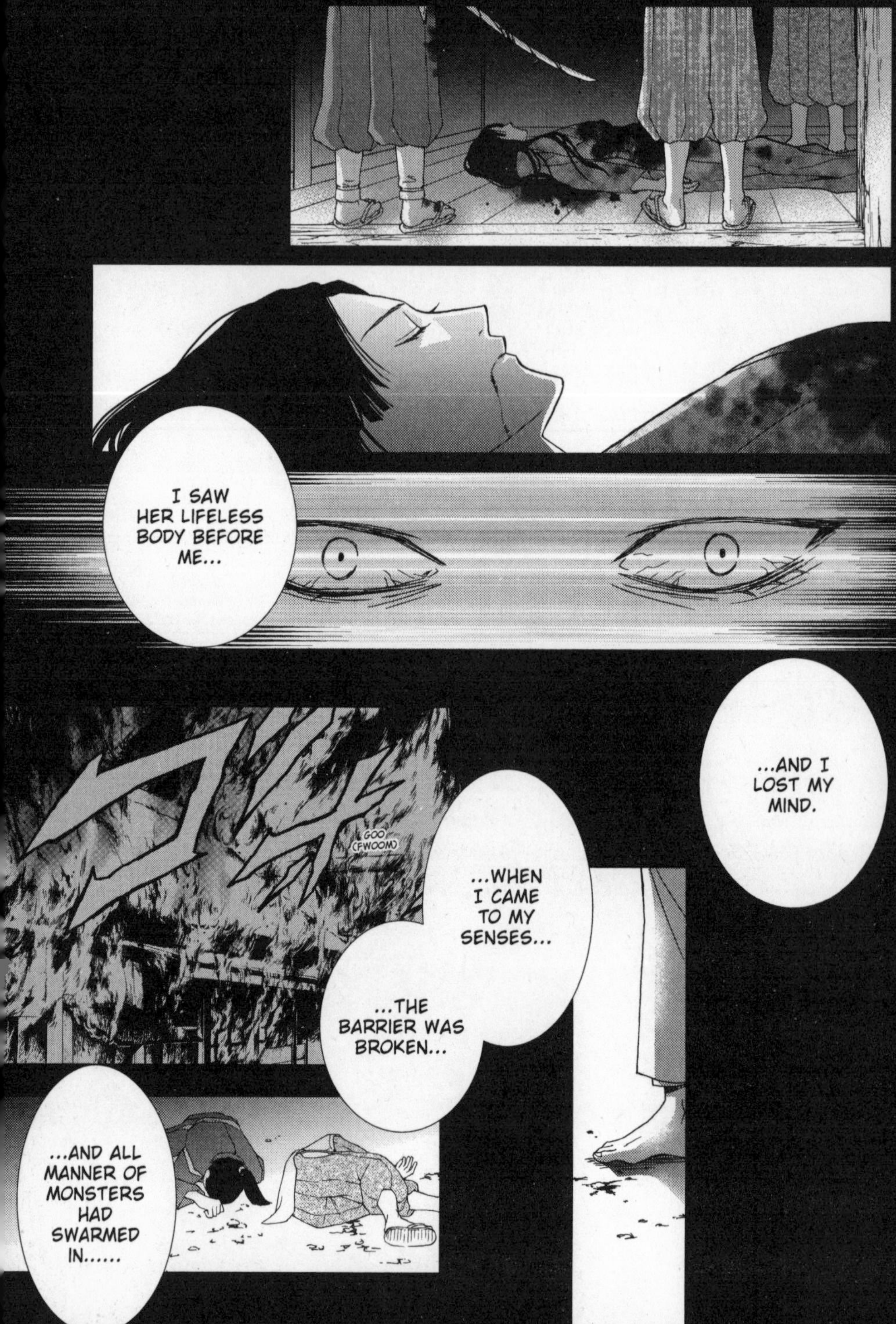
I SAW HER LIFELESS BODY BEFORE ME...
...AND I LOST MY MIND.
...WHEN I CAME TO MY SENSES...
GOO (FWOOM)
...THE BARRIER WAS BROKEN...
...AND ALL MANNER OF MONSTERS HAD SWARMED IN......

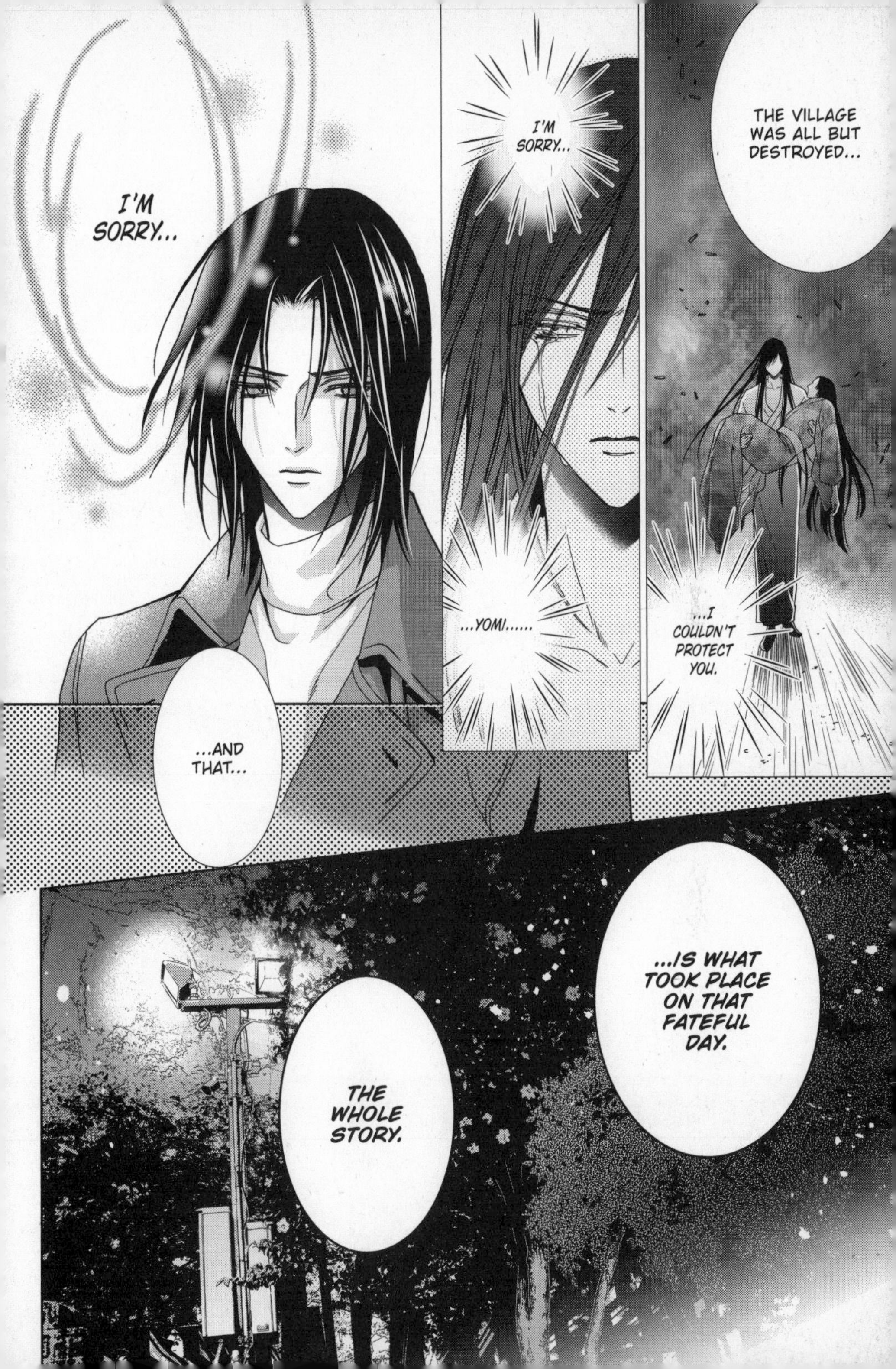
THE VILLAGE WAS ALL BUT DESTROYED...
...I COULDN'T PROTECT YOU.
I'M SORRY...
...YOMI......
I'M SORRY...
...AND THAT...
...IS WHAT TOOK PLACE ON THAT FATEFUL DAY.
THE WHOLE STORY.

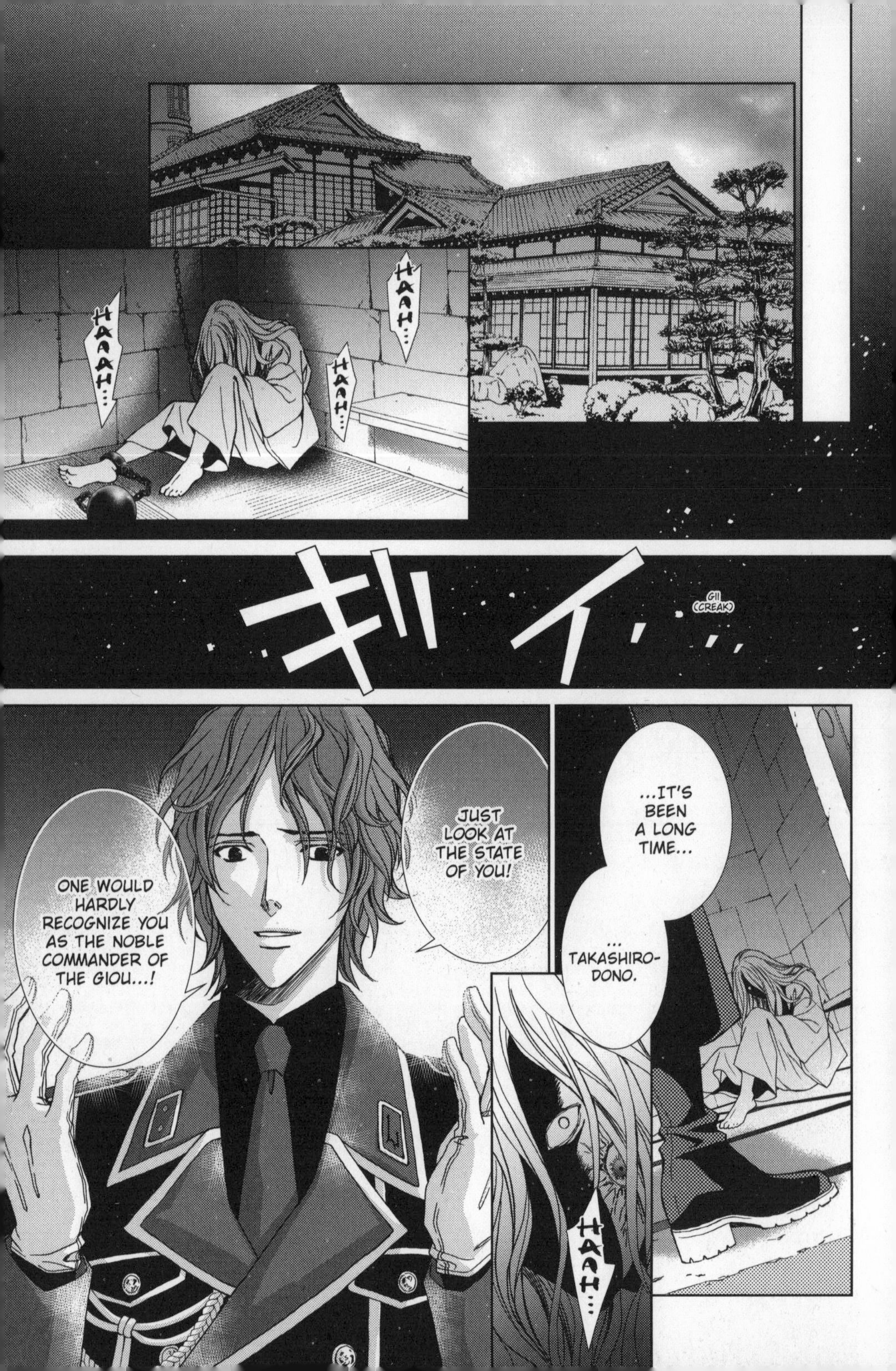
HAAAH...
HAAH...
HAAAH...
キリイ...
GII (CREAK)
...IT'S BEEN A LONG TIME...
...TAKASHIRO-DONO.
HAAH...
JUST LOOK AT THE STATE OF YOU!
ONE WOULD HARDLY RECOGNIZE YOU AS THE NOBLE COMMANDER OF THE GIOU...!

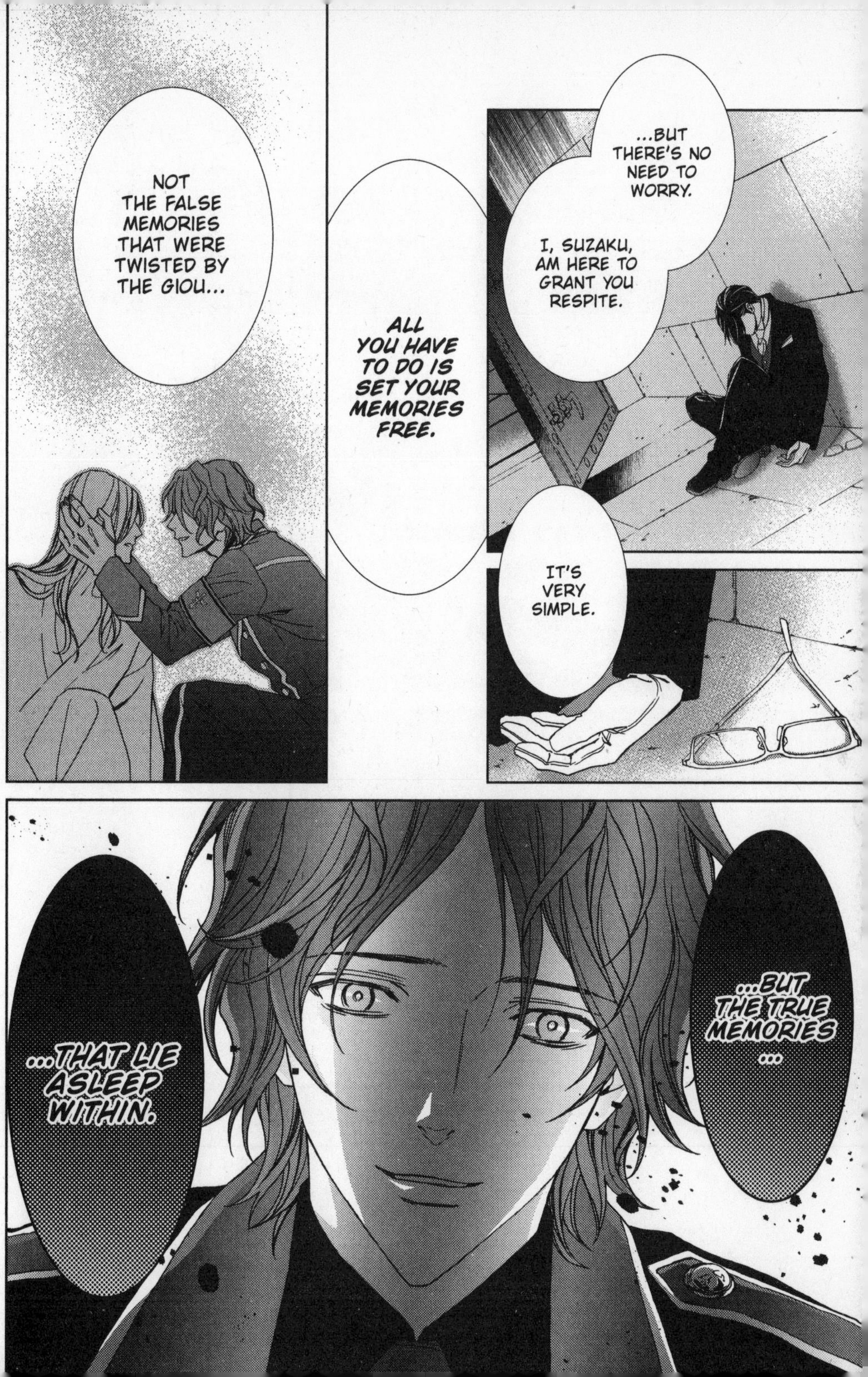

...BUT THERE'S NO NEED TO WORRY.
I, SUZAKU, AM HERE TO GRANT YOU RESPITE.
IT'S VERY SIMPLE.
ALL YOU HAVE TO DO IS SET YOUR MEMORIES FREE.
NOT THE FALSE MEMORIES THAT WERE TWISTED BY THE GIOU...
...BUT THE TRUE MEMORIES...
...THAT LIE ASLEEP WITHIN.

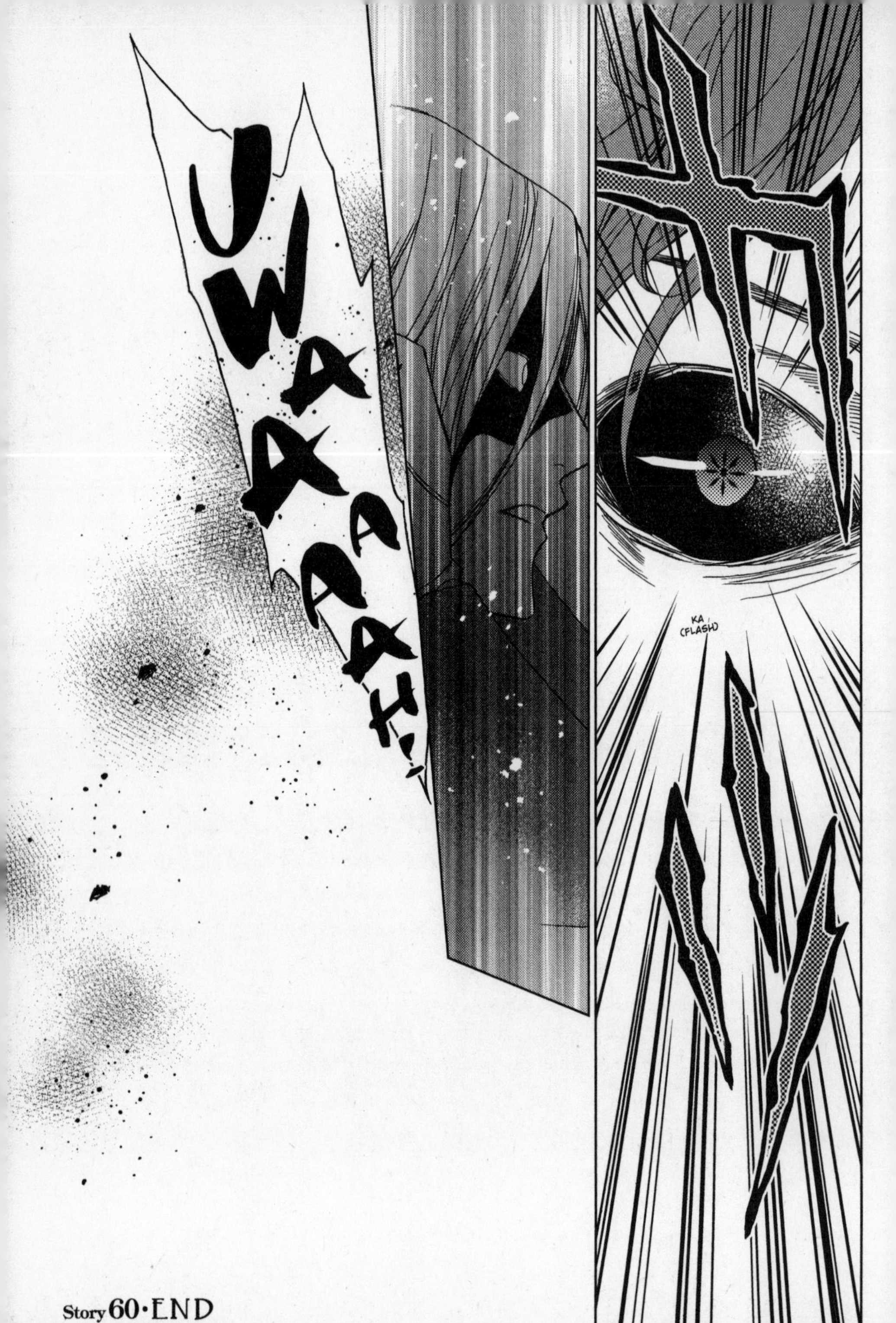
KA
(FLASH)
UWAAAAAH!!

Story 60 • END

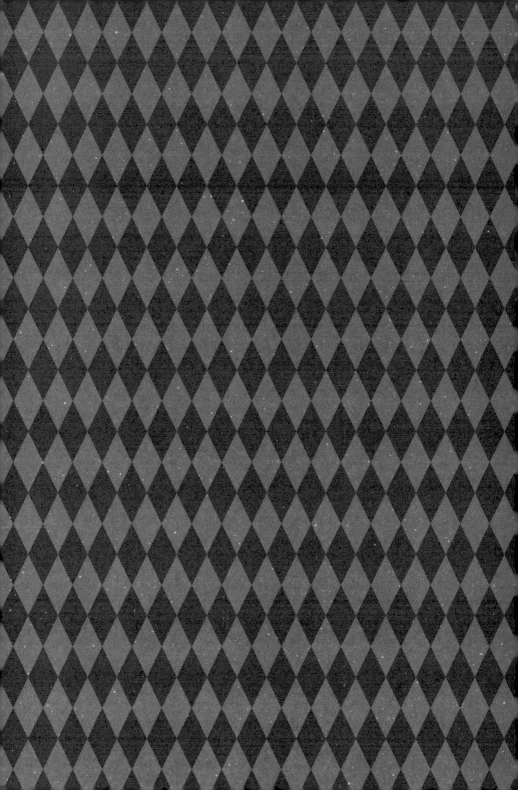

Last Story
AT THE END OF THE BETRAYAL

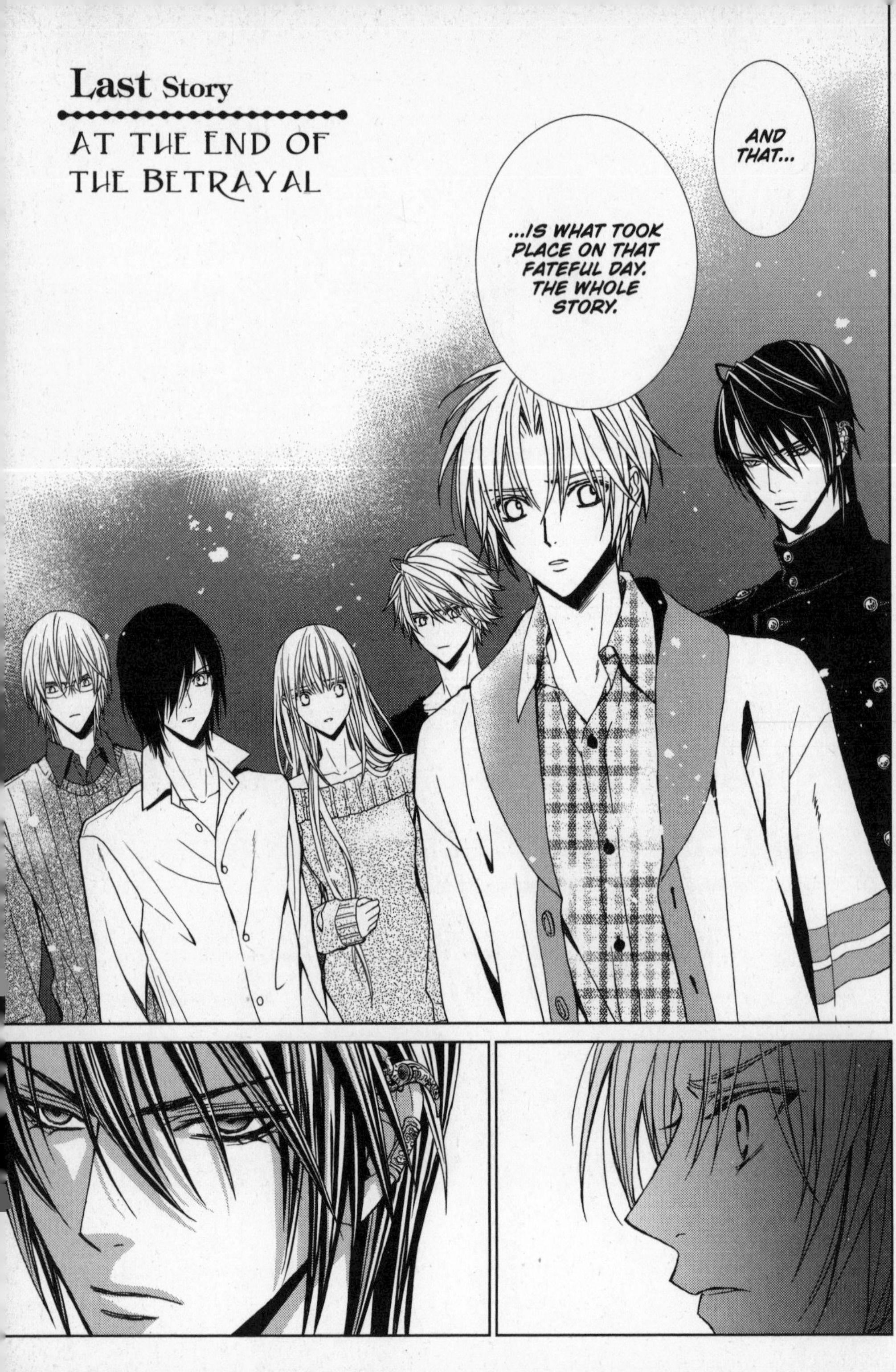
AND THAT...
...IS WHAT TOOK PLACE ON THAT FATEFUL DAY. THE WHOLE STORY.

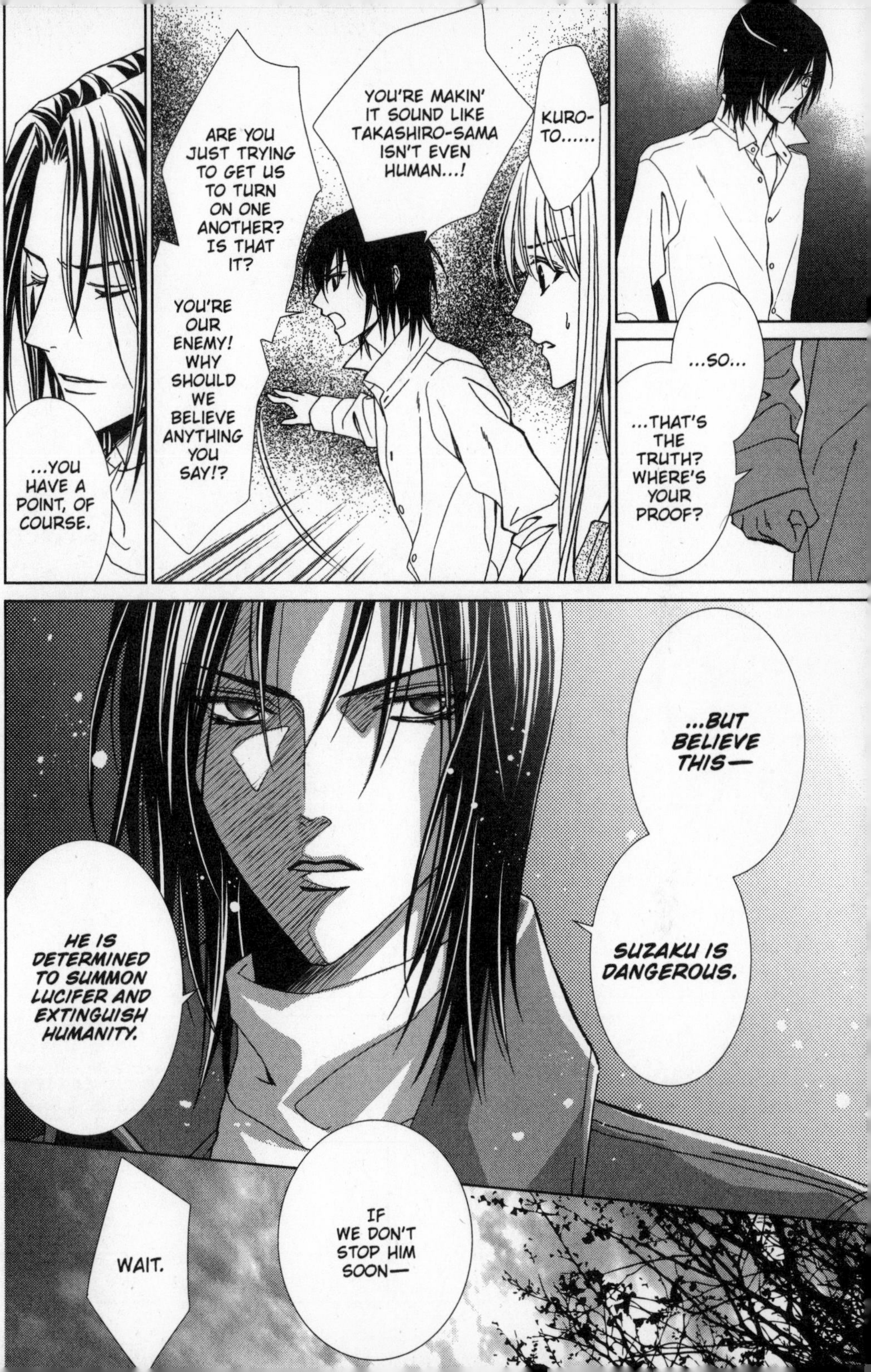

...SO...
...THAT'S THE TRUTH? WHERE'S YOUR PROOF?
KURO-TO......
YOU'RE MAKIN' IT SOUND LIKE TAKASHIRO-SAMA ISN'T EVEN HUMAN...!
ARE YOU JUST TRYING TO GET US TO TURN ON ONE ANOTHER? IS THAT IT?
YOU'RE OUR ENEMY! WHY SHOULD WE BELIEVE ANYTHING YOU SAY!?
...YOU HAVE A POINT, OF COURSE.
...BUT BELIEVE THIS—
SUZAKU IS DANGEROUS.
HE IS DETERMINED TO SUMMON LUCIFER AND EXTINGUISH HUMANITY.
IF WE DON'T STOP HIM SOON—
WAIT.

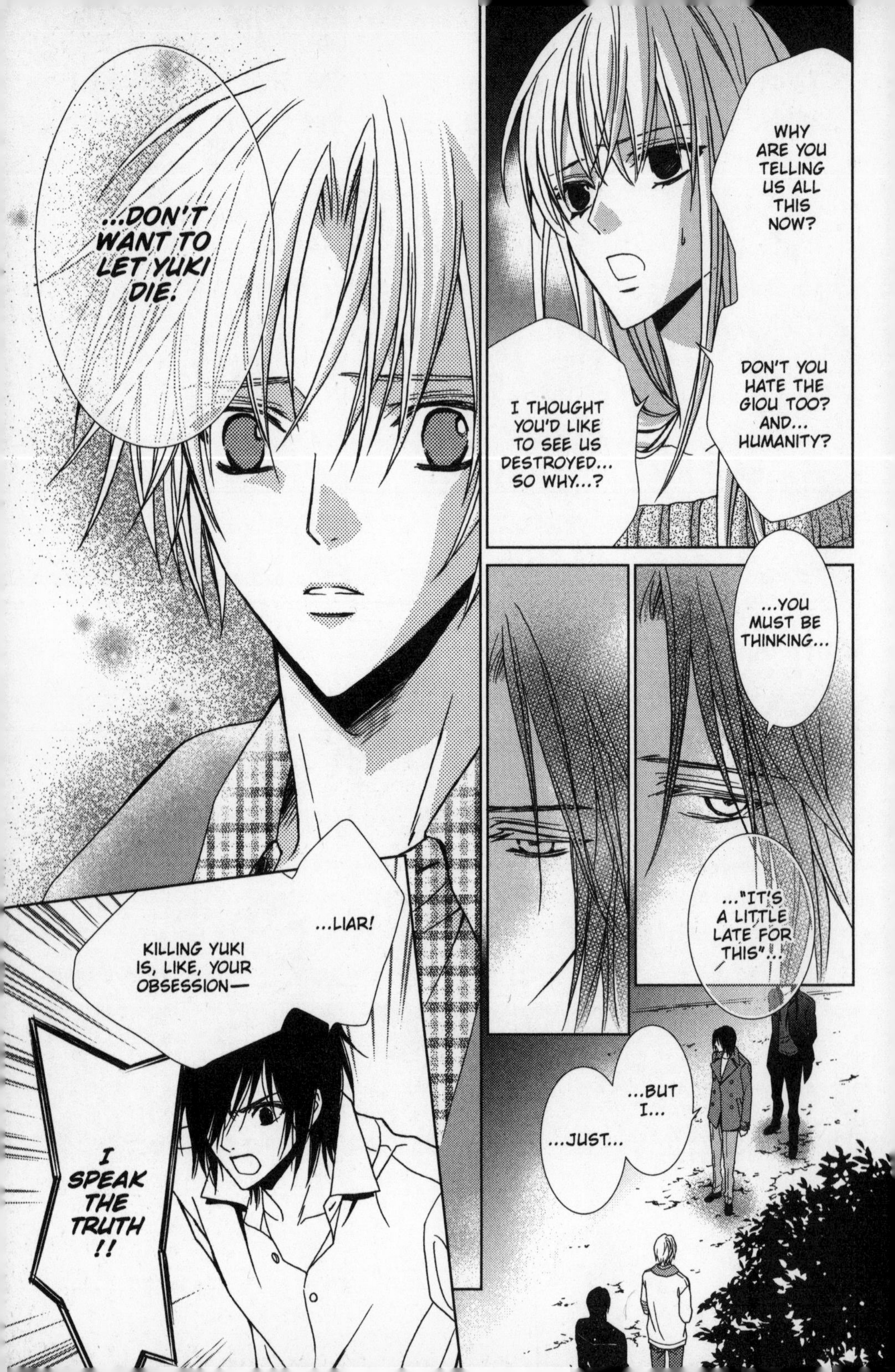
WHY ARE YOU TELLING US ALL THIS NOW?
DON'T YOU HATE THE GIOU TOO? AND... HUMANITY?
I THOUGHT YOU'D LIKE TO SEE US DESTROYED... SO WHY...?
...YOU MUST BE THINKING...
..."IT'S A LITTLE LATE FOR THIS"...
...BUT I...
...JUST...
...DON'T WANT TO LET YUKI DIE.
...LIAR!
KILLING YUKI IS, LIKE, YOUR OBSESSION—
I SPEAK THE TRUTH!!

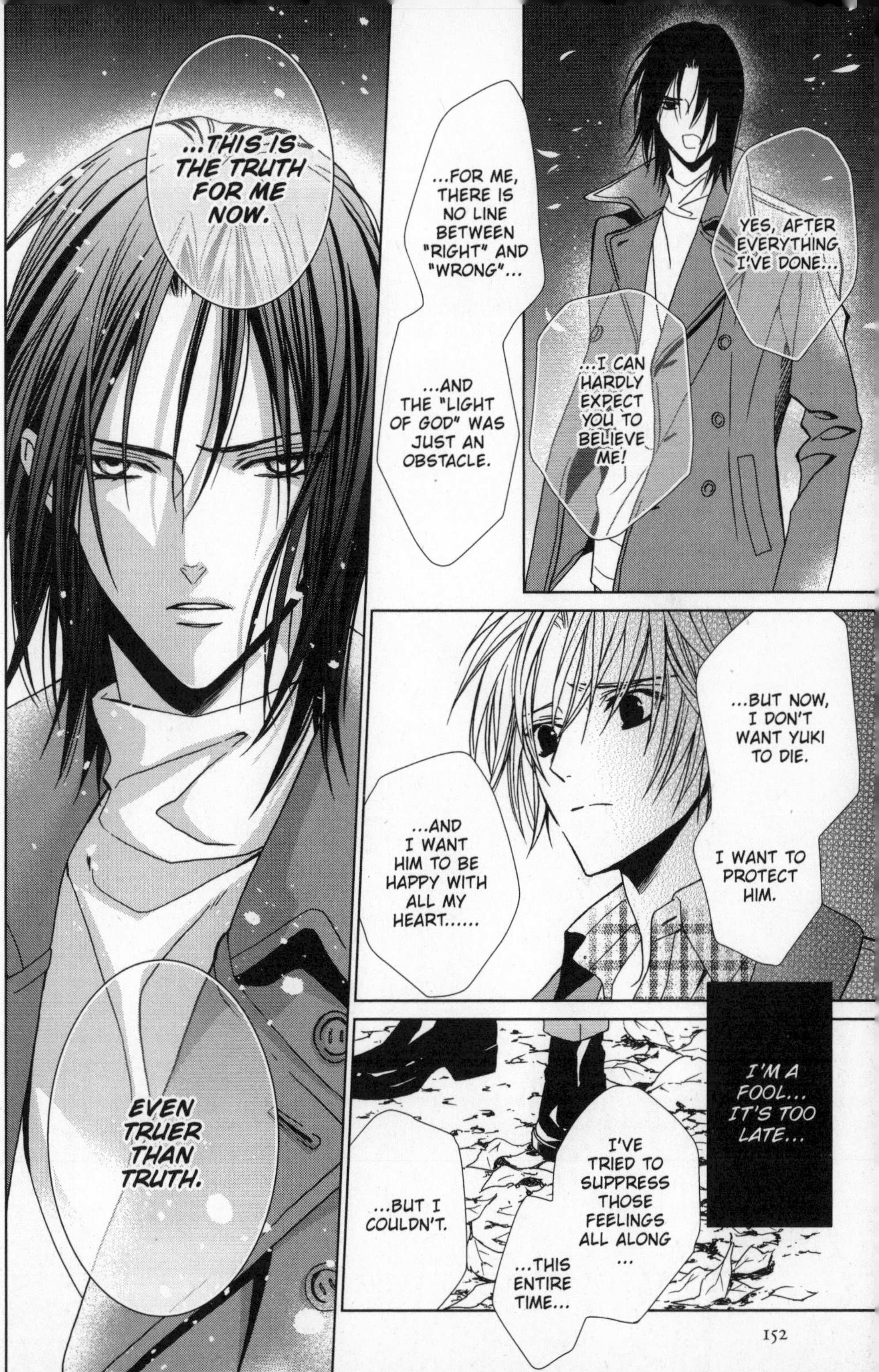

...FOR ME, THERE IS NO LINE BETWEEN "RIGHT" AND "WRONG"...
...AND THE "LIGHT OF GOD" WAS JUST AN OBSTACLE.
YES, AFTER EVERYTHING I'VE DONE...
...I CAN HARDLY EXPECT YOU TO BELIEVE ME!
...BUT NOW, I DON'T WANT YUKI TO DIE.
I WANT TO PROTECT HIM.
...AND I WANT HIM TO BE HAPPY WITH ALL MY HEART......
I'M A FOOL... IT'S TOO LATE...
I'VE TRIED TO SUPPRESS THOSE FEELINGS ALL ALONG ...
...THIS ENTIRE TIME...
...BUT I COULDN'T.
...THIS IS THE TRUTH FOR ME NOW.
EVEN TRUER THAN TRUTH.

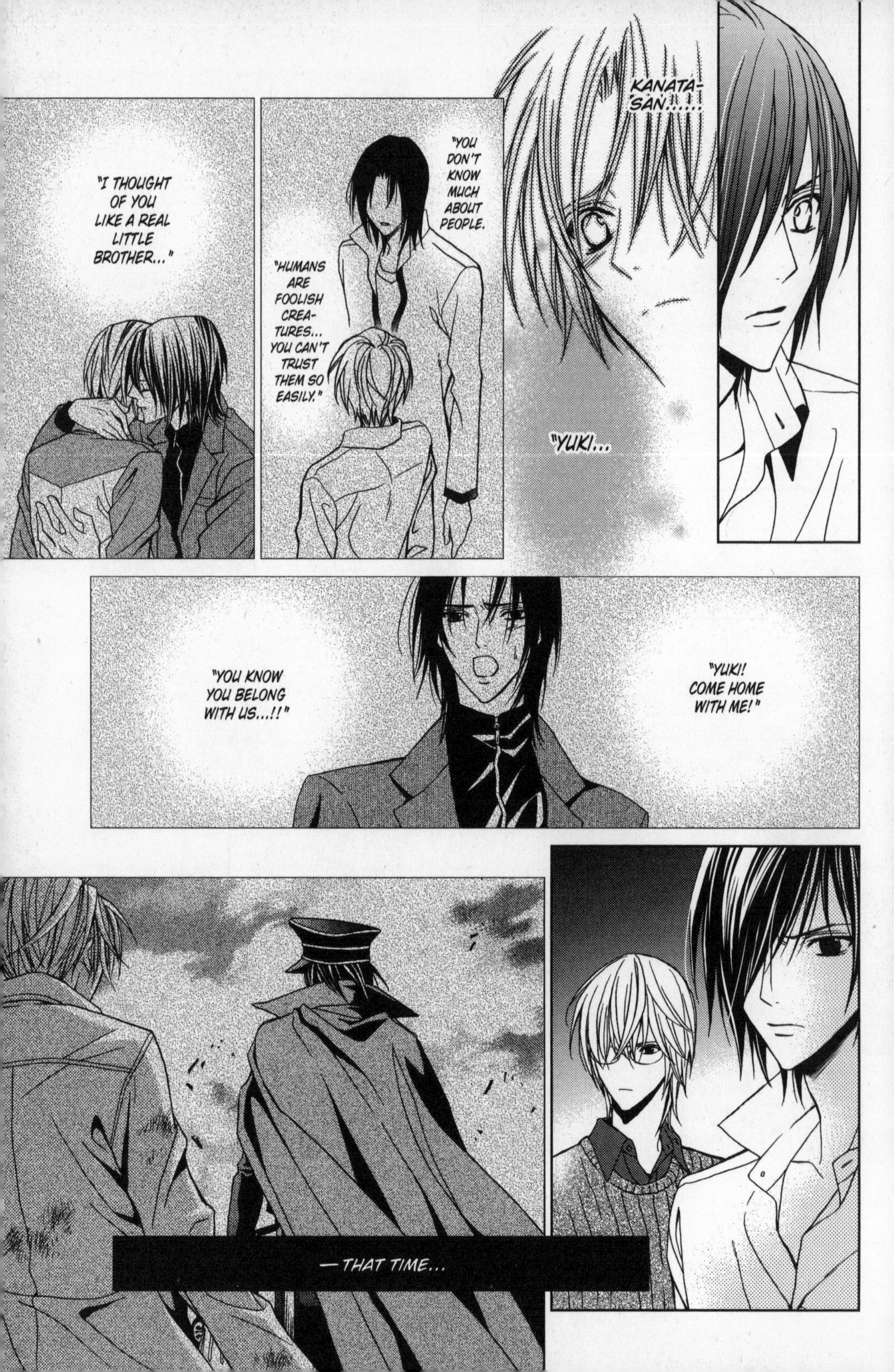
KANATA-SAN......
"YUKI...
"YOU DON'T KNOW MUCH ABOUT PEOPLE.
"HUMANS ARE FOOLISH CREA-TURES... YOU CAN'T TRUST THEM SO EASILY."
"I THOUGHT OF YOU LIKE A REAL LITTLE BROTHER..."
"YUKI! COME HOME WITH ME!"
"YOU KNOW YOU BELONG WITH US...!!"
—THAT TIME...

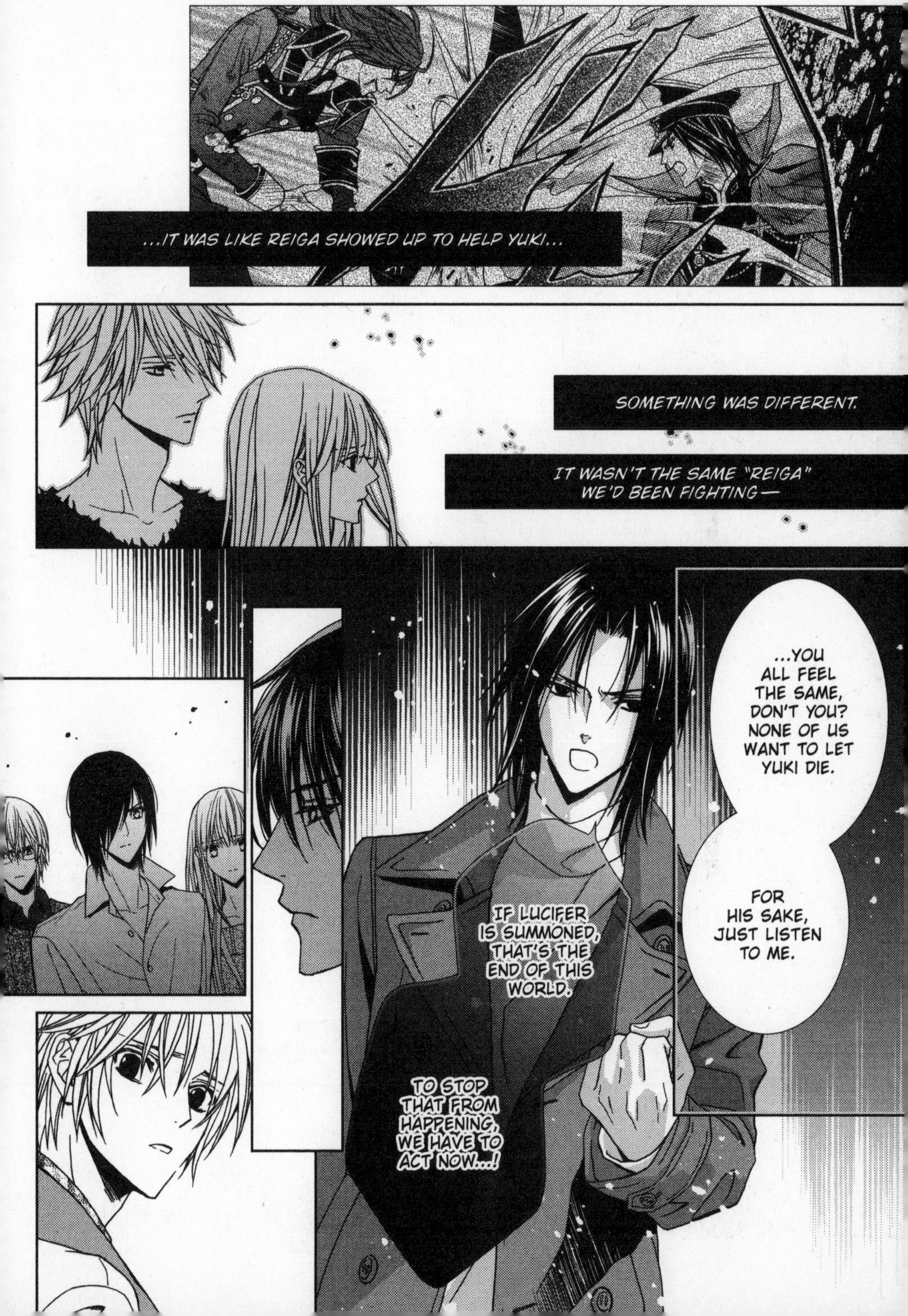
...IT WAS LIKE REIGA SHOWED UP TO HELP YUKI...
SOMETHING WAS DIFFERENT.
IT WASN'T THE SAME "REIGA" WE'D BEEN FIGHTING—
...YOU ALL FEEL THE SAME, DON'T YOU? NONE OF US WANT TO LET YUKI DIE.
FOR HIS SAKE, JUST LISTEN TO ME.
IF LUCIFER IS SUMMONED, THAT'S THE END OF THIS WORLD.
TO STOP THAT FROM HAPPENING, WE HAVE TO ACT NOW...!

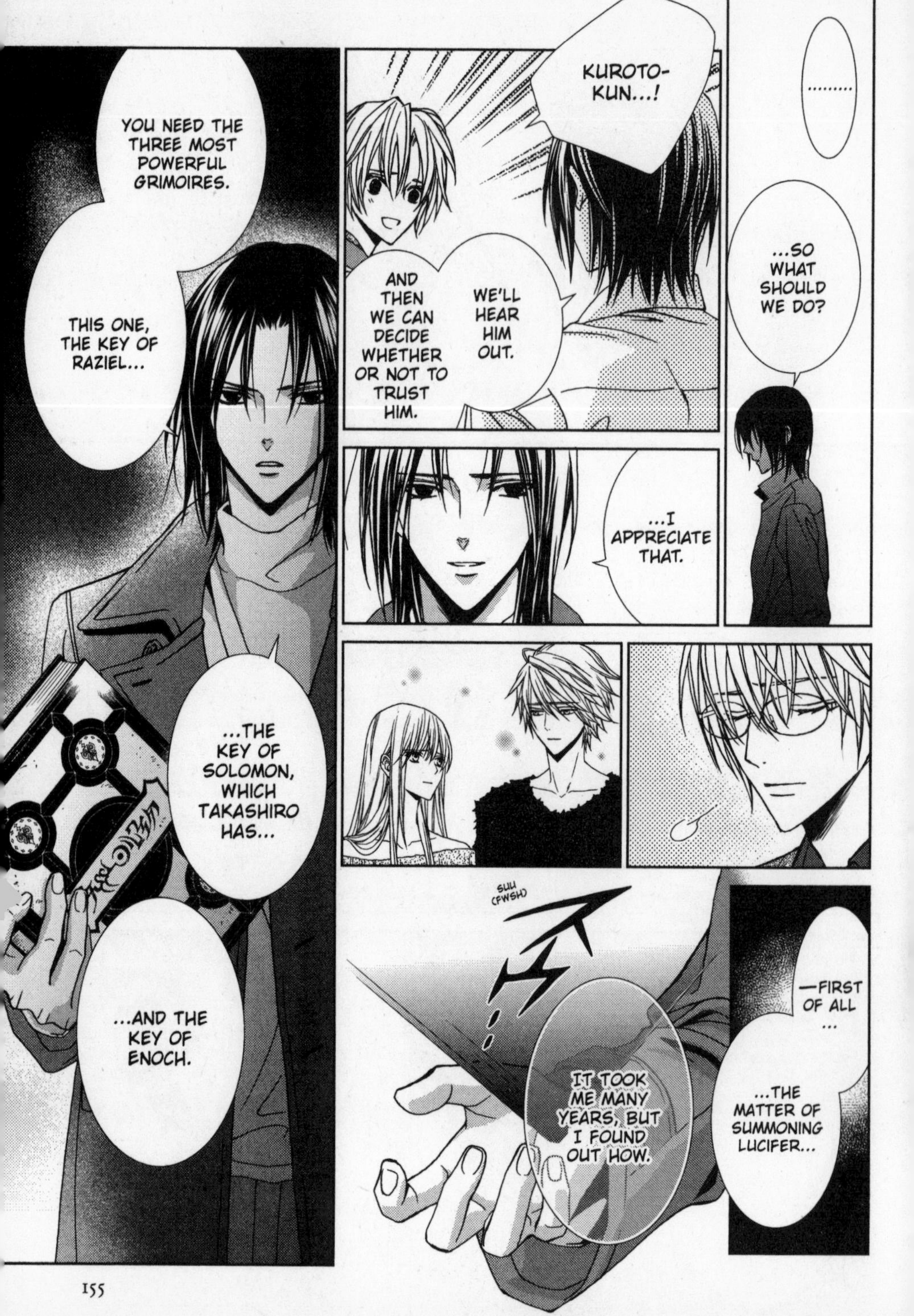
....
...SO WHAT SHOULD WE DO?
KUROTO-KUN...!
WE'LL HEAR HIM OUT.
AND THEN WE CAN DECIDE WHETHER OR NOT TO TRUST HIM.
...I APPRECIATE THAT.
—FIRST OF ALL ...
...THE MATTER OF SUMMONING LUCIFER...
SUU (FWSH)
IT TOOK ME MANY YEARS, BUT I FOUND OUT HOW.
YOU NEED THE THREE MOST POWERFUL GRIMOIRES.
THIS ONE, THE KEY OF RAZIEL...
...THE KEY OF SOLOMON, WHICH TAKASHIRO HAS...
...AND THE KEY OF ENOCH.

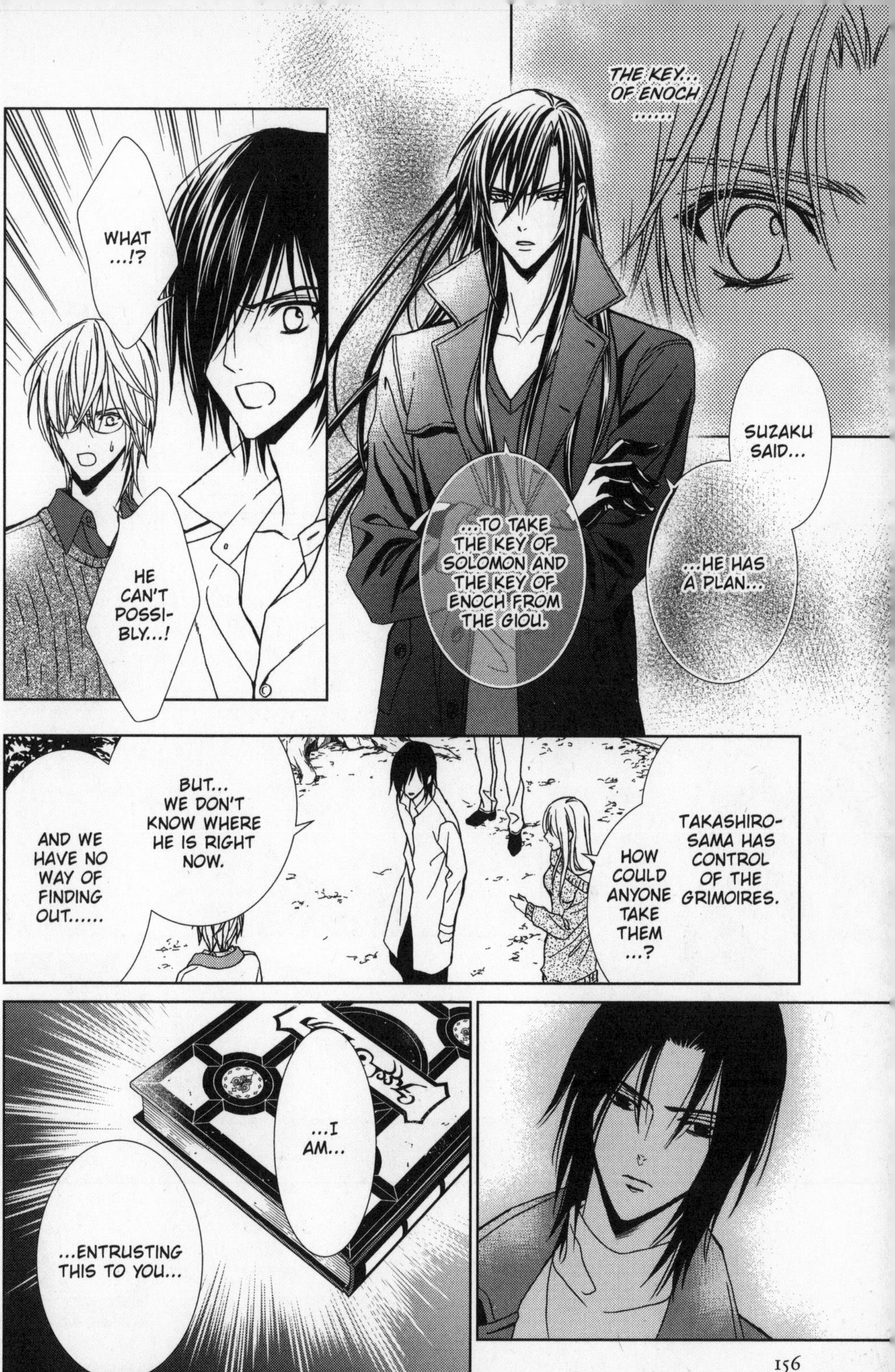
THE KEY... OF ENOCH ......
SUZAKU SAID...
...HE HAS A PLAN...
...TO TAKE THE KEY OF SOLOMON AND THE KEY OF ENOCH FROM THE GIOU.
WHAT ...!?
HE CAN'T POSSI-BLY...!
TAKASHIRO-SAMA HAS CONTROL OF THE GRIMOIRES.
HOW COULD ANYONE TAKE THEM ...?
BUT... WE DON'T KNOW WHERE HE IS RIGHT NOW.
AND WE HAVE NO WAY OF FINDING OUT......
...I AM...
...ENTRUSTING THIS TO YOU...

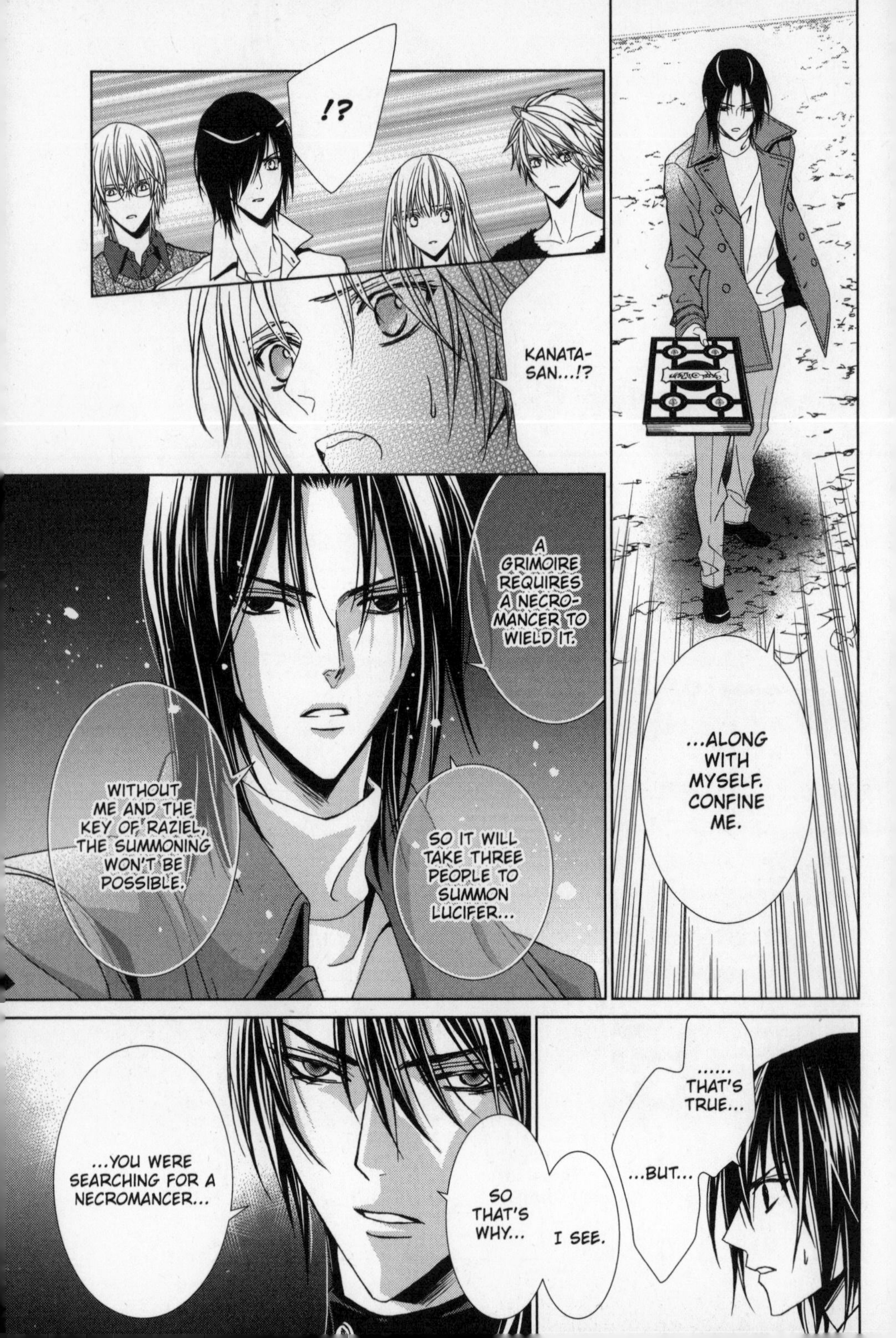

...ALONG WITH MYSELF. CONFINE ME.
!?
KANATA-SAN...!?
A GRIMOIRE REQUIRES A NECROMANCER TO WIELD IT.
SO IT WILL TAKE THREE PEOPLE TO SUMMON LUCIFER...
WITHOUT ME AND THE KEY OF RAZIEL, THE SUMMONING WON'T BE POSSIBLE.
......THAT'S TRUE...
...BUT...
I SEE.
SO THAT'S WHY...
...YOU WERE SEARCHING FOR A NECROMANCER...

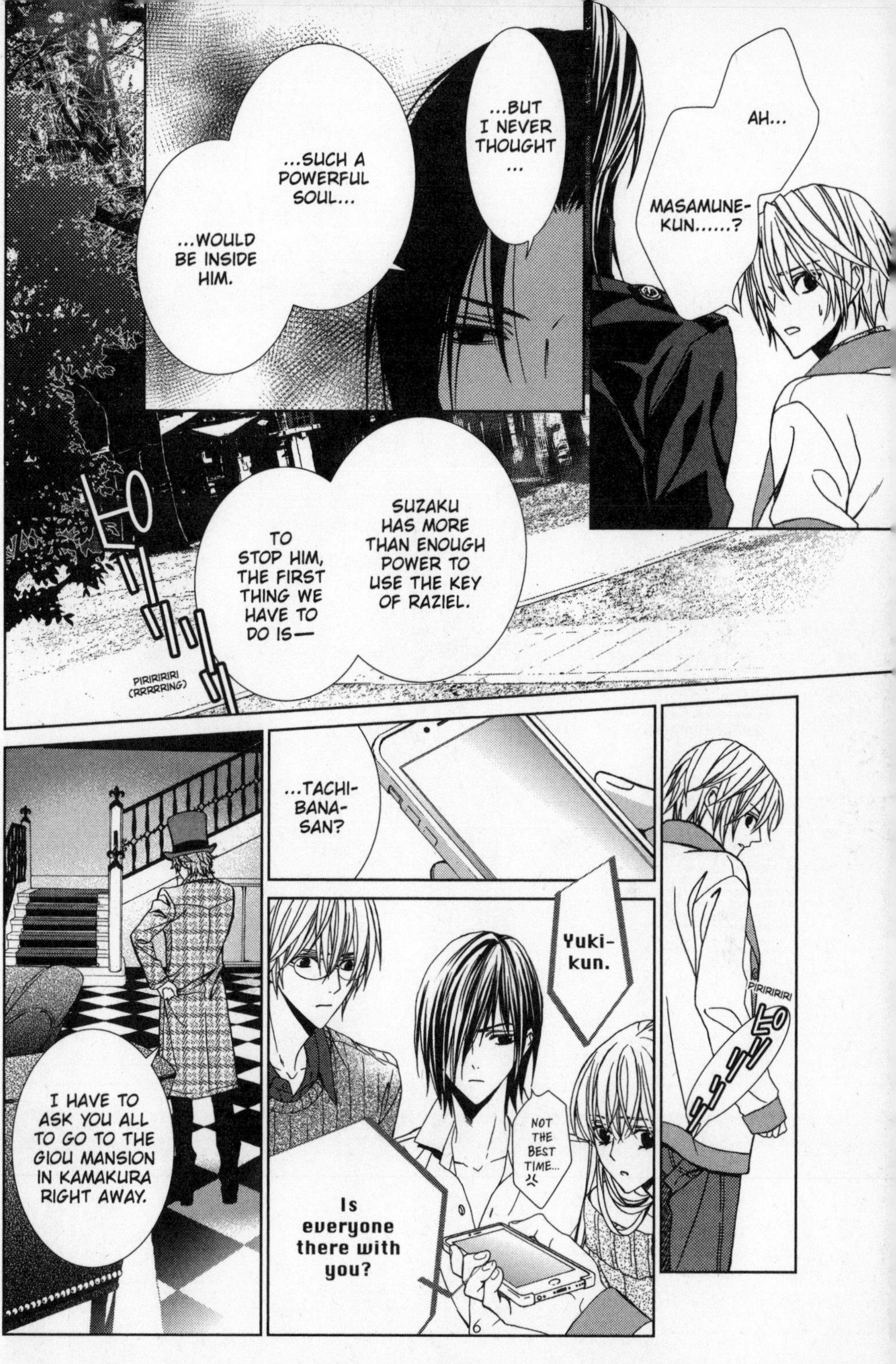
AH...
MASAMUNE-KUN......?
...BUT I NEVER THOUGHT ...
...SUCH A POWERFUL SOUL...
...WOULD BE INSIDE HIM.
SUZAKU HAS MORE THAN ENOUGH POWER TO USE THE KEY OF RAZIEL.
TO STOP HIM, THE FIRST THING WE HAVE TO DO IS—
PIRIRIRIRI (RRRRRING)
PIRIRIRIRI
...TACHI-BANA-SAN?
Yuki-kun.
NOT THE BEST TIME...
Is everyone there with you?
I HAVE TO ASK YOU ALL TO GO TO THE GIOU MANSION IN KAMAKURA RIGHT AWAY.

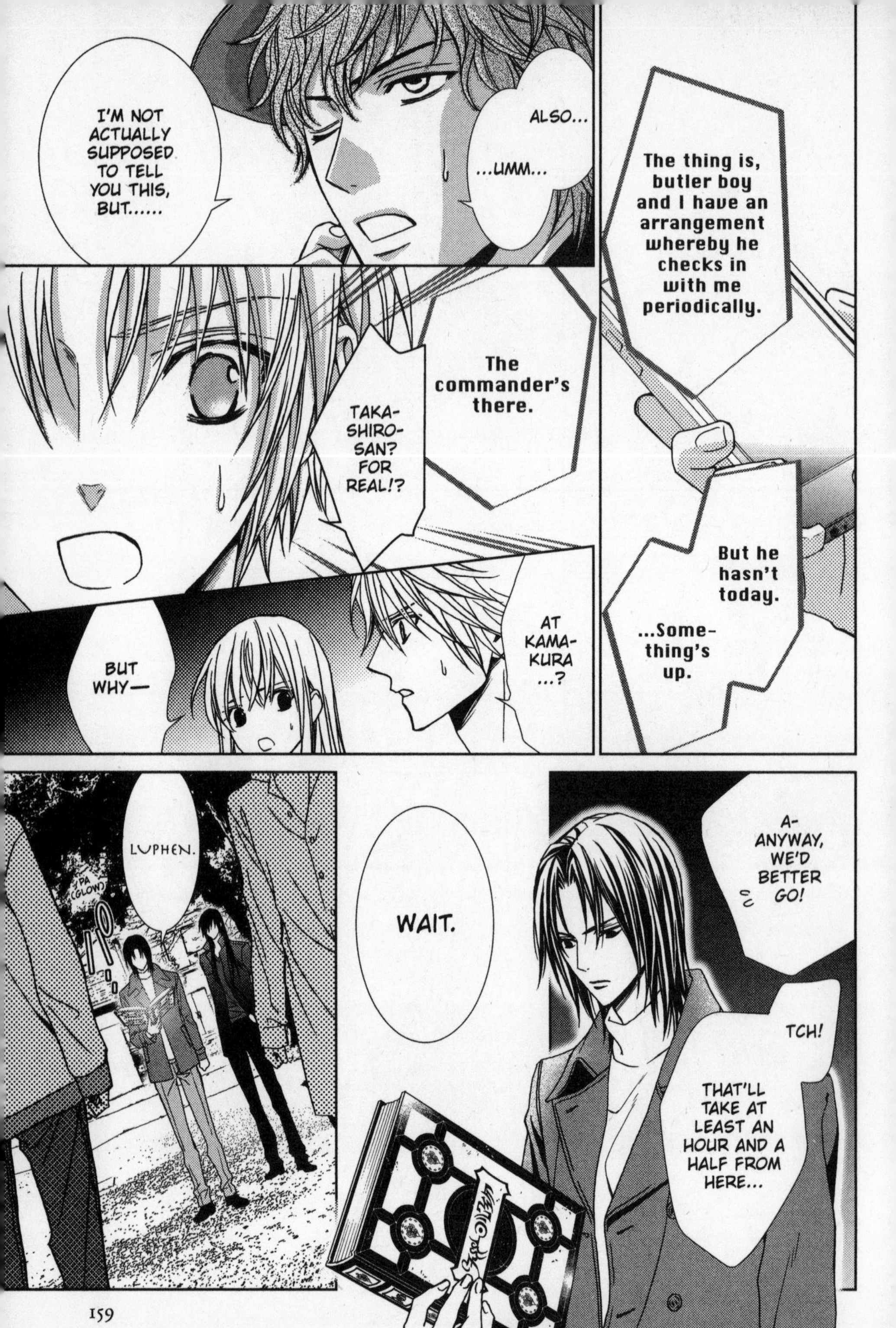
The thing is, butler boy and I have an arrangement whereby he checks in with me periodically.
But he hasn't today.
...Some-thing's up.
ALSO...
...UMM...
I'M NOT ACTUALLY SUPPOSED TO TELL YOU THIS, BUT......
The commander's there.
TAKA-SHIRO-SAN? FOR REAL!?
AT KAMA-KURA ...?
BUT WHY—
A-ANYWAY, WE'D BETTER GO!
TCH!
THAT'LL TAKE AT LEAST AN HOUR AND A HALF FROM HERE...
WAIT.
LUPHEN.
PA (GLOW)

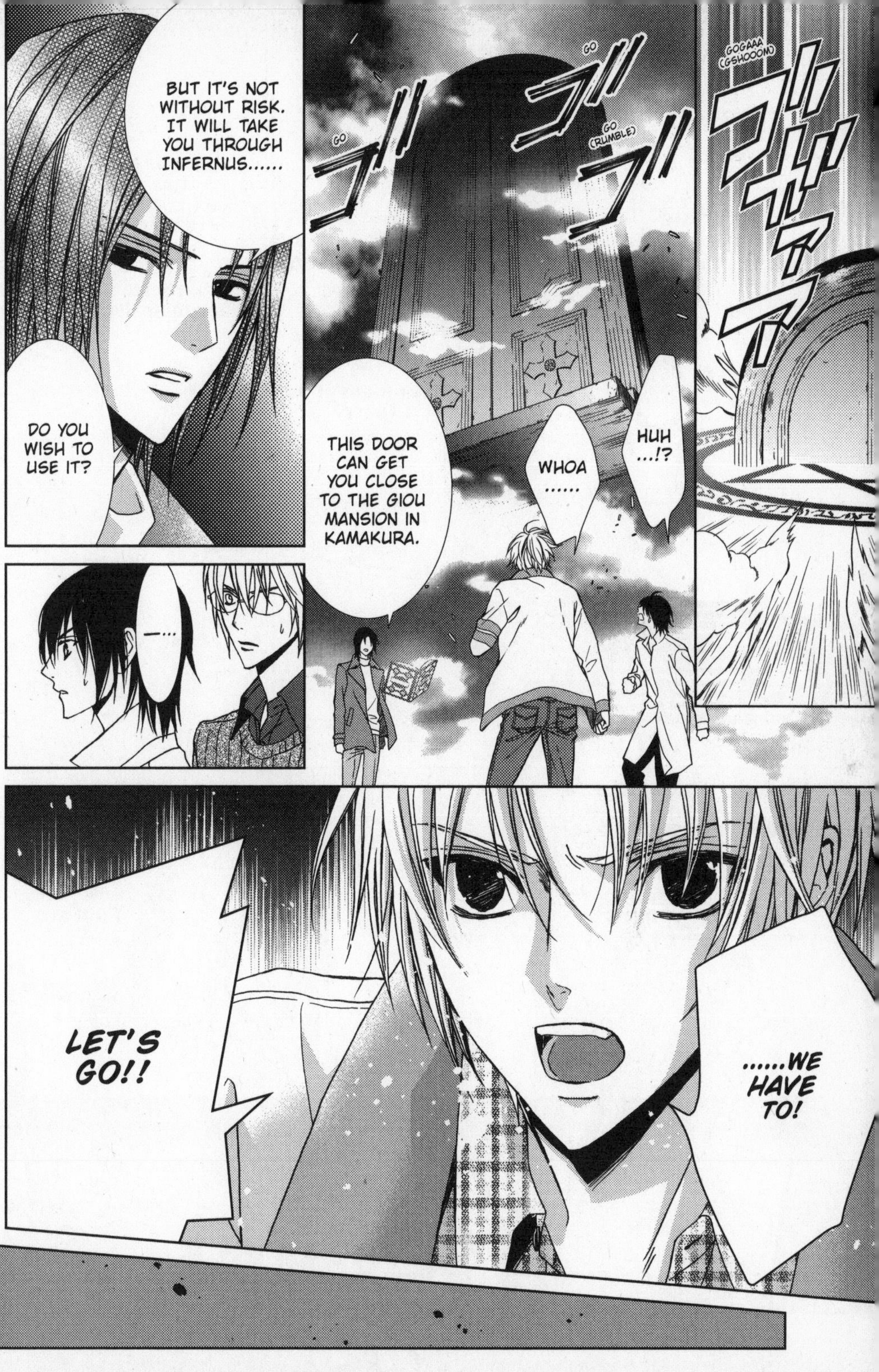
GOGAAA (GSHOOOM)
GO
GO (RUMBLE)
GO
HUH ...!?
WHOA ......
THIS DOOR CAN GET YOU CLOSE TO THE GIOU MANSION IN KAMAKURA.
BUT IT'S NOT WITHOUT RISK. IT WILL TAKE YOU THROUGH INFERNUS......
DO YOU WISH TO USE IT?
—....
......WE HAVE TO!
LET'S GO!!

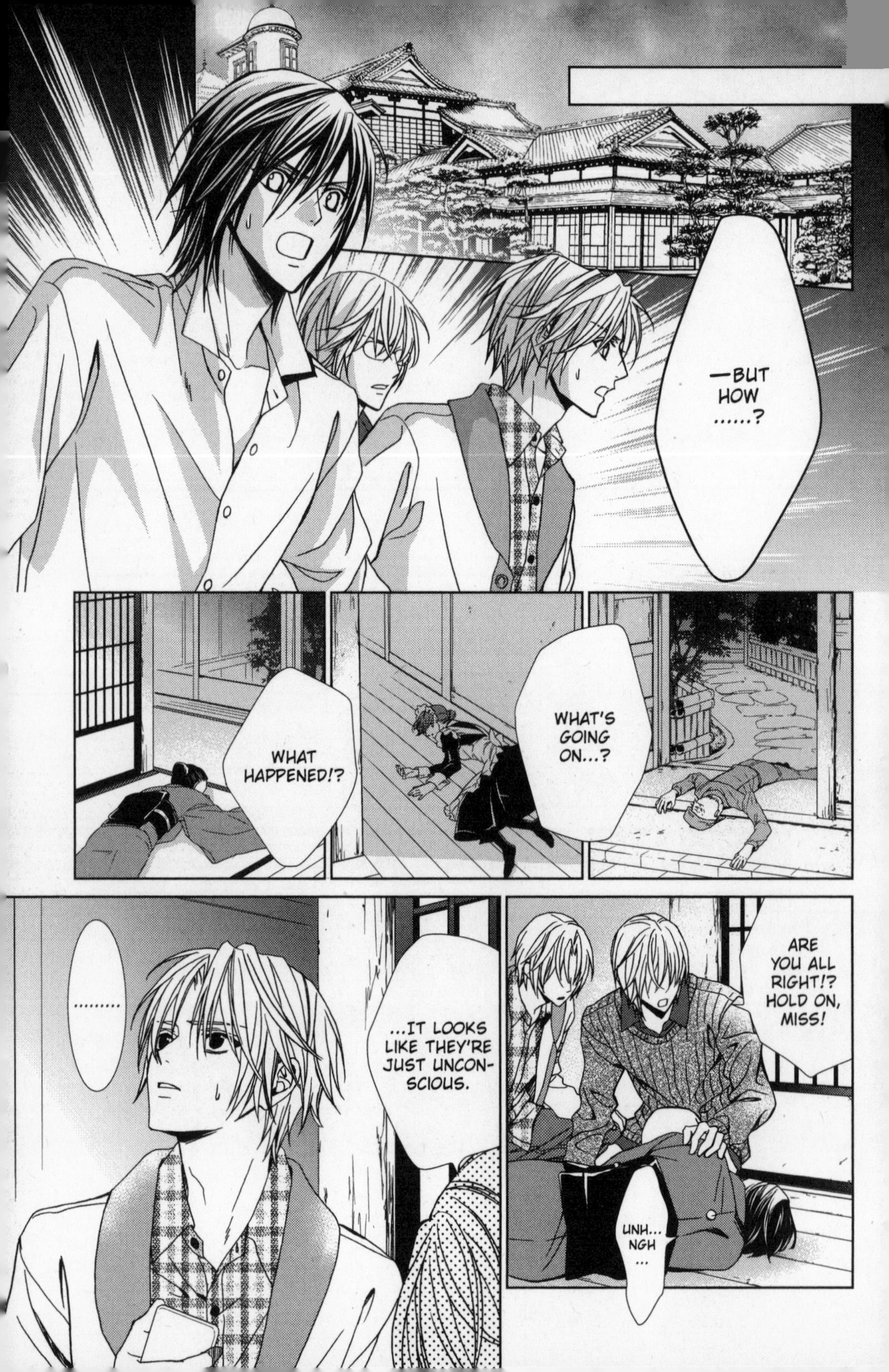
—BUT HOW ......?
WHAT'S GOING ON...?
WHAT HAPPENED!?
ARE YOU ALL RIGHT!? HOLD ON, MISS!
UNH... NGH ...
...IT LOOKS LIKE THEY'RE JUST UNCONSCIOUS.
....

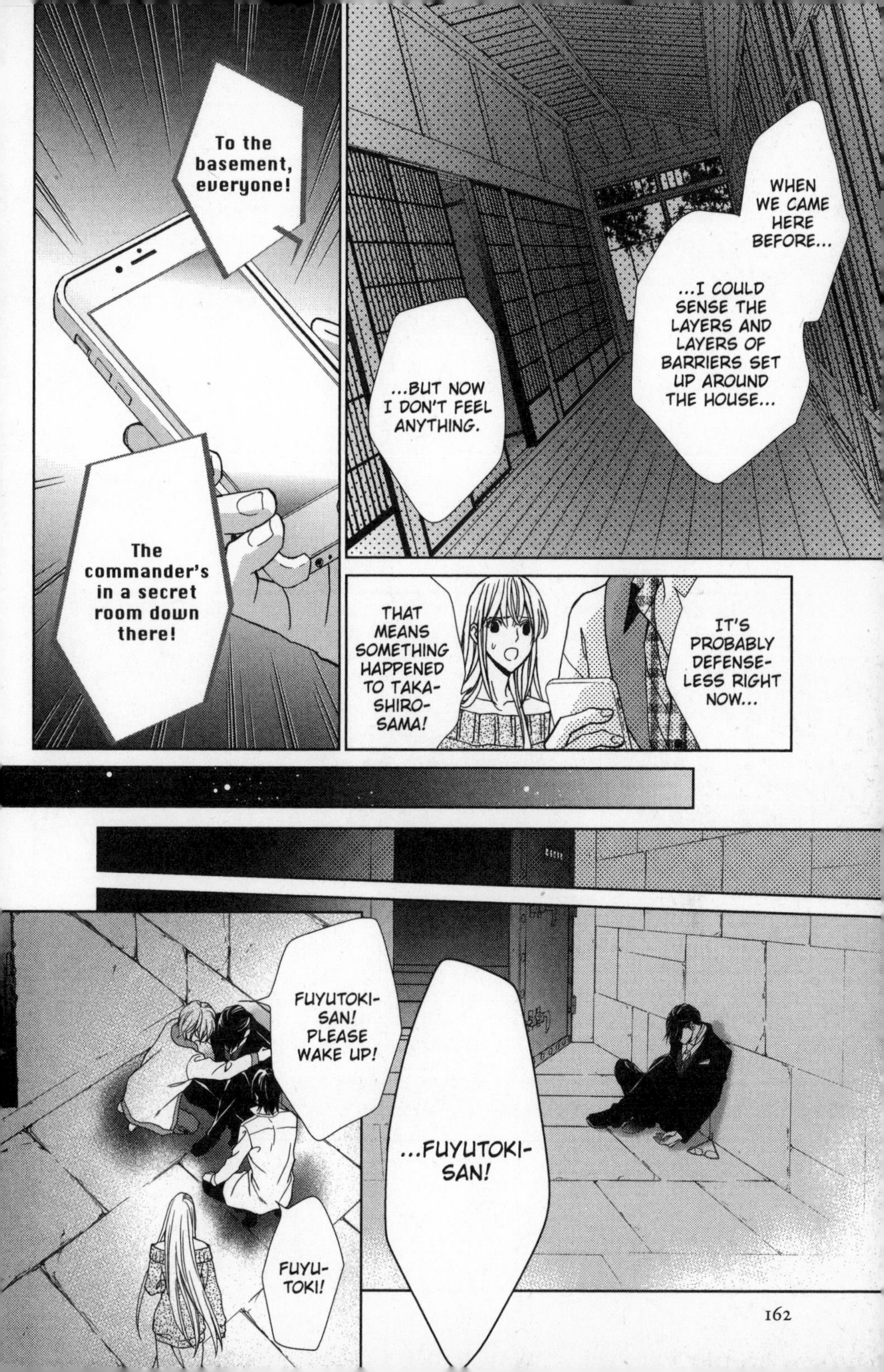
WHEN WE CAME HERE BEFORE...
...I COULD SENSE THE LAYERS AND LAYERS OF BARRIERS SET UP AROUND THE HOUSE...
...BUT NOW I DON'T FEEL ANYTHING.
IT'S PROBABLY DEFENSELESS RIGHT NOW...
THAT MEANS SOMETHING HAPPENED TO TAKASHIRO-SAMA!
To the basement, everyone!
The commander's in a secret room down there!
...FUYUTOKI-SAN!
FUYUTOKI-SAN! PLEASE WAKE UP!
FUYUTOKI!

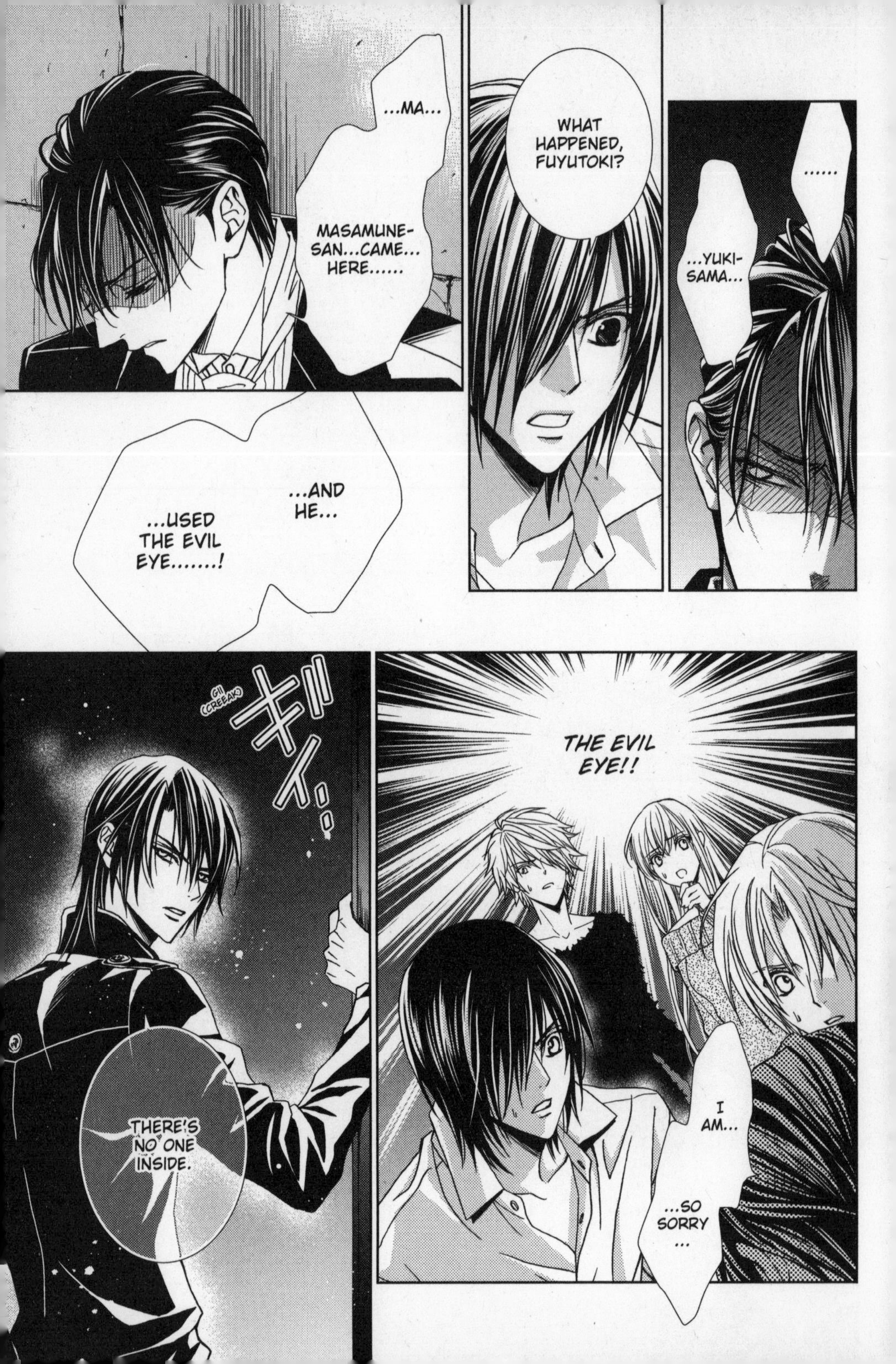
......
...YUKI-SAMA...
WHAT HAPPENED, FUYUTOKI?
...MA...
MASAMUNE-SAN...CAME... HERE......
...AND HE...
...USED THE EVIL EYE.......!
THE EVIL EYE!!
I AM...
...SO SORRY ...
GI (CREEAK)
THERE'S NO ONE INSIDE.

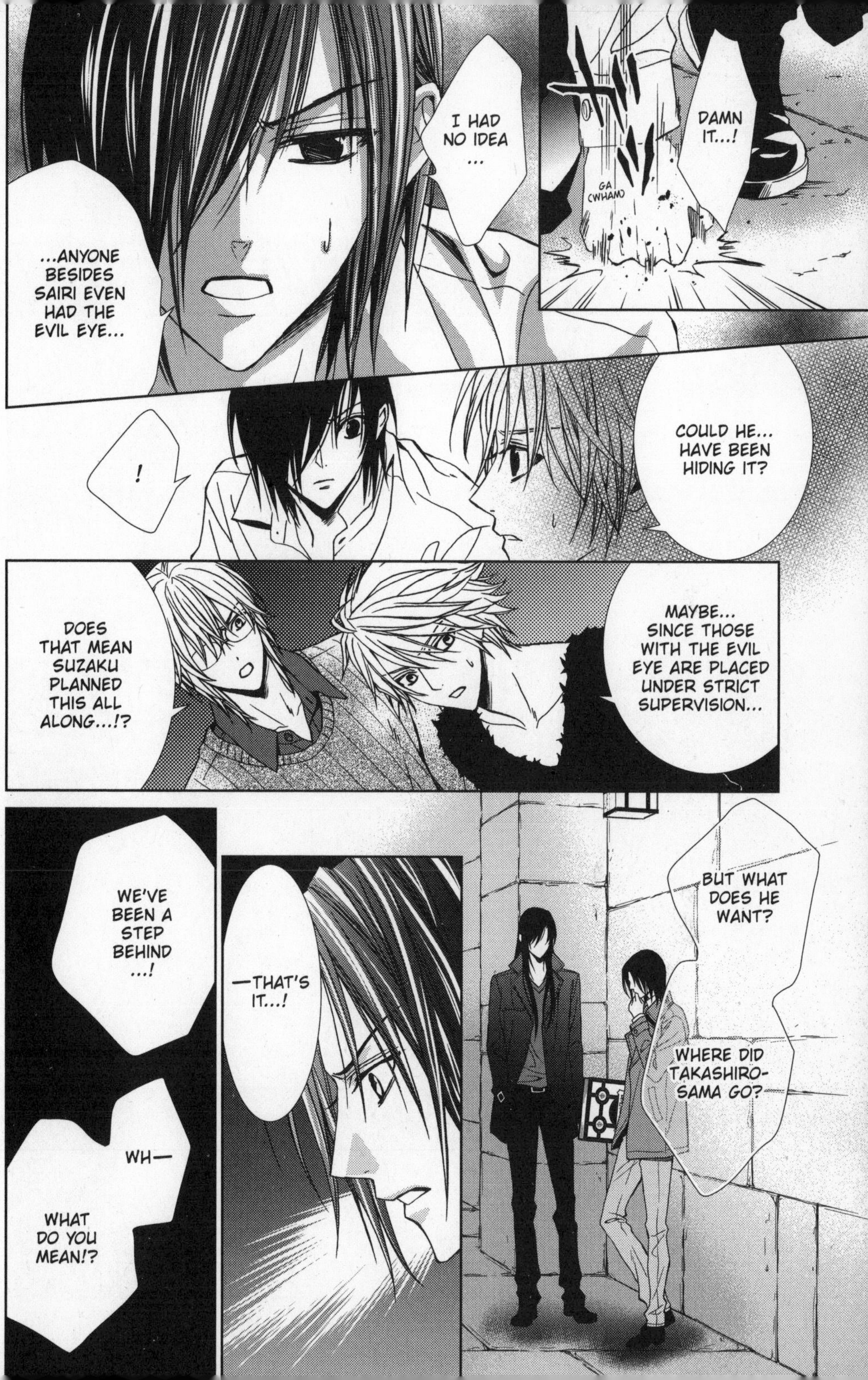
DAMN IT...!
GA (WHAM)
I HAD NO IDEA ...
...ANYONE BESIDES SAIRI EVEN HAD THE EVIL EYE...
COULD HE... HAVE BEEN HIDING IT?
!
MAYBE... SINCE THOSE WITH THE EVIL EYE ARE PLACED UNDER STRICT SUPERVISION...
DOES THAT MEAN SUZAKU PLANNED THIS ALL ALONG...!?
BUT WHAT DOES HE WANT?
WHERE DID TAKASHIRO-SAMA GO?
—THAT'S IT...!
WE'VE BEEN A STEP BEHIND ...!
WH—
WHAT DO YOU MEAN!?

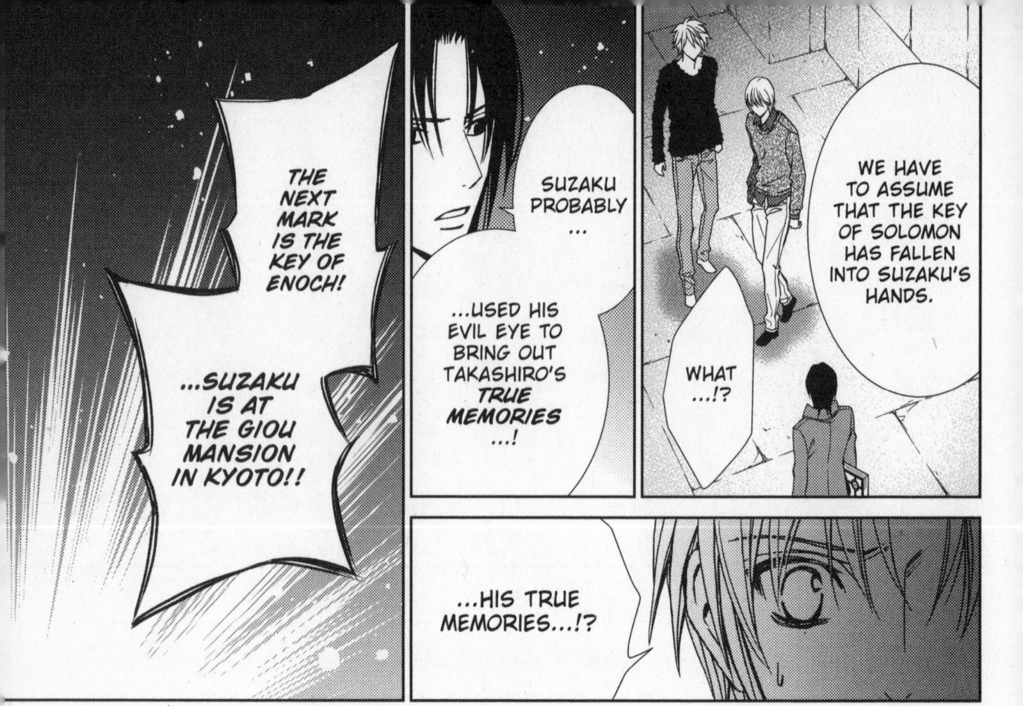
WE HAVE TO ASSUME THAT THE KEY OF SOLOMON HAS FALLEN INTO SUZAKU'S HANDS.
WHAT ...!?
SUZAKU PROBABLY ...
...USED HIS EVIL EYE TO BRING OUT TAKASHIRO'S TRUE MEMORIES ...!
...HIS TRUE MEMORIES...!?
THE NEXT MARK IS THE KEY OF ENOCH!
...SUZAKU IS AT THE GIOU MANSION IN KYOTO!!

GIOU RESIDENCE, KYOTO

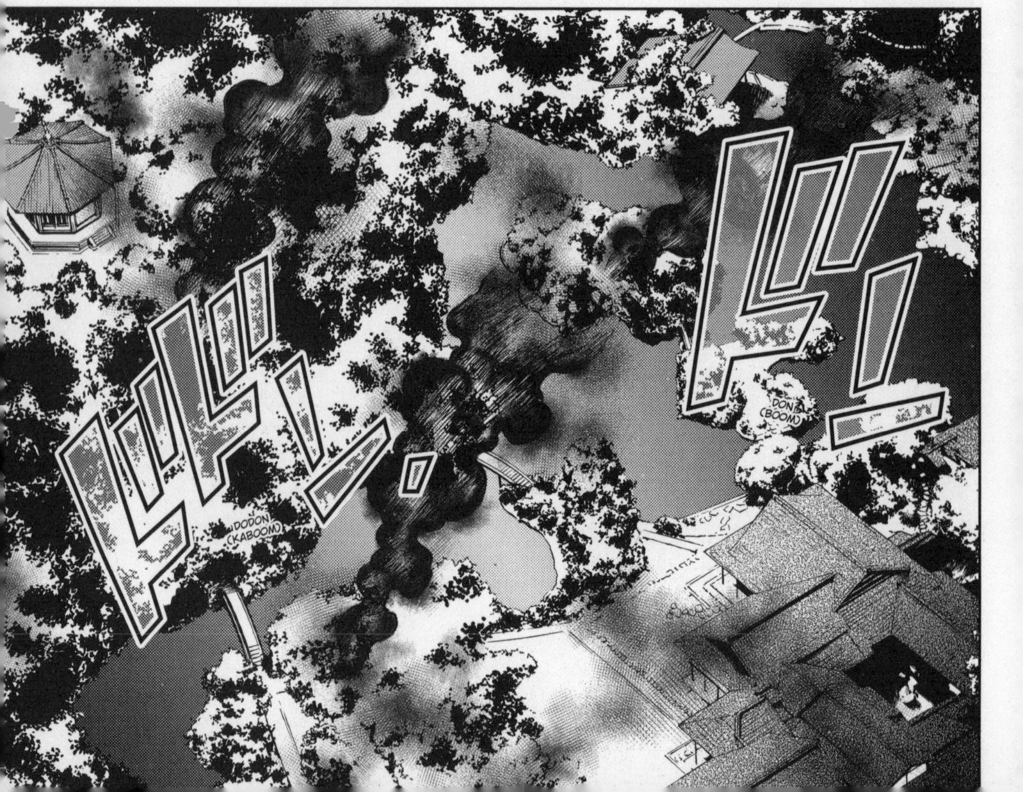
DON (BOOM)
DODON (KABOOM)

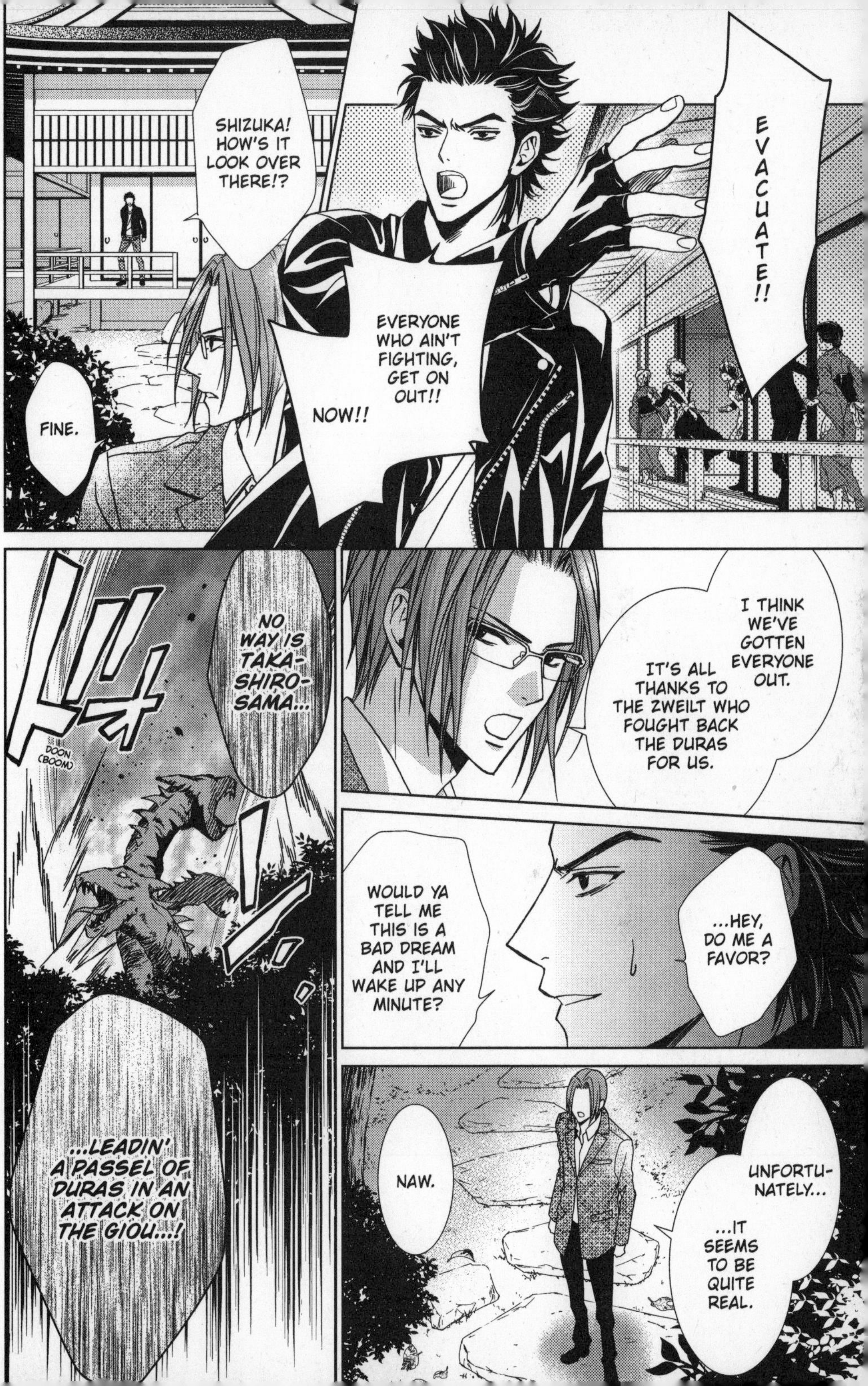
EVACUATE!!
EVERYONE WHO AIN'T FIGHTING, GET ON OUT!!
NOW!!
SHIZUKA! HOW'S IT LOOK OVER THERE!?
FINE.
I THINK WE'VE GOTTEN EVERYONE OUT.
IT'S ALL THANKS TO THE ZWEILT WHO FOUGHT BACK THE DURAS FOR US.
...HEY, DO ME A FAVOR?
WOULD YA TELL ME THIS IS A BAD DREAM AND I'LL WAKE UP ANY MINUTE?
UNFORTU-NATELY...
...IT SEEMS TO BE QUITE REAL.
NAW.
DOON (BOOM)
NO WAY IS TAKA-SHIRO-SAMA...
...LEADIN' A PASSEL OF DURAS IN AN ATTACK ON THE GIOU...!

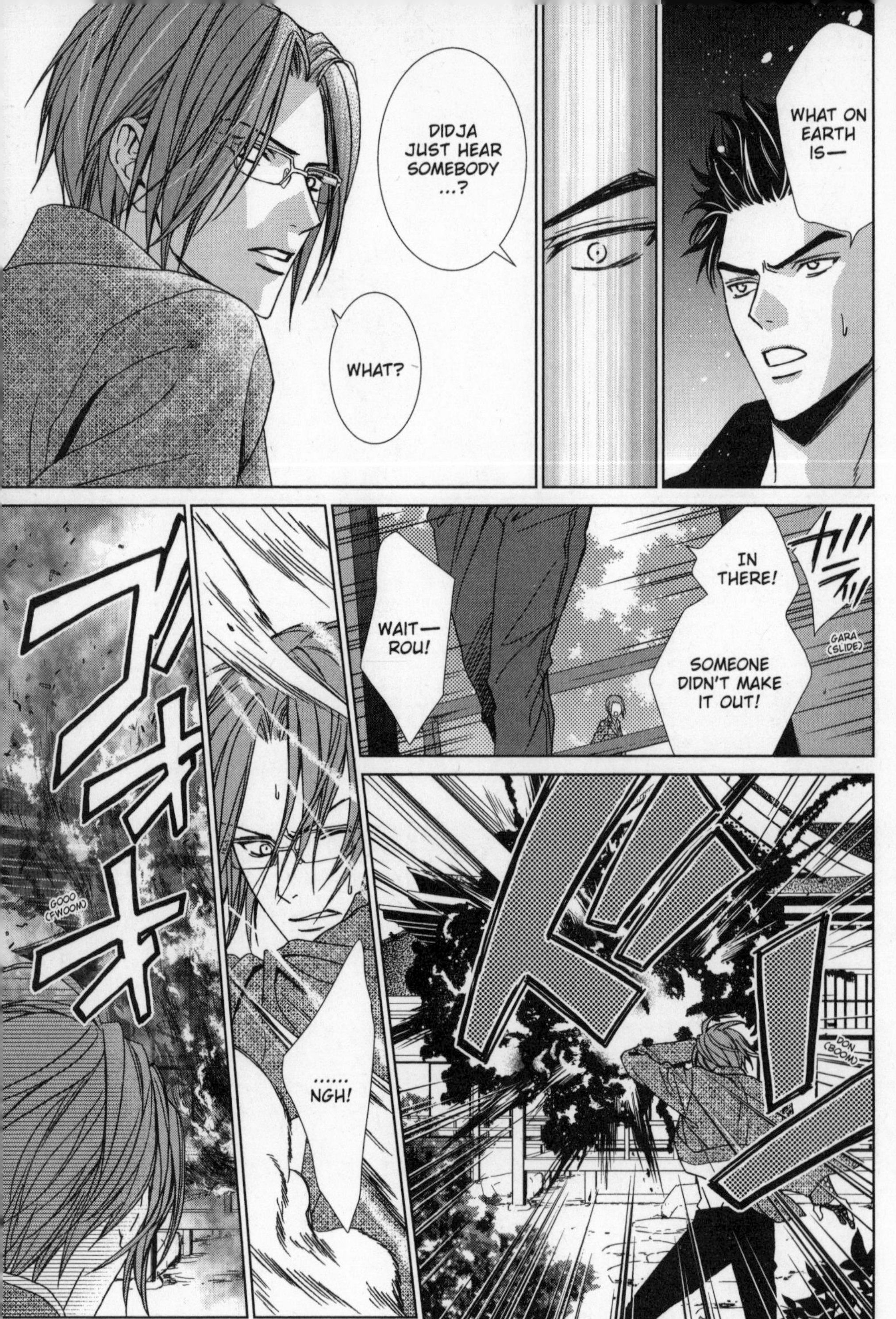
WHAT ON EARTH IS—
DIDJA JUST HEAR SOMEBODY ...?
WHAT?
GARA (SLIDE)
IN THERE!
SOMEONE DIDN'T MAKE IT OUT!
WAIT—ROU!
DON (BOOM)
...... NGH!
GOOO (FWOOM)

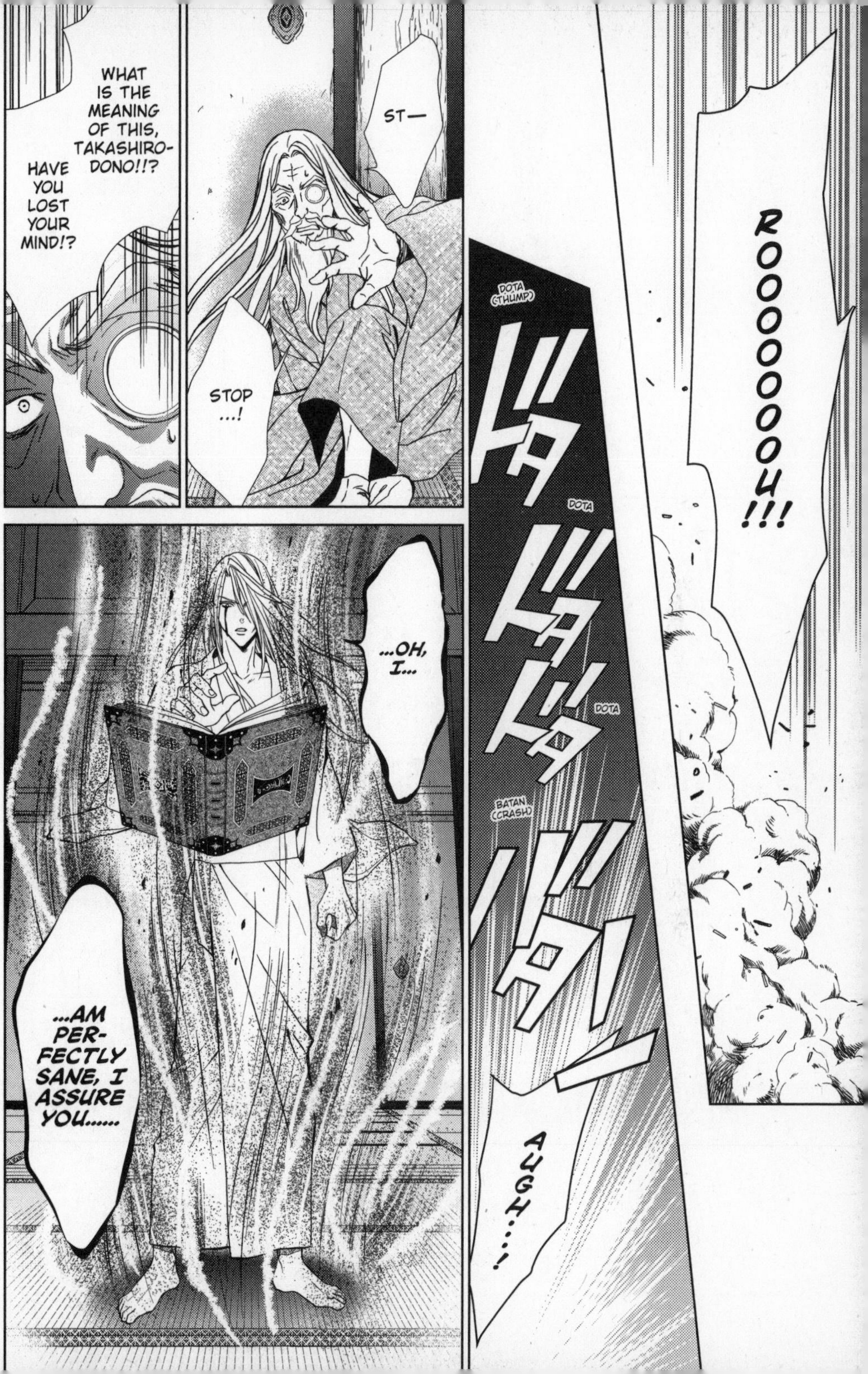

ROOOOOOOOU!!!
DOTA (THUMP)
DOTA
DOTA
BATAN (CRASH)
AUGH...!
ST—
STOP ...!
WHAT IS THE MEANING OF THIS, TAKASHIRO-DONO!!?
HAVE YOU LOST YOUR MIND!?
...OH, I...
...AM PERFECTLY SANE, I ASSURE YOU......

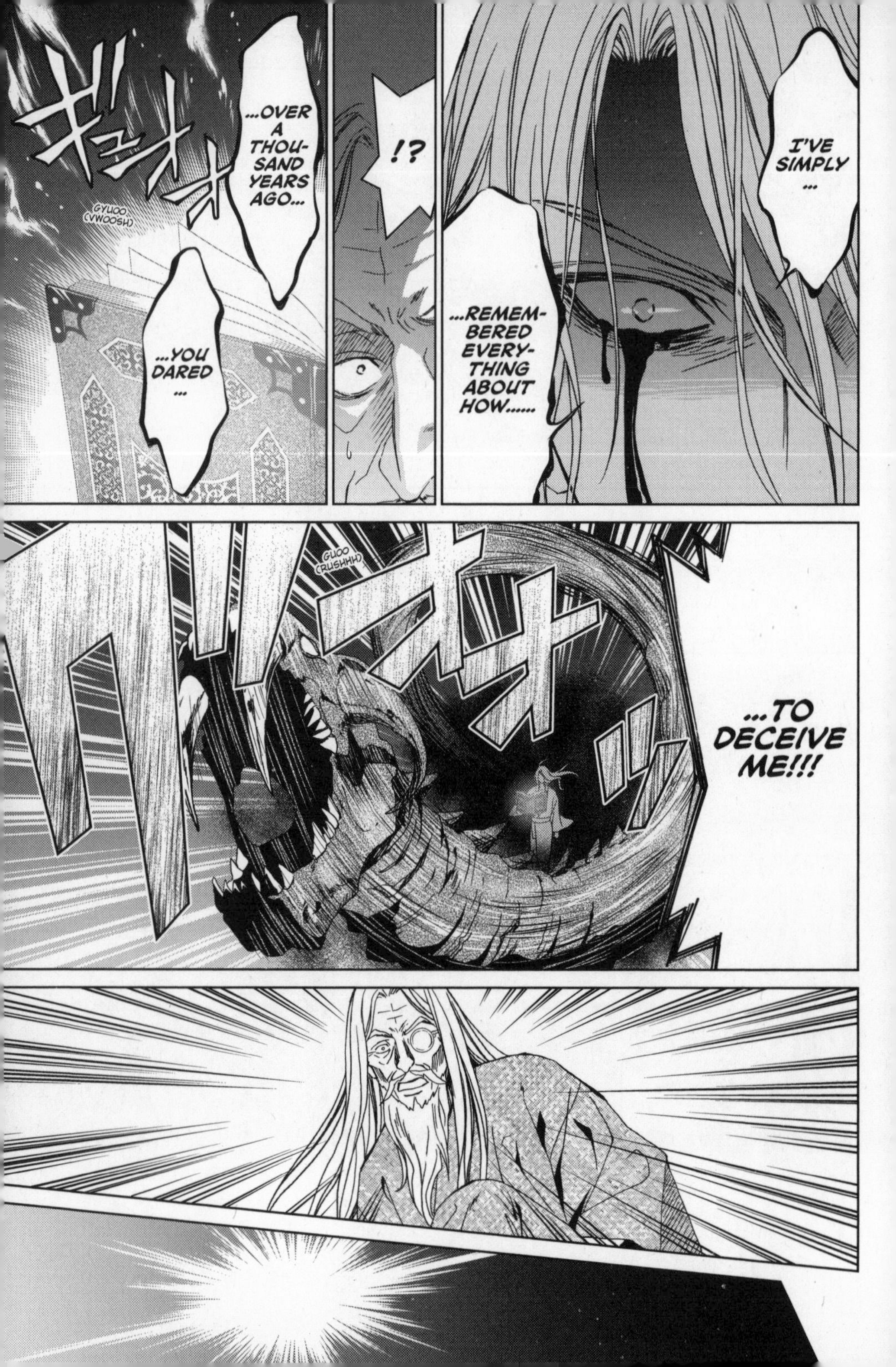
I'VE SIMPLY ...
...REMEMBERED EVERYTHING ABOUT HOW......
!?
...OVER A THOUSAND YEARS AGO...
...YOU DARED ...
GYUOO (VWOOSH)
GUOO (RUSHHH)
...TO DECEIVE ME!!!

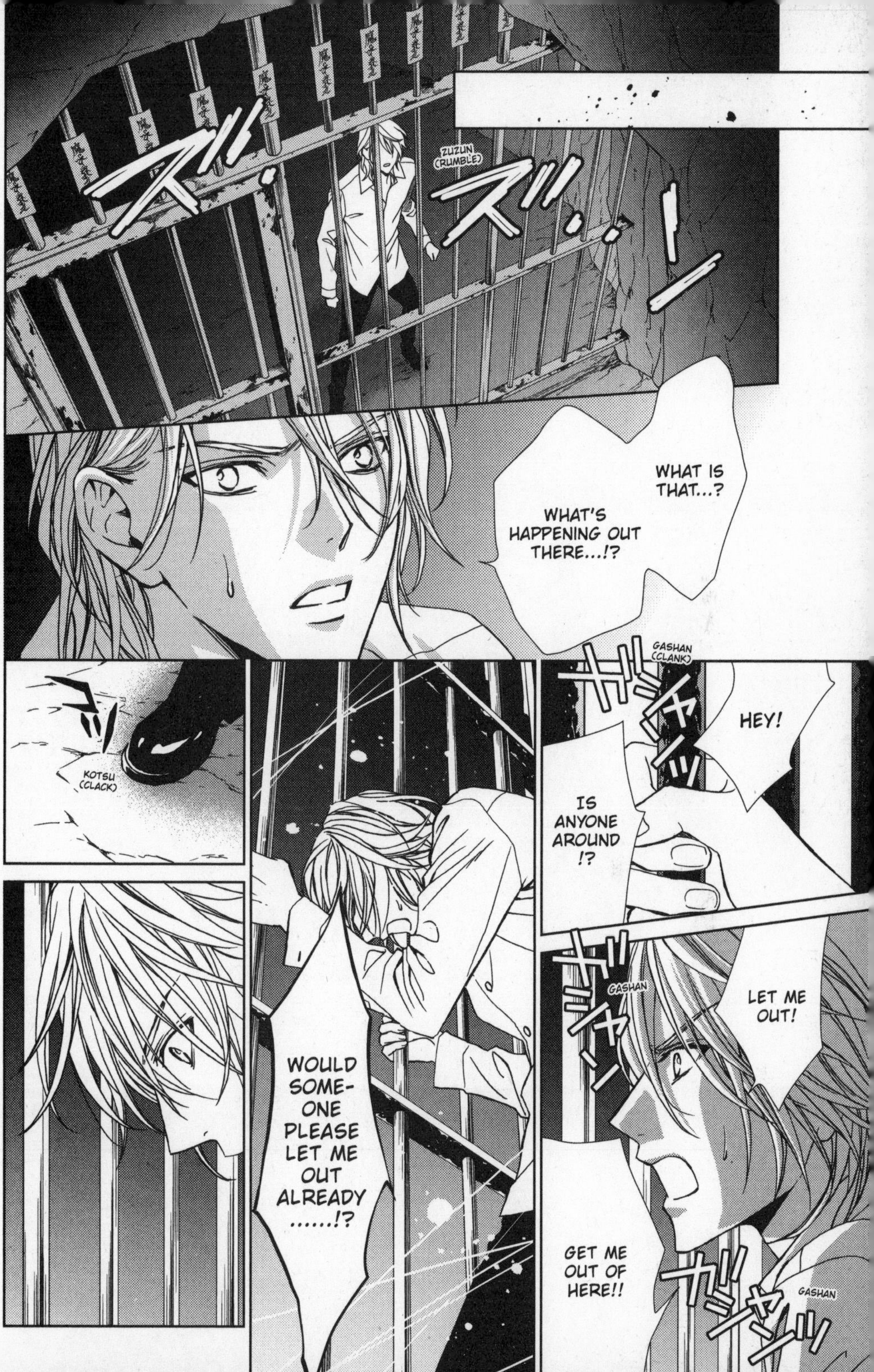
ZUZUN (RUMBLE)
WHAT IS THAT...?
WHAT'S HAPPENING OUT THERE...!?
GASHAN (CLANK)
HEY!
IS ANYONE AROUND !?
GASHAN
LET ME OUT!
GET ME OUT OF HERE!!
GASHAN
WOULD SOME-ONE PLEASE LET ME OUT ALREADY ......!?
KOTSU (CLACK)

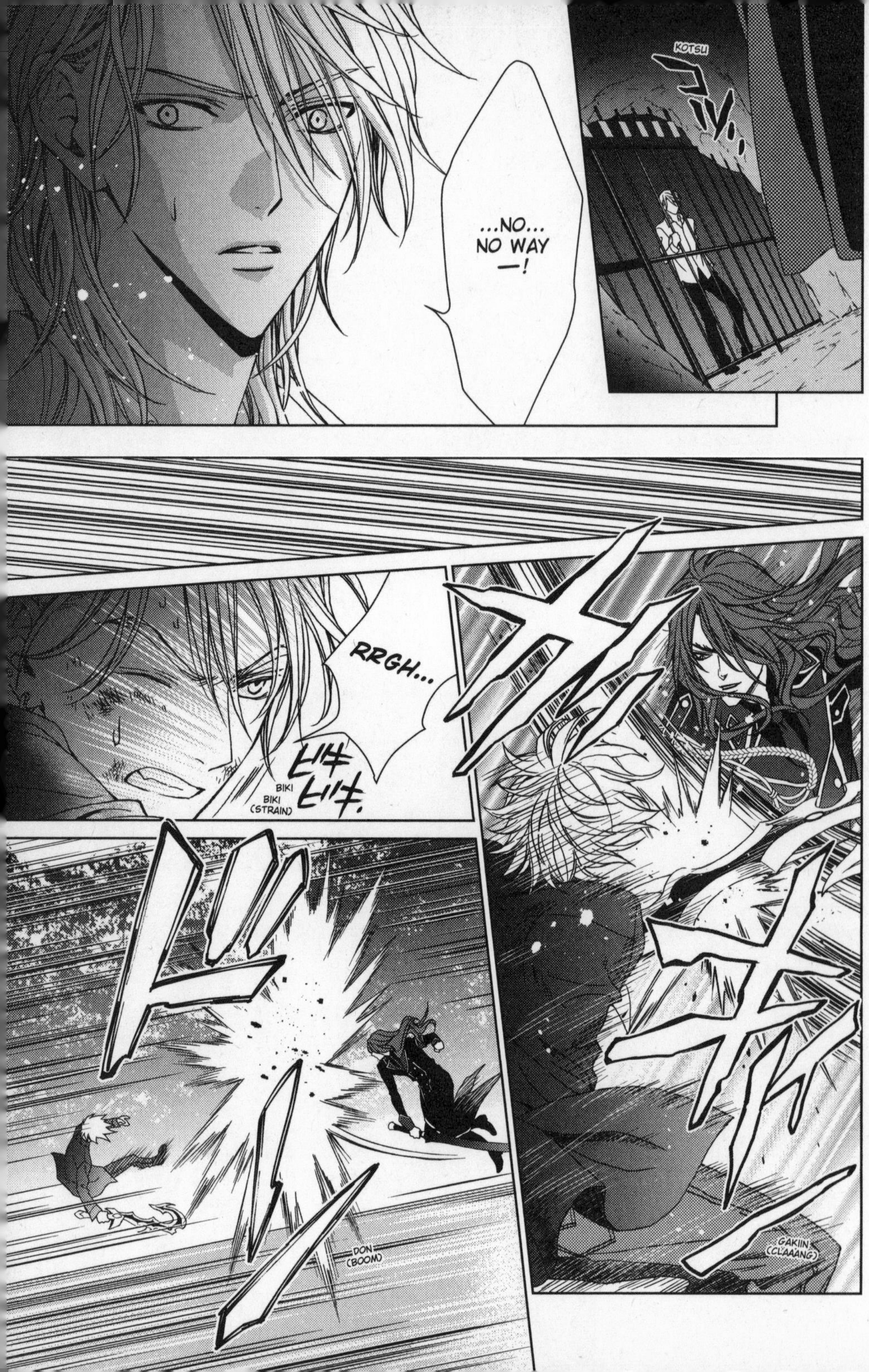
KOTSU
...NO...
NO WAY
—!
GAKIIN
(CLAAANG)
RRGH...
BIKI
BIKI
(STRAIN)
DON
(BOOM)

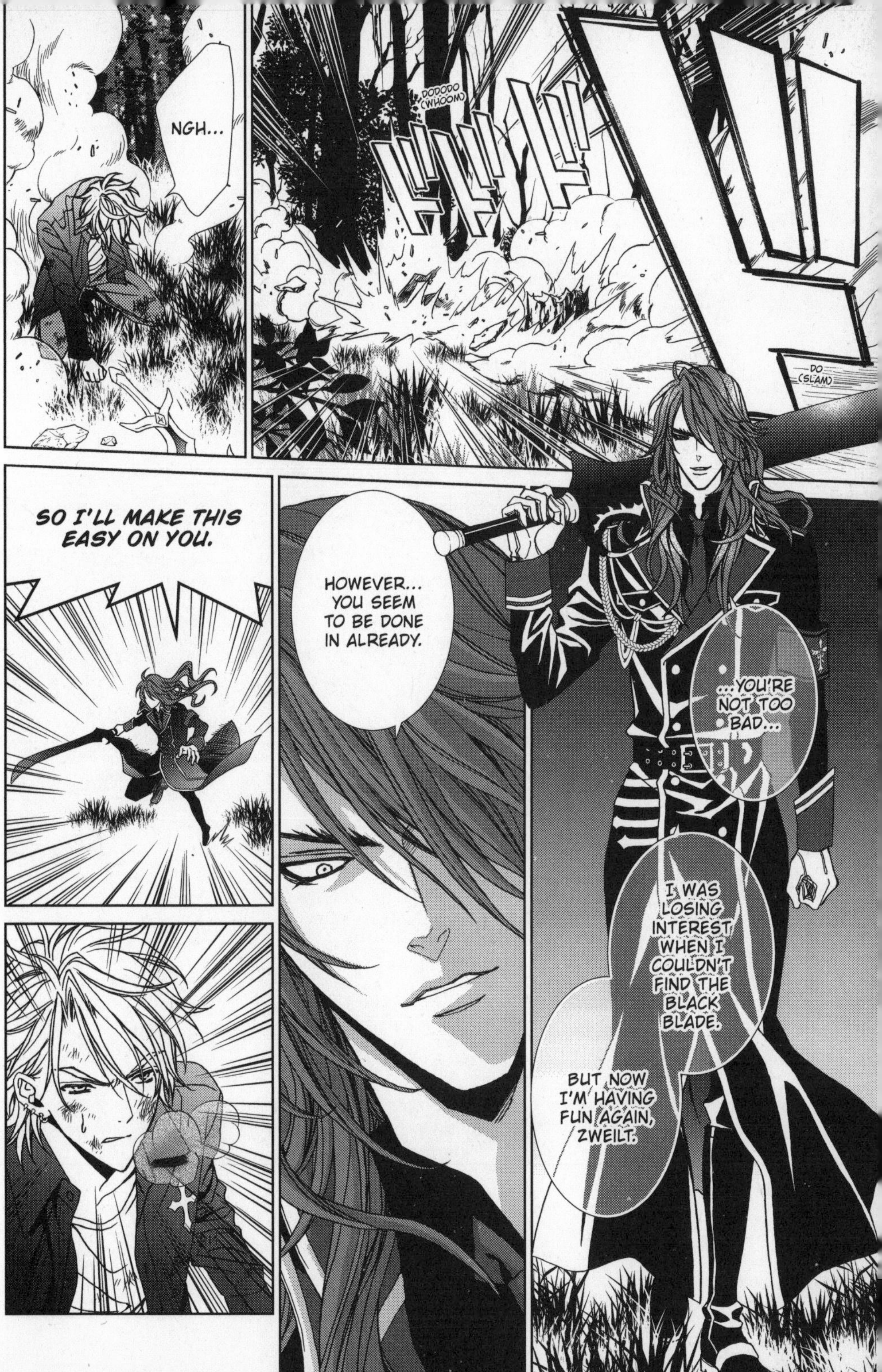
DODODO (WHOOM)
DO (SLAM)
NGH...
...YOU'RE NOT TOO BAD...
I WAS LOSING INTEREST WHEN I COULDN'T FIND THE BLACK BLADE.
BUT NOW I'M HAVING FUN AGAIN, ZWEILT.
HOWEVER... YOU SEEM TO BE DONE IN ALREADY.
SO I'LL MAKE THIS EASY ON YOU.

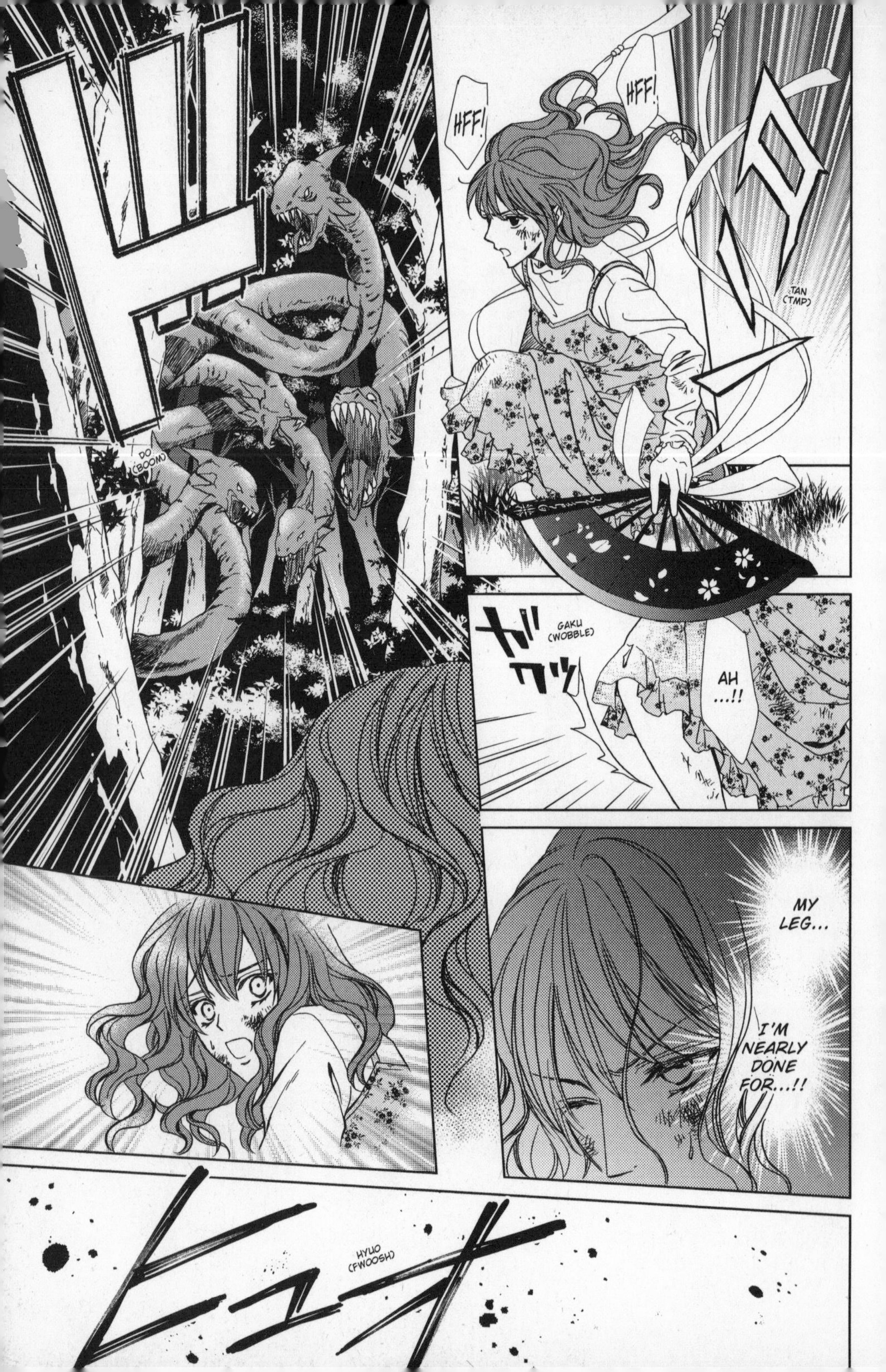
HFF!
HFF!
TAN (TMP)
GAKU (WOBBLE)
AH ...!!
DO (BOOM)
MY LEG...
I'M NEARLY DONE FOR...!!
HYUO (FWOOSH)

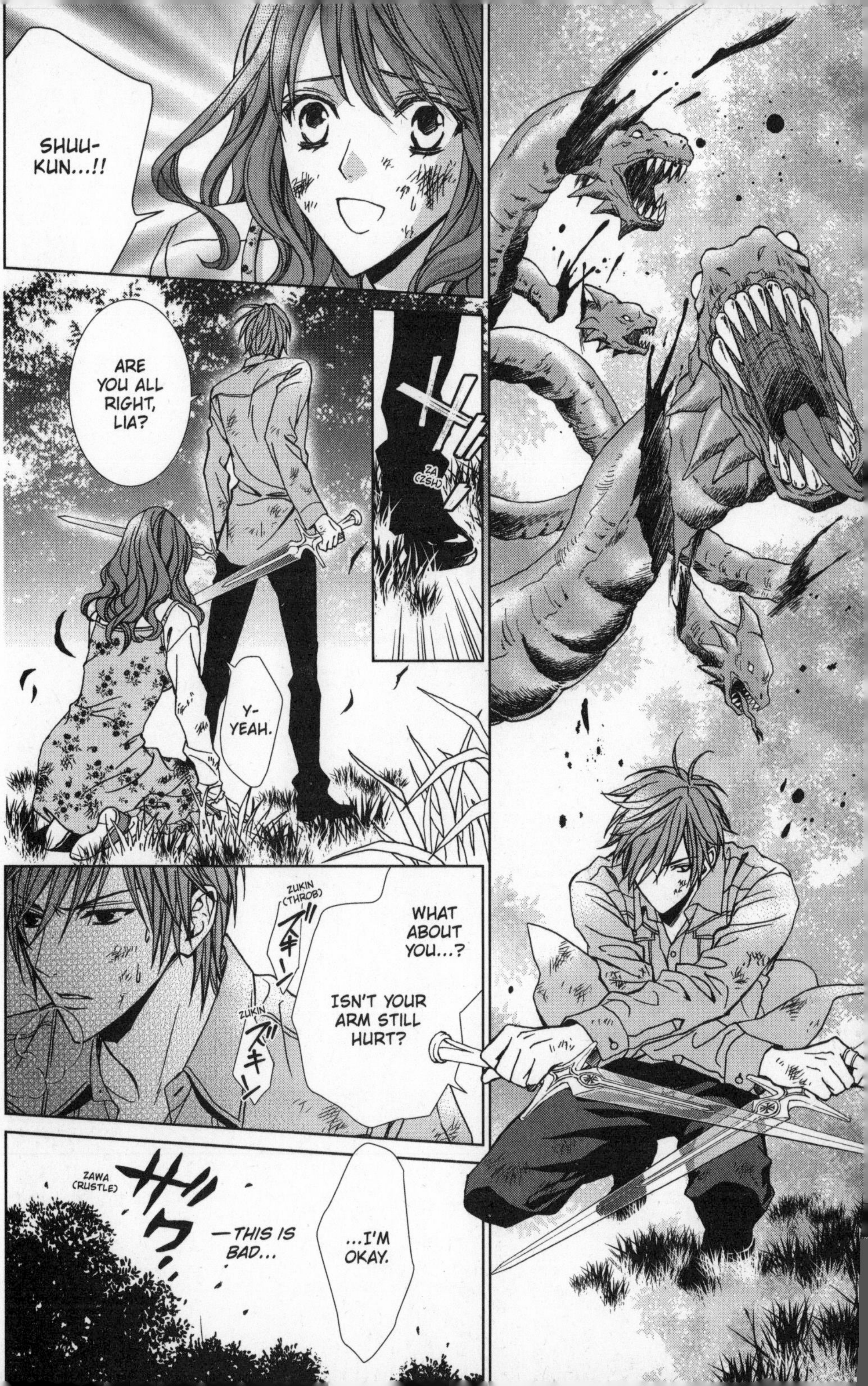
SHUU-KUN...!!
ZA (ZSH)
ARE YOU ALL RIGHT, LIA?
Y-YEAH.
WHAT ABOUT YOU...?
ISN'T YOUR ARM STILL HURT?
ZUKIN (THROB)
ZUKIN
...I'M OKAY.
—THIS IS BAD...
ZAWA (RUSTLE)

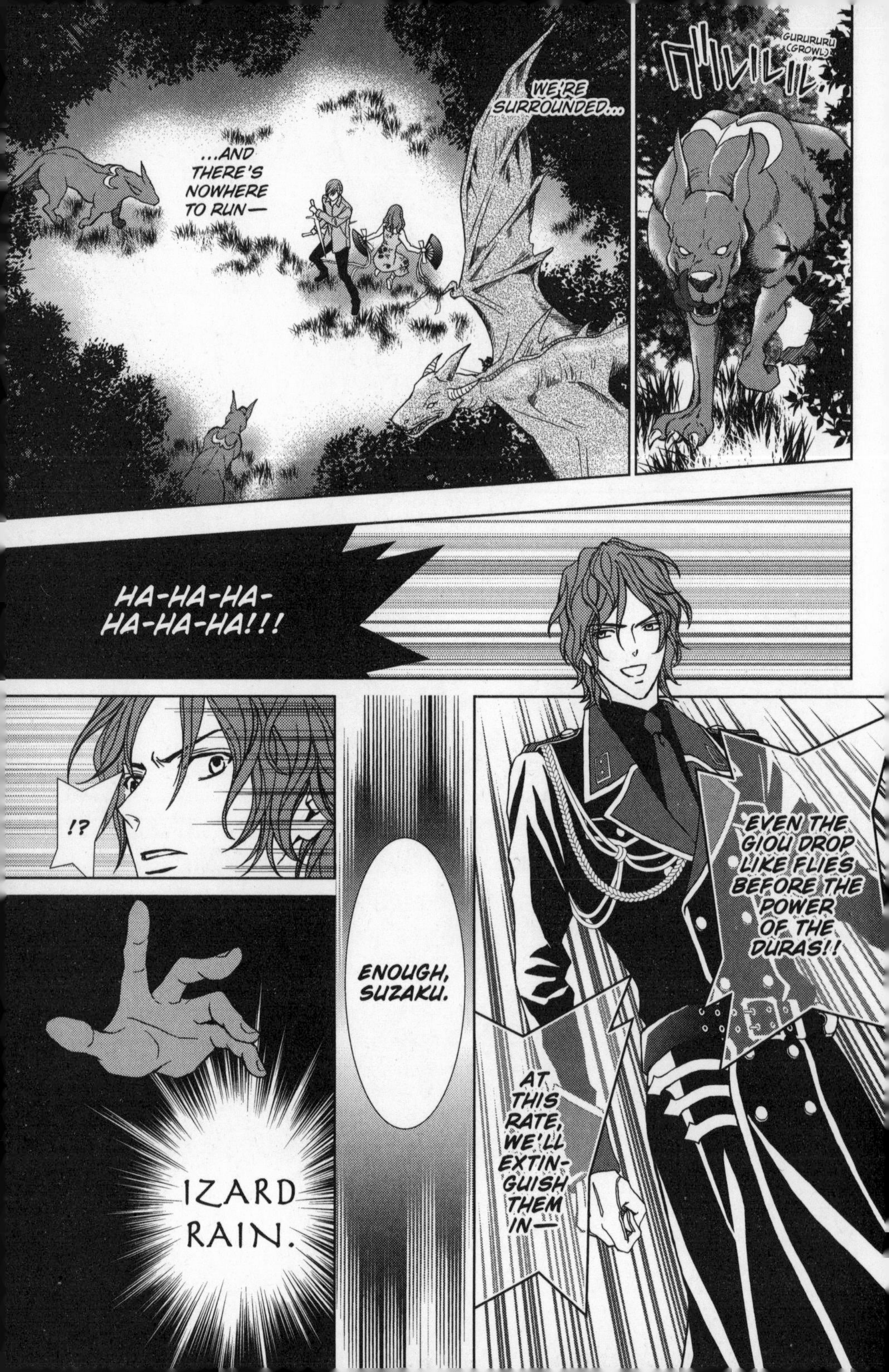
GURURURU (GROWL)
WE'RE SURROUNDED...
...AND THERE'S NOWHERE TO RUN—
HA-HA-HA-HA-HA-HA!!!
EVEN THE GIOU DROP LIKE FLIES BEFORE THE POWER OF THE DURAS!!
AT THIS RATE, WE'LL EXTIN-GUISH THEM IN—
ENOUGH, SUZAKU.
!?
IZARD RAIN.

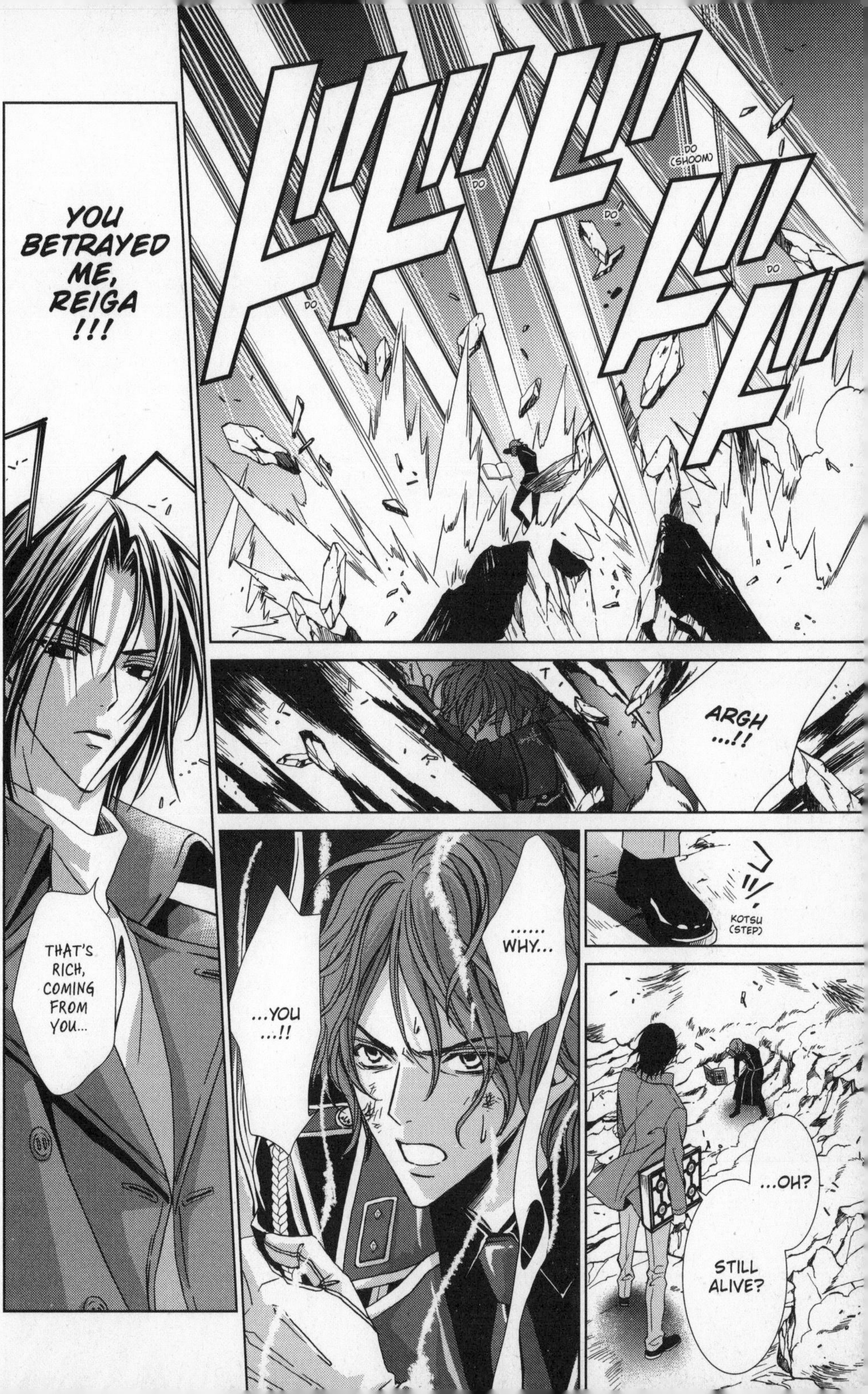
DO (SHOOM)
DO
DO
DO
DO
ARGH ...!!
KOTSU (STEP)
...OH?
STILL ALIVE?
...... WHY...
...YOU ...!!
YOU BETRAYED ME, REIGA !!!
THAT'S RICH, COMING FROM YOU...

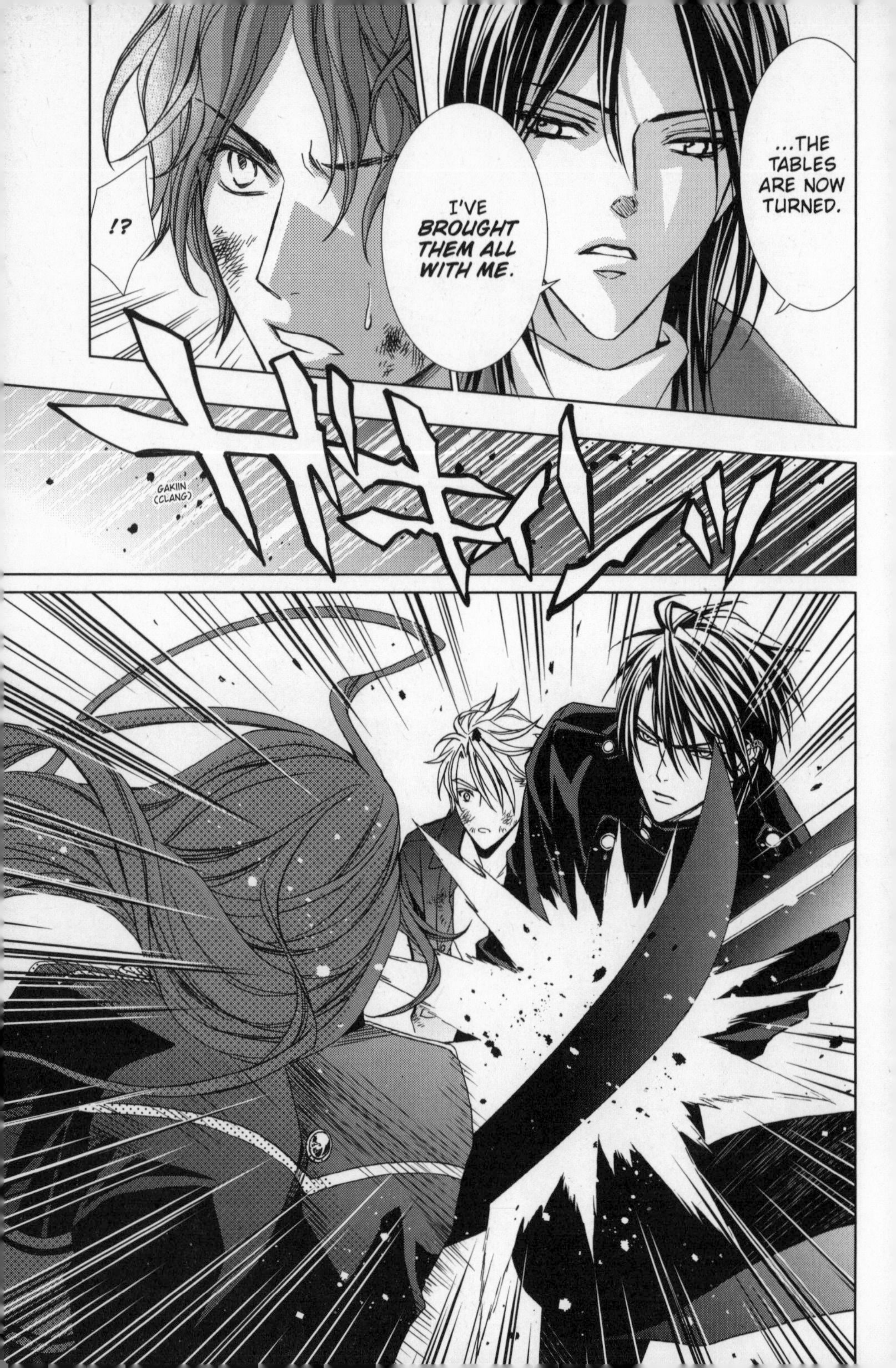
...THE TABLES ARE NOW TURNED.
I'VE BROUGHT THEM ALL WITH ME.
!?
GAKIIN (CLANG)

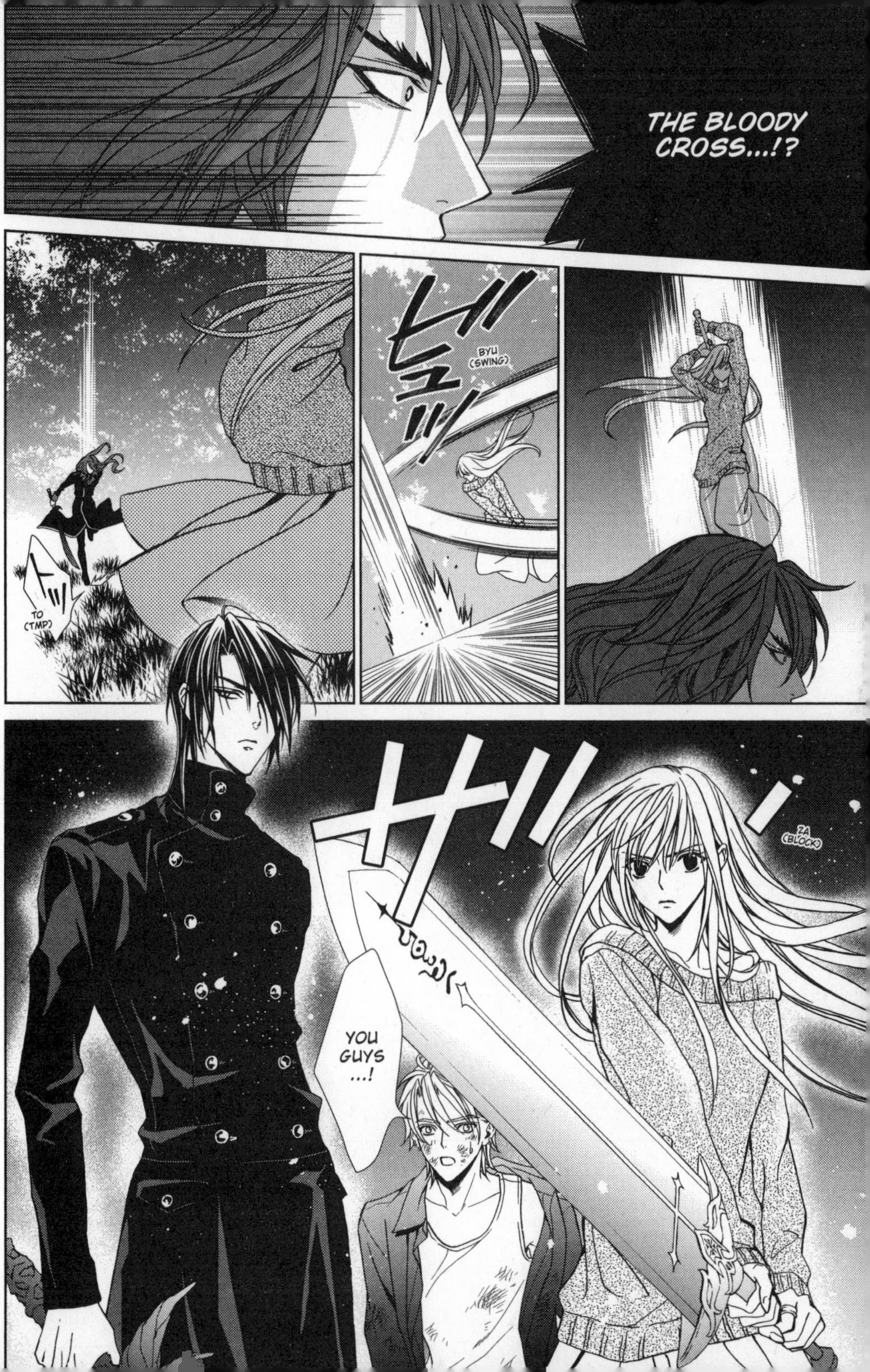
THE BLOODY CROSS...!?
BYU (SWING)
TO (TMP)
ZA (BLOCK)
YOU GUYS ...!

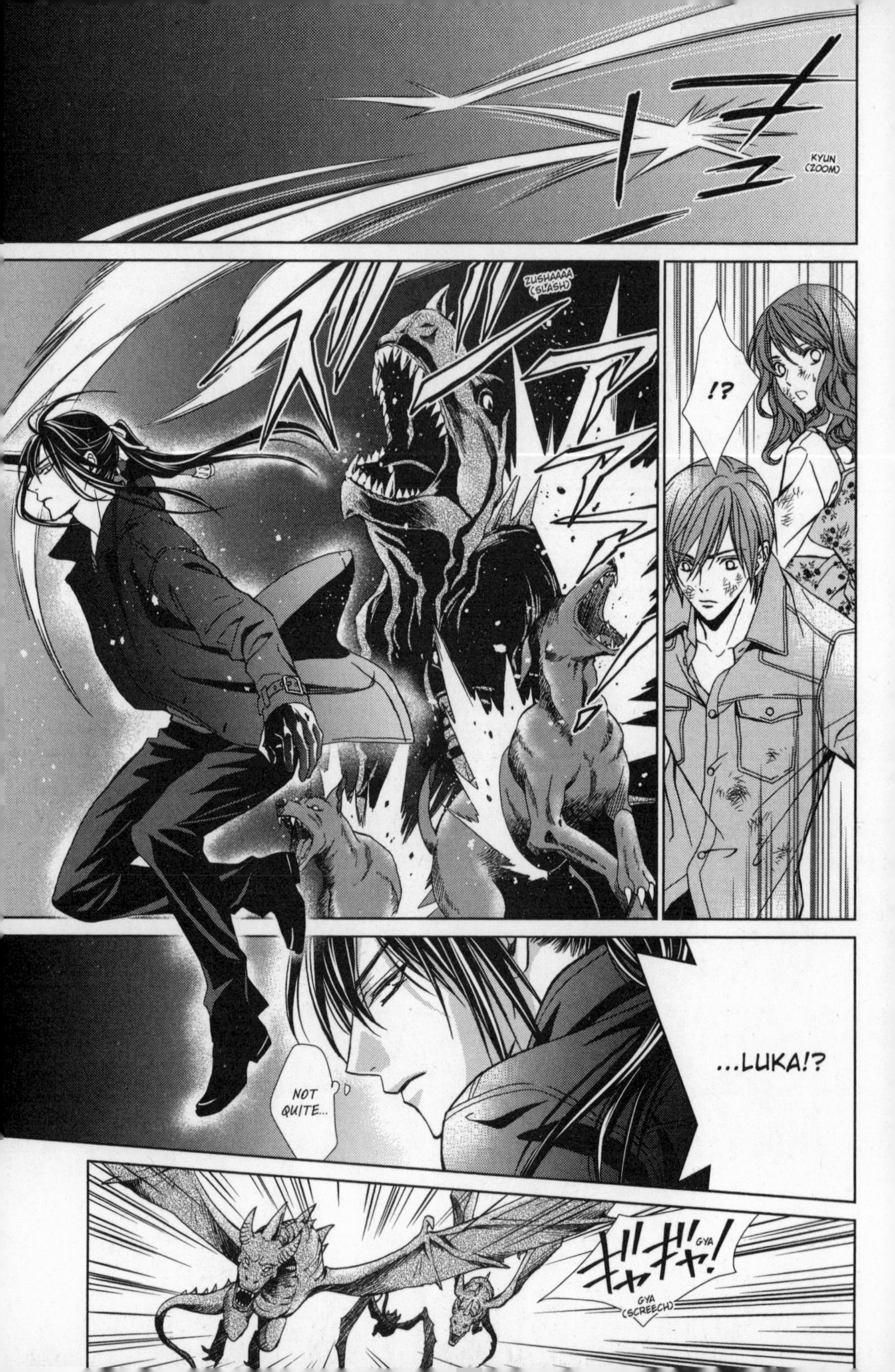
KYUN (ZOOM)
!?
ZUSHAAAA (SLASH)
...LUKA!?
NOT QUITE...
GYA GYA (SCREECH)

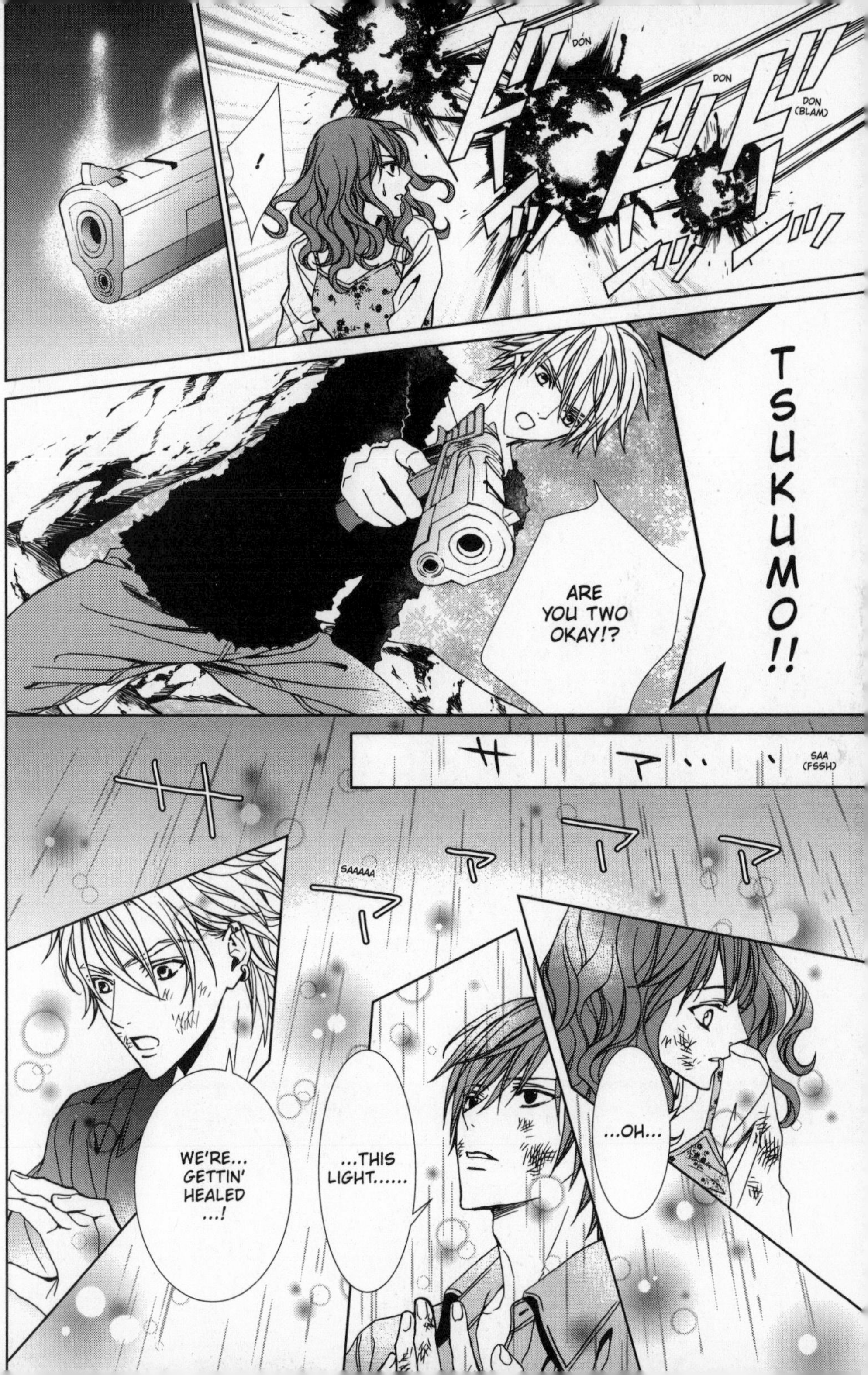
DON
DON
DON (BLAM)
!
TSUKUMO!!
ARE YOU TWO OKAY!?
SAA (FSSH)
SAAAAA
...OH...
...THIS LIGHT......
WE'RE... GETTIN' HEALED ...!

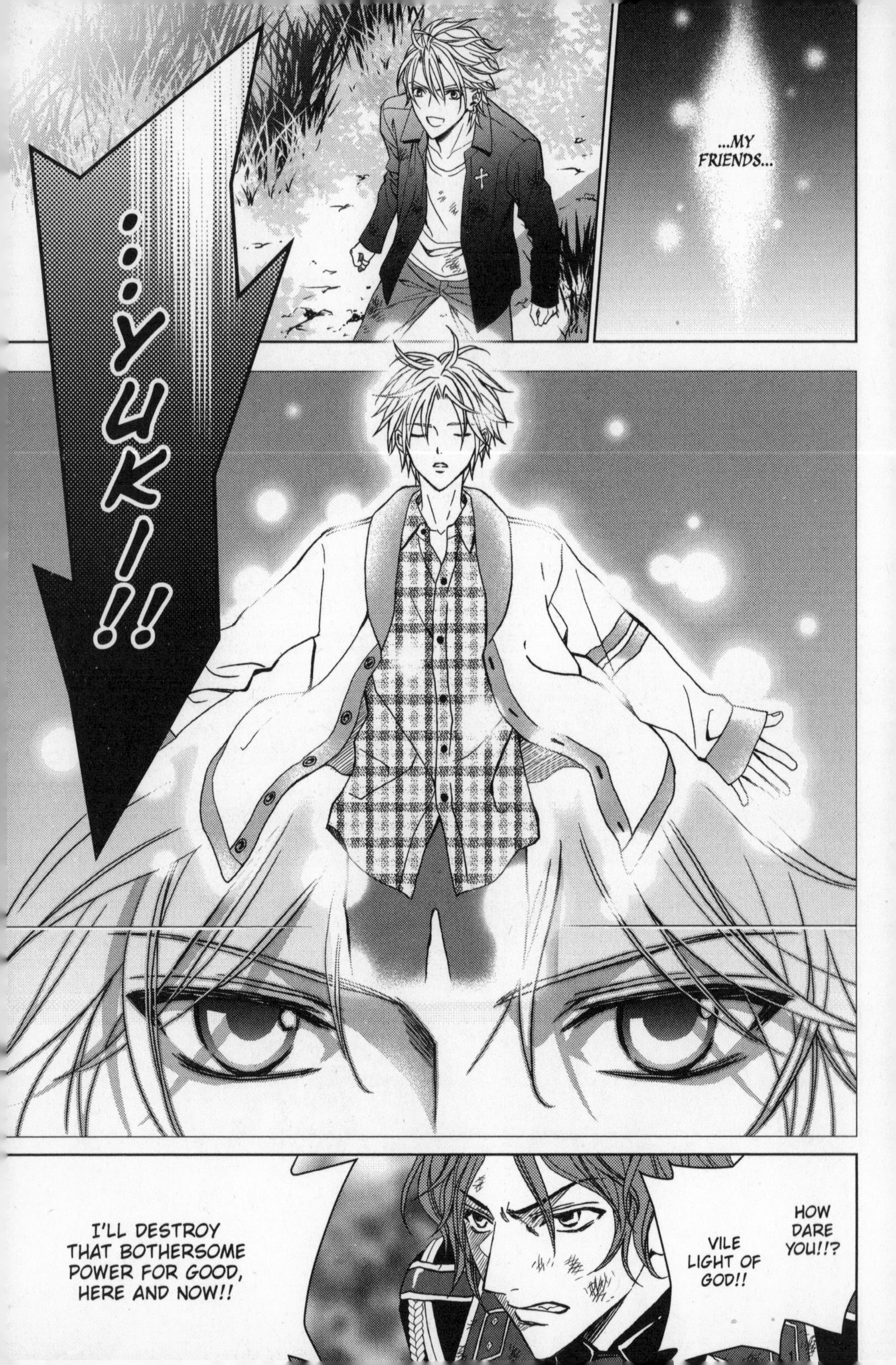
...MY FRIENDS...
...YUKI!!
HOW DARE YOU!!?
VILE LIGHT OF GOD!!
I'LL DESTROY THAT BOTHERSOME POWER FOR GOOD, HERE AND NOW!!

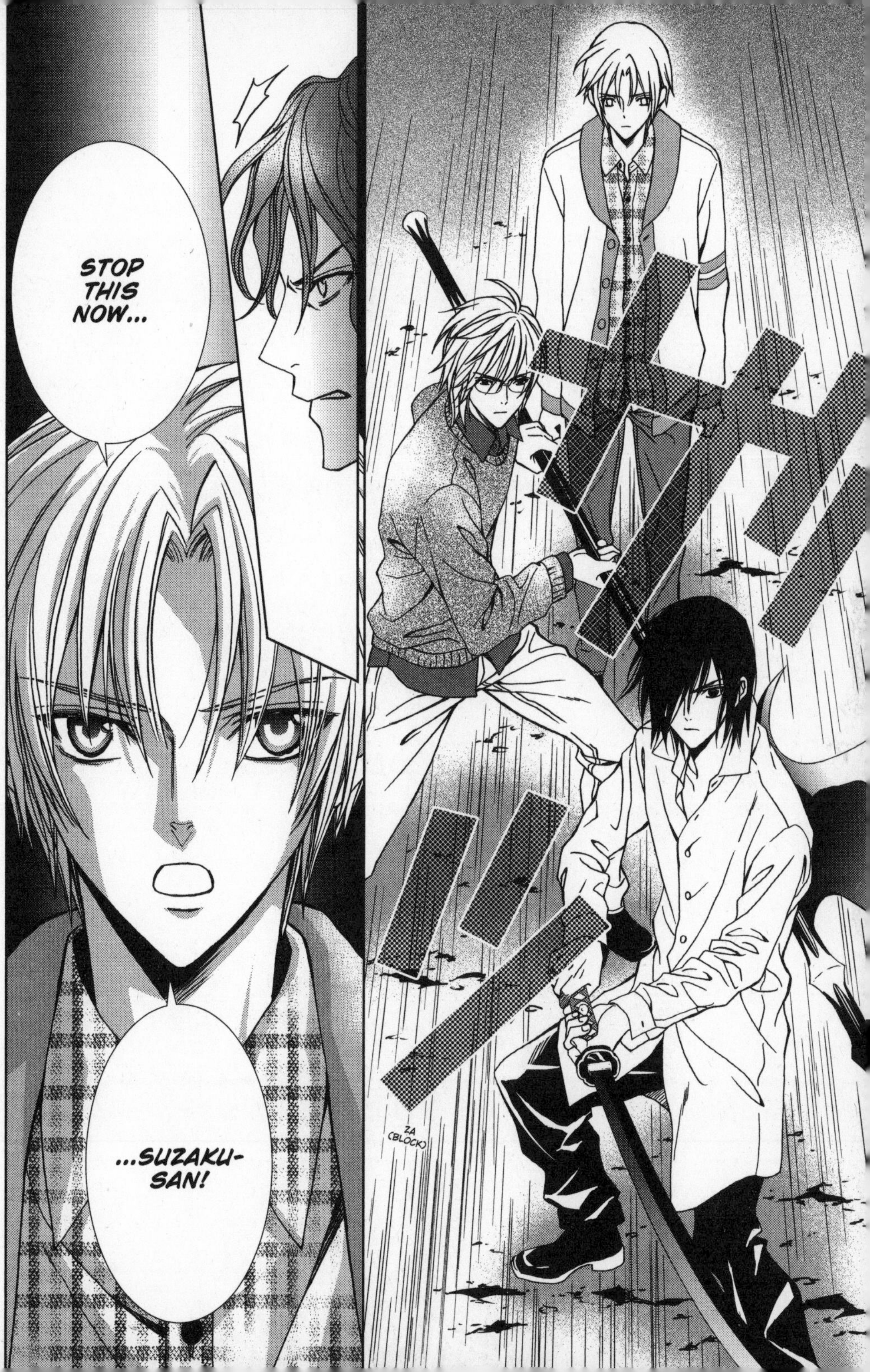
ZA (BLOCK)
STOP THIS NOW...
...SUZAKU-SAN!

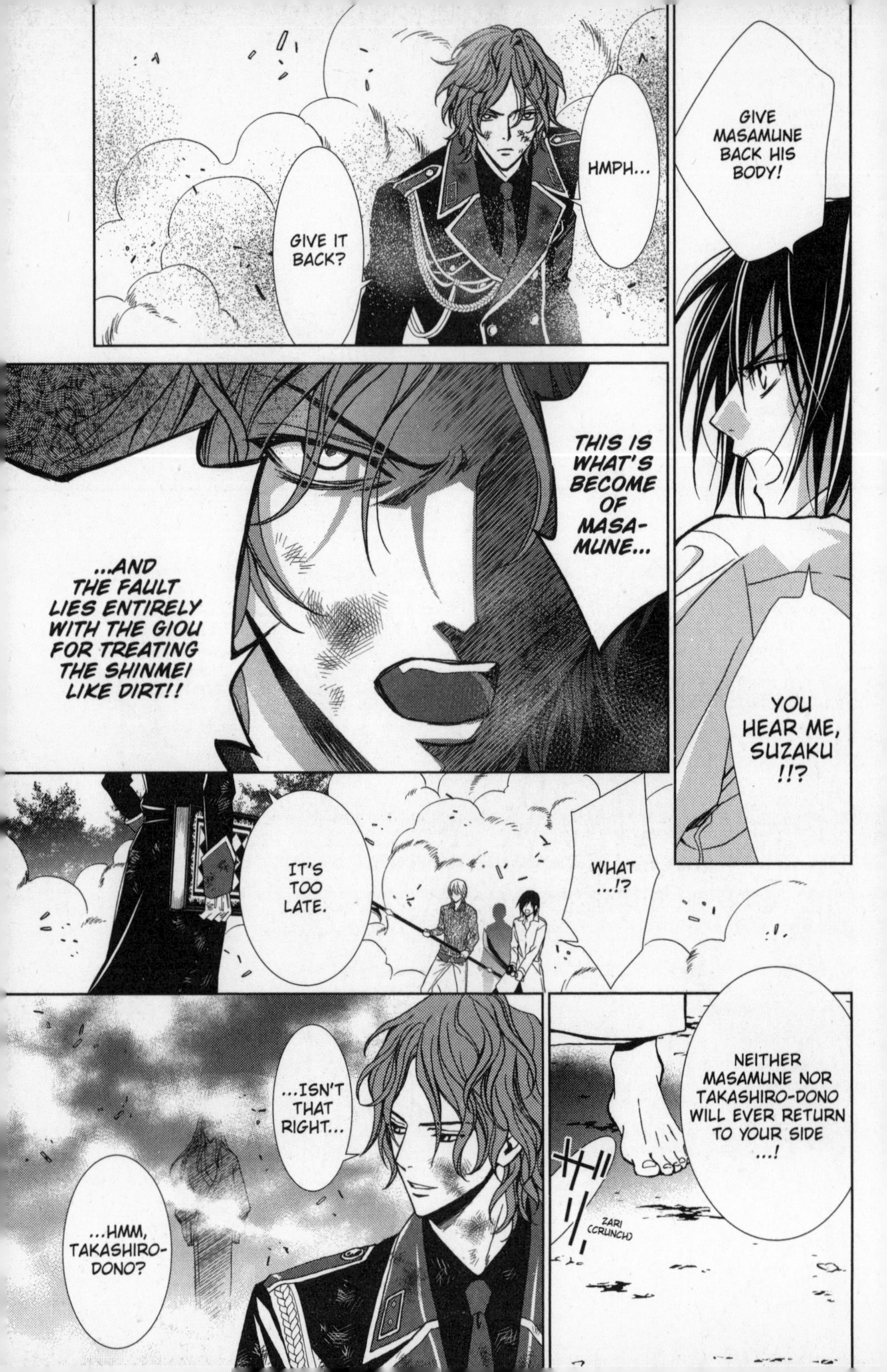
GIVE MASAMUNE BACK HIS BODY!
YOU HEAR ME, SUZAKU!!?
HMPH...
GIVE IT BACK?
THIS IS WHAT'S BECOME OF MASA-MUNE...
...AND THE FAULT LIES ENTIRELY WITH THE GIOU FOR TREATING THE SHINMEI LIKE DIRT!!
WHAT ...!?
IT'S TOO LATE.
NEITHER MASAMUNE NOR TAKASHIRO-DONO WILL EVER RETURN TO YOUR SIDE ...!
ZARI (CRUNCH)
...ISN'T THAT RIGHT...
...HMM, TAKASHIRO-DONO?

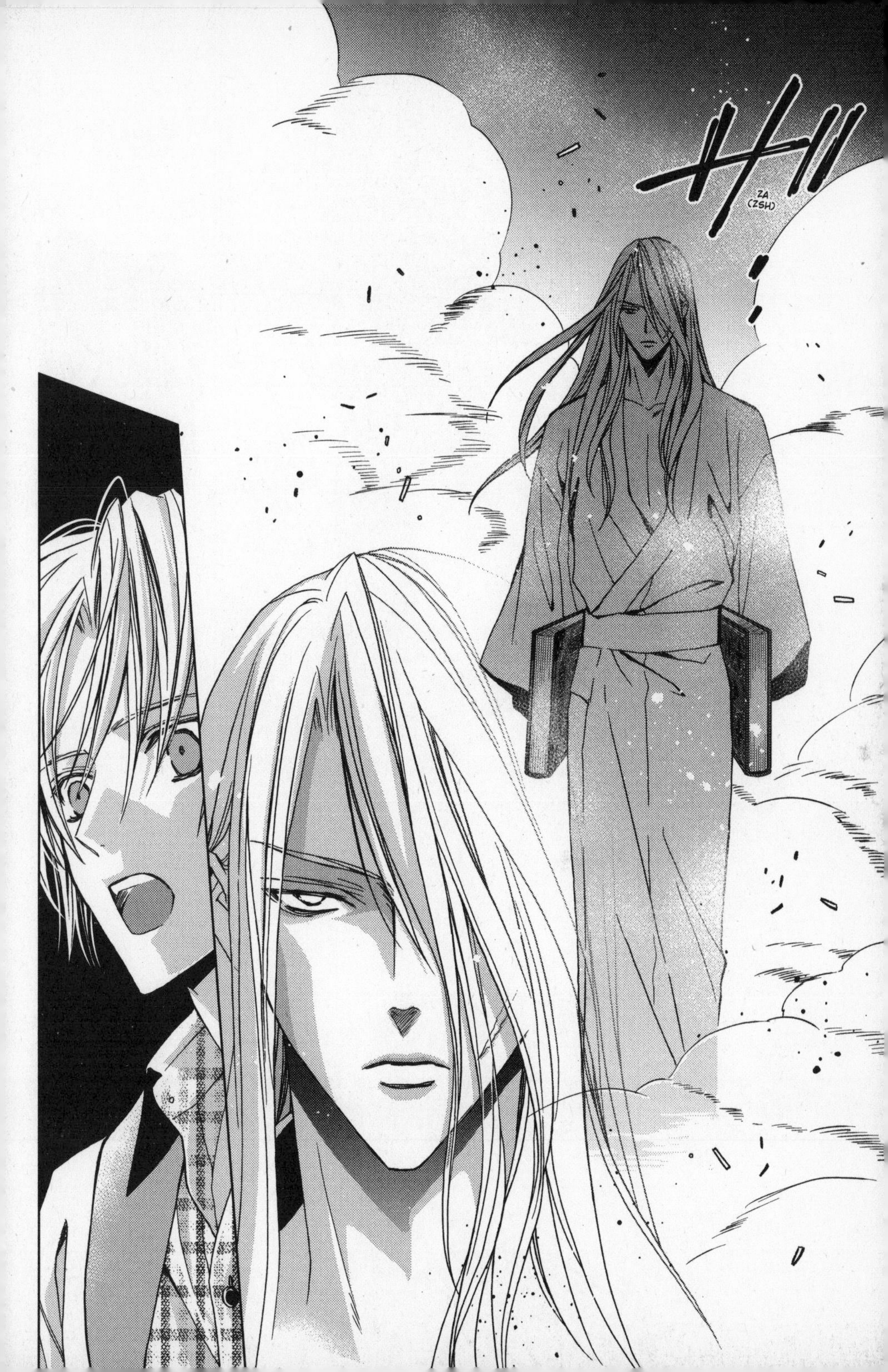
ZA
(ZSH)

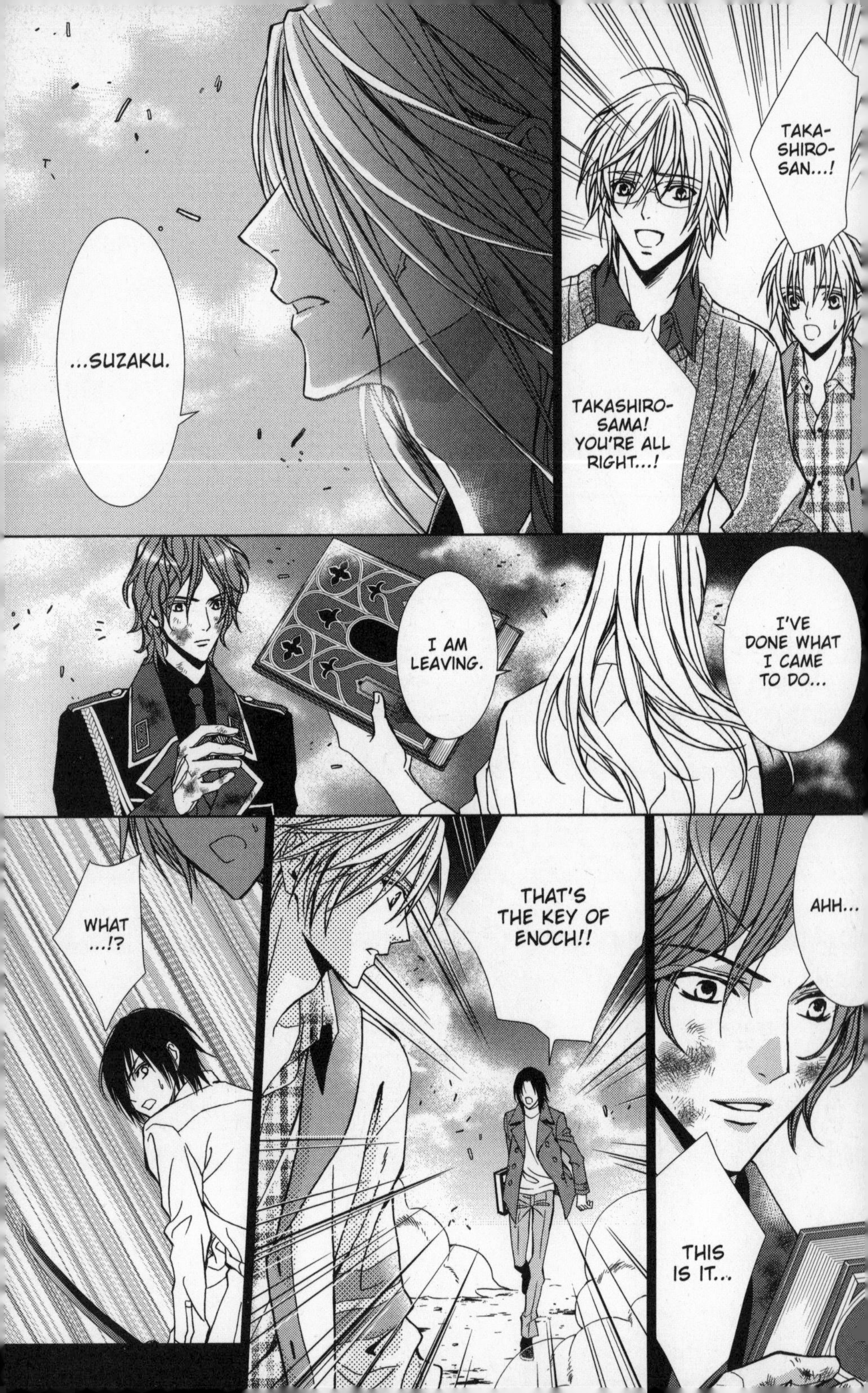
TAKA-SHIRO-SAN...!
TAKASHIRO-SAMA! YOU'RE ALL RIGHT...!
...SUZAKU.
I'VE DONE WHAT I CAME TO DO...
I AM LEAVING.
AHH...
THIS IS IT...
THAT'S THE KEY OF ENOCH!!
WHAT ...!?

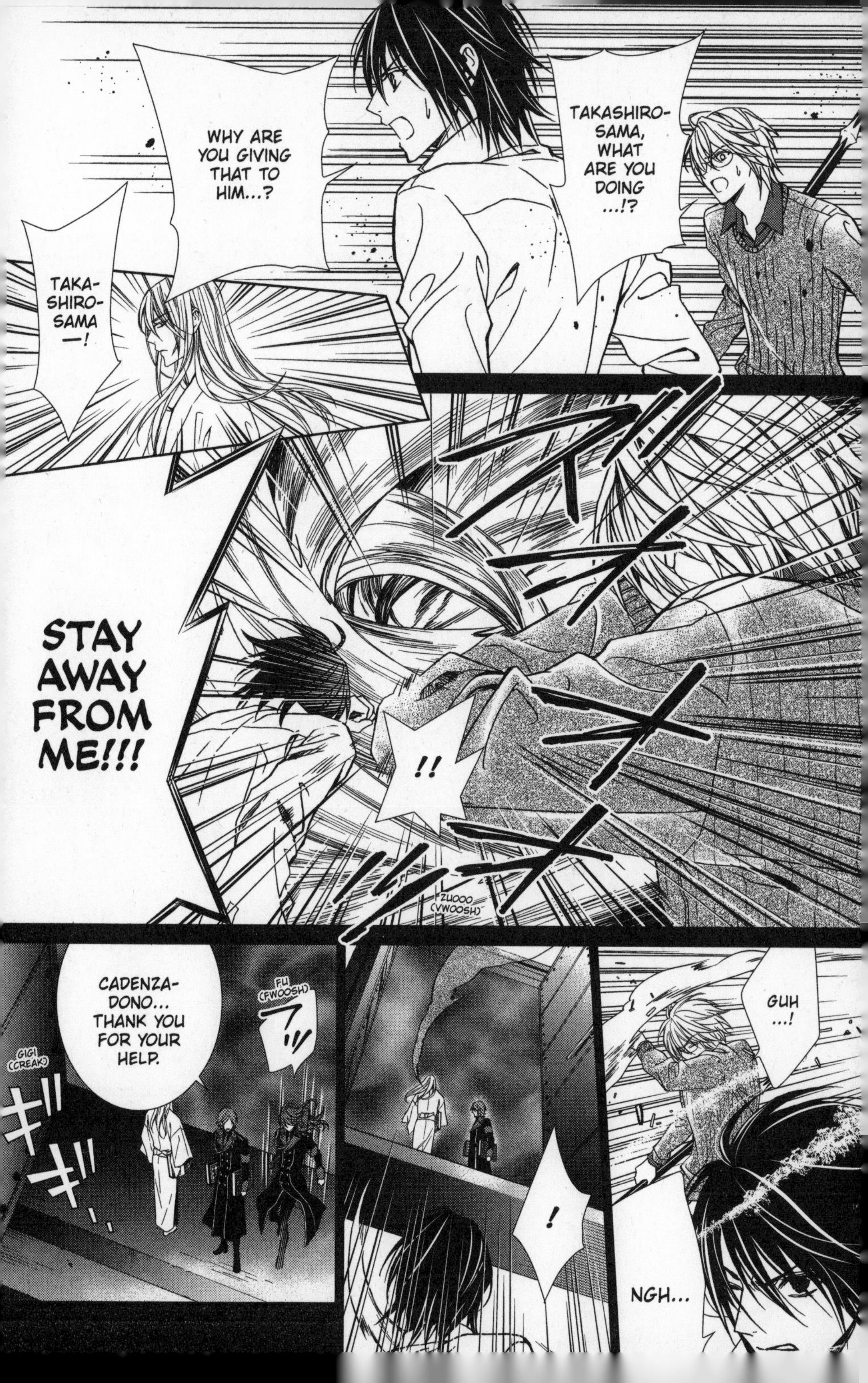
TAKASHIRO-SAMA, WHAT ARE YOU DOING ...!?
WHY ARE YOU GIVING THAT TO HIM...?
TAKA-SHIRO-SAMA —!
!!
ZUOOO (VWOOSH)
STAY AWAY FROM ME!!!
GUH ...!
NGH...
!
CADENZA-DONO... THANK YOU FOR YOUR HELP.
FU (FWOOSH)
GIGI (CREAK)

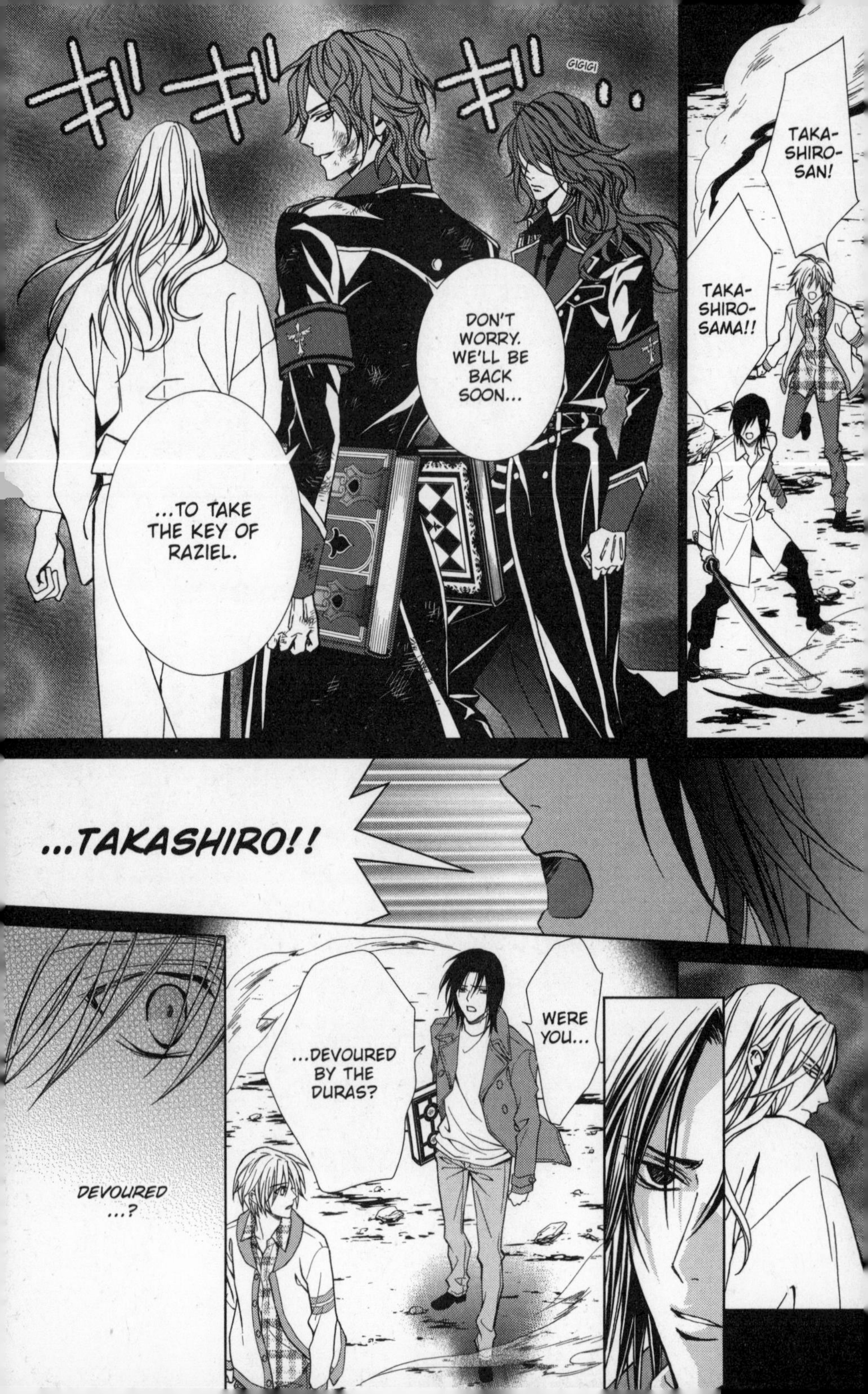
TAKA-SHIRO-SAN!
TAKA-SHIRO-SAMA!!
ギギギ..
GIGIGI
DON'T WORRY. WE'LL BE BACK SOON...
...TO TAKE THE KEY OF RAZIEL.
...TAKASHIRO!!
WERE YOU...
...DEVOURED BY THE DURAS?
DEVOURED ...?

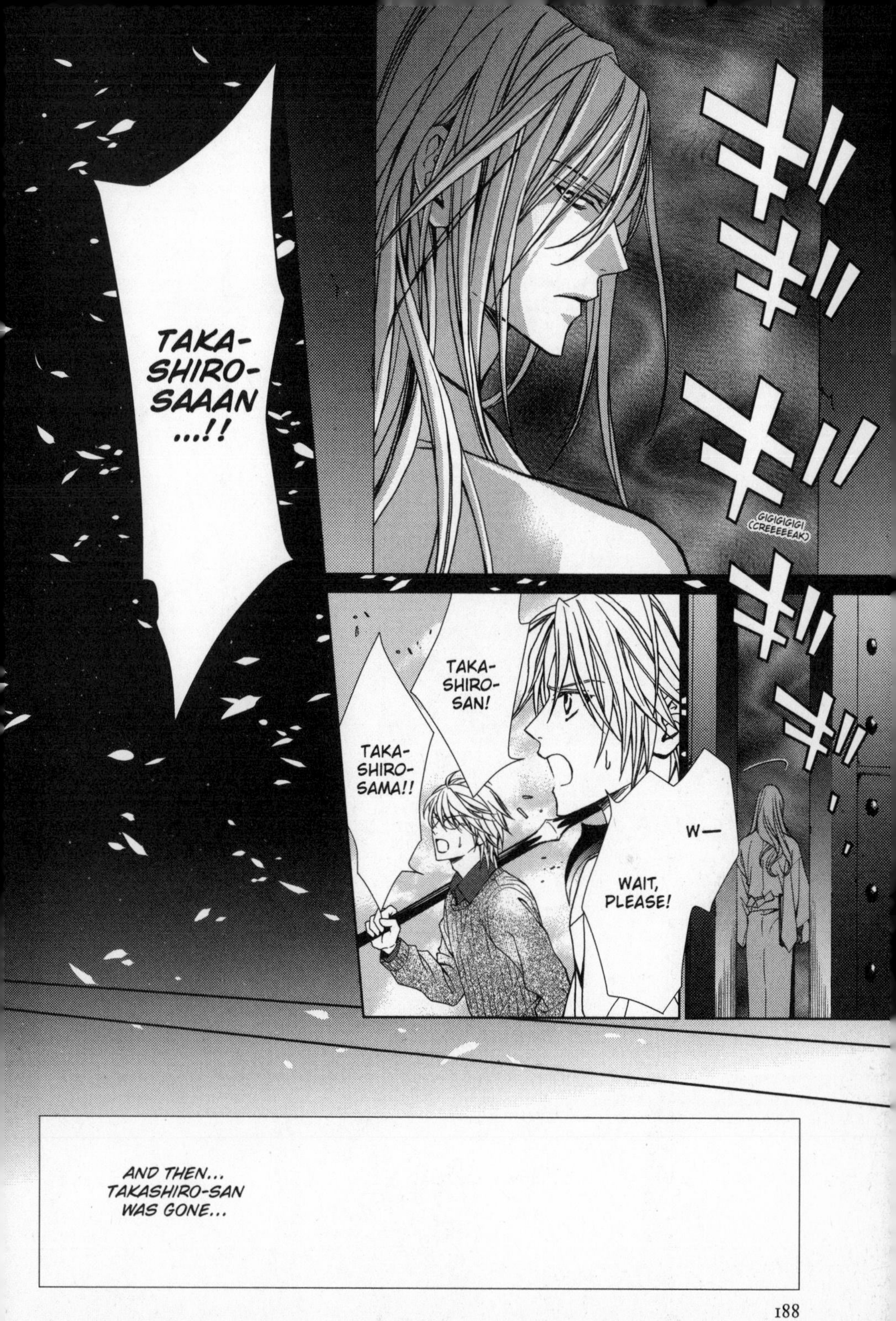
GIGIGIGIGI (CREEEEEAK)
TAKA-SHIRO-SAN!
TAKA-SHIRO-SAMA!!
W—
WAIT, PLEASE!
TAKA-SHIRO-SAAAN ...!!
AND THEN... TAKASHIRO-SAN WAS GONE...

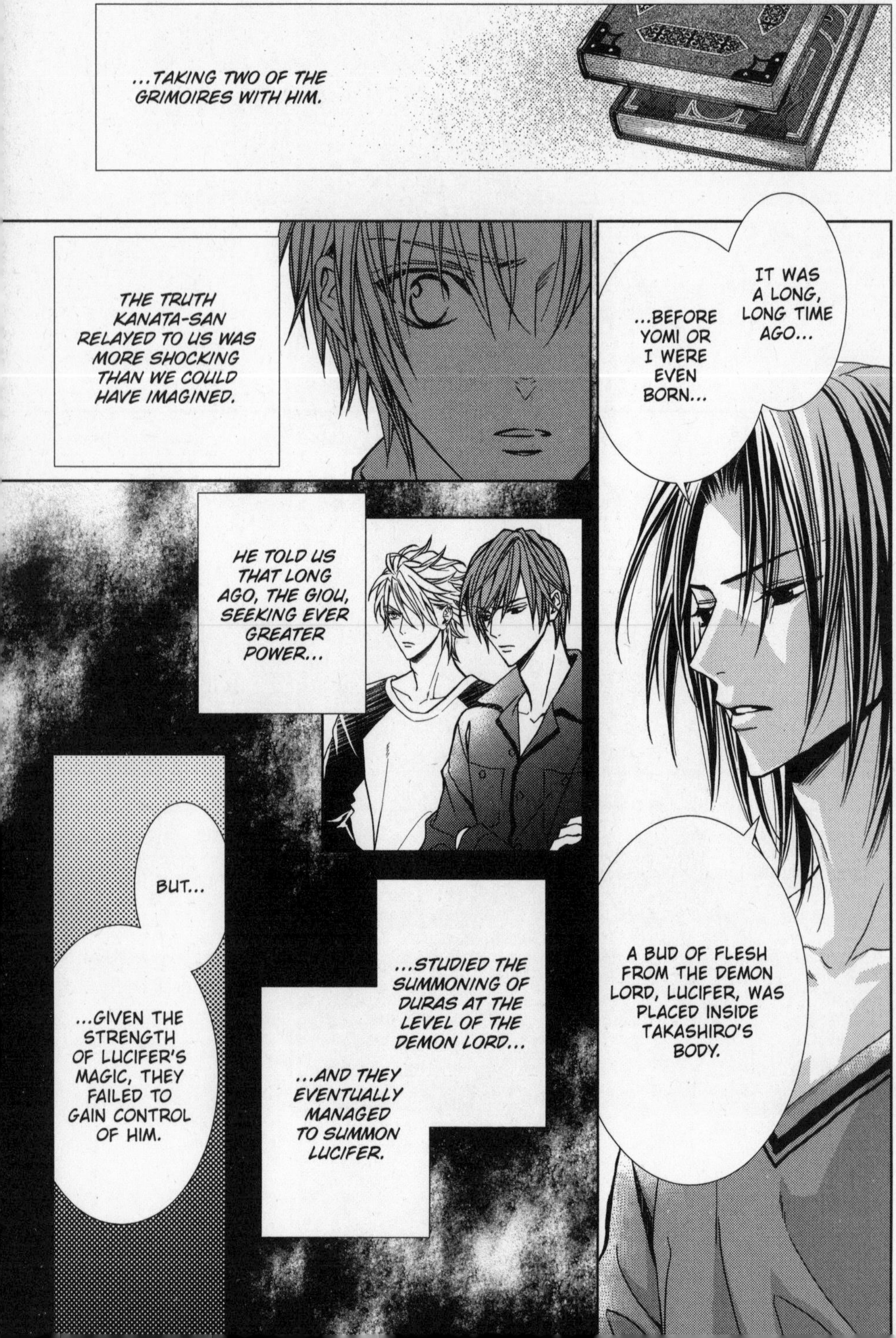
...TAKING TWO OF THE GRIMOIRES WITH HIM.
IT WAS A LONG, LONG TIME AGO...
...BEFORE YOMI OR I WERE EVEN BORN...
A BUD OF FLESH FROM THE DEMON LORD, LUCIFER, WAS PLACED INSIDE TAKASHIRO'S BODY.
THE TRUTH KANATA-SAN RELAYED TO US WAS MORE SHOCKING THAN WE COULD HAVE IMAGINED.
HE TOLD US THAT LONG AGO, THE GIOU, SEEKING EVER GREATER POWER...
...STUDIED THE SUMMONING OF DURAS AT THE LEVEL OF THE DEMON LORD...
...AND THEY EVENTUALLY MANAGED TO SUMMON LUCIFER.
BUT...
...GIVEN THE STRENGTH OF LUCIFER'S MAGIC, THEY FAILED TO GAIN CONTROL OF HIM.

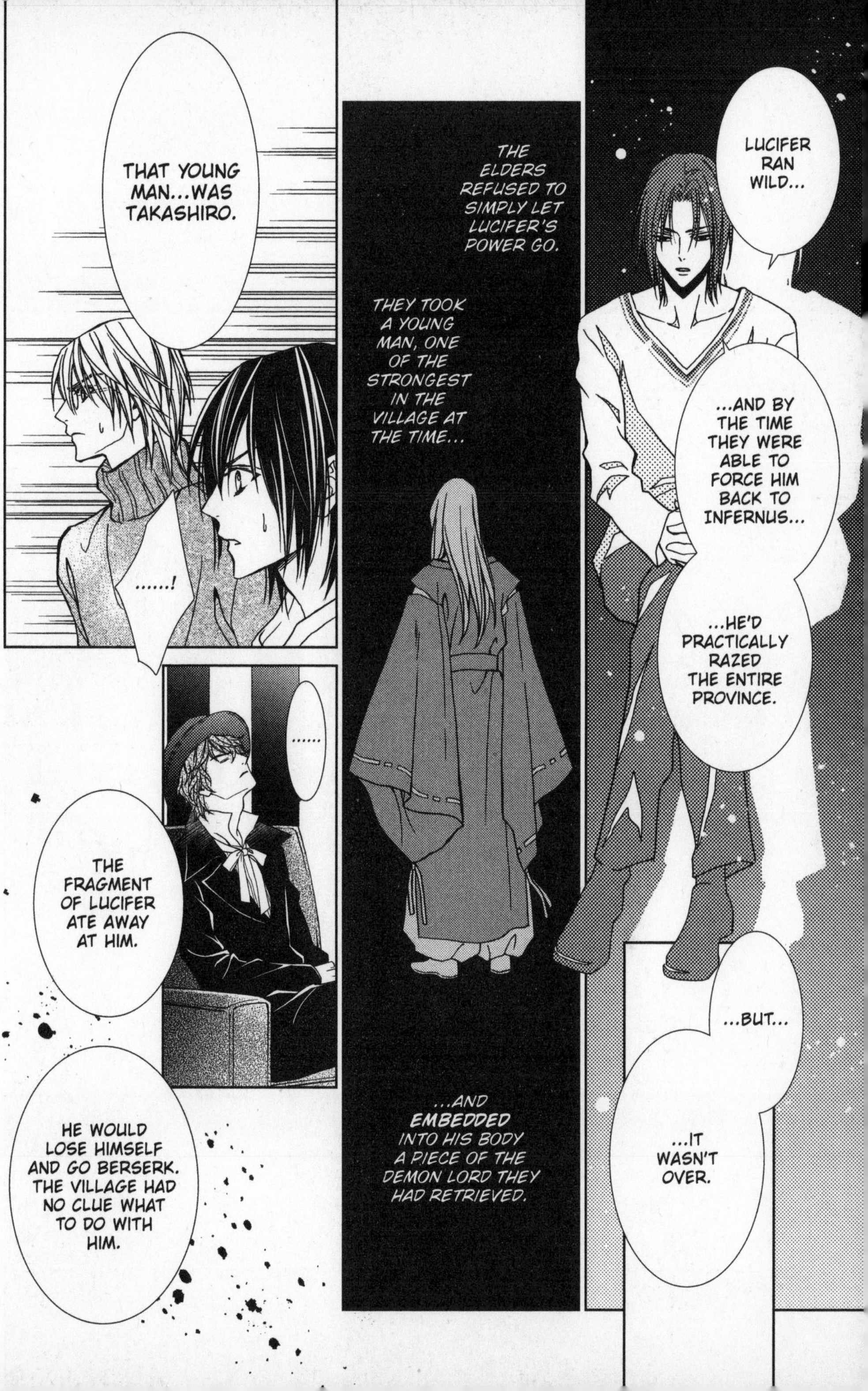
LUCIFER RAN WILD...
...AND BY THE TIME THEY WERE ABLE TO FORCE HIM BACK TO INFERNUS...
...HE'D PRACTICALLY RAZED THE ENTIRE PROVINCE.
...BUT...
...IT WASN'T OVER.
THE ELDERS REFUSED TO SIMPLY LET LUCIFER'S POWER GO.
THEY TOOK A YOUNG MAN, ONE OF THE STRONGEST IN THE VILLAGE AT THE TIME...
...AND **EMBEDDED** INTO HIS BODY A PIECE OF THE DEMON LORD THEY HAD RETRIEVED.
THAT YOUNG MAN...WAS TAKASHIRO.
......!
......
THE FRAGMENT OF LUCIFER ATE AWAY AT HIM.
HE WOULD LOSE HIMSELF AND GO BERSERK. THE VILLAGE HAD NO CLUE WHAT TO DO WITH HIM.

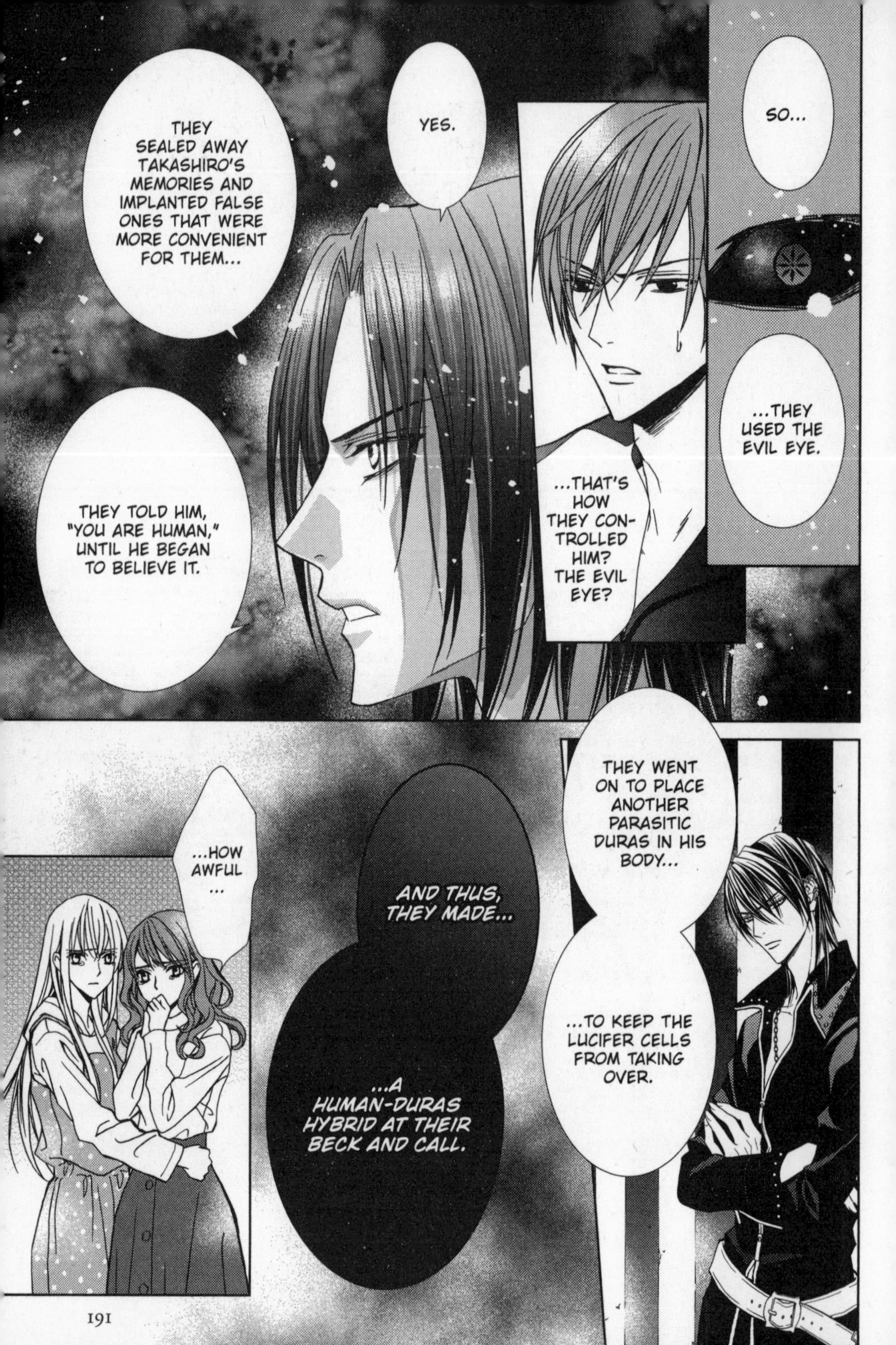
SO...
...THEY USED THE EVIL EYE.
...THAT'S HOW THEY CON-TROLLED HIM? THE EVIL EYE?
YES.
THEY SEALED AWAY TAKASHIRO'S MEMORIES AND IMPLANTED FALSE ONES THAT WERE MORE CONVENIENT FOR THEM...
THEY TOLD HIM, "YOU ARE HUMAN," UNTIL HE BEGAN TO BELIEVE IT.
THEY WENT ON TO PLACE ANOTHER PARASITIC DURAS IN HIS BODY...
...TO KEEP THE LUCIFER CELLS FROM TAKING OVER.
AND THUS, THEY MADE...
...A HUMAN-DURAS HYBRID AT THEIR BECK AND CALL.
...HOW AWFUL ...

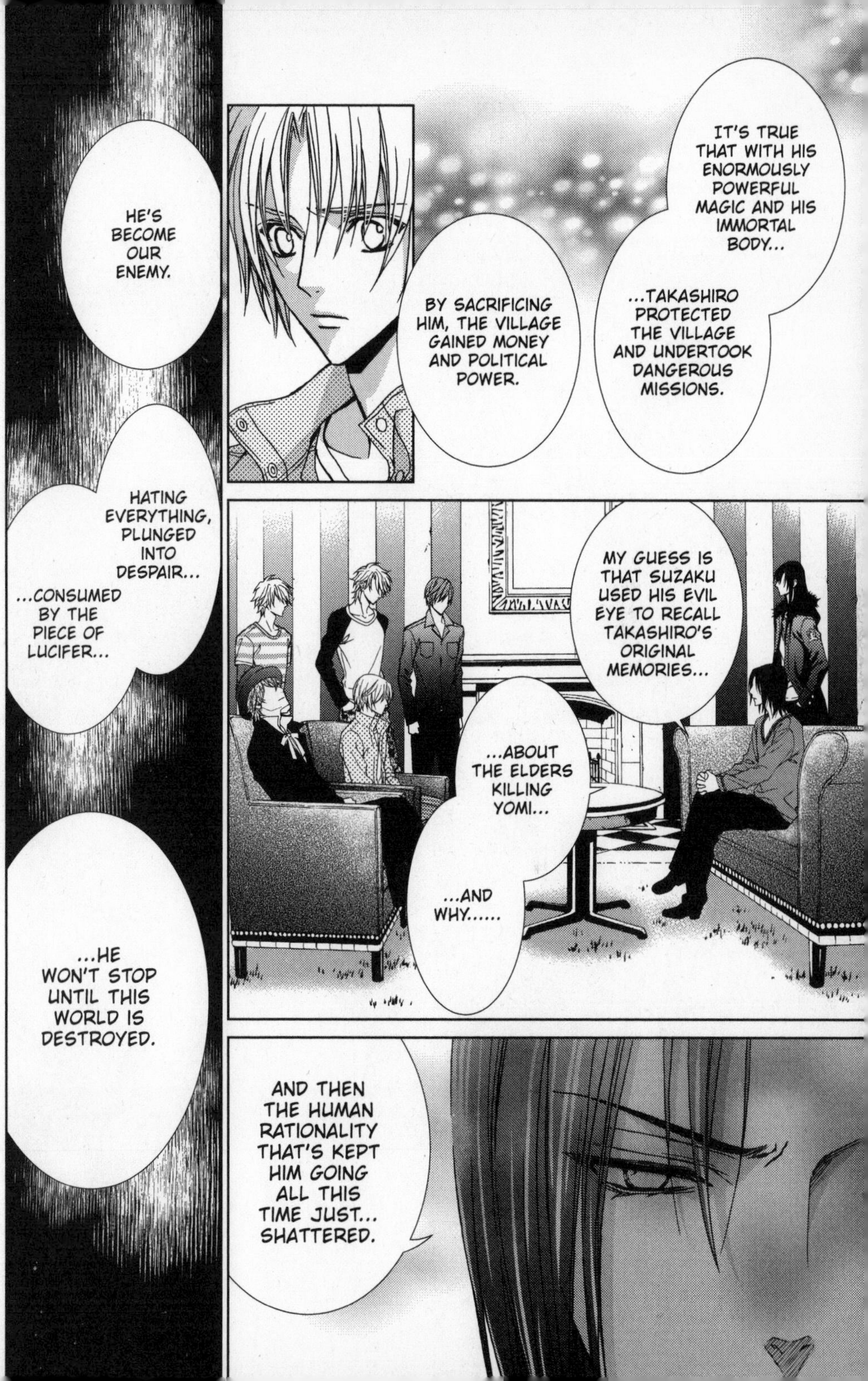
IT'S TRUE THAT WITH HIS ENORMOUSLY POWERFUL MAGIC AND HIS IMMORTAL BODY...
...TAKASHIRO PROTECTED THE VILLAGE AND UNDERTOOK DANGEROUS MISSIONS.
BY SACRIFICING HIM, THE VILLAGE GAINED MONEY AND POLITICAL POWER.
MY GUESS IS THAT SUZAKU USED HIS EVIL EYE TO RECALL TAKASHIRO'S ORIGINAL MEMORIES...
...ABOUT THE ELDERS KILLING YOMI...
...AND WHY......
AND THEN THE HUMAN RATIONALITY THAT'S KEPT HIM GOING ALL THIS TIME JUST... SHATTERED.
HE'S BECOME OUR ENEMY.
HATING EVERYTHING, PLUNGED INTO DESPAIR...
...CONSUMED BY THE PIECE OF LUCIFER...
...HE WON'T STOP UNTIL THIS WORLD IS DESTROYED.

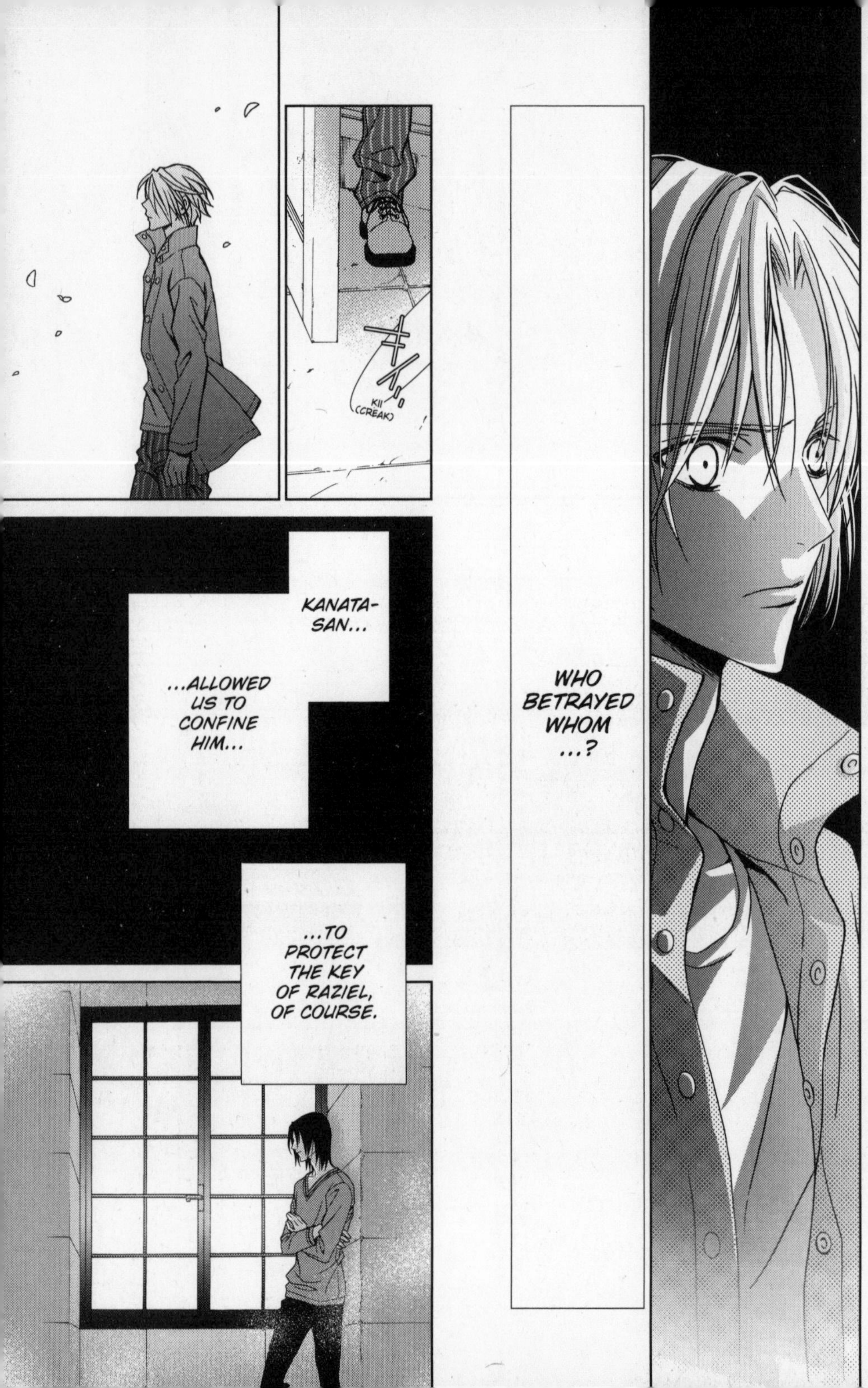
WHO BETRAYED WHOM ...?
KII (CREAK)
KANATA-SAN...
...ALLOWED US TO CONFINE HIM...
...TO PROTECT THE KEY OF RAZIEL, OF COURSE.

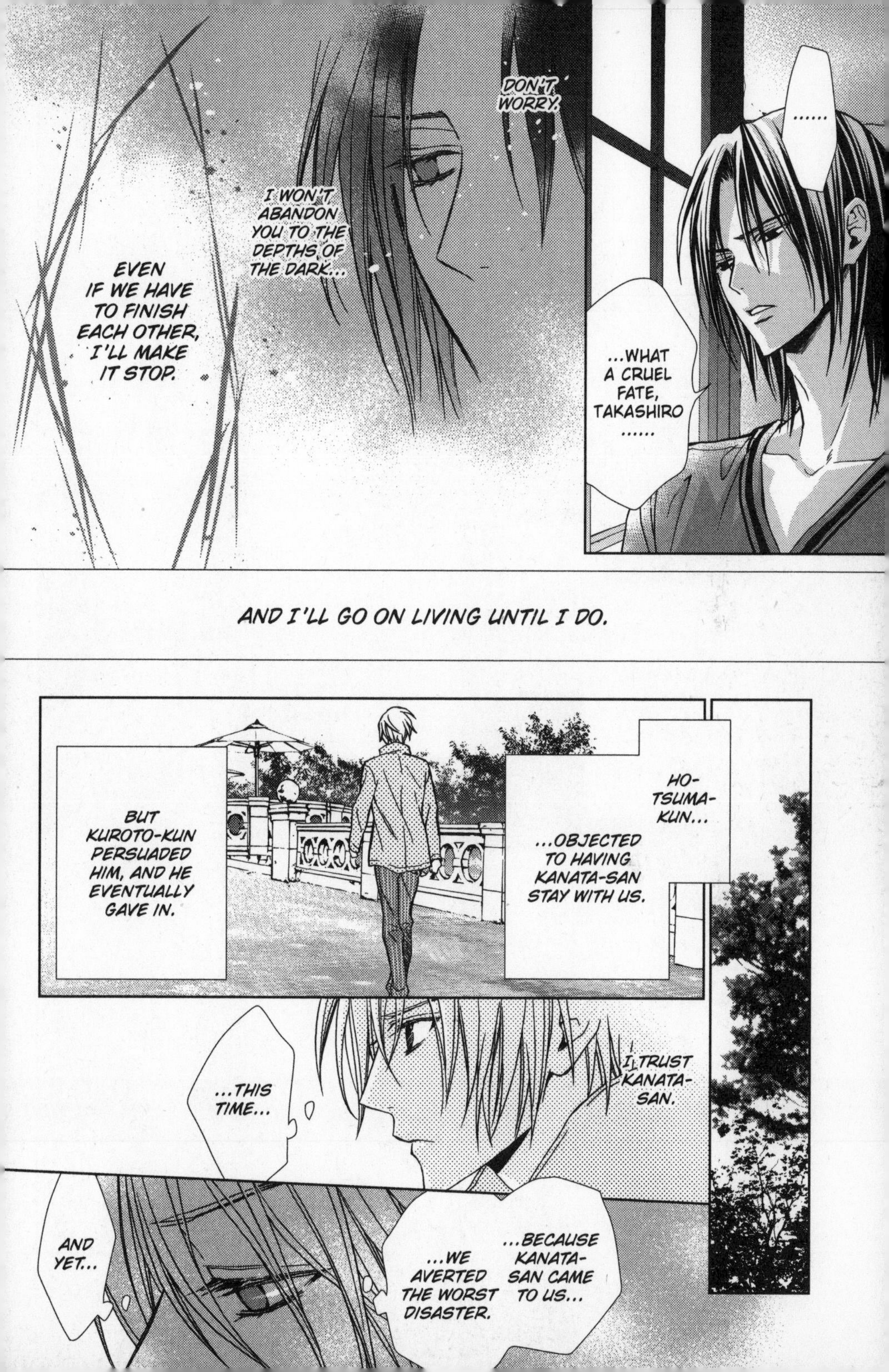
......
...WHAT A CRUEL FATE, TAKASHIRO ......
DON'T WORRY.
I WON'T ABANDON YOU TO THE DEPTHS OF THE DARK...
EVEN IF WE HAVE TO FINISH EACH OTHER, I'LL MAKE IT STOP.
AND I'LL GO ON LIVING UNTIL I DO.
HO-TSUMA-KUN...
...OBJECTED TO HAVING KANATA-SAN STAY WITH US.
BUT KUROTO-KUN PERSUADED HIM, AND HE EVENTUALLY GAVE IN.
I-I TRUST KANATA-SAN.
...THIS TIME...
...BECAUSE KANATA-SAN CAME TO US...
...WE AVERTED THE WORST DISASTER.
AND YET...

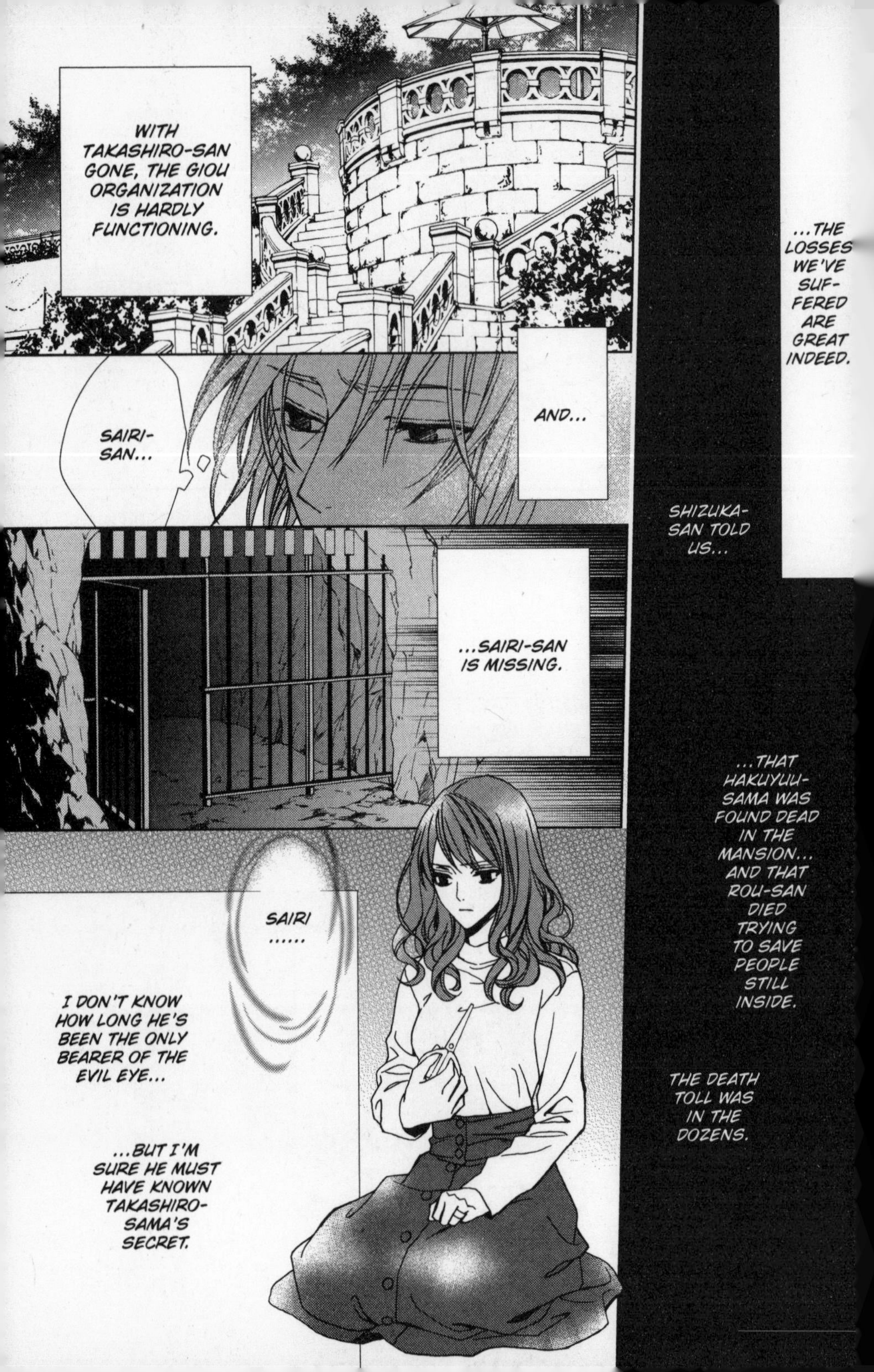
...THE LOSSES WE'VE SUF-FERED ARE GREAT INDEED.
SHIZUKA-SAN TOLD US...
...THAT HAKUYUU-SAMA WAS FOUND DEAD IN THE MANSION... AND THAT ROU-SAN DIED TRYING TO SAVE PEOPLE STILL INSIDE.
THE DEATH TOLL WAS IN THE DOZENS.
WITH TAKASHIRO-SAN GONE, THE GIOU ORGANIZATION IS HARDLY FUNCTIONING.
AND...
SAIRI-SAN...
...SAIRI-SAN IS MISSING.
SAIRI ......
I DON'T KNOW HOW LONG HE'S BEEN THE ONLY BEARER OF THE EVIL EYE...
...BUT I'M SURE HE MUST HAVE KNOWN TAKASHIRO-SAMA'S SECRET.

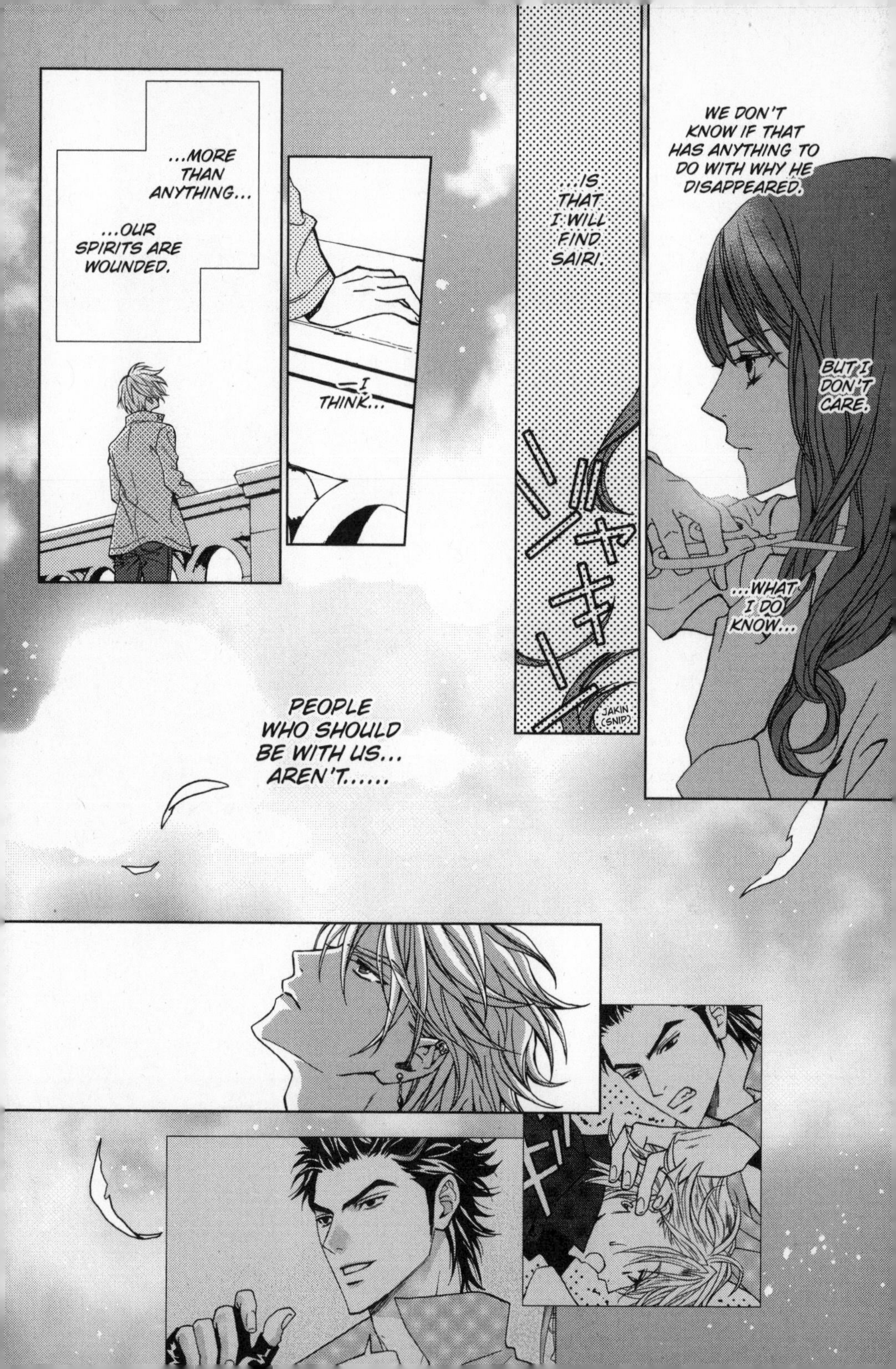
WE DON'T KNOW IF THAT HAS ANYTHING TO DO WITH WHY HE DISAPPEARED.
BUT I DON'T CARE.
...WHAT I DO KNOW...
...IS THAT I WILL FIND SAIRI.
JAKIN (SNIP)
—I THINK...
...MORE THAN ANYTHING...
...OUR SPIRITS ARE WOUNDED.
PEOPLE WHO SHOULD BE WITH US... AREN'T......

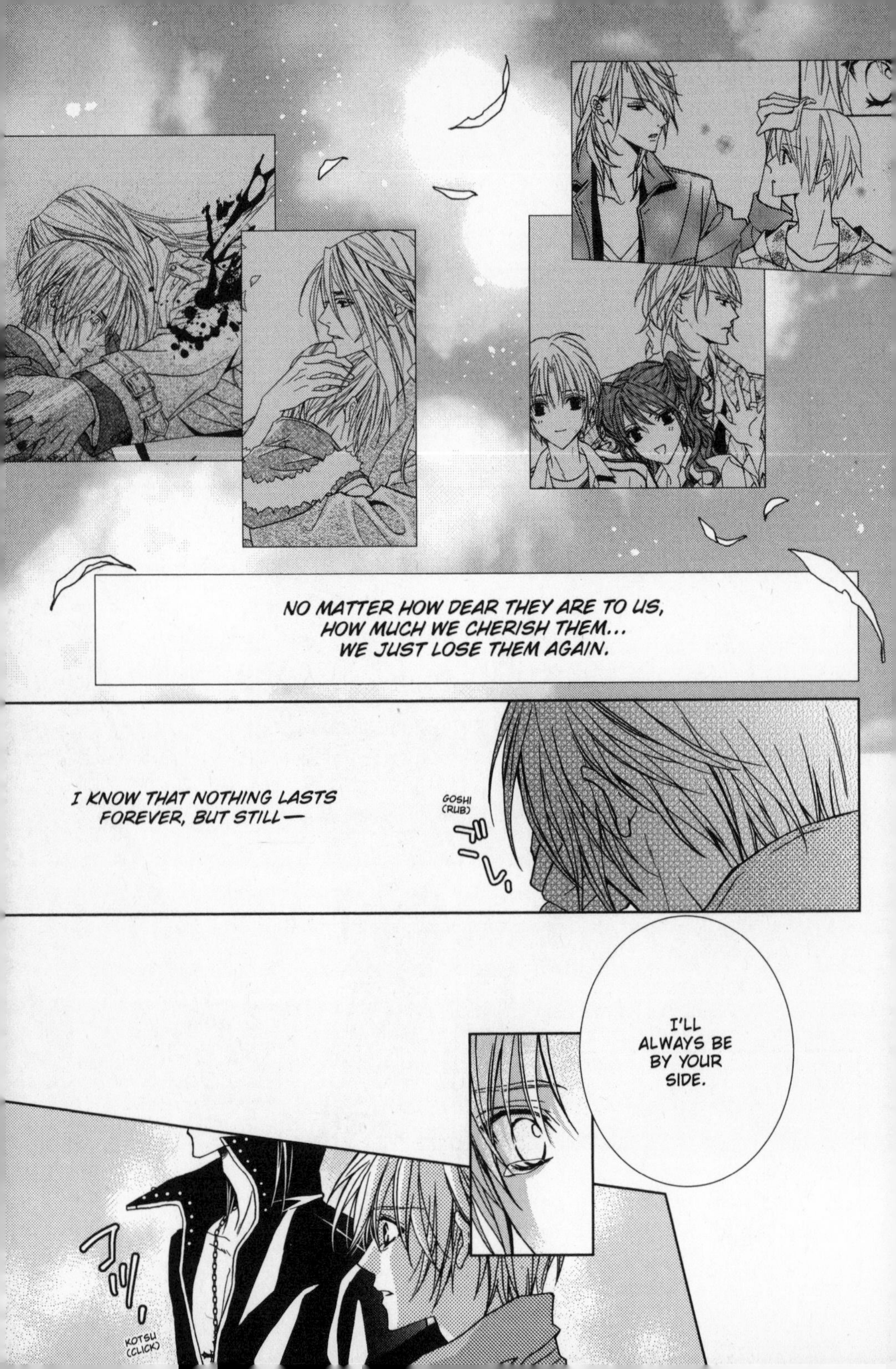
NO MATTER HOW DEAR THEY ARE TO US, HOW MUCH WE CHERISH THEM... WE JUST LOSE THEM AGAIN.
GOSHI (RUB)
I KNOW THAT NOTHING LASTS FOREVER, BUT STILL—
I'LL ALWAYS BE BY YOUR SIDE.
KOTSU (CLICK)

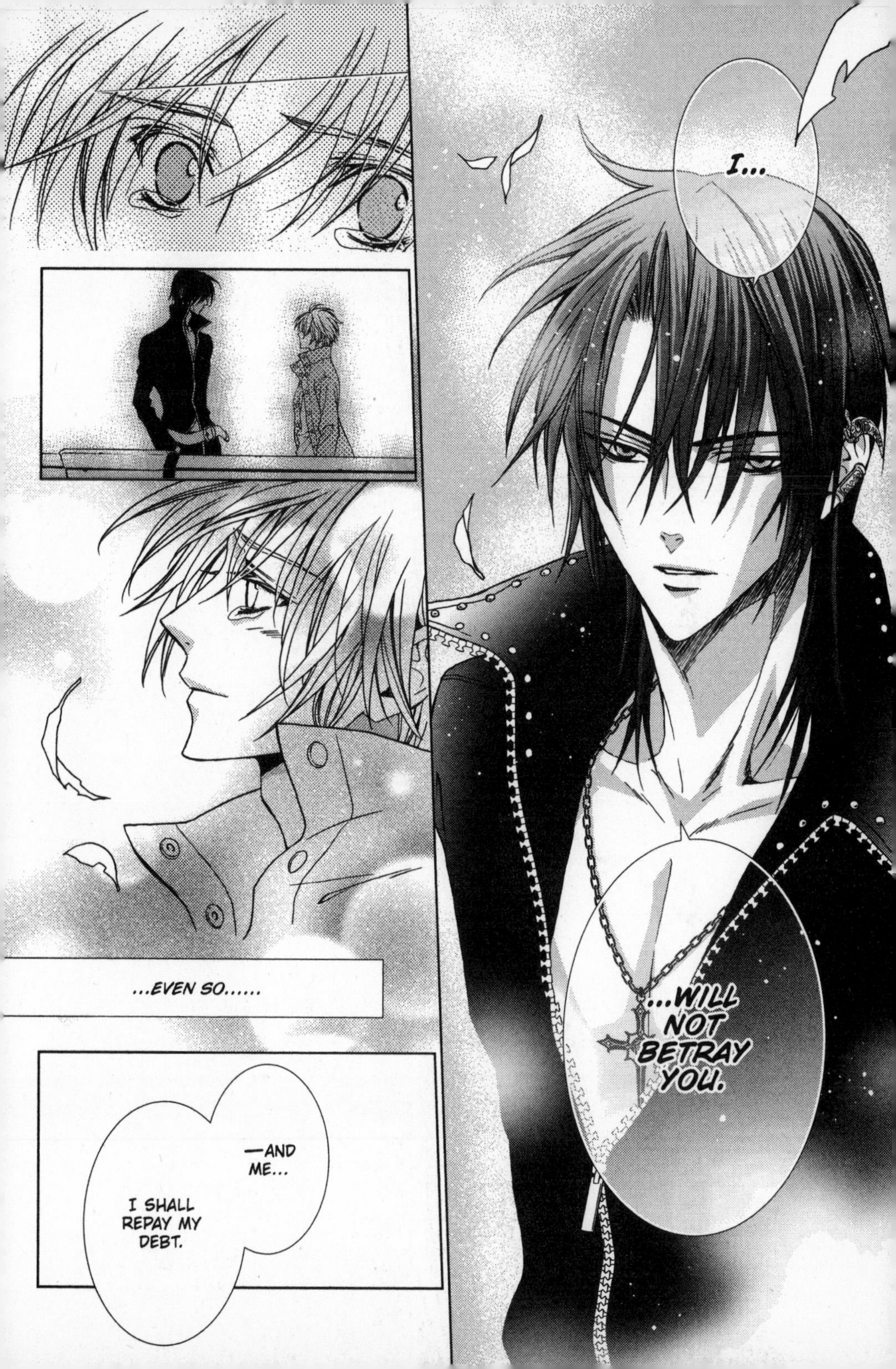
I...
...WILL NOT BETRAY YOU.
...EVEN SO......
—AND ME...
I SHALL REPAY MY DEBT.

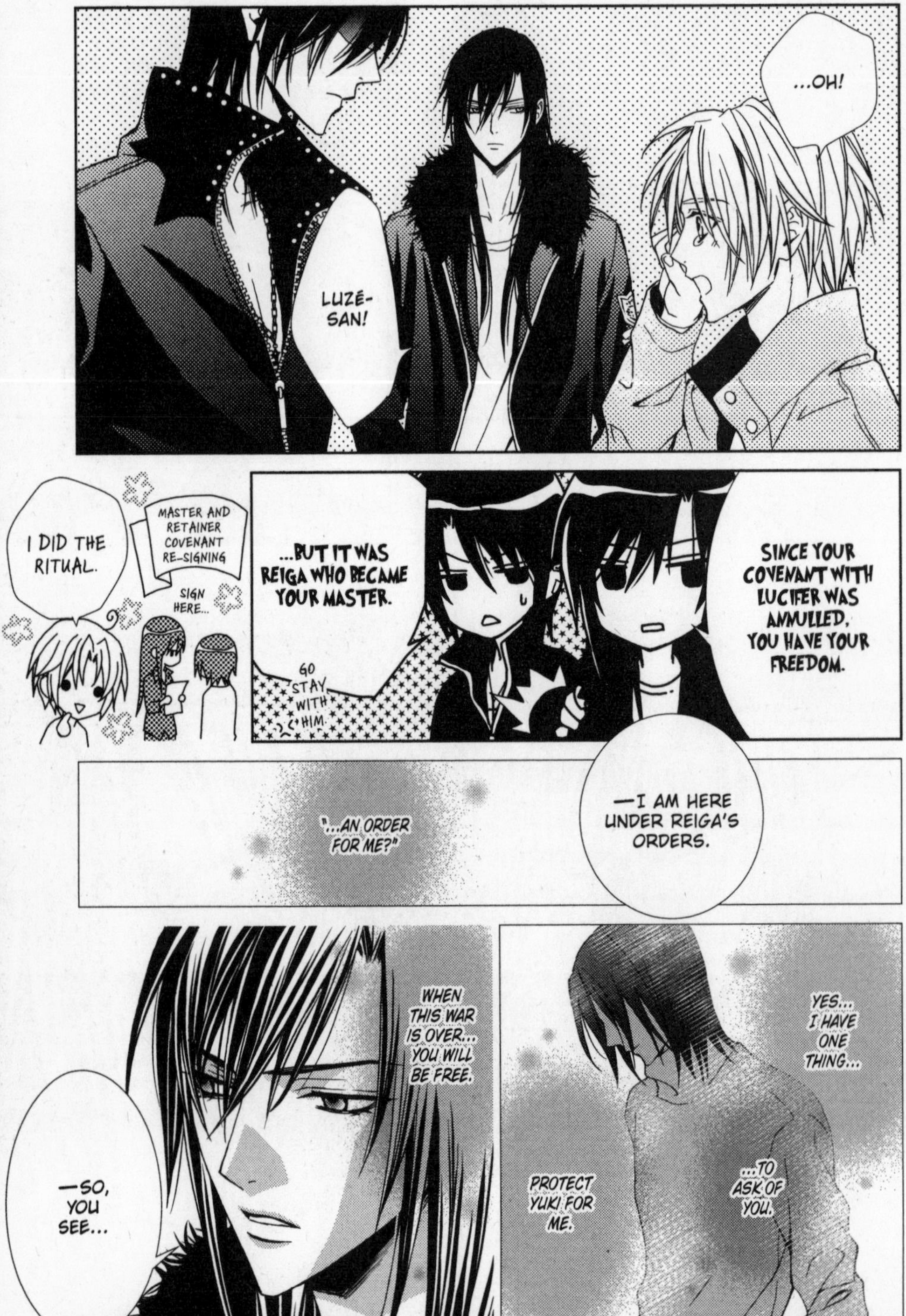
...OH!
LUZE-SAN!
SINCE YOUR COVENANT WITH LUCIFER WAS ANNULLED, YOU HAVE YOUR FREEDOM.
...BUT IT WAS REIGA WHO BECAME YOUR MASTER.
GO STAY WITH HIM.
MASTER AND RETAINER COVENANT RE-SIGNING
I DID THE RITUAL.
SIGN HERE...
—I AM HERE UNDER REIGA'S ORDERS.
"...AN ORDER FOR ME?"
YES... I HAVE ONE THING...
...TO ASK OF YOU.
PROTECT YUKI FOR ME.
WHEN THIS WAR IS OVER... YOU WILL BE FREE.
—SO, YOU SEE...

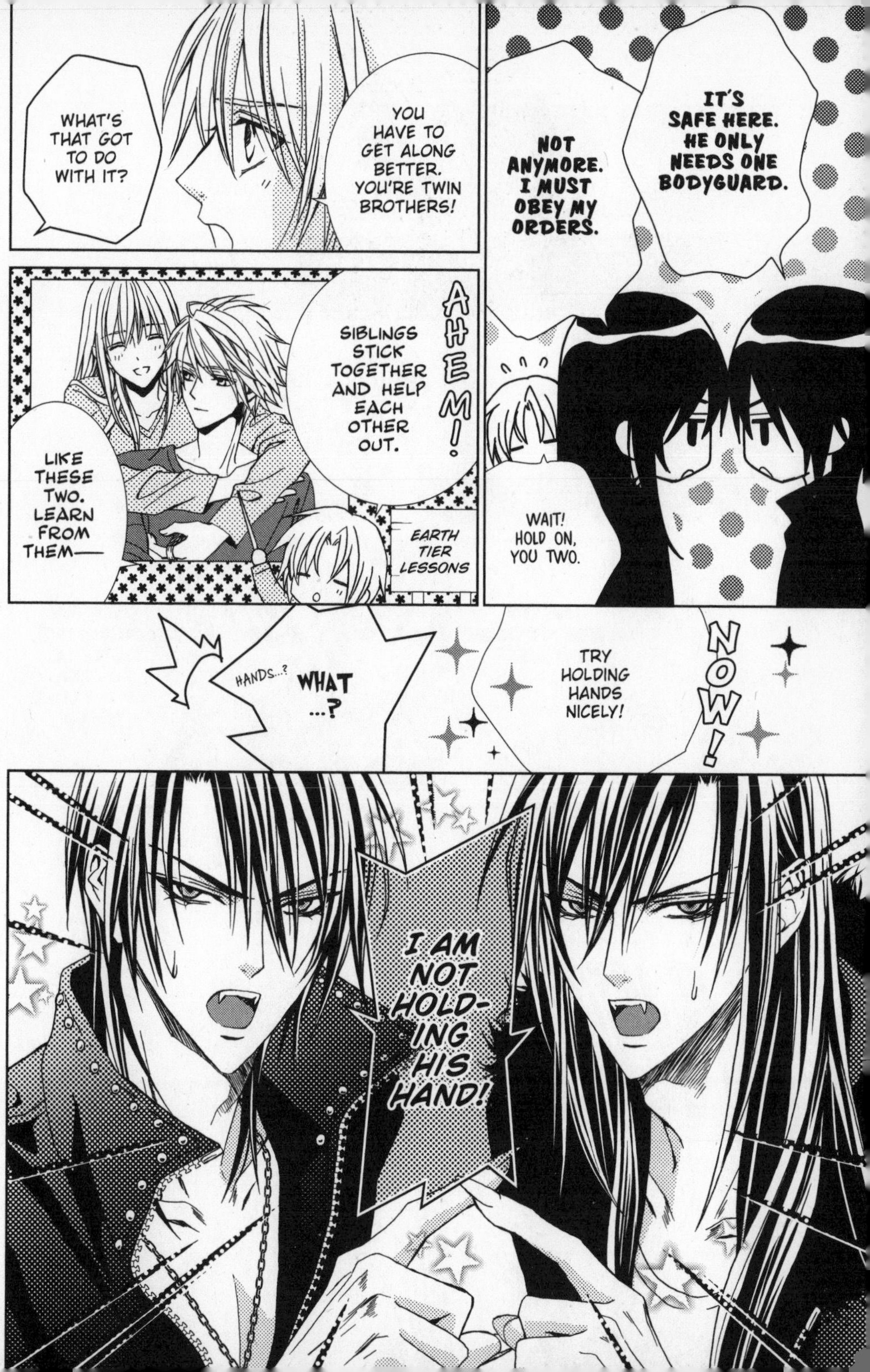
IT'S SAFE HERE. HE ONLY NEEDS ONE BODYGUARD.
NOT ANYMORE. I MUST OBEY MY ORDERS.
WAIT! HOLD ON, YOU TWO.
YOU HAVE TO GET ALONG BETTER. YOU'RE TWIN BROTHERS!
WHAT'S THAT GOT TO DO WITH IT?
AHEM!
SIBLINGS STICK TOGETHER AND HELP EACH OTHER OUT.
EARTH TIER LESSONS
LIKE THESE TWO. LEARN FROM THEM—
NOW!
TRY HOLDING HANDS NICELY!
WHAT ...?
HANDS...?
I AM NOT HOLDING HIS HAND!

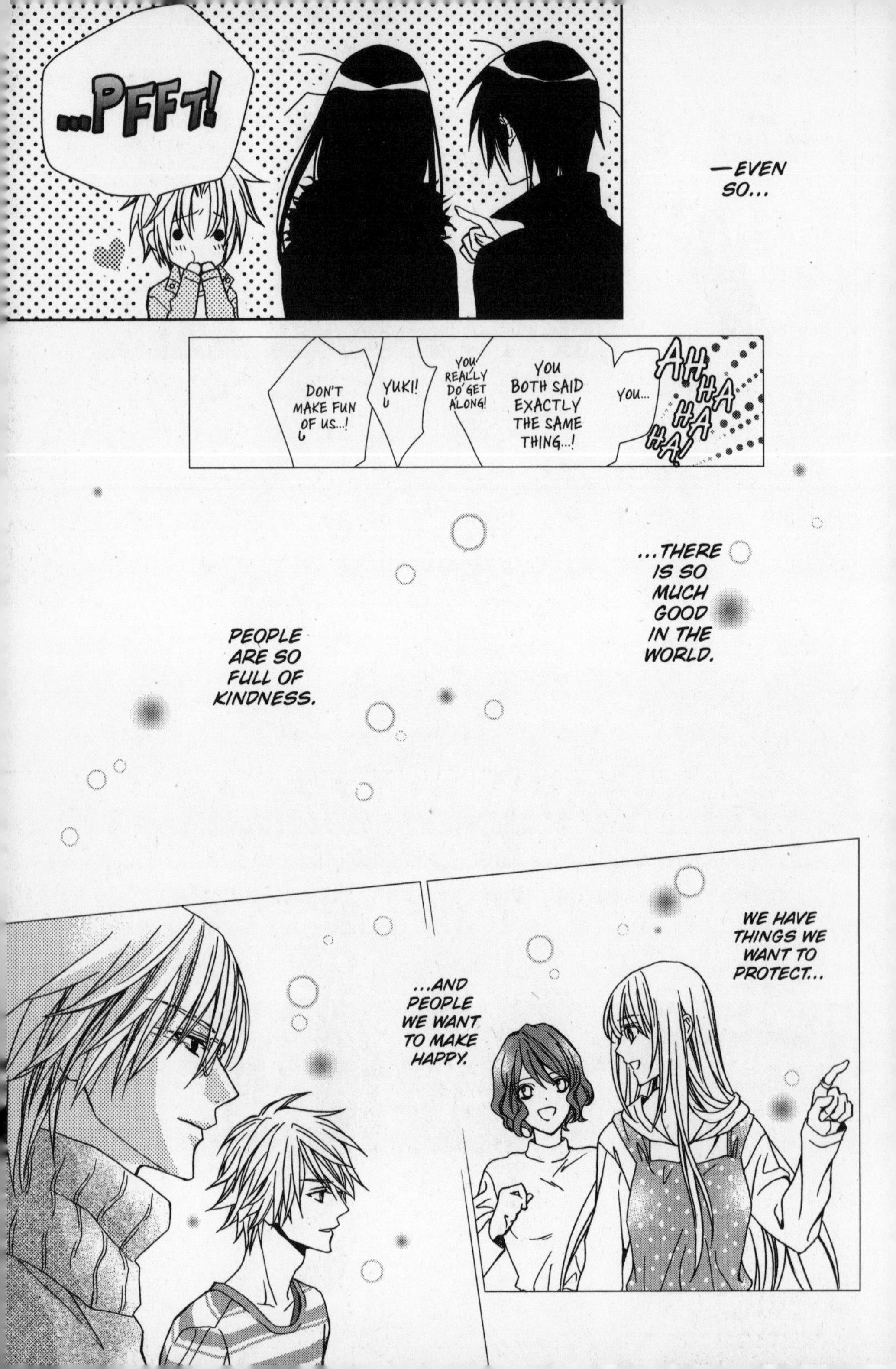
—EVEN SO...
...PFFT!
AHHAHAHA!
YOU...
YOU BOTH SAID EXACTLY THE SAME THING...!
YOU REALLY DO GET ALONG!
YUKI!
DON'T MAKE FUN OF US...!
...THERE IS SO MUCH GOOD IN THE WORLD.
PEOPLE ARE SO FULL OF KINDNESS.
WE HAVE THINGS WE WANT TO PROTECT...
...AND PEOPLE WE WANT TO MAKE HAPPY.

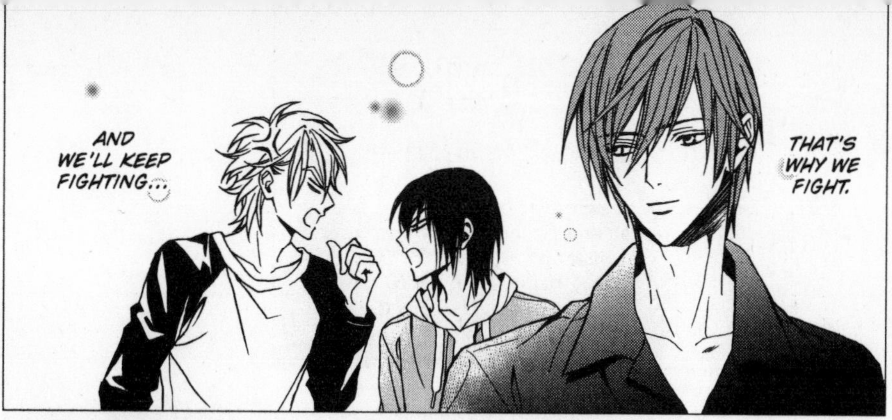
THAT'S WHY WE FIGHT.
AND WE'LL KEEP FIGHTING...
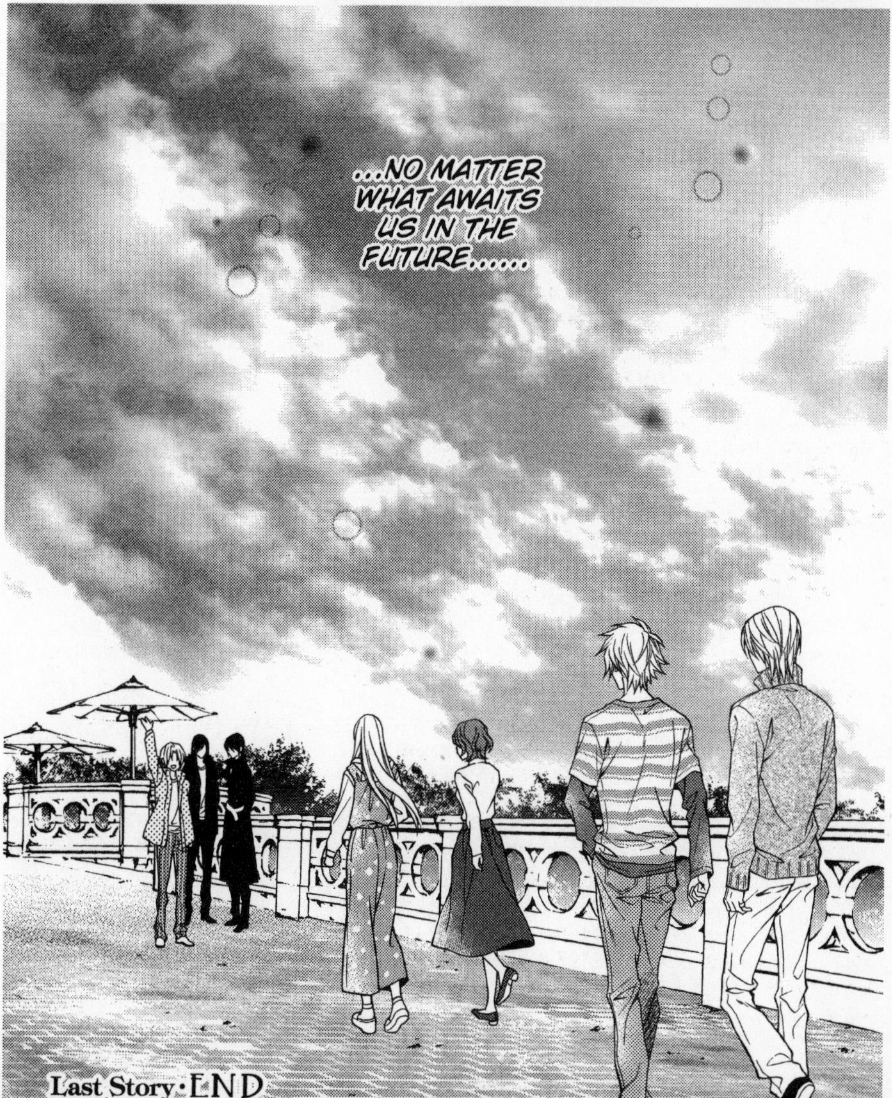
...NO MATTER WHAT AWAITS US IN THE FUTURE......
Last Story · END

Afterword: Part 1

So this is the final volume of *UraBoku*. Thank you for picking it up.

As I mentioned in the previous volume, *UraBoku* is a series that incorporated lots of different suggestions from the editors before it even began. Once it went to print, I wasn't given any specific feedback, but I had to work myself to the bone to keep drawing it, partly because of my lack of experience.

My life revolved around *UraBoku*. I stopped reading, going to movies and concerts, traveling. I wasn't going out with friends or chatting with them on the phone about nothing in particular. There was no time at all to do anything but work.

The expectations of my editors and the hopes of readers kept me going. I wanted to create something the readers would enjoy as much as possible. And no matter how hard it was, this was the life I'd chosen for myself, so I didn't mind.

But my body had different ideas. I've never had the strongest constitution. Ever since I was a kid, I've been bedridden eight months out of the year. Then suddenly I forced my body to take on this grueling schedule, so of course it was going to lash out. My tendonitis got very bad, very quickly, and I had to keep taking breaks from the serialization. I remember crying a lot, miserable and frustrated that my body and my hands wouldn't let me keep drawing as much as I wanted.

I'm always striving to be better than my past self, and knowing that I couldn't draw like I had before affected my mental health too. So that gave me more problems. There are chapters of this volume that I somehow managed to finish and submit even as my vision was spinning from headaches and vertigo.

I kept thinking, "If I tell people this, it'll look awful, like I'm making excuses!" But I've come to feel like it's okay. Now I think maybe it's better to be honest and open about what I'm going through and ask others for help when I need it.

It was only very recently that I started to consider bringing *UraBoku* to a conclusion. *ASUKA* (the magazine where *UraBoku* was serialized) described it as "the end of the third arc," and I think there were people who wondered when the "third arc" had started. But while it wasn't printed in so many words, the delineations were clear in my mind.

- The first arc covers through Volume 4 (of the Japanese editions), up to the big reveal that Kanata-san was an enemy.
- The second arc covers the Kamakura story.
- The third arc starts from there to the final volume you're holding.
This about matches the goal I set out for when the serialization began.

I divided up the story this way from the beginning because I knew there were any number of things that might end the serialization before it was complete. I really feel like it's a miracle that I made it this far. And I started to think that maybe this was a good place to end the story, considering my health and the condition of my hands, and a few other things.

→ *Continued in Part 2*

Our Backstage Comicstrips BOKU-URA!

▶ A Man Named Isuzu Fujiwara ◀

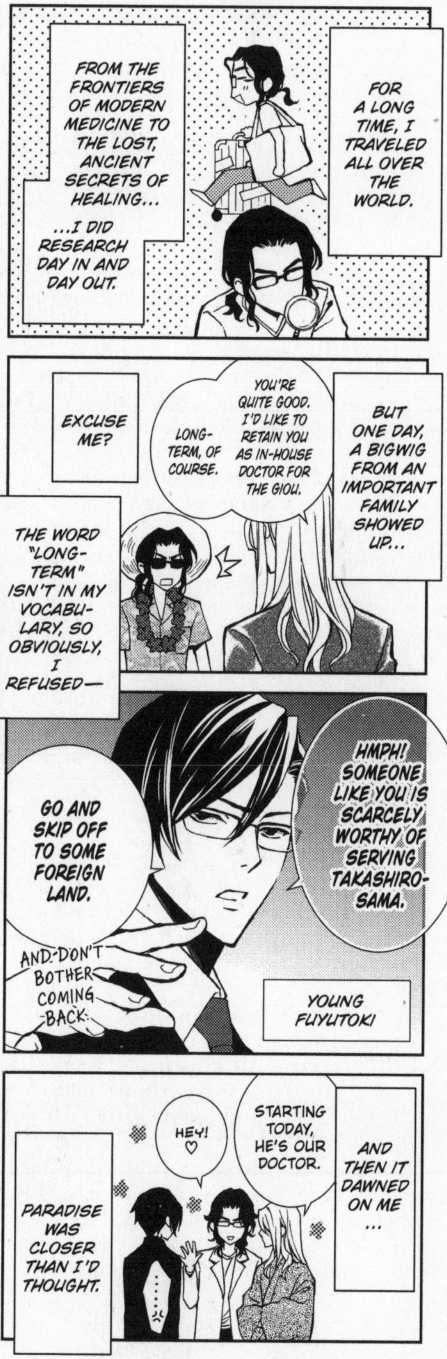

FOR A LONG TIME, I TRAVELED ALL OVER THE WORLD.
FROM THE FRONTIERS OF MODERN MEDICINE TO THE LOST, ANCIENT SECRETS OF HEALING...
...I DID RESEARCH DAY IN AND DAY OUT.
BUT ONE DAY, A BIGWIG FROM AN IMPORTANT FAMILY SHOWED UP...
YOU'RE QUITE GOOD. I'D LIKE TO RETAIN YOU AS IN-HOUSE DOCTOR FOR THE GIOU.
LONG-TERM, OF COURSE.
EXCUSE ME?
THE WORD "LONG-TERM" ISN'T IN MY VOCABULARY, SO OBVIOUSLY, I REFUSED—
HMPH! SOMEONE LIKE YOU IS SCARCELY WORTHY OF SERVING TAKASHIRO-SAMA.
GO AND SKIP OFF TO SOME FOREIGN LAND.
AND DON'T BOTHER COMING BACK.
YOUNG FUYUTOKI
AND THEN IT DAWNED ON ME...
STARTING TODAY, HE'S OUR DOCTOR.
HEY! ♡
PARADISE WAS CLOSER THAN I'D THOUGHT.

▶ The Greatest Joys of Isuzu Fujiwara ◀

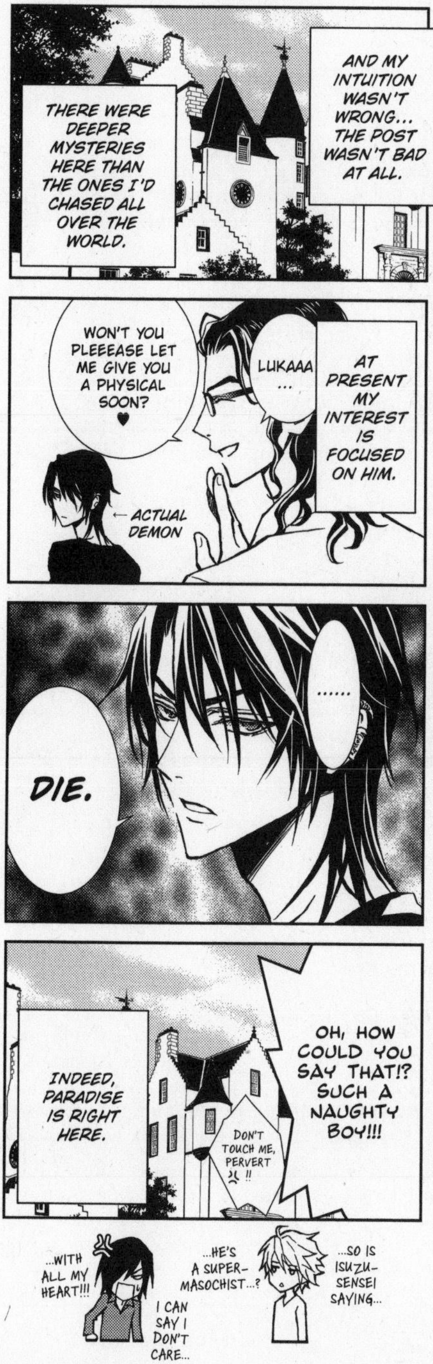

AND MY INTUITION WASN'T WRONG... THE POST WASN'T BAD AT ALL.
THERE WERE DEEPER MYSTERIES HERE THAN THE ONES I'D CHASED ALL OVER THE WORLD.
AT PRESENT MY INTEREST IS FOCUSED ON HIM.
LUKAAA ...
WON'T YOU PLEEEASE LET ME GIVE YOU A PHYSICAL SOON? ♥
← ACTUAL DEMON
......
DIE.
OH, HOW COULD YOU SAY THAT!? SUCH A NAUGHTY BOY!!!
INDEED, PARADISE IS RIGHT HERE.
DON'T TOUCH ME, PERVERT !!
...SO IS ISUZU-SENSEI SAYING...
...HE'S A SUPER-MASOCHIST...?
I CAN SAY I DON'T CARE...
...WITH ALL MY HEART!!!

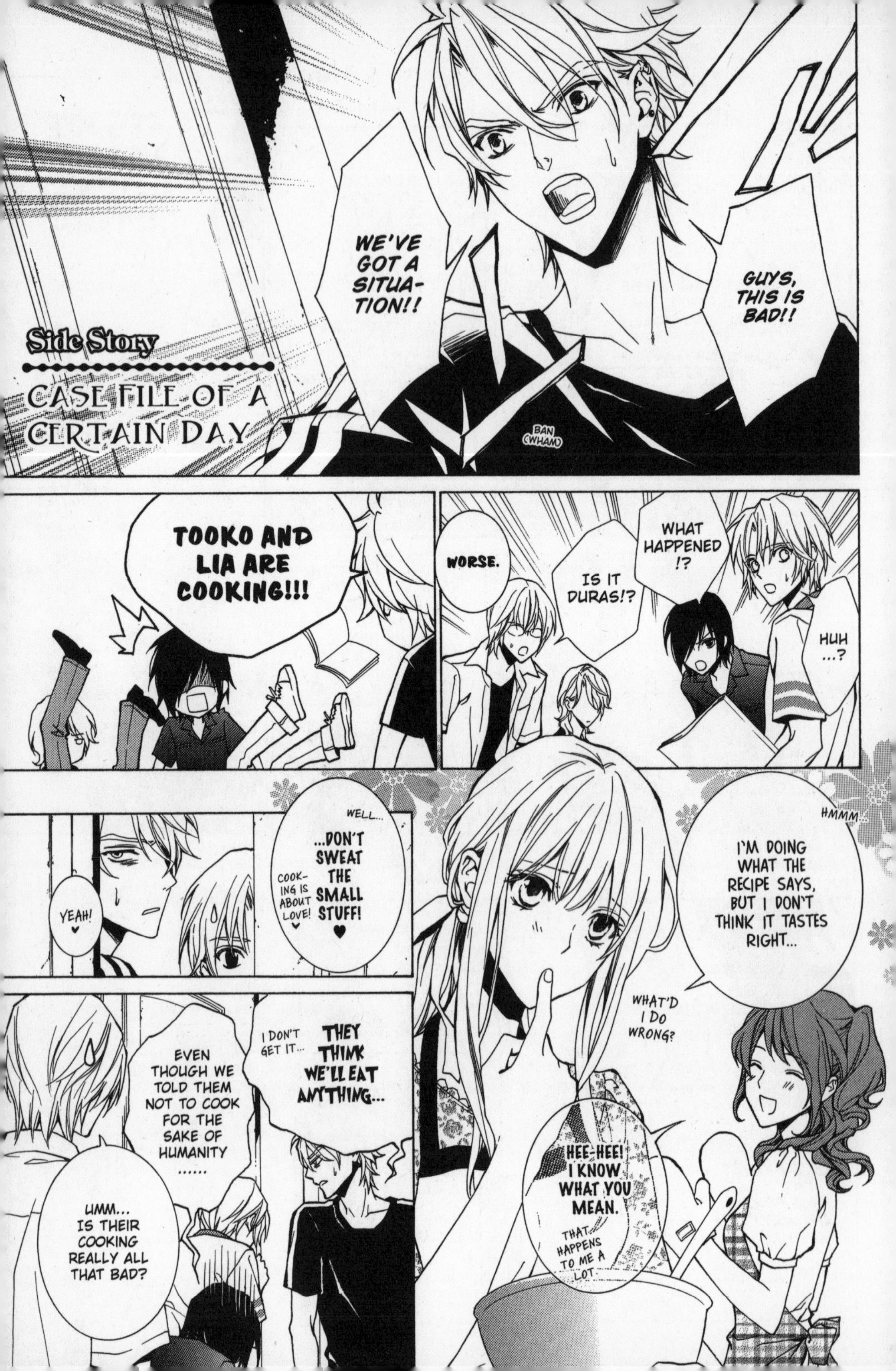
GUYS, THIS IS BAD!!
WE'VE GOT A SITUATION!!
Side Story
CASE FILE OF A CERTAIN DAY
BAN (WHAM)
WHAT HAPPENED !?
HUH ...?
IS IT DURAS!?
WORSE.
TOOKO AND LIA ARE COOKING!!!
HMMM...
I'M DOING WHAT THE RECIPE SAYS, BUT I DON'T THINK IT TASTES RIGHT...
WHAT'D I DO WRONG?
HEE-HEE! I KNOW WHAT YOU MEAN.
THAT HAPPENS TO ME A LOT.
WELL...
...DON'T SWEAT THE SMALL STUFF! ♥
COOKING IS ABOUT LOVE! ♥
YEAH! ♥
THEY THINK WE'LL EAT ANYTHING...
I DON'T GET IT...
EVEN THOUGH WE TOLD THEM NOT TO COOK FOR THE SAKE OF HUMANITY ......
UMM... IS THEIR COOKING REALLY ALL THAT BAD?

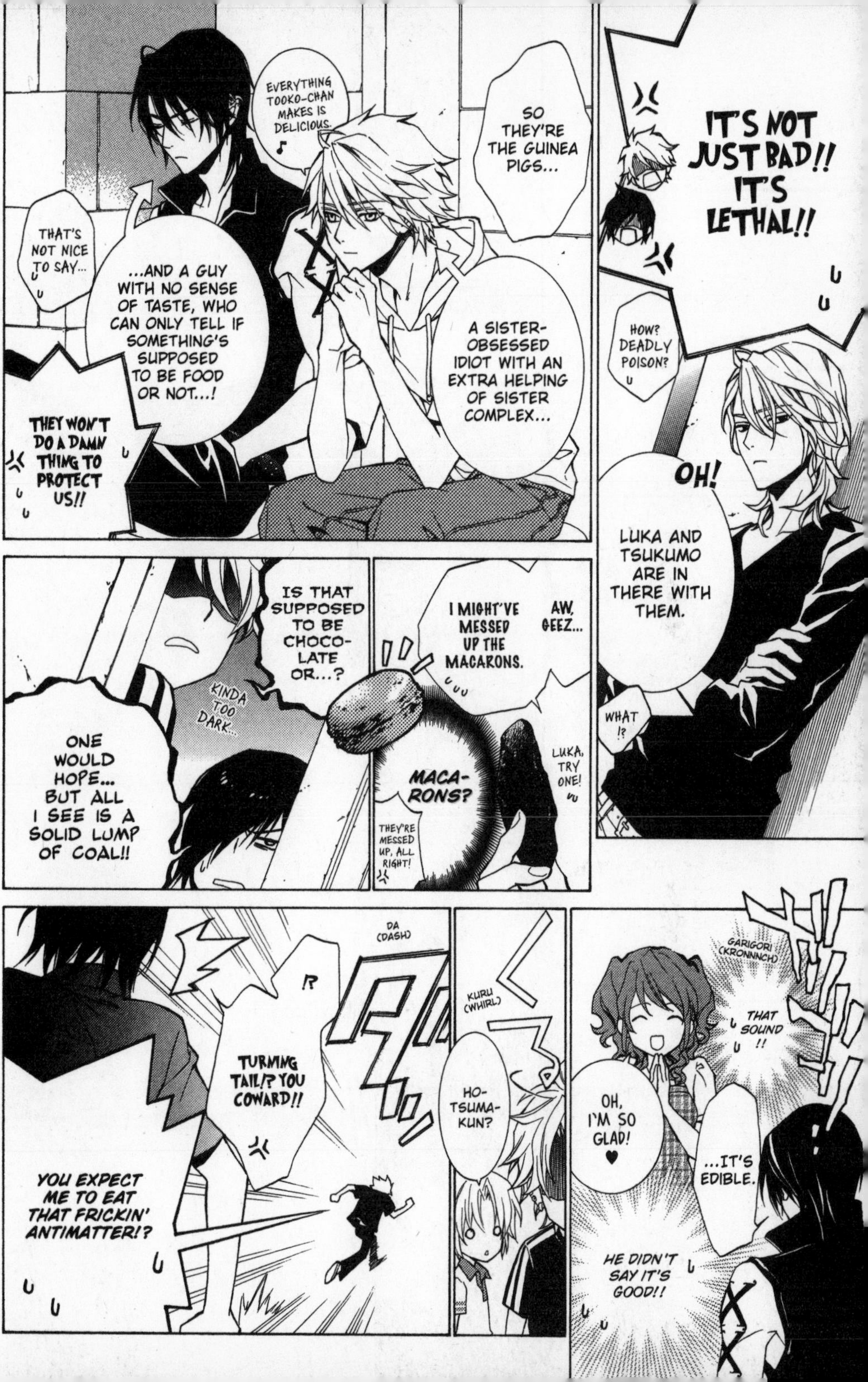
IT'S NOT JUST BAD!! IT'S LETHAL!!
HOW? DEADLY POISON?
OH!
LUKA AND TSUKUMO ARE IN THERE WITH THEM.
WHAT!?
SO THEY'RE THE GUINEA PIGS...
EVERYTHING TOOKO-CHAN MAKES IS DELICIOUS. ♪
A SISTER-OBSESSED IDIOT WITH AN EXTRA HELPING OF SISTER COMPLEX...
...AND A GUY WITH NO SENSE OF TASTE, WHO CAN ONLY TELL IF SOMETHING'S SUPPOSED TO BE FOOD OR NOT...!
THAT'S NOT NICE TO SAY...
THEY WON'T DO A DAMN THING TO PROTECT US!!
AW, GEEZ...
I MIGHT'VE MESSED UP THE MACARONS.
LUKA, TRY ONE!
MACA-RONS?
THEY'RE MESSED UP, ALL RIGHT!
IS THAT SUPPOSED TO BE CHOCO-LATE OR...?
KINDA TOO DARK...
ONE WOULD HOPE... BUT ALL I SEE IS A SOLID LUMP OF COAL!!
GARIGORI (KRONNNCH)
THAT SOUND!!
...IT'S EDIBLE.
OH, I'M SO GLAD! ♥
HE DIDN'T SAY IT'S GOOD!!
KURU (WHIRL)
HO-TSUMA-KUN?
DA (DASH)
!?
TURNING TAIL!? YOU COWARD!!
YOU EXPECT ME TO EAT THAT FRICKIN' ANTIMATTER!?

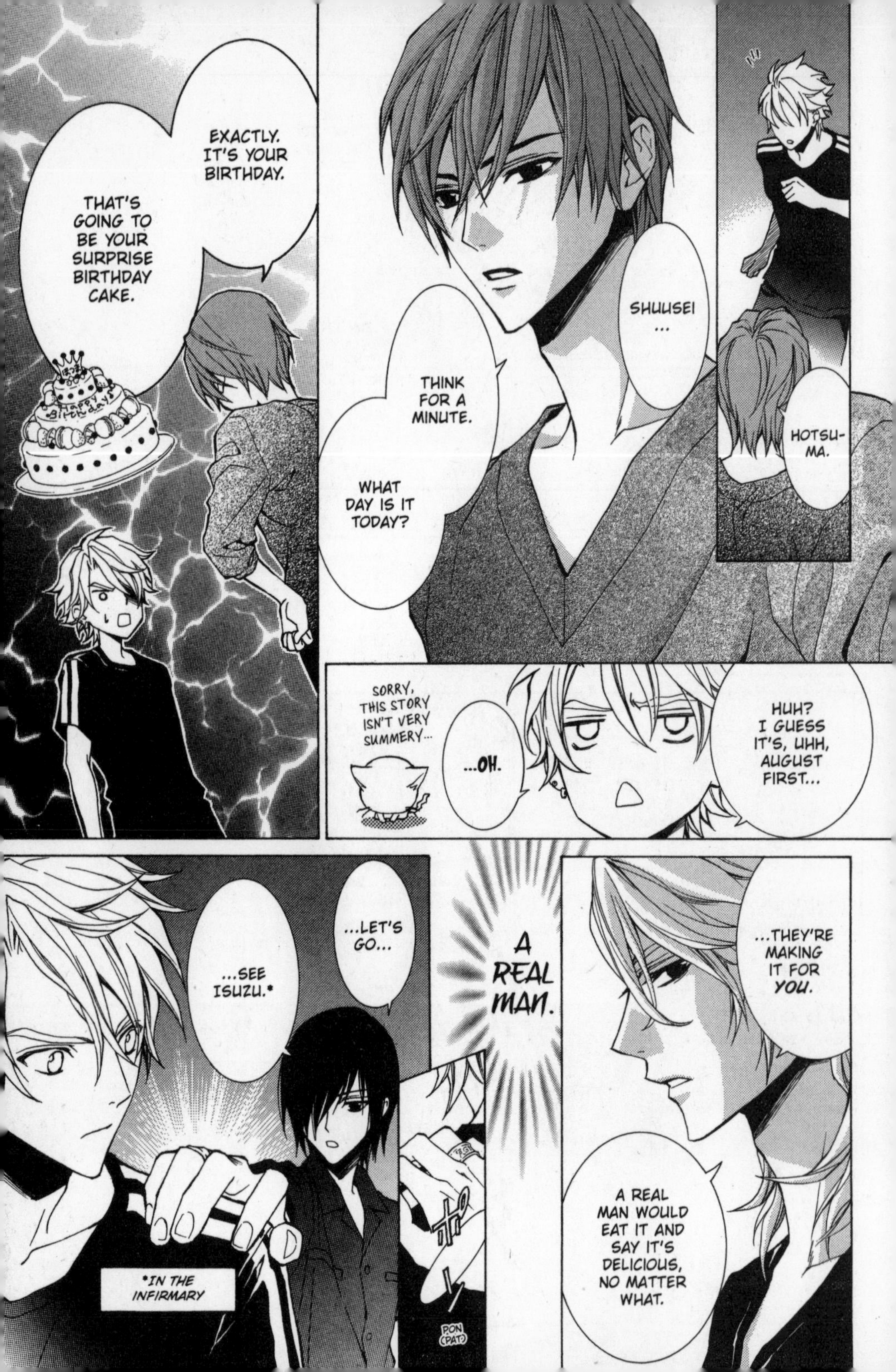
HOTSU-MA.
SHUUSEI ...
THINK FOR A MINUTE.
WHAT DAY IS IT TODAY?
HUH? I GUESS IT'S, UHH, AUGUST FIRST...
...OH.
SORRY, THIS STORY ISN'T VERY SUMMERY...
EXACTLY. IT'S YOUR BIRTHDAY.
THAT'S GOING TO BE YOUR SURPRISE BIRTHDAY CAKE.
...THEY'RE MAKING IT FOR *YOU*.
A REAL MAN WOULD EAT IT AND SAY IT'S DELICIOUS, NO MATTER WHAT.
PON (PAT)
A REAL MAN.
...LET'S GO...
...SEE ISUZU.*
*IN THE INFIRMARY

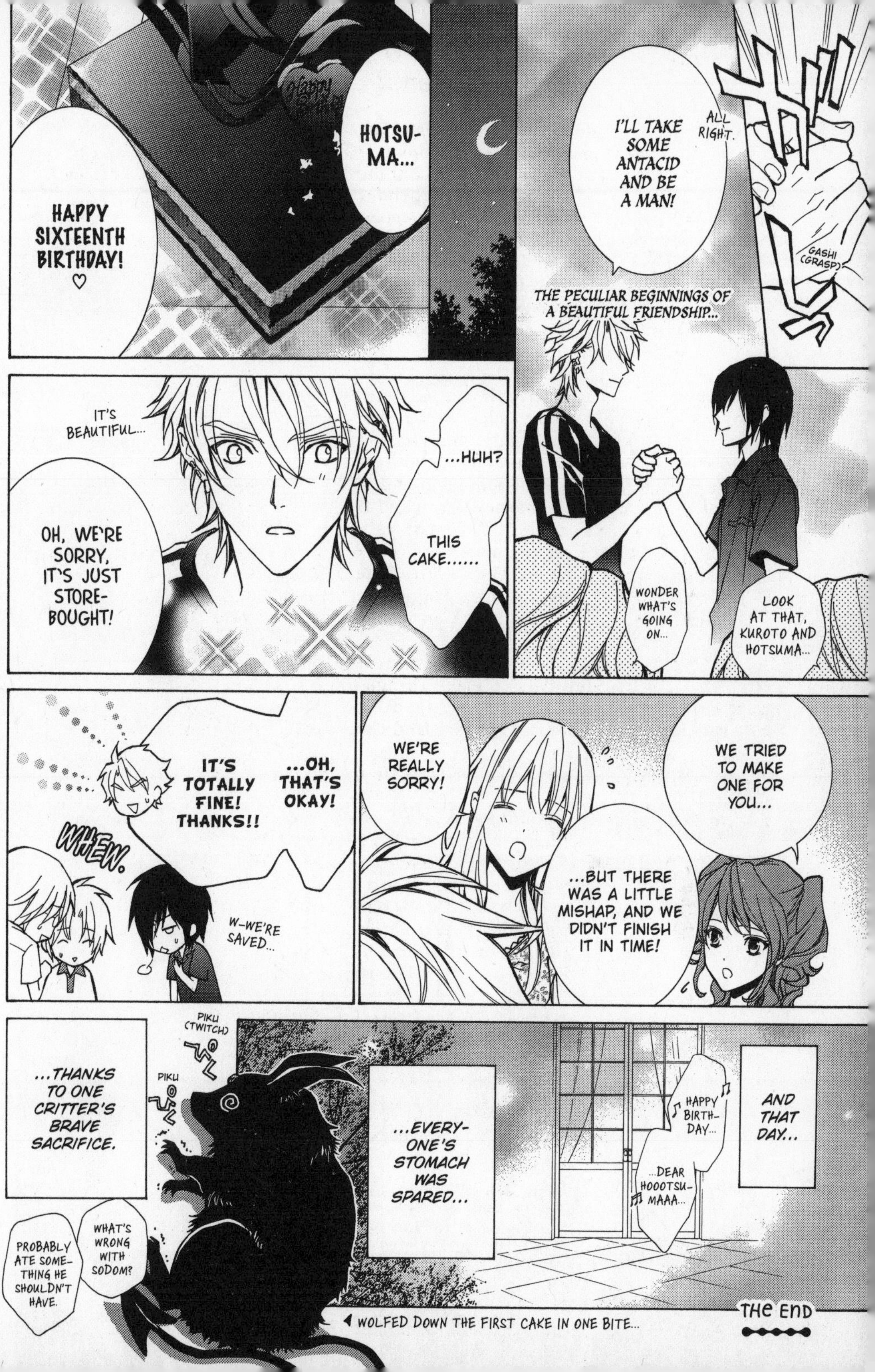

GASHI (GRASP)
ALL RIGHT.
I'LL TAKE SOME ANTACID AND BE A MAN!
THE PECULIAR BEGINNINGS OF A BEAUTIFUL FRIENDSHIP...
LOOK AT THAT, KUROTO AND HOTSUMA...
WONDER WHAT'S GOING ON...
HOTSU-MA...
HAPPY SIXTEENTH BIRTHDAY! ♡
...HUH?
THIS CAKE......
IT'S BEAUTIFUL...
OH, WE'RE SORRY, IT'S JUST STORE-BOUGHT!
WE TRIED TO MAKE ONE FOR YOU...
WE'RE REALLY SORRY!
...BUT THERE WAS A LITTLE MISHAP, AND WE DIDN'T FINISH IT IN TIME!
...OH, THAT'S OKAY!
IT'S TOTALLY FINE! THANKS!!
WHEW.
W-WE'RE SAVED...
AND THAT DAY...
♪ HAPPY BIRTHDAY... ♪
...DEAR HOOOTSU-MAAA... ♫
...EVERY-ONE'S STOMACH WAS SPARED...
PIKU (TWITCH)
PIKU
WHAT'S WRONG WITH SODOM?
PROBABLY ATE SOME-THING HE SHOULDN'T HAVE.
...THANKS TO ONE CRITTER'S BRAVE SACRIFICE.
◀ WOLFED DOWN THE FIRST CAKE IN ONE BITE...
THE END

Afterword: Part 2

After many discussions with my editor, we decided that (at least for now) this would be the final volume of *UraBoku*. I think Yuki and Luka and all the others have fought pretty hard for us. Not only did this puttering little plane get off the ground, it flew higher than I thought possible, and that's given me so much strength. The times when it surpassed my expectations have made me so happy and so thrilled.

Right from Volume 1, I drew all the monstrous Duras and everything myself, but in light of how I've been feeling, I probably won't be able to draw another series with demons and magic flying around like in *UraBoku* again. So in that sense too, this series is really special to me, and I'm so, so glad I got to work on it.

Although I was able to reach the part of the story that I'd set as my goal, there might not be enough closure for readers who were looking forward to the rest. I really feel awful about that. Mostly, I just didn't have what it would've taken. I can't even express how grateful I am to everyone who put up with such a slow-working manga artist.

So many people have sent me letters and filled out the reader surveys and expressed their support in different ways. All of you kept me from falling into that rut of thinking my work is boring and worthless, and I made it to the end. Yuki and Luka, all the Zweilt, Takashiro and Kanata—you've been on this journey with them. Thank you so very much for being here to watch their stories unfold.

...Still, as the author, I haven't really felt like I'm saying good-bye to them. When the time is right, when some things come together...I hope we'll be able to see them again, even if it's in a different form. Nothing would make me happier than to have my readers find them again in another story.

And last but not least—I didn't get this manga out into the world all on my own.

K-san and all of my assistants and staff, you've worked so hard on so many aspects of the series. Thank you so much for supporting me.

To my editor...I know I've been a bumbling lump of trouble. When my body gave out and I suddenly couldn't draw, you'd tell me, "Don't worry, we'll work something out on our end!" And I understood that I wasn't doing this all on my own. Black Bunny, you've been watching over me and *UraBoku* from beginning to end, and it's given me so much strength.

To Maeyama-sama, the designer. Thank you so much for adding your amazing touch to this series.

And to everyone in the *ASUKA* editorial department (I can't list all of your names)—I want to say how grateful I am to all of you for working with me on *UraBoku*.

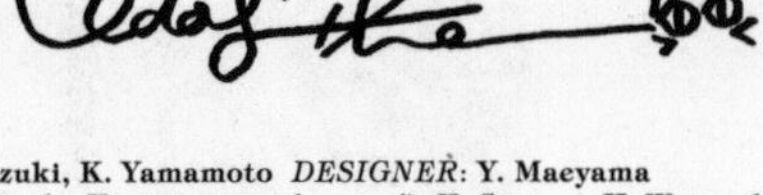

STAFF: K-san, H. Sanbe, H. Matsuo *EDITOR*: Y. Suzuki, K. Yamamoto *DESIGNER*: Y. Maeyama
SPECIAL THANKS: Bishin Kawasumi (I never thanked you for the Kansai accent lessons!), K. Segawa, H. Watanabe

The Black Bunny told me to make an account so people would know I'm alive after this.
So here it is, my twitter account. → @odagirihtr
I haven't kept up with blogging though, so maybe that stuff just isn't for me. It might be for a limited time only. (•_•;)

*Current as of May 2017

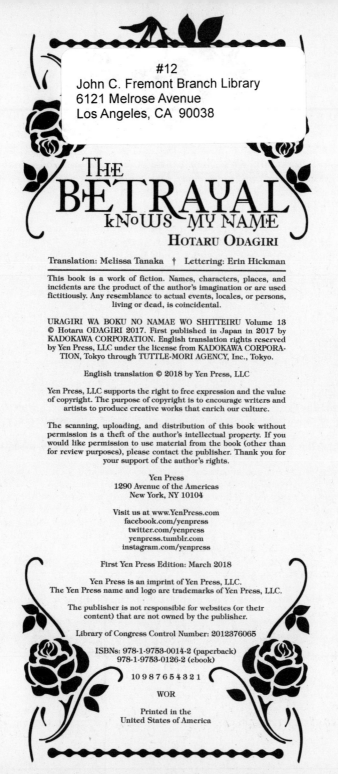

THE BETRAYAL kNoWS MY NAME

HOTARU ODAGIRI

Translation: Melissa Tanaka † Lettering: Erin Hickman

This book is a work of fiction. Names, characters, places, and incidents are the product of the author's imagination or are used fictitiously. Any resemblance to actual events, locales, or persons, living or dead, is coincidental.

URAGIRI WA BOKU NO NAMAE WO SHITTEIRU Volume 13
© Hotaru ODAGIRI 2017. First published in Japan in 2017 by KADOKAWA CORPORATION. English translation rights reserved by Yen Press, LLC under the license from KADOKAWA CORPORATION, Tokyo through TUTTLE-MORI AGENCY, Inc., Tokyo.

English translation © 2018 by Yen Press, LLC

Yen Press
1290 Avenue of the Americas
New York, NY 10104

Visit us at www.YenPress.com
facebook.com/yenpress
twitter.com/yenpress
yenpress.tumblr.com
instagram.com/yenpress

First Yen Press Edition: March 2018

Yen Press is an imprint of Yen Press, LLC.
The Yen Press name and logo are trademarks of Yen Press, LLC.

The publisher is not responsible for websites (or their content) that are not owned by the publisher.

Library of Congress Control Number: 2012376065

ISBNs: 978-1-9753-0014-2 (paperback)
978-1-9753-0126-2 (ebook)

10 9 8 7 6 5 4 3 2 1

WOR

Printed in the
United States of America

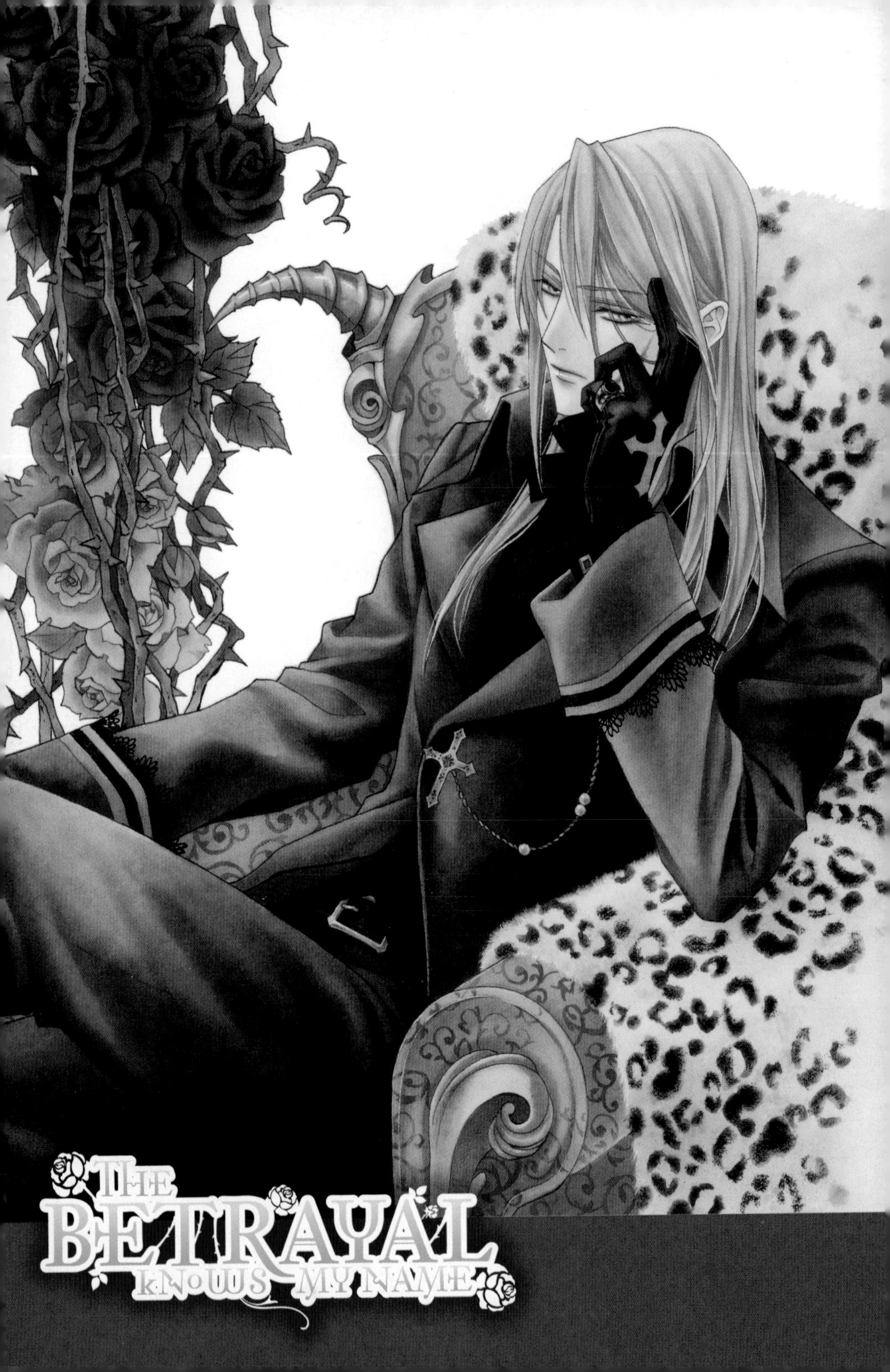
THE
BETRAYAL
KNOWS MY NAME

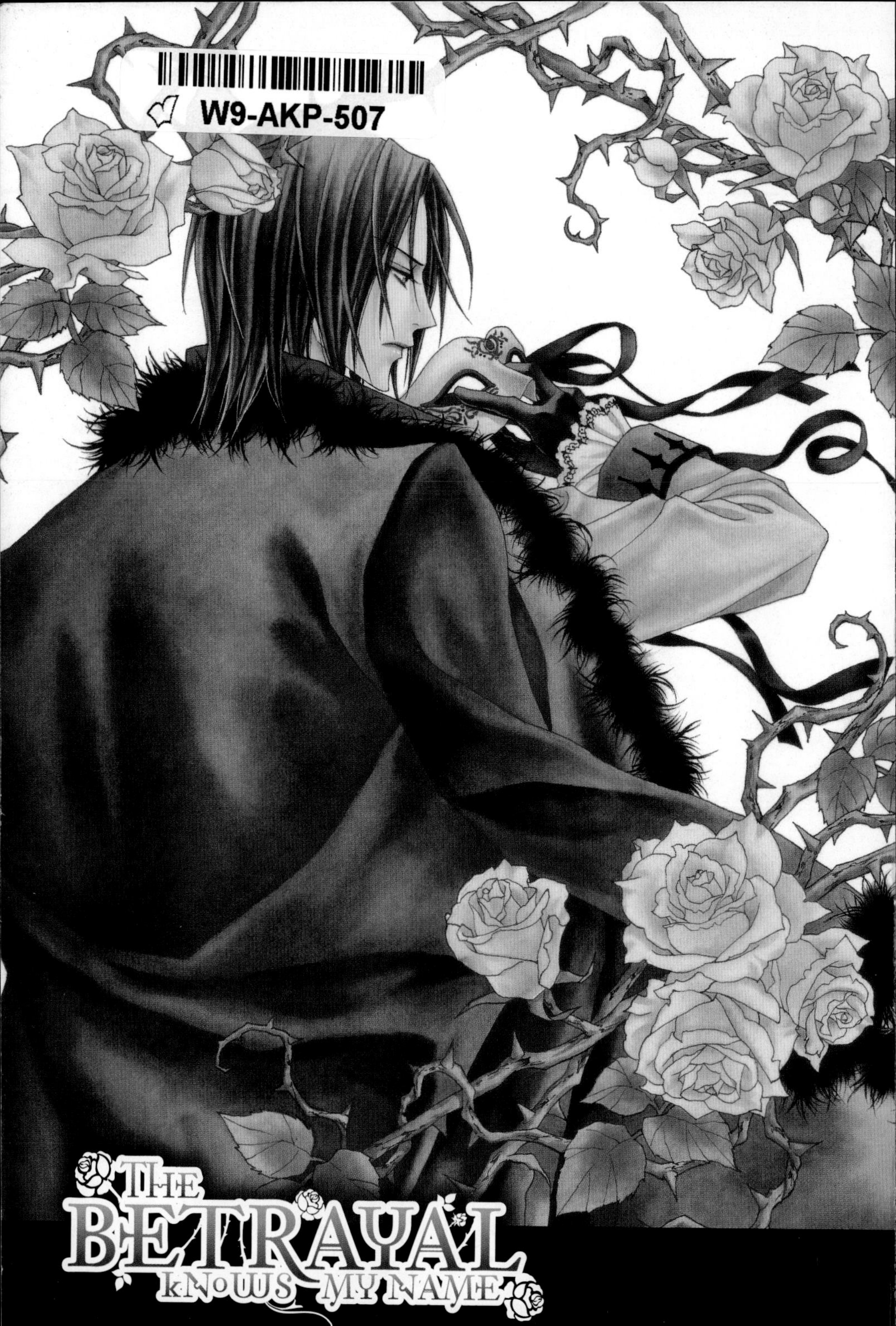
The
BETRAYAL
KNOWS MY NAME